A Life's Catch

Dermot Layden

Dermot Layden
07-03-2008

ORIGINAL WRITING

© 2008 Dermot Layden

All rights reserved. No part of this publication may be reproduced in any form or by any means—graphic, electronic or mechanical, including photocopying, recording, taping or information storage and retrieval systems—without the prior written permission of the author.

ISBN: 978-1-906018-42-9

A cip catalogue for this book is available from the National Library.

Printed in Ireland
Published by Original Writing Ltd., Dublin, 2008

This Book is
Dedicated to
the Memory
and Inspiration
of my
Late Wife
Beatrice

Note from Author

I hope you will enjoy this book. Essentially it is about capturing life in the present, but in doing so it also recaptures memories of the past as an aid to living in the present and facing towards the future. The book is unusual in the varied range of subjects covered and also in the fact that scattered throughout it are many wise sayings from diverse sources and a multitude of photographs. I trust there is a soul to be found in this book and I hope you will find it.

This book does not have to be read sequentially from beginning to end as the different parts and sometimes specific chapters deal with stand-alone topics. The book is at once a family history, a local history, an autobiography, and a reflection on various aspects of our world and of life. So hopefully at least some of the chapters will immediately appeal to you. But as you thumb through the other chapters, you might find nuggets of interest.

Thank you.

Dermot Layden

Proceeds to Charity

All profits earned from this book, for a period of five years from the date of its launch, will be donated to one or more charities or missionary activities or educational projects, or other such worthy causes. Two such worthy causes identified as of now are: St. Patrick's Missionary Society and Bishop McGettrick's Children's Fund, Kiltegan, Co. Wicklow. Both of these causes have been granted charitable tax exemption by the Irish Revenue under the name of the St Patrick's Missionary Society.

Profits for the above purpose are defined as all income arising from the book less the deduction of all costs (including any taxes) incurred in connection with the book, other than the author's time, which is gladly given free of charge.

A reputable firm of accountants will be engaged to oversee the above.

Contents

Foreword by Padraic White *xi*
Acknowledgments *xii*
Introduction *xv*

PART 1 GROWING UP IN LEITRIM IN THE LATE 1930S, 40S AND EARLY 50S

CHAPTER 1: My Parents, Homestead and Country Life *3*
CHAPTER 2: Our Farm and Farm Activities *13*
CHAPTER 3: Family, Sports and Religion *21*
CHAPTER 4: Fishing and Shooting *28*

PART 2 EDUCATION, WORK EXPERIENCES AND THE PEOPLE ENCOUNTERED

CHAPTER 5: Tarmon National School and Rockwell College *33*
CHAPTER 6: UCD, Accountancy Training and TCD *41*
CHAPTER 7: Work at Institute of Chartered Accountants, IDA and EEC *53*

PART 3 MY WIFE, FAMILY AND FRIENDS, AND LATER WORK EXPERIENCES

CHAPTER 8: Married and Family Life in Dublin *69*
CHAPTER 9: Return to the Country and Other Escapades, and a Stint in Africa *83*
CHAPTER 10: Some Conclusions about Achieving Success in Business *107*

PART 4 THE ARIGNA INDUSTRIAL REVOLUTION FROM 1600S TO THE PRESENT

CHAPTER 11: The Arigna Coal Mining Industry and the Earlier Ironworks *113*
CHAPTER 12: Arigna Today *141*

Part 5	The World of Angling
Chapter 13:	Gone Fishing: A Healthy and Absorbing Hobby *157*
Chapter 14:	The Atlantic Salmon and Salmon Angling: The Author's Passion *189*

Part 6	Our Footprints on the Physical Environment
Chapter 15:	Environmental Issues *199*

Part 7	Religion and Spirituality as Part of a Full Life
	Preamble to Part 7 *211*
Chapter 16:	The Material Dimension of Life, False Gods and Problem Issues *213*
Chapter 17:	The God Dimension and the Relevance of Religion and Spirituality *217*
Chapter 18:	Some Deeper Reflections on Religious Practices *225*
Chapter 19:	Family and Other Issues for Society *243*

Part 8	The End Game
Chapter 20:	Conclusions on Life *265*

Appendices

1. Last Will and Testament of Michael Layden (deceased), dated October 23rd, 1916 *273*
2. Beatrice Layden's Favourite Prayer and Some Poems *275*
3. Reflections on Life by Max Ehrmann and Marianne Williamson *281*
4. Fishing *284*

   Bibliography *299*

Foreword by Padraic White

This is a book to savour, enjoy and relax with over many evenings.

It captures the many strands of the life of Dermot Layden, all of them integrated fully in a persona which epitomises the motif "to thine own self be true." There is the young Dermot growing up in Leitrim overlooking Lough Allen in a rustic lifestyle fast fading from our collective memory but with wonderful traditions and mores which are lovingly brought to life in this book. As a member of the extended Layden family based in Leitrim and Roscommon, he witnessed the entrepreneurial drive of that family in developing Arigna coal mines—then one of Ireland's last operating coal mines, which powered the electricity station on Lough Allen's shores. After its demise, he describes the continued application of the family's fuel expertise in forming Ireland's premier smokeless fuel enterprise.

His professional career as a chartered accountant took him to the new IDA-Ireland at its foundation in 1970 and together with his colleague there, Pat Lalor, presented Ireland's unique tax advantages in a simple and persuasive way to incoming investors in conjunction with their counterparts in the Irish Revenue. They made a unique contribution to the success of IDA-Ireland and indeed to Ireland's reputation as a country with an attractive and credible tax advantage. His accountancy expertise drew him as a lecturer to Sligo Regional Technical College which evolved into the Institute of Technology Sligo and brought him back to his beloved native region.

Dermot is also a fisherman of many parts—a game angler for trout and salmon, a coarse angler and sea angler. But his passion as a salmon fisherman dominates all other species. It is truly a passion fuelled by the challenge of mind with the salmon of knowledge and an equal concern for the welfare of this honoured fish whose numbers internationally and those reaching Irish rivers each year have declined dramatically. At Ballycroy in County Mayo, Dermot and the extended Layden family have spent many happy holiday weeks pursuing and enjoying their salmon fishing preoccupation.

Dermot Layden is an essentially spiritual person and that spirituality pervades this book—it is an integral part of his life. His true locus is his immediate family and the love of his late wife, Beatrice, and his children shines through these pages. The death of Beatrice left a profound sense of loss.

Dermot's life and my own have crossed paths in a number of fortuitous ways. When I joined IDA-Ireland in its foundation year in November 1970, one of the first sources of encouragement and re-assurance I encountered was Dermot Layden—he was on the same corridor in Lansdowne House and was a fellow Leitrim man to boot. We were both privileged to have the unique experience of being participants in the foundation days of IDA-Ireland. During those years, my wife Mary and myself had the good fortune to meet his charming wife Beatrice.

Then in 1997, I was invited by Dermot's cousin, Peter—the Managing Director of Arigna Fuels Ltd—to become chairman of the group's companies in smokeless fuel and wind energy. And so, every year since then on the occasion of the annual meetings in the Bush Hotel in Carrick-on-Shannon, Dermot and I meet and reminisce about world affairs.

Our interests overlapped again in 2006 when I was appointed one of a three-person review group by the Government to review the future of salmon fishing in Ireland and particularly the continuance of drift net fishing. I was very conscious of the genuine concern of salmon fisherman like Dermot for the future welfare of the salmon species and I have no doubt that he and like-minded salmon fishermen are committed to all the measures needed to ensure a healthy salmon stock in Irish rivers.

So with these preliminary words, I encourage you to explore the many facets of the life of Dermot Layden as revealed in the following pages.

Padraic White

Acknowledgments

I acknowledge with most grateful thanks the help and encouragement I received from my own immediate family, David, Dervila, Conor, Aisling and Ciara as well as my daughter-in-law, Marina in writing this book. Special thanks to Dervila for her exceptional editing abilities and to Ciara for her help in organising some of the images used. My family's help came under very many guises, not least that of assisting me to overcome the intricacies of the computer. Despite my one-finger approach, I typed the basic script in a surprisingly fast time, at least fast for me.

I acknowledge in a special way the considerable help and encouragement received from my sisters and brother, Imelda, Margaret, Joe and Mary, and also for the encouragement received from my various nieces and nephews. Very special thanks to Beatrice's family, especially, Christina, Una, Michael, and Mary (Pollock).

Most grateful thanks are extended to my first cousin, Brendan Layden, for the very considerable help received from him on the Arigna section of the book. Thanks likewise to my first cousins, Father Leo Layden CSSp, Kitty Kennedy and Mary Layden. Thanks also to Peter, Leo, David and Brendan (sons of Brendan and Doherty Layden) and to the family of the late Micéal and Mary Layden: Anita, Michael, Mia and Sheila. My thanks also go to Seamus Rynn and the staff of the Arigna Mining Museum. A special word of thanks is due to my first cousin, Mary O'Donnell and her husband Barry. Thanks also to various other first and second cousins and relations. A word of gratitude goes to Mary Palmer and Kay Horan of Sligo for background assistance given to me in relation to my mother's family. A special thanks to Sr. Catherine Boland for being able to remember the names of all those old classics we used to play on the gramophone.

My very special appreciation is extended to Padraic White, a fellow proud Leitrim man and an ex-Chief Executive of the Industrial Development Authority. In addition to writing the Foreword, Padraic was most assiduous in his commitment to the book and thus gave me a great deal of help and good advice.

My grateful thanks for the help and encouragement received from many people in Sligo, including that of Frank Murphy and Paddy Smith.

I owe a great debt of gratitude to Mary Conefrey and the staff of the Leitrim County Library, Ballinamore, for their extreme courtesy and help in making accessible to me their very extensive range of papers and other publications relating to mining in Arigna going back as far as the 1600s. Leitrim people have every reason to be proud of their County Library and staff in Ballinamore. Thanks too to the Leitrim Genealogy Centre for their assistance received on family history. I also thank The National Library of Ireland, including the Manuscripts

Department, for information provided on Arigna mining. A very special word of thanks to Seamus Helferty, Principal Archivist, University College, Dublin, for his generous efforts in providing information on the college, not least that relating to the Literary and Historical Society. My grateful thanks too to the library staff of The Institute of Chartered Accountants in Ireland for their help and courtesy.

Many other organizations generously helped in giving me information, including the Industrial Development Authority; the National Board of Accountants and Auditors, Tanzania; Institute of Technology, Sligo; Rockwell College; KPMG; Ernst & Young; Coillte; and Friends of the Earth.

Probably the greatest debt is due by me to the very many sources of information and references I used in compiling this book. All of these sources are listed in the Bibliography. Without these sources the book would have been very much the poorer.

My very genuine thanks to the composers of the many sayings and quotes dispersed throughout the book and particularly for those to which I was not able to attribute a source. If there are sources available for any of those not attributed, I sincerely apologise for the omission of same, and I promise to rectify the situation in any future edition of the book on receiving the appropriate information.

Grateful thanks to all those who provided me with photographs for the book, particularly Derek Speirs, Peter Layden, Father Browne's Collection, the Leland Lewis Duncan Collection, my sisters and brother, and, by no means least, my own immediate family.

I greatly appreciate the very significant help I received from Original Writing Ltd. in Dublin and the printers they worked with in the production of this book, and for the further help they will provide in the distribution and sale of the book.

If through lapse of memory, I have failed to thank any person or organisation who helped me, I ask for your forbearance and I thank you now on the double.

Introduction

This book covers a range of topics so that at once it is a family history, a local history, an autobiography and a reflection on our world and on life, including various social and personal issues.

The principal aim of the book is to inform us of the past and, through reviving this collective past, help us to put the present into context perhaps even providing us with a firmer base on which to build our future. I feel this aim is cogently summed up in a quotation from Archbishop (since Cardinal) Sean Brady: "Without memory we cease to be ourselves, we lose our identity."

I like a bit of sentimentality and emotion in the way we think and act. I feel we need more of these today in a world that can sometimes seem cold in its actions and attitudes. Thankfully, though, there is still a great deal of warmth in the way many people behave, but surely there is room for much more of this. I expressed the hope in the author's note that the reader would find a "soul" in this book. This is what I am getting at here; to me the touch of humanity both indicates the existence of the soul and enables it to connect with daily life, a life that can hopefully be lived unfettered.

In contemporary society there seems to be excessive attention given to the material things of life, the desire for which can be seen to shackle society to this earthly world. Coupled with an almost equal disregard for the higher things of life, this appears to me to be leading today's society and individuals seriously astray. A more balanced approach to life would surely result in a significant reduction in our many societal ills, such as alcohol and drug abuse, violence and so on. Life could then, I submit, be lived without these material shackles.

The following is a brief overview of what is covered in the various sections of the book:

- Apart from some family history, the early section of the book contains quite a deal of information about country life in Leitrim in the war and post-war years into the 1950s. Life in other parts of the country would not have been much different at that time. The role of sporting activities, including fishing and shooting, is also covered, as indeed is the part religion played in our lives.
- The next section deals with the various schools and colleges I attended and also with my various employments up to the 1970s. Even if none of the biographical detail is of interest, there are various insights into the society of the time and the philosophy of work and education.

- The next section deals initially with my own family and then with various other work undertakings until my retirement in 2002. These work situations included: EEC (FEOGA) work to about 1980, then lecturing at RTC, Sligo/Institute of Technology, Sligo, and work in Tanzania for two and a half years. Also in this section is a short account of the career of John Leydon, a family relation, who, together with Sean Lemass, played a very important role in the early economic development of Ireland. Lastly, in this section, I venture to give some hints on the successful conduct of business.
- The next section covers the history of mining in Arigna and the surrounding areas from the 1600s to the present time. I hope readers will be interested in the fascinating industrial history of this area.
- Then there is quite a significant section on angling. Even if you have no interest in angling, you may well enjoy the preamble, the photos and some of the quotes.
- Next there is a chapter on environmental issues, including climate change. The most important conclusion to be drawn from this chapter is that the time has come now for each of us to take action, and not just talk about taking action.
- The penultimate section deals with social and spiritual issues. Much of what is contained in this section comes from the pen of other people. I believe this to be the most important section of the book and I hope it offers guidance for living life today. One commentator has referred to the serious "pruning of the family tree" that our new social and family structures are giving rise to. If we continue the way we are going, many of us will become detached from both our ancestry and our wider families, losing that sense of connection which can make life so meaningful. Finally, I hope you will find the Reflections of the 2007 class of graduates of the Girls and Boys Town, Nebraska to be moving.
- This brings us to the last chapter dealing with conclusions on life. It is an extremely short chapter, but perhaps very long when it comes to putting it into practice.
- Lastly, the appendices include a copy of my grandfather's last will and testament (1916); my late wife's favourite prayer and some poetry; reflections on life by Max Ehrmann and Marianne Williamson which have some good advice for living; and lastly an appendix on fishing.

Part 1

Growing Up in Leitrim in the Late 1930s, 40s and Early 50s

. . . .

"Without memory we cease to be ourselves, we lose our identity."
— Archbishop Sean Brady

. . . .

Family Tree

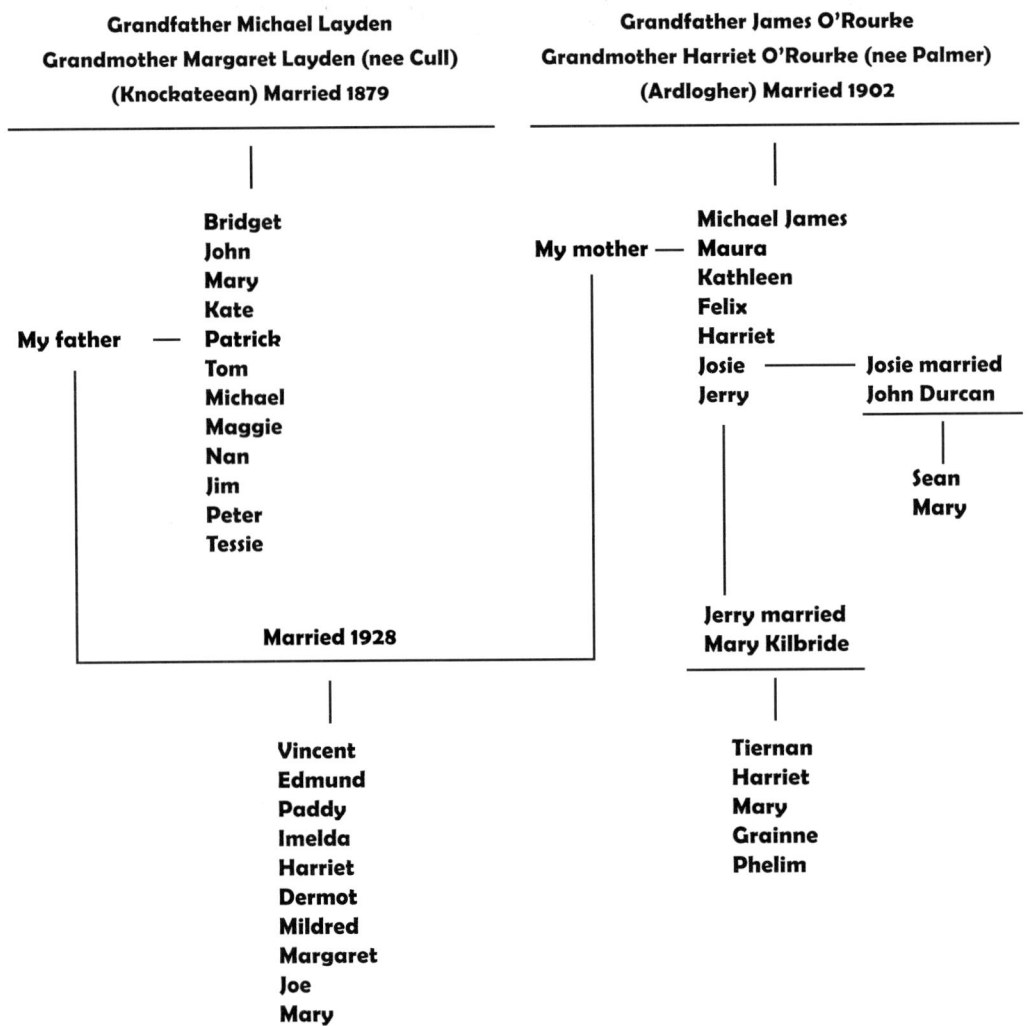

Note: Of my parent's siblings, all except four of my father's siblings married. However, for convenience, details are not provided here. Neither are those of our generation.

CHAPTER ONE

My Parents, Homestead and Country Life

My Parents and Family History

My devoted parents, Patrick Layden and Maura Layden (née O'Rourke) were married in 1928, having met one another some years earlier as teachers in the local primary national school at Tarmon, County Leitrim. I was born in January 1937, the sixth in a family of ten of five girls and five boys. Sadly, one of the girls, Mildred, died at the age of six months from pneumonia. All ten of us were born at home, which was the common practice at that time. Most of us were delivered by the renowned and much sought-after Dr. Roden from Keadue (a town which, many years later, became notable for its tidy town successes). In my time, Dr. Roden was assisted by an efficient and caring midwife, Kathleen Gilhooly, from nearby Tarmon. Home for us was Lecarrow House close to Spencer Harbour, County Leitrim, on the shores of beautiful Lough Allen.

Spencer Harbour had been one of the ports of call and departure for boats plying coal, flour and other cargo along the Shannon river, and probably also to Dublin via canal, prior to the harnessing of the river Shannon for electricity in the late 1920s. Spencer Harbour apparently got its name from the fact that the Harbour was officially opened by the Earl of Spencer at some stage in the past. Today one can still see the old red brick chimney tower at Spencer Harbour which was used in a previous era for firing clay bricks, and which for us as children seemed to reach the sky as we played hide and seek through its openings beneath. The local post office was also located at Spencer Harbour. I have a clear vision as a youngster of the postmaster, the very aptly named Gerard Ovens, baking big cakes of bread on the open fire in a black pot hanging over the fire, with hot embers placed on the lid of the pot. The smell of the baking bread permeated the post office, which was a room in his home. In more recent years, The Board of Works erected a fine marina at Spencer Harbour but when we lived there, the old harbour was in a state of disrepair and disuse. Spencer Harbour features again in Part 4 of this book.

My father, Patrick Layden, was born fifth of a surviving family of twelve, of six girls and six boys. Sadly, a number of the family members did not survive into old age; two died young in their early forties. However, Mary lived to ninety-two, Maggie to eighty-three and my father almost to eighty. My father's parents were Michael Layden and Margaret Layden (née Cull), both of whom came from Arigna. Michael was prominent in the coal-mining business in the Arigna area and after their marriage Michael and Margaret lived and raised their family at the Colliery House at Knockateean on the lower slopes of the Arigna mountains. Michael died in 1916 at the age of sixty-three and Margaret died in 1924 at sixty-two years of age. I never knew my grandparents, but Michael's legacy survived long after him as can be seen from the account of the Arigna mines in Part 4.

My mother, Maura was born second in a family of seven. All seven lived to fairly reasonable ages, my mother reaching sixty-eight. My mother's parents were James O'Rourke and Harriet O'Rourke (née Palmer). They lived and raised their family at Ardlogher, County Leitrim, where they operated a grocery business and farm. Ardlogher was the family homestead of James O'Rourke and was located beneath the slopes of the Arigna mountains overlooking Lough Allen, some two miles uphill from Tarmon catholic church. Access thereto was by a steep road that we called "the black road." In frosty conditions, or if one was not too confident about the power of one's car engine, a detour with less demanding climbs would be taken. Ardlogher, the birthplace of my mother, is only a few miles from Knockateean, the birthplace of my father. Despite this short distance separating them, it appears that they did not meet until they started teaching together as adults.

James O'Rourke could in all probability claim some family lineage with the O'Rourkes of Breffni.[1] His wife, Harriet Palmer, came from Drumkeerin, County Leitrim (otherwise known as Innismagrath), where her family were farmers. James O'Rourke died in early 1941, while his wife Harriet survived until early 1950. Unfortunately, I have no recollection of knowing grandfather James O'Rourke, thus grandmother Harriet O'Rourke was the only grandparent I remember. Later, some of the Palmer family moved to Sligo and Mary Palmer, who is very hale and hearty, still lives at Lord Edward Street, Sligo. She is a first cousin of my mother Maura—but, may I add, very many years younger. Mary's father, Jeremiah, was a brother of my grandmother Harriet. Mary's brother, the late Tom Palmer, was at one time editor of the county newspaper, The Sligo Champion. Tom and Mary's uncle, John Palmer, was at one stage the owner of O'Neill's public house at the corner of Church Hill and Wolfe Tone Street, Sligo. There are Sligo connections on the O'Rourke side of the family also; the late Jerry O'Rourke, who was well known in Sligo's insurance circles, was my uncle. Jerry O'Rourke married Mary Kilbride and had a family of five (see Family Tree). So the latter and I are first

---

1. The O'Rourkes of Breffni are an ancient Gaelic clan who can trace their ancestry to Brian, a 4th century King of Connaught. The O'Rourkes of Breffni were themselves Kings of Connaught in the 10th and 11th centuries; indeed present-day County Leitrim was, until 1565, called Breffni O'Rourke.

> *"When you were born you cried and the world rejoiced.
> Live your life so that when you die the world cries and you rejoice."*

cousins. I have another first cousin, Sean Durcan, who is married to Kathleen and living in Sligo. His mother, the late Josie Durcan from Castlerea, County Roscommon, was a sister of my mother. A close associate of the O'Rourke family from Ardlogher, Kay Horan, also lives in Sligo town. Myself and my family moved to Sligo in 1976; indeed it seems that Sligo has been a point to which many members of my extended family have gravitated.

As my granny, Harriet O'Rourke, lived until 1950 I have fairly clear memories of her. I would describe her as a very formidable and highly respected but very kind lady. I remember her visiting the houses of her children to provide practical help with the rearing of the grandchildren. She usually went on annual pre-Christmas holidays to her daughter Josie and son-in-law John Durcan in Castlerea. On these occasions my father invariably drove her. Her son Michael James (my uncle and father of Carmel Murray and the late Father Raymond O'Rourke) usually accompanied them on the day's car trip. Frequently, I was taken on the outing and I have very happy memories of these trips. I particularly looked forward to the culinary delights that would be provided when we arrived at Durcan's house!

My father, having previously trained as a primary school teacher in Waterford at the Training College there, was the Principal at Tarmon National School for many years, and as such was highly respected in the area. He also worked in his spare time on secretarial and administrative affairs in the local family coalmining business in Arigna. My mother also qualified as a teacher at a very young age and was considered an excellent Irish speaker. Her first teaching job was in Sligo town but after a year, when a vacancy came up near home, she joined my father at Tarmon National School. She had a great flair for singing and took pride in training a mixed choir at Tarmon Church. One of our early memories of mother was of her playing the harmonium at Mass on a dark Christmas morning to the light of two candles shining from jam-jars placed on either side of her. What wonderful strains came from that choir as they sang Silent Night, Adeste Fideles and Gloria in Excelsis Deo! For us children, this all added to the enchantment which filled the air and added much to the joy and mystery of those first Christmases. Mother gave up teaching later on to rear her family, only doing occasional locum work.

The Homestead and Country Life

Our family house at Lecarrow, Spencer Harbour, where I and all my siblings were born and reared, was a big house by local standards. It had a basement, ground floor, a return and a first storey. There were six bedrooms, two large

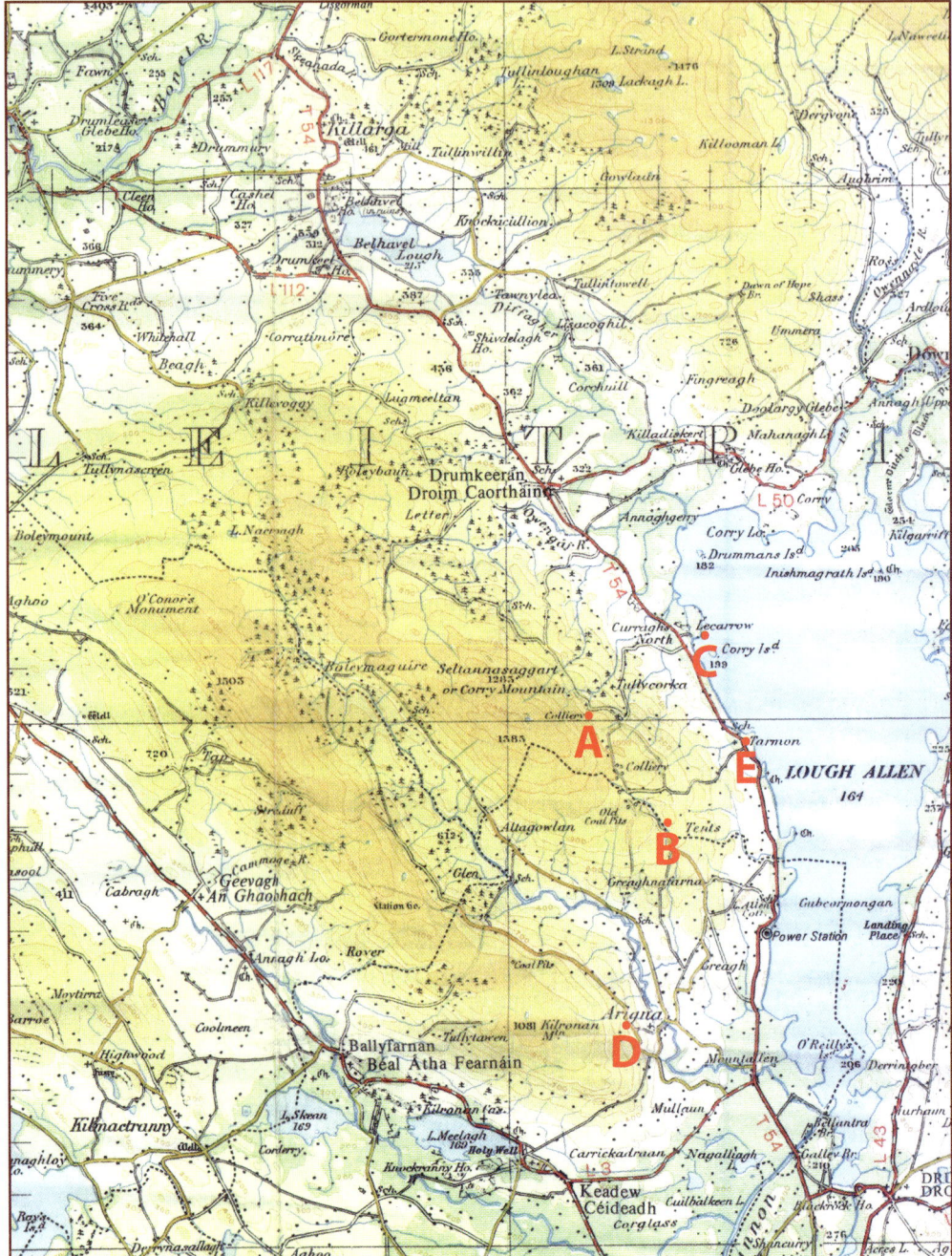

LEGEND. A – KNOCKATEEAN: Birthplace of author's father, Patrick Layden, and homestead of grandfather Michael Layden, coal mining entrepreneur; B – ADLOGHER: Birthplace of author's mother, Maura O'Rourke; C – Location of LECARROW HOUSE, purchased by the Layden brother from Major General Fawcett in 1921, and birthplace of author. Also location of SPENCER HARBOUR (port), old CLAY WORKS, and JETTY HOUSE built by Michael Layden in early 1900s; D – Arigna: Coalmining hub. Coalmining was dispersed widely in the general Arigna area; E – Location of TARMON CHURCH, TARMON NATIONAL SCHOOL and the JOHN McKENNA (flute player) MEMORIAL.

> *"Happiness is a direction, not a place."*

reception rooms and a very large hallway and staircase as well as the working area of the house—the kitchen, utility and storage rooms. It was built in the mid 1800s, and its outer walls were three to four feet thick. My father, together with his five brothers, Michael, John, Thomas, James and Peter, purchased Lecarrow house with some one hundred acres of low land and other property rights in 1921 for £4,000 from William James Fawcett, a Major General in His Majesty's Army. The other property rights included in the sale consisted of mountain land at Moneenatieve, mineral and mining rights at Seltanaskeagh and some sporting rights. In later years, some time after my parent's marriage, my father's five brothers transferred their interests in the house and lands to my father at a mutually agreed consideration. It would appear from the title deeds of the Lecarrow property that the mineral and mining rights of lands at Greaghnaslieve, some four miles towards the mountain from Spencer Harbour, were transferred in 1904 from the Fawcett holding to (grandfather) Michael Layden. It appears that the Fawcett family owned at one time some 1,000 acres of land locally (Patrick Flanagan, "Some Notes on Leitrim Industry," p. 411), which presumably included the properties referred to above. Prior to the acquisition of the Lecarrow lands, grandfather Michael Layden built a new house of moderate size on an adjoining site (which was close to the old Spencer Harbour) in the early 1900s. The house became known as the Jetty House.

Some of grandfather's family moved to this house from their homestead at the Colliery House at Knockateean. Later this house was occupied by unmarried members of grandfather's family. This house also became a favourite meeting place for all members of that family, their extended families and their children. My siblings and I have many happy memories of visits to the Jetty House; here in particular we got to know our cousins. One of our enjoyments was watching the guinea fowl fly off into the trees, no doubt aided by our antics. Then there were the famous white yeast loaves which Aunt Kate baked in post-war years and we always hoped we might have one such loaf home with us. As I reminisce about nice people, it would be very remiss of me not to mention my Aunt Madge (wife of Tom Layden) who was my godmother and who lived about one mile from us at Drumasuane. She was a most gracious and kind lady and very good to me. I have very happy memories of many visits to her house and family. Aunt Madge's apple tarts were just out of this world. Sr. Maureen, Monica and Bernadette thankfully still survive from this family.

In our house at Lecarrow there were fireplaces in all the living rooms and bedrooms. There was no central heating in those days and electricity did not arrive in our part of the country until the rural electrification programme of the late 1950s. Wax candles and paraffin oil lamps were the usual source of light. We also had a gas plant that came with the house which provided light in certain rooms. This plant converted petrol into gas by means of huge weights that were hoisted up on a pulley and then gradually descended over a week or so, creating the pressure that converted the petrol into gas; such a plant would have been relatively unusual in a private house. Local coal, turf, wood and culm balls (a type of briquette, see chapter 11) were the fuels used for fires. There were no telephones until about the mid 1950s, when open party telephone lines became available, meaning that anybody with a telephone on the line system could listen into telephone conversations if they so wished, merely by lifting their receiver. Telegrams, delivered by hand via the local post office, were the main method of communication. There was always a sense of anticipation associated with telegrams; sometimes they brought good news, sometimes bad news, such as a death or serious illness of a close relative. There were no televisions either as they did not arrive until the 1960s. Even the radio was a scarce commodity, as every house did not have one.

Radios in those days were clumsy affairs for, apart from being large in size, they required a combination of a wet battery (containing electrodes laid in acid) and a dry battery to power the radio. You were in serious trouble if you spilt the acid from the wet battery on the carpet—it simply rotted it. I remember well being glued to Michael O'Hehir's broadcast of the All Ireland football final in 1947 from the Polo grounds in New York. The final was between Cavan and Kerry and Cavan duly won. John Wilson who died recently was on that Cavan team, as was Mick Higgins, who attended the former's funeral. My father particularly treasured the radio and you would be unwise to make noise as he listened to the news programmes and to Michael O'Hehir. Another big item in the communication scheme of things was the gramophone, which was a substantial piece of furniture, including its movable arm to which was attached the needle for playing the records, invariably long playing records. Many houses had gramophones together with a good stock of famous classical records of the day, such as John McCormack's "I Hear You Calling Me," "Mother Machree" and "Machushla"; Benny Goodman's "Somebody Stole my Gal"; Vera Lynn's "We'll Meet Again" and "White Cliffs of Dover"; Ella Fitzgerald's "Paper Moon"; Delia Murphy's "The Spinning Wheel" and "The Moonshiner as well as various other records, including those of Duke Ellington, Louis Armstrong, Bing Crosby and Frank Sinatra.

Perhaps the most important source of communication and entertainment was what we called rambling; that is one neighbour visiting the other for a chat and a cup of tea, and often for traditional music and a sing-song. This indeed was the heart of community life in the country at that time. On our home scene, I cannot pass on without mentioning our Sunday afternoons and evenings as we gathered with many locals at the river bridge just outside our avenue gate to toss coins, chat and fish. This was a real meeting place and my father loved to join the group to discuss the passing news and enjoy a good old "healthy" smoke. As children we were delighted to have the opportunity to be with the grown-ups. In addition to the above, there were infrequent travelling cinema shows and also the occasional local parish concerts and

> *"It is said that many who plan to seek God at the eleventh hour die at 10.30."*

bazaars. Of course there was also the annual wren boys rendezvous on St. Stephen's Day when the young and not so young dressed up in unrecognisable attire and, armed with tin whistles, or whatever, entertained the neighbours both near and afar, usually receiving some monetary reward for their efforts.

Generally speaking large families were the standard for this era. Infant mortality was higher then due to lack of modern facilities and medicines. On top of that there was the scourge of TB (tuberculosis). However, to offset all of this there were many local cures available for various ailments, and also some self- made medical practitioners, whom we referred to as "quacks." There was one such highly regarded person in our locality by the name of Gilbert who cured numerous people and animals. Generally there was high emigration from Ireland in those days due to lack of job opportunities at home. Fortunately, emigration was not a very big issue in our region due to employment being available in the local coal mines.

Needless to say, motor cars were scarce commodities. Walking ("shanks mare" as we called it) and cycling were the main modes of propulsion. Those who were more fortunate had a trap pulled by horse which could take four to six people. As one was walking the road to Mass, or wherever, it was quite a treat to be given a lift in one of these sedate traps, particularly if the horse was able to keep up a good steady speed and wasn't giddy. My father did have an old Dodge car but it was jacked up in the garage during the duration of the war (1939-1945) because of unavailability of petrol. I remember distinctly after the war was over my father's brother Michael (who was affectionately known as Mick and who managed the Layden coal mines in Arigna at that time and had, among other attributes, a great mechanical brain) coming to our house and working on the car and getting the engine started and the car running again. It was a time for celebration.

In fact the end of the war was a time for celebration in many senses, particularly because of the renewal of peace in the world. Also, of course, food and many other household and industrial commodities which had been unavailable during the war gradually became available again. I remember the ecstasy I felt in eating a banana some time after the war ended. With the help of the US Marshall Aid programme for the purpose of rebuilding Europe, life gradually got back to normal. There was food rationing during the war which was very well and fairly administered by John Leydon, the then Secretary of the Department of Supplies. Another aspect of the war was compulsory tillage. Generally all farmers had to sow and till a prescribed portion of crops to enable Ireland to be self-sufficient in foodstuffs during the war. In addition, farmers normally grew all their own potato and vegetable requirements, and frequently also grew oats, particularly to feed their horses which were used to work the land, as tractors had not yet arrived on the scene.

Grandfather Michael Layden

Grandmother Margaret Layden (nee Cull)

Grandmother Harriet O'Rourke (nee Palmer)

Father and mother, Patrick and Maura Layden (nee O'Rourke) on their wedding day, 1928.

Father and mother nearly forty years later.

My sister Imelda (Marist nun) with my father in the early 1960s, together with red setter dog. (Note: Nuns generally wear more practical attire today, and likewise so does Imelda.)

Cousins and some siblings at the Jetty House in 1939

Lecarrow House, Spencer Harbour

Colliery House, Knockateean, as it stood in the 1980s

CHAPTER TWO

Our Farm and Farm Activities

The Farm

The land in our part of North Leitrim was rather poor in that the soil was heavy with an impervious daub base. Thus it tended to be wet and rushes grew fairly abundantly on it. Yet with good management it produced good crops of potatoes (spuds), oats, meadows for hay, and later for silage when that became fashionable. We were one of the first people in that part of the country to make silage in the early 1950s. I remember us having meadows in prime condition for silage (i.e. young grasses of the right variety) at around the 24th of May and making very good silage there from in a silo tower specially built for that purpose. That was particularly early for that part of the country. My father had a great interest in farming, mostly though as a hobby and he employed men to work the land, and loyal men they were: John Daniel and later his son Johnnie, Hughie Flynn, Michael Keegan, Mick Smith, Cathal Keavney and others, at various times. He took great satisfaction in walking the land after his day at school and viewing the state of the fields and the stock. He could name and recognise probably every type of grass that grew on his land, such as the clovers, the rye grasses, crested dogstail, cocksfoot, timothy, and so on. He could do likewise with trees and shrubs.

Father also had a great interest in fruit trees and at one time we had one of the best orchards in that part of the country. He was probably one of the few people in the vicinity who knew how to properly prune young apple trees. He was particularly interested in monitoring the progress of young fruit trees, and myself and my older sister Imelda were on one occasion warned, in an Adam and Eve type situation, not to pick fruit off a particular tree. However, the apples were very enticing and I decided it would be alright to shake the branches and then pick the apples off the ground. So I am confessing at last and can confirm that the forbidden fruit did indeed taste wonderful! During summer and autumn, one of our jobs as children was to pick lots of apples and some pears for school, as my father had an arrangement that the other children would bring some turf from their homes, in exchange for the fruit, to help with the school fires in the winter.

We kept six to eight cows for their milk and calves and dry cattle stock, usually of the Shorthorn and Angus breeds, or crosses thereof. Father was a good judge of a beast and a comment such as, it is "too high in the pins," meant the beast was not up to scratch in terms of frame and conformation. Calving was an event that got special attention. The impending signs of a cow ready to give birth were noted and someone would be ready to be in attendance, checking the cow every so often. The cow didn't always choose a convenient time; night time or early in the morning was quite a possibility. I might add that I delivered many a calf on my own. Once you got the head of the calf coming you were generally in business. Then on the odd occasion you got the pleasant surprise of a twin calf following.

Another fairly significant event on the cattle front at that time was the release of the winter-housed stock to the fields. On a particular day in spring, with nature pushing forward new life, the young cattle were let out into the fields. The way they chased madly around the fields with their tails up was a real spectacle—they had won their freedom. Perhaps they were a lesson to us humans to be more appreciative of our freedoms and of the many dawns presented to us in life.

We had two horses, Terry and Paddy. One often hears the phrase "a great workhorse" being used today to describe a machine, more likely an old machine. Well, Terry and Paddy were truly great workhorses and the man behind the plough appreciated this as the two horses worked in unison. Naturally there was great sadness when eventually each of them in turn (Paddy was the oldest) died of staggers, a common cause of death then in old horses. Horses are very special animals and of course a great bond develops with their handlers over a span of up to twenty years. The horse had to have its periodic outing to town, specifically to the forge for its new pairs of shoes and manicure of its hooves. There was quite a bit of ritual involved on the part of the blacksmith in the shoeing operation. The forge was a great place for the people to meet and socialise, as invariably one had to join a queue of horses. It was regarded as a day out in town. A sojourn to a local hostelry would not be unknown.

The Fair Day

The local fair day, in Drumkeerin village in our case, was a big event both commercially and socially. Sometimes we travelled further afield to Drumshanbo. Cattle walked the main roads in those days to the fairs, usually under the escort of at least two drovers. The bargaining between buyer and seller (mostly between farmers but sometimes one would be a middleman) and the tactics used were very entertaining. Even if the buyer was dead keen to purchase, he couldn't show his interest in too obvious a way. So a sojourn to a public house for some nourishment or perhaps for breakfast would be fairly standard practice. If he returned to the person selling then it was a time for the seller to get serious and usually there would be a third party to help out, who would invariably require each of the two combatants to stretch out one of their hands with palm upright and get each side

"Life is fragile, handle with prayer."

to come closer to one another in price and finally suggest a splitting of the difference and a clasping of the palms, maybe with a spit of excess saliva to seal the deal. Then of course there was the question of the "luck penny" whereby the seller would have to give some small recompense back to the buyer. The third party who helped clinch the deal would often earn something as well.

I thoroughly enjoyed those fair days, particularly the ones in Drumkeerin because my father always visited, and had lunch with, his sister Maggie Dolan and her husband Patrick, who incidentally was a very shrewd judge of cattle and all things farming as well as running a very successful grocery and a well controlled bar. In this he was ably assisted by his son Frank. The four course lunch served up on these occasions left absolutely nothing to be desired. The soufflé for dessert was truly divine. Later generations of the Dolan family have continued this great catering tradition in the Bush Hotel in Carrick-on-Shannon.

Saving the Hay

Hay making was a huge event at that time, or at least that is the way it appears now. It was a truly social event as well as a serious working occasion. Generally, the summer in those days seemed to be of almost endless sunshine, or perhaps that is my fond recollection. The hay making process started with mowing the grass with a one- or two-horse drawn mowing machine. The blade for the mowing machine had to be sharpened beforehand with a particular sharpening stone and repeated at intervals thereafter if a large area of grass was being cut. Very small plots of grass or awkward spots of meadows would be cut by hand with a scythe. One or two days after cutting, depending on the weather, the grass was manually shaken out using two-pronged pitch forks, and it was important to give it a proper shaking. A second shaking of the grass, now drying towards the hay stage, might be necessary over the next day or so.

All going well the hay would be ready for cocking after about four days, maybe a bit less in very good weather. So the hay was gathered with pitch forks and the leftovers hand-raked into piles of appropriate quantities for each individual cock of hay. Typically the cocks were eight to ten feet high and of circular dimension and cone shaped. The circular base would be around nine feet wide and the point at top a mere two feet or less. The cocks then had to be tied down with ropes, invariably wound (woven) from the hay by the young members of the family, using a very simple winding device. Later these hay ropes were superseded with hemp ropes. Also the manual shaking and gathering of hay would eventually be mechanised, but it is doubtful if the mechanical shaking of hay was ever as well done as the manual shaking, which could deal more readily with the specific conditions. With no threatening weather on the horizon, time could be taken out to partake of hot tea taken out into the hay field in beautiful shiny tin cans, smithed by the skilled tinsmiths of the itinerant clan, who were a significant part of rural life in those days. Tea was poured from the tin can into drinking "pongers" (mugs), also fashioned by the same tinsmiths. To accompany the tea there was lots of bread generously lathered with butter, both of which were likely to be home-made. Tea and buttered bread never tasted so good, unless perhaps you were cutting/saving turf on the bog, usually on the lower slopes of the local moors. Incidentally, the home made butter would have been made using the traditional churning process, whereby after much whirling around the butter separates from the milk, and the milk that was left over was buttermilk, which was a very popular drink.

However, not all hay making was as idyllic as this, and probably the worst scenario was when a good judge of the weather would predict that the rain would come before the carefully spread-out hay would be ready for cocking. Then a major strategic decision had to taken involving three options: do nothing (and hope the rain would not come), make the hay into hand-shakings or, the least palatable option, make the hay into laps—usually when the hay was not dry enough for hand-shakings. The hand-shaking was really a miniature cock which, when the weather permitted, would be shook out again to dry fully before making proper cocks. Basically the same was done with the laps but the problem with the laps was that their making involved back-breaking work. To make a lap, one bent down and gathered a quantity of well teased-out hay with both arms and moulded it sensitively and placed it back on the ground with a channel for the air to go through it, the channel being the space occupied by your arms.

In the 1950s when I was home for summer holidays from boarding school and later from university, I worked continuously and with great enthusiasm on the land. My father exposed me to farm management at a very early age and in the context of lapping hay appointed me one day, when I was probably around fifteen years old, to be the bearer of back-breaking news to some four men, who had laboured hard all day preparing about six acres of hay for cocking in Gubb meadow along the lake wood, to say to them that the most appropriate option was to start making laps. It was a big ask but they were decent men and the field was lapped that evening.

Something one associated with hay making in high summer in those days was the corncrake. As you lay in bed at night ready to sleep and the window of the bedroom wide open, one was invariably lulled to sleep with the craking of not just one but several corncrakes. Alas, it is a sound rarely heard now! Another memory is that of bats circulating around your room, which were attracted in by a light in the room. Thankfully, we still have some bats, but of course some people now have a fear of bats getting tangled in their hair. I don't think we ever had any experiences like that.

The hay is not quite finished yet. Perhaps, the biggest event of all in the hay making operations was the gathering in of all the cocks of hay in the fields into

> *"A great man is one who has not lost the heart of a child."*
> — Menicius

the haggard or house yard where a big rick of hay was made from them. The rick was of rectangular shape and rising to a slanted head rather like the roof of a house. The dimensions of the rick would depend on how much hay one wished to put into it. A farmer may have one or more ricks depending, not just on the quantity of hay available, but also the locations from which stock would be fed in the winter period. As an alternative to ricks, we sometimes made what we called pikes; pikes were basically very big cocks of hay with a pike, i.e. a timber support, sunk in the ground around which the hay was built. Occasionally there were hay sheds available into which the hay was put (building it up on a layered basis so as to maximise the capacity of the shed) rather than making ricks or pikes.

Various methods were used to bring the cocks of hay into the rick area, the most popular perhaps being the float, a flat-bottomed carriage on wheels which was drawn by horse. The back end of the float was tipped to the base of the cock and, with the aid of a strong rope worked on a pulley device, the cock was dragged on to the float. It was off to the haggard then where by tipping the float and pulling it away the cock was dislodged. The float was a great favourite with youngsters because free rides on the float seemed always to be available, with or without cocks of hay. Another popular method of bringing in cocks of hay was what we called snigging, where, by putting a strong rope around the cock and coupling the rope to a flange at the back of the cock which was attached to the horse's harness, the cock was dragged in by horse to the haggard. Often as youngsters we would jump up on the moving cock, sometimes causing it to fall over; then we were in trouble! Instead of either of these methods of drawing in hay, the hay cocks could be forked onto a cart or trailer in the field and then forked off again in the haggard. This involved a lot of handling but sometimes it was the only option available. The gathering of hay into ricks, pikes or sheds usually took place in September.

Hay balers and the many other forms of mechanization were not a feature of farm life in these days and the tractor had not yet replaced the horse. However, the scene gradually began to change in the late 1940s and early 1950s. I had the privilege of driving and working one of the first Massey Ferguson tractors to appear in those days in North Leitrim. I can boast of ploughing a field for oats all on my own at fourteen years of age. Was this the beginning of the end of the real physical connection with farming, as horses began to be replaced with mechanical power? Probably yes, but I continued to enjoy the summer work with the tractor for another seven or eight years until another career outlet dictated a different way of life for me. Talking about tractors, I have the fondest of memories of Bertie Christie from Arigna, who to me was Mr. Tractor and who taught me everything I knew about tractors, not least the intricacies of reversing a trailer.

The Pig

Any look back in time would be incomplete without considering the vital role that the pig played in Irish rural life. Nearly every family kept a pig and often two pigs as we did. The basic food for pigs was boiled potatoes and generally the pigs were allowed to range freely. Killing the pig was a very big event and proper planning had to be put in place, usually involving a team of people, some hired and some family or extended family. The actual killing of the pig (which to my young eyes seemed like a very cruel operation, involving slitting the pig's throat) and the drawing and retaining of the blood in a clean vessel was usually done by a hired specialist from the locality, assisted of course by others. After killing, the pig was cleaned and the hairs removed with a shaving knife. It was then hung from the hind legs for some days to mature. In the meantime, the black pudding specialist (for many years my Granny Harriet) made the pudding, using the freshly drawn blood and a mixture of cereals and other ingredients. Unfortunately, I don't have the recipe but I can say that no black pudding has ever since tasted so good and this is not fantasy.

The next stage in the pig process was to cut away the ribs from the rib cage, and these were referred to as spare ribs, which were usually cooked fresh, but sometimes were salted and stored for preserving. No more than the black puddings, the fresh spare ribs duly cooked and served with apple sauce tasted awesomely good. The next and final stage of the pig operation was to cut the carcase into appropriate-sized pieces suitable for future consumption. While a small number of the pieces might be kept for immediate consumption over the next week or two, the bulk thereof was preserved through salting as there were no fridges or freezers at that time and would be eaten over the next six to twelve months. This preserving process was achieved by placing the pig pieces between layers of salt in suitable containers, generally empty tea chests of light plywood in which loose tea would have been shipped from abroad to merchants and shopkeepers in Ireland. The product that emerged later was bacon as compared to the initial fresh pork product.

Needless to say, salted bacon as prepared above was one of the staple items in the food diet of that period. Generally before cooking the salted bacon would be steeped in water to remove the salt, or at least some of it. Sometimes it might be boiled slightly to remove more salt. A most popular use for this bacon was to boil it with cabbage and combined with floury potatoes one truly had what was probably the most sought after meal of that time. Of course it is still a great favourite today. Some of the salted bacon was sliced into rashers for breakfast, tea or otherwise. A great favourite was to fry the rashers with slices of boiled pup boxty, particularly popular in North Leitrim.

Boxty was one of the many food uses to which the humble potato was put. In addition to boiled pup boxty there was also what we called pan boxty, which is still readily available today, but I do know of one Leitrim firm that currently makes boiled pup boxty. Potato and flour were the basic ingredients for both types of

> "Late have I loved you, Beauty so ancient and so new: late have I loved you."
> — St. Augustine

boxty, but the process used was different. Another very popular dish for which the potato was the principal ingredient was what we called cally. This was basically mashed potato with ingredients added such as home-made creamery butter, scallions, and presumably salt. This was served on a plate in a rounded mound with a hole in its centre in which was placed a piece of butter and on top of which was poured hot milk. For kids this was a delight and trying to bank in the milk that was breaking out from its surrounds made the eating experience very exciting.

Apart from pigs, most farmers also kept fowl, particularly chickens, but sometimes ducks, geese and turkeys also. The chicken and ducks were normally kept for their fresh free range eggs, but sometimes also for killing for the table, while the geese and the turkeys were kept for slaughter at Christmas, some of which may be sold. Frequently eggs would also be sold. When the laying days of the hens were over they were normally used (i.e. boiled) to make chicken or, more correctly, hen broth. It was also normal practice for every farmer to be self-sufficient in cow's milk, some of which may also have been sold to the local creamery. There was also the odd goat kept for milk.

As you can see, farming was not merely a job or a business but was a major part of everyday life in rural Ireland. This connection with the land and the communal aspect of it were very much enjoyed by all, despite the hardship that it could, at times, entail. Perhaps the mechanisation that has taken place since my childhood has made this connection with land and community a less salient part of rural life today.

"If only I may grow: firmer, simpler, quieter, warmer."
— Dag Hammarskjold

CHAPTER THREE
Family, Sports and Religion

My Siblings and I

So much for farming and the food we ate, it is now time to return to our family as we grew up in those early years of my life. We were a family of nine after Mildred's death at six months of age. The first of the family, Vincent, arrived in 1929, and the last and best, Mary, arrived in October 1948 when I was nearly twelve years old. This was the year after the big snow of 1947—I don't think there was any connection! In passing, it might be said that the snow falls of 1947 were of historical severity and the only mode of transport we had for quite some time to secure outside supplies was Terry the horse. Our family had five sons and four surviving daughters in the following order of age; Vincent, Edmund, Paddy, Imelda, Harriet, myself, Margaret, Joe and Mary.

Our house was a busy place and a healthy competitive environment prevailed in the interest of successful survival, whether in work or play. We played a lot together as a family and no doubt we played our fair share of pranks on one another. The one that comes to mind now is that I woke up one morning with a very black face much to the amusement of all onlookers. I realised the cause of the amusement when I looked in the mirror and I think I identified the culprit as Paddy who used the black polish on me during my sleep. We probably had the usual squabbles but generally nothing too serious and certainly nothing that seems significant at this remove.

Lough Allen was a great focal point for us in the summer months, not just for fishing as will be mentioned later, but for playing on the sand beaches and also for swimming. For us, the Lough Allen tide went out once a year in the summer, thus laying bare large stretches of shoreline and beaches, and then came back in the winter. This was because Lough Allen acted as a reservoir of surplus water in the winter months which was used up in the summer to drive the electricity generating plant at Ardnacrusha. This was operated by sluice gates at the outlet of the lake.

We had various chore allocations and I suspect that the girls may have come off worst in this matter, particularly in regard to in-house work. However, I have a recollection of often helping in cooking and doing various other jobs in the house, even at quite a young age. I remember cooking a turkey meal at the age of fourteen, when my mother was sick and some of my older siblings were away at boarding school. Fairly normal practice in those days was that the older members of the family helped in the tasks of rearing the later arrivals. I would claim I did my part in this, whatever about the quality of my efforts. Regardless of my input, the outcomes were excellent.

Handball and Football Enthusiasts

Regarding sporting activities, handball and football were prominent pastimes for the family mainly, it must be said, among the male members, but not exclusively so. In addition, my oldest brother Vincent was a good hurler and played for Rockwell College, Co. Tipperary, where practically all the male members of our family and those of our cousins attended, mostly in the 1940s—I finished there myself in 1955. As a family, we played a lot of handball using the gable-end of our house as a handball alley and we found this facility quite adequate. Handball was a very popular game in the country that time, and I have a recollection of there being a handball alley in most country towns, including Drumkeerin, some three miles away. Again Vincent was the most capable of the handballers amongst us and was most proficient in hitting a ball dead from a serve. There were some very good matches between him and a local expert, Arthur Gorman, from Drumkeerin. My father was quite a good handballer as well and, while we all had our moments, Paddy would have been the best of the rest of us.

We all believed that we had good gaelic football talents, such beliefs not necessarily being well-founded in all cases. In any event, we played a lot of football among ourselves, using a proper leather football. Keeping the ball properly pumped could be an issue sometimes. Edmund, the second-eldest, was definitely the most prominent of the footballers in the late 1940s, and did represent the Leitrim senior team on some occasions. Joe, the youngest brother, managed to soak up the football skills that most of the rest of us failed to do and became a skilful footballer and played for both Leitrim and the Connacht teams. When transport became more available in the early 1950s, travelling to the various football matches, accompanied usually by our cousin Frank Dolan, and perhaps others, were big events. Sadly, only Joe and myself remain alive of the five brothers; Vincent, Edmund and Paddy all have passed to their eternal rewards, somewhat before their time. All my deceased brothers worked with their cousins in the family coal mining business in Arigna. Happily, my sisters have fared better. Harriett died relatively young from a heart attack but the other three are still hale and hearty. Imelda the oldest, nearing her mid-70s, is a Marist sister and is now on her second tour of duty in Brazil. Our very good wishes and prayers go to her. My other two sisters, Margaret and Mary, are happily retired from work and living in Dublin, but keeping themselves active

> *"For neither man nor angel can discern hypocrisy,*
> *the only evil that walks invisible, except to God alone."*
> — Milton

with various activities. Joe is also living in Dublin with his family, and is a successful and caring businessman.

Sunny Days in Bundoran

As a family, the annual summer holiday to Bundoran was special. Bundoran in the 1940s was especially good, and I don't think that this was an illusion of youth. Nice accommodation and food, plenty of swimming, watching (as well as some participation in) the diving from the top of the rocks at Rougey, walking, some visits to the Church, variety shows in the evening and then the high spot of the day, beautiful tea and pastries (they were exquisite) in Crowders Restaurant, and a good walk home to our accommodation, all contributed to a full and satisfying day. I remember a great future singing star who cut her teeth on the variety show scene in Bundoran—she was the one and only Ruby Murray, who became a big star soon afterwards. Another great star to have graced the stage in Bundoran was our own Bridie Gallagher, immortalised with her rendering of "The Boys from the County Armagh." My mother just loved the fresh whiff of the sea. Sometimes she would go away for a week on her own (would you blame her for getting some release from us lot?) to beautiful Strandhill in Co. Sligo where she soaked up everything the open Atlantic could offer.

Higher Things

Religious practices were very much part of life in our family as was the case generally. Regular prayers, particularly the family rosary at night (with plenty of trimmings), Mass on Sundays and Holydays, and occasional church missions were all standard. To receive Holy Communion at morning Mass (no evening Masses in those days) one had to fast from all food and water from the previous midnight. Fasting in Lent (where only one substantial meal was allowed daily) and abstinence from meat on Fridays were all standard practices. Going to Lough Derg in Co. Donegal on three-day pilgrimages was a pretty common practice also. While there, one was barefooted and had one meal per day of black tea and dry toast and stayed up one night. My siblings and I (for our sins) did Lough Derg on several occasions. My father used to cycle to Lough Derg, a distance of some fifty miles, with some of his siblings and with a very good humoured brother-in-law,

Tom Morahan. It is noteworthy that my father and mother did the Lough Derg pilgrimage together before they were married.

Both my Mum and Dad died within two months of one another in April and May 1974 (RIP). As indicated earlier, Dad almost reached eighty years of age, while Mum was sixty-eight. They were very good and loving and caring parents, who generously shared their time and resources with us. When it came to controlling his family, his sons in particular, Dad had it just right in the sense of imposing appropriate discipline and perhaps applying the odd punishment or sanction.

We had a great respect for our parents. The memory of good parents is very special. I believe that we in our turn must ensure that we pass on similar cherished memories.

Father and my three older brothers and myself.

"*One never stands as tall as when one kneels to help a child.*"

My sister Imelda, cousin Bernadette and two friends at school in Carrick-on-Shannon.

My brothers Edmund and Paddy

My sister Harriett

FAMILY, SPORTS AND RELIGION 25

Jerry O'Rourke's (my uncle) wedding to Mary Kilbride, with my brother Vincent as best man and Evelyn Kilbride as bridesmaid.

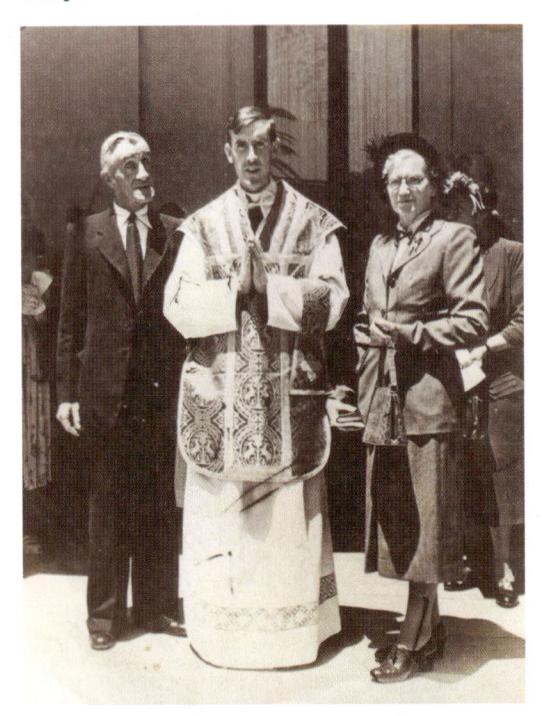

My cousin Father Leo Layden CSSp at his ordination in Rome in 1952, with his father Michael (Mick) Layden and mother Katie Layden.

My cousin Father Raymond O'Rourke with his sister Carmel (right) and Kay Horan (left).

Beatrice's (my wife) family, Thomas George Hunt, Bridget Hunt (nee Kilcoyne) Christina, Una, Beatrice and Michael, and her aunt and uncle Annie and Ernie Nolan and Mary Nolan. (Late 1940s)

Beatrice's family (Early 1950s). Front from left: Beatrice, Michael and Una. Standing: Mother, Father and Christina.

CHAPTER FOUR
Fishing and Shooting

A Fishing Apprenticeship

This section would be incomplete without mentioning two passions shared by our family and, indeed, by several of our relations as well as by many others in the area. These were fishing and shooting. Our family's first introduction to fishing would have taken place at the very young age of four or five on the shores of Lough Allen, a mere few hundred yards from our house. We caught perch and bream in plenty, but also eels and pike and possibly the odd trout. All these fish were highly prized and there was no such thing as catch and release in those days. We fished from the shore where the water was fairly deep or at the mouth of the river which ran through our land. We used long one piece hazel or other rods cut from the local wood, to which was tied some twenty yards of strong fishing line, attached to about a size four hook. We didn't have rod reels then. The bait generally used was the blackhead worm, if you could get them, otherwise one would make do with the red soft worms (earthworms). We often fed the area of water we wished to fish with cooked oaten meal balls (with a stone or ball of daub in their centre to make them sink) so as to attract the fish to the vicinity. Fishing here was quite a social occasion as quite a number of neighbours also congregated to fish. Often we would leave our rods set at night, and there would be a scramble to be the first to lift the rods in the morning as there was always a great expectation of having a catch overnight. One had to resist the temptation of lifting someone else's rod, particularly that of a neighbour.

We fished for trout in our early days in the small river that flowed through our land, from the relatively nearby mountain, under Scardan Bridge. The rods we used were shorter than those used in the lake, and in addition to worm for bait, we used white grubs (found in dock stems) and corbetts (which were the grub or the larva stage of sedge flies, found in the caddis shells under stones in the river). In low water when the trout were unlikely to bite, we often dirtied the river with mud from the bank upstream from the pools we wished to fish, so as to give the trout the sensation that a flood was on the way. This proved very successful. No one ever seemed to question the legality of this type of fishing. Not alone did we fish as such, but we also participated in a method of fishing called crooking. This

> *"All art is but imitation of nature."*
>
> — Lucius Annaeus Seneca

was surely poaching but again no one was aware of it being so. Crooking involved catching trout under the stones with your hands. Often you would chase the trout to the stone or stones that you could fairly easily manage to get your hands under. My brother Edmund, and another local man who lived nearby, were dab hands at crooking, and had the courage to put their hands under stones where there might, on rare occasions, be a water rat in residence. There was another "fully legal" method of fishing called teeming, whereby in low water we dammed up the water above a pool that we expected trout to be in, and then teemed out the water from the pool with containers to maroon the trout in dry dock and then pick off those worth taking. Frequently, the dam burst before the teeming was finished. It was quite a labour-intensive operation.

So much for that type of fishing! Our authentic entry to fishing was fly fishing on the local medium-sized rivers i.e. the Arigna river, Irwin's river and the Yellow river, all of which flowed into Lough Allen. We would have started fishing these rivers at ten or eleven years of age. We had proper fly rods, coupled with reels, fly lines and gut casts (these were pre-nylon days). Our favourite flies were the Hare's Ear, March Brown and Greenwell's Glory. Others such as the Cow Dung, Blue Bottle, Priest and so on were also used. These rivers were in pristine condition and held big stocks of trout up to two pounds. These were pre-forestry and pre-artificial fertiliser days. We certainly had many great days fishing on these waters, sometimes fishing into the heart of the mountain and often involving long walks maybe in addition to a long cycle. The excitement in rigging up the rods for fishing, particularly on days when fishing conditions were just perfect, was sometimes too much to bear as youngsters and one failed to tie the fly knot correctly with, of course, disastrous results later. The trout were very tasty when rolled in flour and cooked on the pan with butter. Salmon fishing, with the very odd exception, had not yet arrived on the scene for us. But it was to come later.

Dog and Gun

Shooting was the other big attraction for us. Nowadays I do not shoot and have not done so for many years. I stopped shooting after one of my daughters, concerned about what she perceived to be my cruelty to animals, said to me "Dad, never do that again" after I proudly brought home quarry I had shot. I think it is fair to say that my own appetite for shooting had already diminished by that time so it was not such a big sacrifice. Anyway, in my formative years the biggest event in the shooting calendar of those days was the grouse shooting which opened on

August 12th each year—"the glorious 12th" as it was known. Everybody that shot in the locality was probably out that day, most likely from early dawn. The mountains were packed with grouse (a clutch of grouse was referred to as a pack). The good shots picked off "doubles," ideally a left and right, meaning a brace of birds were shot, as the grouse flushed and took off. My father and Vincent were particularly good shots, Paddy was pretty good too, and the rest of us were somewhat behind. There would be an equal variety of shots among my uncles and cousins and others that shot. In any event, the really big thrill was walking the moors in glorious scenery on a good day with others, with good working dogs (Irish setters were our choice) and watching and walking with them as they searched and sniffed out the grouse, and then to see them go on a "dead set" as they closed up on the birds. Irrespective of what the results were when the grouse rose, the experience was pure magic.

Sadly, today grouse have almost disappeared from Irish moors and bogs. Their demise is probably due to a combination of factors such as overgrazing by sheep, afforestation, vermin, and so on. Grouse chicks require young ling heather in their diet to survive, thus overgrazing and exclusion of large tracts of moors by afforestation were major problems. I got a pleasant surprise in the summer of 2006 when, walking to the source of the Owenduff river, I encountered three grouse. Hopefully, they will multiply for posterity. Incidentally, the grouse made a very tasty meal and it is many the meal fit for a king that my mother, and indeed my sisters, prepared for us gang.

Pheasant shooting also had a particular calendar date. It opened at one time on 1st October and later it was moved to 1st November. While it was attractive shooting, it did not have the ambience of grouse shooting on the moors. Nevertheless, and particularly around Christmas when pheasants were in full bloom and possibly in frosty conditions, we used to have some exciting days of shooting, often with extended family members. Indeed, I have recollections of some great extended family get-togethers and sing-songs after the meal, with my mother on the piano (which was father's wedding present to her in 1928) and various efforts by others at singing, by far the best being that of my father's brother in law, Tom Morahan. "Sitting on the Bridge below the Town" was sure to feature. Tom was a much better singer than he was a shot. He was a lovely man. My mother was an accomplished pianist and had a lovely voice. Many's the time she lulled us to sleep with that most popular song "In the Shade of the Old Apple Tree." Another favourite bed-timer of hers' was "Come Back to Erin Mavourneen Mavourneen." The famous singer Peggy Dell, who my mother knew, was one of her great favourites.

Incidentally, we also shot woodcock and snipe on these pheasant outings. On less auspicious occasions we would shoot duck, pigeons and rabbits all of which were prized foods. On rare occasions we shot wild geese which were in season at that time. Thus, as the wild geese fly back to Greenland, we conclude this look down memory lane, perhaps with a certain amount of nostalgia on my part. But we must move on.

Part 2

Education, Work Experiences and the People Encountered

CHAPTER FIVE
Tarmon National School and Rockwell College

Tarmon National School

I attended Tarmon National School from about 1943 to 1951. I have happy recollections of those school days. I cannot remember any great pressure being put on us students and generally our teachers, including my father for the senior years, were caring people and made school as attractive as possible. It was a two-teacher moderately sized school with a student roll of about seventy. Usually the infants and juniors were taught by a lady teacher and the more senior pupils by a male teacher, who for most of my years was my father. The big important events at our school were, on the academic front, the preparation of the students for the visits to the school of the school inspectors who would examine us orally on our acquired knowledge, and, on the religious front, the preparation for Holy Communion and Confirmation. In relation to the latter, the local parish priest would normally visit the school periodically to examine us, but also to help us in our preparation. Then on the odd occasions, there were parish plays or other forms of entertainment performed in the school, when local people and families of the students were involved in various roles.

Physical facilities at our school were relatively modest, as was typical for that time. There was no electricity or running water and toilet facilities were basic, being of the pit type, which had to be emptied manually every so often. In relation to heating our school did better than most as we had good fires due to a plentiful supply of local turf and coal. Students brought their own lunches which usually consisted of bread and butter and a bottle of tea, cocoa or milk. We usually put our bottles of tea and or cocoa beside the fire in the morning, with the cork loosened to avoid an explosion, so that they would be warm at lunchtime. It was a great treat to walk barefooted to school in the summer period towards the latter part of the school year and perhaps also in September. The school was about two miles from our house. Short trousers were the order of the day for us boys. When we eventually made it to long trousers, probably at about the age of twelve, it was a significant milestone in our lives.

In the meantime, picking strawberries on the way home from school in the summer months and collecting them on grass straws was a compulsive pastime, which often made us late for dinner. Wild strawberries seemed to be very plentiful along the roads in those days and they tasted exceptionally sweet. Meandering along the roads in that period was quite safe as motors cars were still a fairly rare sight.

Rockwell College

I set off for Rockwell College in county Tipperary in September 1951 and spent four years there as a boarder. All my elder brothers and many of my cousins had gone there before me and had finished by 1951, except my cousin Joe Dolan who was in his final year in 1951. Usually my brothers and cousins were driven to Rockwell by that most affable of hackney drivers, Micky Guihen from near Arigna. However I had to make my own way, but at least I had my cousin Joe with me for the first year. My journey lived up to the song "It's a Long Long Way to Tipperary" as my travelling logistics were fairly complicated. These consisted of a car to the railway station in Carrick-on-Shannon, a train to Dublin, several hours wait in Dublin for a train connection to Thurles in Tipperary and then a bus to Rockwell College. The long day on the road meant a late arrival in the college and also a late pick of the beds in the dormitories.

I cannot say that I ever looked forward to going to Rockwell at the beginning of each school term, except perhaps when I saw the end in sight in the last year. I can certainly vouch for the fact that I really looked forward to my return home to Leitrim at the end of each school term. Boarding schools were harsh environments in those days with few creature comforts. Food was pretty basic, discipline strict and the senior dormitory was so cold that we aptly named it Siberia. Nevertheless, we always looked forward to getting to bed at ten o'clock after a long day. We did not have radios and television had not arrived on the scene in those days. We did however have newspapers in the common room. Some teasing and bullying went on among the students. I didn't do too badly on the receiving end in this regard, and I hope I never inflicted the same on others. Why do some students bully their colleagues? I don't really know, but I suspect they often regret doing so in later life.

There was also the isolation of being away from home and family for up to three months at a time. There was no such a thing as phoning home as most homes did not have phones. Letter writing was thus the mode of communication. Visits from family members living long distances from the college would hardly ever happen. I had one visit during my four years in Rockwell and that was from my cousin Monica Daly (nee Layden) and her husband Paddy, while on their honeymoon to the "deep south." I must not forget to thank my parents and put on record the great exhilaration that I got every so often on receiving generous parcels of food or goodies from home. This was pretty common practice for students living a long way from home. Occasionally my excitement was dulled somewhat on discovering that

> *"The boy goes where his father goes. He does what his father does, not what his father says he should do."*
> — Father Flanagan

the two pound glass pot of strawberry jam enclosed had broken in the post.

Boarding schools where they still exist today have undoubtedly changed much for the better, both in terms of physical conditions and in the provision of an all round supportive environment for bringing up young people. Notwithstanding my somewhat negative comments, I have proud memories of my days in Rockwell College and I strongly suspect that the disciplines imposed by boarding school can have very positive influences on one's character and approach to life. As Father Flanagan of Boys Town fame said: "Character is formed by doing the thing we are supposed to do, when it should be done, whether we feel like doing it or not." Father Flanagan was a great believer in keeping boys busy, including taking an active part in sports, and here Rockwell College excelled.

Rockwell students, with very few exceptions, participated actively in the college in-house rugby, gaelic football and hurling league competitions. Matches were played twice a week in a competitive spirit and the winners announced in various divisions at the end of the term/year. We also had the opportunity to play basketball, handball and participate in athletics. All of these activities greatly helped in neutralising the isolationist effects of being away from family and home for long periods. A fellow Rockwellian colleague of mine who lives in Sligo, Dermot Treacy, reminded me recently of the "dab" dinners that the winning teams in the various competitions gorged on. These dinners consisted of huge piles of mashed potatoes and sausages (bangers) and copious amounts of ice cream and jelly afterwards. After this the senior boys were allowed to go to the smoke room for a puff. But there was also the very special bonus of missing evening study time, as the dinners took place then.

To keep our muscles toned up we had regular drill exercises outside in the quadrangle. This was not always appreciated in the cold weather. We also had regular walks around quite a beautiful lake near the college—although at the time the lake may not have seemed very beautiful to us. Indeed, at certain times in the summer months we were allowed to swim in the lake. Sadly there was a student drowned in the lake, but not during my time. We also had frequent outings or walks to nearby New Inn village or further afield. Any positive benefits from such walks were probably more than nullified by the consumption of sweets and other trash, assuming pocket money permitted. We also had our annual outing to the Rock of Cashel.

The real sporting excitement in Rockwell wasn't to do with in-house competitions but rather with the inter-schools sporting events, particularly the senior and junior Munster Rugby Cups. Although Rockwell catered for all sports, it was first and foremost a rugby college. However, it also had a fairly decent hurling team. I don't remember it having a gaelic football college team. In my day, but with no help from me, Rockwell had an envious record in the winning stakes of rugby. Of great importance to the students was the fact that a win in these competitions meant a free day or at least a half-day off classes and perhaps off study as well. As might be expected, Rockwell had its share of famous rugby and sporting personalities, including Irish rugby internationals. Rockwellians capped for Ireland since the 1950s were: Bertie O'Hanlon, Michael Dargan, Dave McSweeney, Tim McGrath, Mick English, Frank Byrne, John Moroney, Pat McGrath, Willie Duggan, Paul Mc Naughton, Garry Halpin, Jack Clarke, Michael Fitzgibbon, Gabriel Fulcher and Denis Leamy, our current 2007 international (Rockwell College Union Diary 2007). I just happened to be writing this part of the book when Denis Leamy and the whole Irish team gave that epic performance against England in Croke Park on the evening of Saturday February 24th, 2007, which Ireland won 43 to 13 before a packed stadium of over 82,000 people and millions of television viewers. What an emotional scene the whole Croke Park spectacle was that evening, particularly during the singing of "God Save the Queen" and "Amhran na bhFiann" when grown men on the Irish team, not least the gentle giant John Hayes, openly shed tears. Ireland surely became a nation among the World League of Nations under the Croke Park lights on that unforgettable evening. One justly felt proud to be Irish.

Courtesy of Irish Times Newspapers

> "Life beats down and crushes the soul and art reminds you that you have one."
> — Stella Adler

Rockwellians have also featured prominently in many other home and international sporting activities, as well as in the broad arena of public and business life in Ireland and elsewhere. Most notable among these is Patrick Hillary, EEC Commissioner and later President of Ireland. Although not a Rockwellian in the sense of being a student at Rockwell, a very notable personality who taught mathematics in his early career at Rockwell College, was Éamon de Valera, who subsequently became Taoiseach and President of Ireland. De Valera was a keen mathematician and also played rugby for Rockwell and later for Munster at full back. He had a close relationship with the Holy Ghost Order, and particularly with Blackrock College where he attended as a student. It was in Rockwell College that de Valera was given the nickname of "Dev" by a teaching colleague, Tom O'Donnell.[2]

In particular, Rockwellians have featured prominently on the mission fields in Africa and elsewhere. Perhaps this is the cue to say something about the Holy Ghost Fathers who run Rockwell College, as well as various colleges in Dublin, including Blackrock College and St. Mary's College. The Holy Ghost Order was founded some three hundred years ago by French priests. It spread its missionary zeal both for the word of God and for education throughout every continent of the world, and particularly in West and East Africa. Today there are some three thousand Holy Ghost priests worldwide. The heroic and unselfish commitment made by members of the Order on the mission fields over very many years is legendary. Perhaps one of the greatest legends is Bishop Joseph Shanahan. Bishop Shanahan left Rockwell College around the beginning of the 1900s for Nigeria in West Africa. His impact on the mission fields there was truly immense. He, along with so many other Holy Ghost fathers, certainly roared out into the deep. Bishop Shanahan also founded the Holy Rosary Order of nuns. I am honoured to have a first cousin, Father Leo Layden, CSSp, who is a Holy Ghost priest and who did his missionary stint in Nigeria.

I might add that one of the great past Presidents of Africa, Julius Nyerere, who was President of Tanzania, is reputed to have been a pupil at one of the Holy Ghost colleges. I had the privilege of seeing President Nyerere at close quarters in church in Tanzania some twenty years ago—a little more about that in a later chapter. I would like to finish this chapter by saying a little about the Rockwell College of today. Rockwell was in my day one of the premier secondary colleges in Ireland. I am happy to say that this is still the case. A recent newspaper article,

---

2. Further information on de Valera's early life is available on Wikipedia (http://wikipedia.org).

"Rockwell College Still Living Up to Its Motto," gives a sense of the Rockwell of today and also contains what I consider to be important statements as to the role of education:

> The prestigious Dublin schools may capture much of the educational spotlight, but, in Rockwell College, outside of Cashel, there is a school that has as much tradition as any in the greater Dublin area, and facilities to rival any second-level educational establishment in the country. Rockwell College is a Catholic, co-educational boarding school which can trace its roots back to 1864. It was founded by the Congregation of the Holy Spirit and, to date, it retains a strong focus on the values that underpinned its establishment. The Holy Ghost Fathers had not only a strong missionary ethos, but also focused on each student as an individual, seeking to maximise their potentials, whatever their talents were. This tradition is continued throughout the school even today and is a signal example of the college's motto in action—"Inter Mutanda Constantia", which translates loosely as "Constancy in the Midst of Inevitable Change".
>
> To achieve the intellectual, social, cultural and physical development of each pupil, the school provides a wide range of subjects, including religious education, and aims for a high academic standard while preparing them for a broad range of professions and occupations. But, important as formal education and exam results are in modern Ireland, at least as important (and probably more so) is the moral and spiritual development of the individual—and this attention to the holistic development of the student is a feature that sets Rockwell College apart from many of the career-focused schools of the 21st century.
>
> Even outside of this noble ethos, the attractions of Rockwell College are obvious. Its location in the heart of the Golden Vale, could not be more apt for a college with a strong pastoral focus. The magnificent house, which passed into the possession of the Holy Ghost congregation in 1864, overlooks idyllic wooded grounds and farmland (including a 23-acre lake). But within this majestic estate has been created a modern school campus fit for the 21st century, complete with the sorts of sports facilities that one would expect to find at a university.
>
> The list of sports and leisure features at Rockwell College is comprehensive, in keeping with the Holy Ghost tradition of allowing students to develop through security and ordered freedom. Facilities include an indoor, heated 25-metre swimming pool, a nine-hole golf course, a modern gymnasium complete with squash, badminton and volleyball courts, a weights room and perhaps most importantly, about 20 acres of playing pitches. Of the playing fields, these include tennis courts and a new all-weather pitch for hockey or football. These are just some

> "They are never alone that are occupied with great and noble thoughts."
> — Sir Philip Sydney

of the facilities that the 500-plus students can enjoy throughout their time at Rockwell. This number is split between day boarders and full boarders, and has truly an international dimension—pupils from more than 20 countries are represented at Rockwell. But the facilities can also be enjoyed by teenagers from all over the country during the Summer months at Camp Rockwell, which is a unique summer camp that makes use of many of the attractions of the campus, and is a safe and enjoyable way for youngsters to develop during the long holidays.

(*Sunday Tribune* 13 May 2007, Supplement on Tipperary)

Tarmon National School pupils in late 1940s. Can you spot yourself and others?

Some shots of Rockwell

CHAPTER SIX

UCD, Accountancy Training and TCD

UCD

I attended University College Dublin (UCD) from 1956 to 1959. I studied Commerce and qualified in 1959 with a B. Comm degree. UCD had not moved its academic facilities to Belfield at that stage. The commerce faculty was, along with the main college campus, based at Earlsfort Terrace. This is now the site of the National Concert Hall.

Undoubtedly, of all my educational endeavours, UCD stands out as a shining light. I enjoyed every minute of my time at UCD; I felt I learned a lot academically and had the privilege of meeting many very fine people, both at staff level and fellow-student level. What other perspective would one expect of the fairly simple unsophisticated country lad that I was, being exposed to the country's intelligentsia in Ireland's metropolis? I have no negative recollections whatsoever of my time in UCD or life in Dublin, which at that time was fairly easy-going compared to now. You could walk the streets of Dublin at any time of the night then without the slightest worry of there being an incident. It would be nice to see a return to this situation, not only in Dublin but in all the cities and towns of Ireland.

We students got on very well with one another. We probably all appreciated that we were very privileged to be there, and privileged we certainly were, as free university fees had not even reached the political agenda at that time and accommodation costs were beyond the reach of most parents. The result was that only a very small percentage of secondary school graduates progressed to university then. The regional colleges (later the Institutes of Technology) were only established at the beginning of the 1970s, thus the range of third-level options available today did not exist. While the transition from secondary school to university was, in chronological terms, a mere three months or so, it would appear that we matured very quickly as young adults. School boy pranks and teasing were left behind and we suddenly became grown up. Finding ourselves in an environment free of the customary discipline of secondary schools, we had to make it largely on our own; thankfully most of us did. We had of course the help of the college chaplains and the good advice of our lecturers. We also had the various college societies to become involved in and these societies provided us with great opportunities to get immersed in other pursuits, whether they be sporting, academic, political, religious, or whatever. All the societies hung out their wares and actively recruited new members on Freshers' Day. Friendships made at university were usually very genuine ones. Occasionally acquaintances made became more real in later life. For instance in my first year in UCD, I was aware of someone in my class, possibly because of her good humour and smile, who turned out in later life to be the very jovial and much-acclaimed writer Maeve Binchy. Maeve did Arts at UCD and Arts and Commerce had some common classes in the first year, although I am quite certain Maeve never spotted me—she would have had no reason to.

As regards the lecturers, we probably had some of the best academics in the land, many of whom had business experience also. Some of the names that come to mind are: George O'Brien, James Meenan, Paddy Lynch and Garrett Fitzgerald. I remember Garrett as a relatively young, budding, fast-speaking lecturer on transport, who worked in Aer Lingus at the time. It is great to see Garrett still very active and obviously enjoying a second springtime in his life. Powerpoint presentations were not heard of at that time and the overhead projector was not used. Lectures were read by the lecturers from their notes and the blackboard and chalk used where appropriate. I don't remember any handouts either—probably photocopying facilities hadn't really developed then. So one made sure to attend lectures, and if one was missed for any reason, it was vital to get the notes from a reliable student colleague (with legible handwriting!). Incidentally all our lecturers were very dependable and would turn up on time and duly perform. In the rare instance of unavoidable absence, the head porter, Paddy Keogh, would come into the class to announce the absence, and usually pandemonium would break out, unless Paddy agreed to speak or lecture to us on some appropriate topic, the choice being up to Paddy. He was a great character and much admired by the students. I reckon he could hold his own on any podium! It was good to learn that Paddy was awarded an honorary Master of Arts degree after his retirement. I feel Paddy probably felt he had a moral responsibility to look after the students' welfare. There was the very odd exception, in another faculty or two in the college, of lecturers not being able to make it to lectures on time, or maybe missing a lecture due to a slight over-indulgence in a particular brew. Both students and college authorities were generally understanding in these situations.

Other UCD personalities that come to mind are Father P. Tuohy and Father Joe Dunn, both of whom were college chaplains and were very affable people. Father Joe Dunn later became a household name with his Radharc television programmes, broadcasting footage he took of various humanitarian and political situations from around the world. He made a huge personal commitment, on a fairly frugal budget if I remember correctly, to this work. Father Joe sometimes used to join us on our Legion of Mary social outings to the beauty spots of Wicklow and elsewhere. The social side of the Legion of Mary, of which I was a member while in UCD, was just as important to us as the spiritual side. I had the great privilege of meeting Frank

> "The most beautiful thing we can experience is the mysterious."
> — Albert Einstein

Duff, who founded the Legion of Mary in 1921, many times in the Morning Star Hostel. I made a lot of good friends in the Legion of Mary; great people like the late Michael O'Donnell, who became a very senior figure in educational circles in Dublin, Michael McGrath and many others. Another personality I recognised in my college days in UCD was Brian Farrell who was on the college staff and involved in the Appointments Bureau. I did not know him personally. He of course became a household name for his popular television and radio work.

While in UCD, I participated fairly actively in gaelic football. I played for the UCD junior gaelic football team, assuming I was picked on the day. The high point of my football career was when I scored two goals in succession in a competitive league match in the Phoenix Park. Perhaps the goalie had taken a break! Anyway, we enjoyed the football and the companionship. I have particularly pleasant recollections of having the privilege of meeting some of the greats of our country's senior county footballers, both in the college pavilion and on the playing fields at Belfield. Names that come to mind are: Jim Brosnan of Kerry, Jerome O'Shea of Kerry, Jim McDonnell of Cavan, Cathal Young of Cavan, and the late Sean Murray of Longford but there were many others. They were all lovely people and, despite their athletic reputations, were all very down-to-earth. I used to meet Jerome O'Shea frequently on the campus at Earlsfort Terrace. A big yet unassuming man, Jerome won three All Ireland senior medals with Kerry in the 1950s.

Among the most exciting memories of all of my UCD days are the goings-on at the Literary and Historical Society (L & H) weekly debates held in the Physics Theatre in Earlsfort Terrace and which one could attend free of charge. Needless to say, like most of the audience, I never dared to speak at these debates—that would take real courage and might be likened to being thrown into the lion's den. But the debates provided wonderful weekend entertainment with speakers for and against the motion (whatever that may be for the evening), dressed in formal attire, totally convincing with the power and intrigue of their words, even if they had no substance whatsoever. Words were often played upon to highlight the apparent inconsistencies and contradictions of reasonable statements genuinely made by the opposing speaker. A speaker could be literally devoured, so this stage was certainly not for the faint-hearted. These young tigers in formal dress looked awesome; humility was certainly not part of their attire. Although much of the bravura was for entertainment purposes, serious topics were often debated.

The L & H debates had such enormous impact that two books recounting their history have been written: *The Literary and Historical Society 1955–2005* edited by Frank Callanan and *Century History of the Literary and Historical Society of University College Dublin 1855–1955* by James Meenan. A reprint of the latter history was included with the edited history by Frank Callanan.

L & H debates were chaired by the auditor duly elected yearly by the UCD student body, usually after a bruising and hard-fought election. The auditor had the services of a committee of students to help out with the organisation and running of the debates. Usually outside personalities of note would be invited to participate in the debates; these included Government ministers and Church personalities among many others. Some of them were probably wise enough not to accept the invitation to speak. All invited speakers wore formal dress, as did the auditor and committee members. There was an assumption at the time that those who wore the auditorial chain of office were destined for high political office thereafter. However, according to Callanan's edited history, this was generally not borne out in practice; indeed it was much more likely that ex-auditors would make it big in the legal profession. Many of them reached the very highest echelons of that profession. These auditors were invariably young men, whom I suspect were of the liberal viewpoint and probably in a hurry to change things. At any rate the topics for debate had to be cleared with the College authorities, and particularly with Dr. Michael Tierney who was President of UCD in my time. There were constant tug-of-wars in regard to getting clearance for L & H motions. The interesting thing is that probably many of these so-called young liberals became conservatives in later years. Indeed what is new about that?

As Callanan's "Introduction" points out, the L & H seemed to be a crucial barometer of the country's historical and political scene:

> The history of the L & H has tracked the course of modern Ireland, the period after the famine when Catholic Ireland looked chiefly to the redress of specific grievances within the union; the emergence of home rule, the rise and fall of Parnell, the long electoral ascendancy of Redmond's Irish party; the victory of Sinn Féin, the civil war, the establishment of the state, the Cumann na nGaedheal governments, and thereafter the long hegemony of Fianna Fail punctuated by the intermittent alternance of coalition governments. (p.1)

> A sense of history of the Irish state, often veiled, but sometimes palpable, hung over the L & H and inflected its rhetorical practice. Overwhelmingly nationalist, the society bore the impress of the shifts and schisms within nationalism from the Parnell split onwards. (p.1)
> Some of the society were to play a significant role in the creation of the independent Irish state, notably Kevin O'Higgins, Hugh Kennedy, Patrick Mc Gilligan, James Fitzgerald-Kenny and John A. Costello. The society was preponderantly pro-treaty (although for example Cearbhall O Dalaigh and Vivian de Valera, both Fianna Fail, were auditors in the early thirties) and the displacement of Cumman na nGaedheal by Fianna Fail at the general election of 1932 left deep scars. (p. 2)

> *"Art teaches nothing, except the significance of life."*
> — Henry Miller

Thus it seemed that the early history of the L & H was involved in some very serious business. Callanan also points out the extent to which the L & H moved ahead of the times:

> Broadly the L & H was always moderately modernising, situated within a national consensus, while seeking cautiously to push out its boundaries. Its position within that consensus paradoxically permitted a freer play of ideas, and certainly a greater irreverence of humour, than might otherwise have been possible. [...] The game in the L & H was less to shock than try to situate oneself in the centre, or rather what one anticipated would shortly become the centre. (p. 3)

> A history of the L & H is an exercise in retro-futurology, laying out a series of prophecies across time. Speakers in each session believed they understood the future because they were the future. The debates were propelled by what was, although rarely expressed in such terms, an immense sense of confidence in the possibilities of Irish statehood, undercut of course by indignation at how those possibilities had been thwarted by the regime of the day. There is a sense in which every speech delivered in the L & H was an address to Ireland in coming times. (p. 3)

Various L & H personalities of the past were asked to submit their recollections of the society to Frank Callanan for inclusion in his edited history. I have given extracts from some of these below in order to convey the flavour and excitement of the debates—and indeed of the university experience more generally.

"Much more than a show 1953–58" Myles McSwiney

Myles McSwiney, who was auditor from 1957 to 1958, gives some sense of the wonder felt by those attending the debates:

> It was often said that UCD was no more than a very big secondary school - but there were some differences. Girls were present in numbers, one could skip lectures without punishment and the L & H provided free entertainment on Saturday nights—it was a Late Late Show long before RTE came on the scene. Because the topics for debate frequently concerned major public issues, the L & H was much more than a show. I concluded that it was unmissable when I attended a debate on parti-

tion in 1953, which was chaired by Mr. W. T. Cosgrave. As Mr. Cosgrave had retired from public life many years before and as I assumed he had gone to heaven, I was amazed to see and hear a person who had led the first government of the new state.

Debates were regularly reported by the Sunday newspapers, although summaries such as "Mr. Murphy said the future of Ireland depended on its young people" did not fully convey the scope and brilliance of one's contribution. Opinions ranged from Redmondite to militant republican and from conservative Catholic to suburban socialist. (p. 16)

However, not everything was high-brow and serious. McSwiney recalls the following incident during a debate in his period as auditor:

I heard the sound of an engine coming from the corridor. A scooter driven by Oliver Moylan, with several passengers draped on it, entered through one archway, proceeded to the centre where all on board bowed to the auditor, and departed through the other archway. (p. 17)

McSwiney notes that society members included notables such as "the playwright Mr Denis Johnston, the scientist Professor Ernest Walton, Mr Sean MacBride and lords mayor Byrne, Larkin and Briscoe" (p. 20). However, not all were natural orators; he observed that although speaking at the L & H "was considered to be a fearsome ordeal" yet he recalls "several earnest speakers without flair and others who had great difficulty in finding a full stop" and concludes that "the mob must have been not only fair but restrained as well" (p. 20).

"The golden age for debating" Hugh O'Flaherty

Hugh O'Flaherty, who first came to the L & H in 1955, aptly describes the awe with which the L & H officers were regarded: "At first seeing these demi-gods of the committee in dinner jackets, I slunk away having decided I could not live with them" (p. 28). Yet its attraction is demonstrated by the fact that he "picked up the courage to return a year later in the reign of Desmond Windle" and duly "climbed the ladder to speechify and intrigue with the best" (p. 28). Hugh O' Flaherty remembers with particular fondness another former auditor, Dermot Boucher-Hayes, whom he described as having "the biggest heart of all" (p. 29). He notes that Dermot would not "walk on the other side" preferring to "to identify with those in trouble" and laments his tragic and untimely death after a mountaineering accident in 1969 (p. 29).

"We acted extravagantly" Peter Smithwick

Peter Smithwick reflects upon both the excitement of the L & H and the way in which youthful protest becomes assimilated into respectability. In particular, he

> *"The most crippling failure disease — excuses."*

mentions Adrian Hardiman (L & H auditor 1972–73) who has since become a pillar of Ireland's legal profession.

> It was in the month of October 1955 when I had my first sight of the L & H ... There was no television in Ireland then, sex had not yet been invented and drink was beyond my modest allowance, so I reported to the L & H for exciting entertainment. There was raw anarchy during private business and public debate that was light years ahead of my polite school debating society. Most speakers seemed to be lawyers and, as lawyers are really actors who choose a more lucrative stage, we acted extravagantly.
>
> [...] How little did we think our revolutionary fervour would disappear. Even (from a later generation) Adrian Hardiman has become distressingly respectable.
>
> If I appear respectable and dull it is merely a pose. I have never really outgrown my L & H days and I hope not to (p. 30).

"The sex of the fifties" Maeve Binchy

Maeve Binchy says of her time at the L & H that "if you weren't there not only would you not know, you literally would not believe it. The debate at the L & H was the sex of the fifties." She goes on to recall her time there as follows:

> What did I love so much? The sense of drama as the crowds filled in, shuffling in their duffle coats and long striped scarves, smoking, looking and being looked at, being waved at, people keeping you a seat, hissing against someone who was a bore, shouting against the affected person, cheering the hero who defied the college authorities and invited a speaker of whom the college president mightily disapproved.
>
> [...] In my first year 1956-57, I looked at the auditor and committee as if they were greater stellar creatures, no boys' band or football team could have got as much adoration.
>
> [...] I ached to be part of it all, something much nearer than just sitting in those ascending benches (p. 31).

Maeve then explains how she became part of the inner circle, as it were, when she later spoke at a debate and was asked in the following year by the incoming auditor, Myles McSwiney, to serve on his committee. Maeve regarded that as the greatest proposal she ever got, other than the proposal of marriage in later years.

Maeve finishes her piece as follows:

> You always think your time is the best; I know those years nearly a half a century ago were magic. But just as I thought my father's generation fairly sad and pathetic back in the twenties, so too do people laugh an embarrassed laugh at our antics.
>
> It doesn't matter. It's only lent to you, that time. And we loved it (p. 32).

"No audience as frightening" Owen Dudley-Edwards (auditor 1958-9)

Owen Dudley-Edwards' two page contribution to the history of the L & H makes for interesting reading, accentuated by the fact that stand alone sentences and full stops are a rarity. The following is some of Owen's contribution:

> The dark-brown-benched amphitheatre ('physics') in Earlsfort Terrace, north end, ground floor, convenient to the convenience [...] the voracious, saliva-dripping, vulpine jaws of the semi-slaked three hundred ensconced, awaiting their victims [...] kamikaze glean in the eye of the maiden speaker [...] the irrelevant, mindless flak fatal to answer [...] the mortal wound prematurely tearing itself open to house the one lethal heckle that must be answered [...] the transfiguration of audience into a noble Olympian band of judicious arbiters as appreciative roars greet an interpolation capped and a witticism capsized [...] the gleaming fangs yet undrawn as the death-or- glory lion cub claws its way through the murderous Christians mollified but still choplicking [...] the illustrious persons of whom the L & H was no respecter (p. 37).

Now you really know what went on at the L & H!

Of course, there were varying assessments of the merits of those involved in the L & H. Finola Kennedy observed: "To my young eyes, L & H men were either impossibly clever, as handsome as Greek gods, or both" (p. 83). Vincent Browne expressed a widely divergent opinion:

> Several of those now fully registered as astounding national idiots 'graced' the L & H in the mid sixties. Full of verbiage, gesticulation, presence and, above all, themselves, they managed to say nothing at all with spectacular panache. Many of them said nothing since either. It was a factory for windbaggery (p. 117).

The L & H played its part in debating the important political issues of the day, furthermore those involved in such debates were sometimes connected (or later

> *"If you want a better world get busy on your little corner."*

became so) to the realities of political life.[3] For example, John Dillon, the nationalist politician and Home Rule advocate was auditor of the L & H in 1874–75. His son, James Dillon, at one stage the leader of Fine Gael, was an invited speaker in October 1970 addressing the motion that "parliamentary democracy is the opium of the West" (there is a photograph of this occasion on page 15 of the picture section of Callanan's book).

Accountancy Training

Having graduated as a Bachelor of Commerce from UCD, I joined the firm of Griffin Lynch & Co, Chartered Accountants, Lower Baggot Street, Dublin, as an articled clerk in the autumn of 1959. The firm at that time could be described as medium sized with four partners, William Sandys, John L. Kealy, Maurice Tempany and Brendan Devine, all of whom were highly respected in the accountancy confraternity. An articled clerkship was effectively an apprenticeship agreement where the clerk would be articled to the principal (one of the partners, in my case William Sandys) for a period of three years. At that time, an articled clerk—or more likely his/her[4] family—had to pay a fee of some hundreds of pounds for the privilege of getting an apprenticeship with a firm of chartered accountants. The articled clerk was paid a nominal salary; however, over the three years, it probably did not amount to much more than the fee paid on taking up articles.

Work in the early stages of articles was fairly routine and mundane, which included the (manual) checking of tots in large manually kept accounts books—pocket calculators had not hit the stage at that time. However, as time went on one got more responsible work to do and eventually became responsible, or partly so, for auditing or other accounting assignments, reporting directly to a partner or a senior manager of the firm. Griffin Lynch had a number of large clients when I joined them, including Irish Life Assurance Company and I.B.M. They also had a good range of other clients, but of course there were the usual small so-called shoe box clients, meaning literally that all the client's accountancy records were delivered in a shoe box. My articles therefore gave

---

3. As noted above, the L & H was by no means a springboard to a political career; in fact it was more likely to lead to a legal one. Nonetheless, the sense of being politically aware was crucial to the members of the L & H.
4. There were very few female articled clerks at that time. Subsequently, women have become much more involved—and very successfully so—in the accountancy profession.

me the opportunity to get a wide range of experience. Incidentally the shoe box clients provided a good training ground in the preparation of a set of financial accounts, often from incomplete records, where sometimes one had to use a bit of imagination (and perhaps intrigue!) to get more information from the client.

During articles, the articled clerk was given time off to study for the various accountancy examinations which had to be passed in order to qualify as a chartered accountant. So work and study went hand in hand during the period of articles. This was not an easy combination, particularly at that time, as the accountancy educational facilities were very meagre and mostly consisted of correspondence courses provided from outside the country. However, some short-term night classes were provided by the Institute of Chartered Accountants in Ireland. Some notable accountants lectured on these courses, including Ian Morrison,[5] Russell Murphy, David Rowe, Gerard Wheeler, John Lowe and others. The accountancy examinations were difficult with high failure rates. Having tripped up a couple of times, I passed my final accountancy exam, I think, in late 1963, and was admitted a member of the Institute in 1964.

As might be expected, the payment of a fee to secure articles is now long gone; it was discontinued shortly after my time and the profession is happily a much more accessible one now. In fact trainee accountants are now paid relatively handsome salaries. Also the educational back-up for students preparing for accountancy exams of the Institute has been greatly enhanced and now there is no need to avail of foreign-based correspondence courses. Fully qualified accountants can command very good salaries today, whether they go to work in industry or finance or remain in the profession i.e working with firms of auditors and accountants. It is generally accepted that the training and the exposure to business and management systems and operations that trainee accountants receive during their training equips them well afterwards for careers in business and associated areas. But maybe not everybody thinks so, because when I asked one of my sons after his Leaving certificate, whether he would be interested in doing accountancy, his answer was unequivocal: "Dad I would be wasted in accountancy." That finished that conversation!

After qualifying as an accountant I worked for about eighteen months in the auditing department of the well known firm of auditors and accountants, Kennedy Crowley & Co, Westmoreland Street, Dublin, where Vincent Crowley and his sons Niall, Conor and Laurence were the principal partners. I have a lot of good memories of my time in both Griffin Lynch & Co and Kennedy Crowley & Co. There was very good camaraderie between members of the staff and we had our share of pranks to lighten the burden of work.

In line with the mergers and amalgamations that took place in the accountancy profession in Ireland from the late 1960s onwards, both Griffin Lynch & Co and

---

5. A profile of Ian Morrison can be found in Howard Robinson's book *A History of Accountants in Ireland* (see bibliography).

> *"To the world you might be one person—
> but to one person you might be the world."*

Kennedy Crowley & Co have joined with other firms. Griffin Lynch & Co is now part of the Ernest & Young group, while Kennedy Crowley & Co is part of the KPMG group. Both of these groups are major international firms, providing a range of services, including auditing, accounting, taxation and management consultancy.

TCD

I gave up work in Kennedy Crowley & Co in autumn 1965 to attend a one-year full-time Masters programme in business studies in Trinity College, Dublin (TCD). Most of the students on the programme had previous experience in the work place. It was a pleasant and worthwhile year, but naturally it didn't have the emotional connotations that UCD had for me nearly ten years earlier when I was a raw country lad being exposed to the big smoke of Dublin city for the first time.

I passed my final TCD examination at the end of the academic year, and also my project thesis report, notwithstanding that I had the little matter of attending to some arrangements for my wedding to Beatrice Hunt on the 1st October, 1966, the day after the deadline for handing in the thesis report. Incidentally, my thesis concerned the Role of Joint Consultation in Industrial Relations and, as part of the work involved therein, I interviewed some twenty business managers and representatives of employer and employee organisations. I interviewed all of these people in person in their work places, except one such manager that I was not able to meet in person, but instead I conducted a fairly lengthy telephone interview with her. I did not state in the thesis that this interview was by telephone, assuring myself that the difference did not much matter. As luck would have it my project tutor, Dr. Bill Murray, met this lady purely by accident at Dublin Airport and took the opportunity of thanking her for meeting me and giving me the interview. She explained that it was no problem as it was only a telephone interview. This could have spelled trouble for me but Dr. Bill didn't hold it against me and believed me, I think, when I assured him that I interviewed all the other people in person. The lesson I learned was to never tell a lie of any sort.

I enjoyed my year in TCD, and importantly I got to see the historic location on which that very entertaining film *Educating Rita*, starring Michael Caine and Julie Walters, was shot. Incidentally, as a Catholic I had to get the permission from the then Archbishop of Dublin, Dr. John Charles McQuaid, to attend Trinity. Thankfully, that requirement has long since been dispensed with.

"Some heights can only be reached by the heart."

Beatrice and myself at TCD graduation.

CHAPTER SEVEN
Work at Institute of Chartered Accountants, IDA and EEC

Institute of Chartered Accountants in Ireland

I started work in the Institute of Chartered Accountants in Ireland in late 1966 as an Assistant Secretary. I now found myself working within an institution that as a student some years earlier I was fearful of, thinking of it as a somewhat soulless body which did not care greatly about its students. This was probably a natural reaction to any such examining body which had to maintain high standards. However there was possibly a grain of truth in it, because in later years, subsequent to the implementation of the Whelan Report on the review of the Institute's activities, the Institute became much more proactive in providing for the needs of the students.

I quickly got involved in the work of the Institute which was varied and interesting. Robin Donovan was the Secretary of the Institute at that time, and Ben Lynch was an Assistant Secretary (as was I, but he had been there long before I started). Eleanor Jenkins was the Librarian and there were about six other staff, including its most senior member, Carmel Leggett. All the staff members were very affable so I soon began to change my views about the soulless Institute. I also discovered that a great deal of the Institute's work was done through a range of committees, with the Council of the Institute at the head i.e. it acted as the governing body. The President and Vice-President of the Council were elected by the votes of the Institute's members for a one-year term and also a portion of the ordinary members of Council were voted in annually. Membership of the various Institute committees was chosen by the Council. All the members of the Council and the various committees were members of the Institute, i.e. chartered accountants, except with the very odd exception in the case of the committees. There was a huge range of committees which effectively mirrored the range of activities that the Institute was involved in. There were no less than eighteen committees in the Institute in the 1960s. These were as follows: Charter and Bye-Laws Amendment; Courses; Disciplinary; District Societies; Editorial; Education and Training; Examination; Finance and General Purposes; Future Plans; Hospitality;

Industrial and Administrative Members; Investigation; Library; Parliamentary and Law; Policy; Premises; Public Relations; and Taxation.

The Council and the various committees listed above were serviced by the staff of the Institute, particularly by the Secretary and the Assistant Secretaries. I quickly came to meet many of the members of the Institute who sat on the Council and on various committees that I was involved with. I was very honoured and privileged to have the opportunity to get to know these people and see them work at first hand. Certainly, they were not soulless and indeed they were very hard working and conscientious, who by and large give their services free of charge. Many of these people (who were practically all men at that time, but that has of course changed now) were very prominent in accountancy and business circles in Ireland, including banking. They always treated me with courtesy and I learned a great deal from them.

There were two specific committees that I was heavily involved with; the Courses Committee and the Taxation Committee. The Courses Committee oversaw the development and implementation of a fairly comprehensive range of new courses directed at qualified members of the Institute. My recollection is that we called these courses Post Development Courses; this was a new departure at the time and is echoed in the continuing professional development undertaken by all professions today. They covered a range of topics falling under the general headings of auditing, management accounts and services, finance, taxation and so on. The organisation of these courses was one of my principal functions in the Institute. We liaised with the Irish Management Institute in the provision of some of these courses. I greatly enjoyed this work and it gave me the opportunity to meet other members of the Institute.

I have fond memories of John Love (snr) and Alex Spain[6] who were very active on the Courses Committee. Alex was a great man to get things done and cut through the red tape. He became President of the Institute in 1975 at the young age of forty-two. I have also very pleasant memories of Niall Crowley[7] who was very active on the Taxation Committee. He was very courteous and hard-working. The Taxation Committee involved itself, inter alia, in making pre-budget submissions to the Minister of Finance. Niall Crowley became President of the Institute in 1971. I merely mention the above people in passing, but I can assure you that there were a great many other accountants that I was very fortunate to have had the opportunity to know and learn from.

There was a clear realisation in the 1960s at the Council level of the Institute, that the Institute needed to re-position itself in the public eye, and particularly to re-organise itself so as to provide a more extensive range of services to its members and the public generally. Accordingly, in June 1968 the Council appointed

---

6. A profile of Alex Spain can be found in Howard Robinson's book *A History of Accountants in Ireland* (see bibliography).
7. Robinson also gives a profile of Niall Crowley (see above note and bibliography).

"Never put off until tomorrow the smile you can give today."

Brian Whelan, a member of the Institute and a senior staff member of the Irish Management Institute, to carry out a review of the Institute's activities. Brian reported within nine months in March 1969; his report became quickly known as "The Whelan Report." In this regard, I quote from H.W Robinson's *A History of Accountants in Ireland*:

> The Whelan Report [...] dealt with the impact of change; change in the role of the accountant; the use of modern management techniques; the extension of a practising accountant's functions; the demand for a wider range of services not only from the bigger firms; changes which required a continuous review of professional and educational standards; changes in the structure of the profession with the trend towards bigger units through amalgamations and the consequent increase in specialization; the raising of entry standards and the movement towards a graduate profession; the increased demand from Industry and Commerce for qualified accountants; the need for harmonisation of accounting principles and practices with other countries; the need to project a new image to the general public; and the increasing role of the state in economic life. (p. 259)

Brian Whelan also identified specific objectives and functions for the Institute, making particular recommendations as to central co-ordination, planning, and delivery of services to members and students. Robinson notes that he

> criticised the educational efforts, which were at that date still in the hands of the District Societies, as too disparate; the lack of overall planning for the development of educational facilities; the insufficient training of teachers; the unsystematic attitude to revision of the syllabus and the insufficient research into the examination performances of students and guidance to principals.
>
> [...] Finally he proposed an organisation structure under which the eighteen existing Council Committees would be reduced to nine (p. 260).

He also recommended new full-time appointments, including a Director of the Institute. The Council accepted and implemented the Whelan Report in full. One of the appointments emanating from this was the appointment of Ben Lynch as Director of Education. Ben was highly successful in this position and was very popular with the student body, as indeed he had been for many years before that. Ben always had the full interest of the students at heart and his appointment within the restructured and increasingly professional Institute was one of many which married personality with systemisation, allowing the profession to develop and meet the challenges of a changing Ireland. In this respect, the Institute of Chartered Accountants in Ireland owes a great deal to the ability and integrity of Brian Whelan.

I wish now to return to the aforementioned History of Accountants in Ireland by Howard Robinson. Howard was a highly esteemed accountant, businessman and banker and was involved in various organisations, including the Irish Red Cross. He gave wonderful services to the Institute and, judging from his written history, was clearly a gifted writer and researcher. One wonders how he managed to get the time he gave to it; perhaps the old adage of asking a busy person if one wanted something done applied in his case. The first edition of the History was published in 1964 to mark the 75th anniversary of the founding of the Institute and a second edition was published in 1983. I am most grateful to Dr. Robinson and to the Institute for the opportunity to paraphrase or use extracts from the second edition.

Dr. Robinson notes that accounting (or, more correctly, bookkeeping) dates back to Babylonian merchants in 4000 BC, subsequently moving to Egypt when it became the world's commercial and cultural centre. Bookkeeping was even a school subject in Egypt as early as 1700 BC (p. 3). Later banking developed in ancient Greece, with the Greeks being "the first people to mint gold coins; issued about 600 BC" (p. 3). Dr. Robinson points out that the development of commerce in Italy, which happened much later, depended heavily on the banking system. The Bank of Venice is, he said, reckoned to have been founded in 1157, followed later by other Italian banks. These banks gave a great impetus to accounting and bookkeeping.

The birth of double entry bookkeeping is, according to Robinson, generally accepted as having occurred in the year 1494 when a Franciscan Monk, Luca Paciolo, published his treatise containing various elements of mathematics and bookkeeping. It is likely that Paciolo was describing a system of bookkeeping that had evolved in Italy over the years, rather than conceiving a system. Dr. Robinson further points out that the first society of accountants in the world was formed in Italy in 1581. However, there are much earlier references to accountants; they are first mentioned in English Statutes in 1285 and are first mentioned in Ireland in the records of the City of Dublin in the year 1316 (Robinson, chapter 1).

However, accountants were not a numerous profession; Dr. Robinson notes that by 1820, the number of accountants in Dublin had increased to sixteen and then fell for some years, before increasing again (chapter 2). It was in the late 1800s that the profession really began to develop and firms of accountants and auditors began to appear in Dublin. Many of the big names in the modern accounting and auditing firms date from about this time. The accounting profession developed in response to a commercial need "for accounts and statements of affairs in connection with bankruptcies, failures, frauds and disputes" (Robinson, p. 26). Robinson

> *"It is only if you have been in the deepest valley that you can know how magnificent it is to be on the highest mountain."*

notes that the work of accountants as auditors generally came later; the profession were clearly aware of the need for dialogue among themselves and the establishment of standards of practice and *The Accountant* (the world's first accountancy publication) which was first published in London in 1874 provided such a forum.

With the rapid rise of the commercial class in the post-Industrial revolution period, it is perhaps not surprising that "the nineteenth century in Britain, and to a lesser extent in Ireland, was a period of wild speculation, of failures and crashes, of booms and crises, of embezzlements and frauds" (Robinson, p. 32). One might be surprised to hear that the early history of Irish banks was one largely of failures. There were several such failures in the 1700s in Ireland, according to Dr. Robinson; however, he notes that the Bank of Ireland was successfully established in 1783. The failures of many smaller banks continued into the nineteenth century:

> The Irish failures [...] were in the main the result of mis-management and misfortune, but the failure in 1856 of the Tipperary Joint Stock Bank was due to fraud [...] The last failure of an Irish bank occurred in 1885 when the Munster Bank closed [...] Rumours about the bank caused a run on the bank, which resulted in its closure [...] The creditors of the Munster Bank were ultimately paid in full and while the company was being liquidated a new bank, the Munster and Leinster Bank Limited was formed [...] Wild speculation, dishonesty, failures, were perhaps inevitable children of the Industrial Revolution" (Robinson, p. 34–35).

Such failures demanded greater regulation of business enterprises and Dr. Robinson notes that the passing of the Companies Act of 1845 gave a big impetus to company formation. Prior to that, companies were formed by Royal Charter or an Act of Parliament. There were also large partnerships in Ireland, but they did not have a corporate existence. The Consolidating Companies Act of 1862 confirmed the principle of limited liability for shareholders. This Act however omitted requiring directors to present statements of accounts to their shareholders or requiring any audit to be carried out—but the Companies Act of 1900 rectified these omissions. With the growth of limited liability companies, came the gradual separation of ownership and management of companies. All of this gave impetus to the growth of the accountancy profession.

Dr. Robinson notes that the formation of the Irish Institute was initiated by Robert Stokes, an Irishman trained in England. This led to a petition, signed by thirty-one people (all men), being presented to His Excellency the Lord Lieutenant "praying [...] that Her Majesty might be graciously pleased to grant a Royal Charter, incorporating the petitioners and such other persons as might thereafter be admitted into a body corporate under the name and style of The Institute of Chartered Accountants in Ireland" (p. 54). The petition was accepted and a Royal Charter, dated 14th May, 1888, was granted. Several of the petitioners' names such as Robert Gardner, Henry Brown, Robert Stokes, Edward Kevans, Michael Crowley, and so on, survive in firm names today and more so in firm names of 1970s and 1980s, before the amalgamation trend of more recent years. Yet accountants were still a small but growing coterie and by 1909 "the membership of the Irish Institute had grown to 106" (p. 61). Some accountants became better known in other fields and Dr Robinson observes that

> the most famous member of an Irish firm of accountants so engaged was, of course, Michael Collins, who came from London to work with Craig, Gardner and company so as to be in Dublin when the rebellion broke out in 1916. He was only a few months with that firm but among his colleagues on the same staff, although they never met, was Joseph McGrath, later Minister for Industry and Commerce in the Cosgrave Government and founder and chairman of the Irish Hospital Sweepstakes (p. 113).

Of course the political situation at that time affected every walk of life and the accounting profession was not exempt from this. Dr. Robinson praises the ability of the Institute during the 1920s and 1930s to adapt to the social and political conditions, observing that it "succeeded in keeping together as a single body, without internal struggle or bitterness despite the political and military battles that were raging around it" (p. 122).

Dr. Robinson recounts how income tax, having been introduced by William Pitt in 1799 to finance the Napoleonic wars, became part of the work of accountants (Chapter 13). Another important part of the accountant's work is cost accounting; this acts as "an aid to management by ascertaining the cost of each article produced or service rendered" (p. 144), although Dr. Robinson notes that England and Ireland were slow to adopt cost accounting in comparison with other developed economies. Dr. Robinson referred further in this chapter to the need for costing records, for the purpose of proper management, particularly in the developing iron, coal and engineering industries in Britain, who were leading the world in the Industrial Revolution. Indeed I will return to this issue in relation to Ireland's own mining industry in Part 4 on Arigna. Robinson suggests that during the Industrial Revolution "British firms were 'having it so good' that little attention was paid to costing methods. While the demand for their products was great and competition slack, there was no need for economy" (p. 147). In any event, cost accountancy became a necessary part of the accountant's armoury, and is par-

"The most prized possession is integrity."

ticularly necessary to maintain accurate pricing and competitiveness—issues that became more important as markets became globalised and transport costs fell. The Irish Institute was involved in the development of cost accounting standards to enable Irish businesses to meet these challenges.

I was attracted by this growing and dynamic profession. Dr. Robinson indicates that the membership of the Institute increased from 417 members in 1938 to 1,770 members in 1963, with the greatest part of this increase occurring after the end of the Second World War. I suppose I felt that I was joining an important profession which could assist in Ireland's economic development.

I finish this section by stating once again that I greatly enjoyed my time in the Institute and I was privileged to have had the opportunity to work there. Undoubtedly very many changes have taken place in the Institute since I worked there, and, as part of life on this planet, many of those very good people in the accountancy profession who I had the privilege of meeting have passed to their eternal rewards. Having been offered an attractive opportunity to join the Industrial Development Authority, I left the Institute in 1969 to join that body.

IDA

I joined the Industrial Development Authority (IDA) around mid-1969 as a financial advisor. I struck up a great relationship with my immediate boss, Pat Lalor, and we encountered many happy successes, particularly in relation to advising IDA clients on the availability and operation of Export Sales Relief, but a little more of that later.

When I joined the IDA, it was in the process of major change both in its structure and in the role and services it would provide in the future to meet a new vision for the industrial development of the Republic of Ireland. The old IDA, established in 1950, mainly to promote industry and advise the Minister for Industry and Commerce thereon, and An Foras Tionscal, established in 1952 to administer the payment of grants to industry, were combined to form the new IDA under the Industrial Development Act, 1969, which became operational on 1st April, 1970. The old IDA and An Foras Tionscal were staffed by civil servants, and they were free to change over to the new non-civil service IDA. Most of the staff did in fact change over, and let me hasten to add that they were great people, very much "salt of the earth" solid people such as John Walshe, Ted O'Neill, Pat Lalor and so on. Because of the planned expansion in the activities and services of the new IDA, considerable numbers of outside (non-civil servants) personnel were recruited to the new IDA, which I will from now refer to as the IDA. Thus I joined the IDA in this context. It was an exciting time to be in an organisation concerned with the industrial development of our state, but first let us look at some background of our economy at that time.

The 1950s were very dark times in Ireland in terms of economic activity. Unemployment was high with little job creation while emigration to Britain, the U.S. and elsewhere was draining the country of its young people. Prospects for economic recovery did not appear good. Our protectionist industrial policy, intended to support and protect home industry, which had by then been in operation for several decades was definitely not producing the desired results. Undoubtedly, the single greatest factor to signal a change in national economic policy, was the adoption of a national strategy for economic planning, which was spearheaded by Dr. T. K. Whitaker, the then Secretary of the Department of Finance. This resulted in the first five-year Programme for Economic Expansion to be published in 1958, covering the period 1959 to 1963. The programme was based on the disbandment of protectionism for Irish industry in favour of a free trade environment and one where exports would play a pivotal role. Crucial to this strategy was the provision of state support for the establishment of productive activities (such as manufacturing industry), which would in turn provide employment and tax revenues to enable the government to undertake social investment. Apart from being a complete policy change, this new strategy, I suspect, boosted the Irish people's self-confidence and gave them a new goal to reach. Thankfully, economic performance greatly improved over the next five years. Thus second and subsequently third Programmes for Economic Expansion followed and an aspiration of full employment was being conceived for the 1980s. Hence the basis for a sound economy was being firmly laid down.

Thus while the 1950s were years of economic stagnation, the 1960s were ones of considerable expansion. In excess of five hundred new factories were established in our state in this period (IDA Report 1969/70, p. 17). There had been a marked increase in employment in the industrial sector and emigration fell from an annual rate of 44,000 in 1960 to 6,000 in the year ended March 1970. During this period 43,000 new jobs were created in industry, including mining (p. 23). The principal promoters of the new industrial projects were industrialists from Britain, the U.S., Germany and the Netherlands, but there were also Irish indigenous projects (p. 17).

So there was a lot of good work done on the industrial development front in the 1960s, but a lot more remained to be done. With the good track record of the 1960s behind them, the future planners envisaged a much expanded role for the IDA. As already indicated, the structure of the IDA was re-organised and expanded with considerable additional recruits of new personnel, including Michael Killeen who became its first Chief Executive under the new regime. Michael, like all the Chief Executives who followed him (Padraic White, Kieran McGowan and the present incumbent, Sean Dorgan) filled that position with distinction. Promotion of foreign industry was greatly enhanced through the expansion or opening of new IDA offices in various strategic locations abroad. Furthermore, various IDA

> "Colour in a picture is like enthusiasm in life."
> — Vincent Van Gogh

offices were established strategically in the various regions in Ireland, so as to provide the necessary industrial support in the regions and also to help achieve balanced economic growth. Certain areas in the country which suffered economic disadvantages were designated as eligible for higher investment grants or other supports. The range of incentives to attract industrial development were extended, and in some cases enhanced. The range of incentives thus offered, mainly comprised the following:

- Export Sales Relief, which was introduced in 1957 and originally due to run out in 1977, but was then extended to 1990. This relief gave fifteen year's exemption from tax on profits derived from exports and a further five years' reducing relief. This relief proved to be a major incentive in attracting foreign industry and also in encouraging exports, both by foreign owned and indigenous based industry. Later, the relief was extended to cover the export of services, as well as of goods.
- Non-repayable grants towards the cost of fixed assets, including plant and equipment, invested in new industries up to a maximum of 50% in designated areas of the country and 35% in other areas.
- Non-repayable grants towards the cost of modernising existing industry, known as re-equipment grants, at rates of 35% and 25% of fixed assets, respectively in designated and other areas.
- Non-repayable grants towards the costs of establishing or expanding small viable industries up to a maximum of 65% and 45% of fixed assets respectively in designated and other areas.
- A range of other incentives including labour and management training grants; research and development grants to research new products and processes; guarantees of loans and subsidisation of interest on loans; grants towards reduction of factory rentals; provision of ready to use advance factories throughout the country; and grants in respect of leased plant and equipment. In the latter case, the grants were paid direct to the lessor, normally a finance house, who passed on the benefit of the grant to the industrialist in the form of reduced leasing rentals.

In addition to the foregoing incentives there were two other important factors that were influential in the attraction of industry to Ireland. The first was our country's entry into the European Economic Community (EEC) on 1st January, 1973, which made Ireland an attractive base for industrialists located outside the EEC, who wished to get access to EEC markets. Secondly, there was a ready supply of labour available in Ireland at relatively cheap rates. Furthermore, through the efforts of AnCo (the Training Authority) and the newly established Regional Technical Colleges, this labour pool became increasingly skilled. As great emphasis was being placed on exports, Córas Tráchtála was very active in assisting businesses to market and distribute their products and services in overseas markets.

On the negative side, we had some shortcomings in our infra-structural facilities, particularly in communications and transport. These were in due course largely attended to, although the economic successes of the Celtic Tiger and consequent expansion in population have again exposed inadequacies in these areas. However, at that time, Ireland was on the whole very well poised to develop its industry and this it did extremely well in the following decades. The IDA succeeded in attracting some of the world's leading companies to set up industry in Ireland, with the result that Ireland became a leading global producer in sectors such as pharmaceuticals and electronics. Thus the base for our Celtic Tiger economy of the late 1990s and early 2000s was being solidly established.

To digress into a little detail, the largest grant approved in my time in the IDA was something over eleven million Irish pounds for Ferenka Ltd to produce steel tyre cord in Limerick. This project was established by the large AKZO Group based in Holland. As part of the evaluation process for this major project, a team of personnel from the IDA under the leadership of Ray McLaughlin went to Holland to carry out the necessary investigations. I happened to be a member of that team. We were duly impressed with what we saw and were able to recommend the project to the IDA board of directors. The Ferenka project was thus established in Limerick and commenced production in 1971. Everything seemed to be running smoothly under its very able Chief Executive, Dr Tiede Herrema and at its height, the company provided 1,400 jobs. Sadly however, Dr. Herrema was subsequently kidnapped by the IRA while on his way to work in Limerick in October 1975. In late 1977, the Ferenka plant closed, but I am not clear as to what the reasons for the closure were. I understand that Dr. Herrema has visited Ireland on a number of occasions since the plant closed, because of his affinity to Ireland. He expresses no animosity towards his kidnappers and certainly seems to have come through his two-week kidnap ordeal without any ill-effects.

Over the subsequent years from 1970 onwards, there were a number of closures of IDA assisted projects which on the surface may seem to be due to failures and bad decisions by the IDA. Possibly the IDA did make some bad decisions, but business investments always involve an element of risk and it is never possible to achieve a 100% success rate—or to do so would have involved approval of a far lower number of projects and the creation of many less jobs. It is often said that people who never make a mistake invariably make very little else; this certainly holds true in the case of business investments. In addition, the IDA had to compete for its new projects, often against strong competition from other countries, so it had to make timely decisions.

> *"Nothing but the name of Jesus can restrain the impulse of anger, repress the swelling of pride, cure the world of envy, bridle the onslaught of luxury, extinguish the flame of carnal desire, temper avarice, and put to flight impure and ignoble thoughts."*
> – St. Bernard of Clairvaux

I would argue that many of these so-called failures by the IDA were not failures at all, often having operated and provided employment for some fifteen years or so, which would be a typical time span for evaluating new investments. Technology and other conditions are always changing so I think the trick is to make the best decision available at any one time, rather than waiting until everything about the project's future is clear—effectively it can never become clear because there will invariably be always some new factor impinging upon it. Obviously, one would prefer a project that would continue successfully for fifty years rather than fifteen or twenty years. But we must not forget that the projects that closed down after say fifteen years probably gave a great economic boost to both the local and national economies, and thus provided the basis for further economic activity. The alternative of doing nothing would certainly not have created the foundations for our Celtic Tiger. The closing of our labour-intensive industries because of cheaper labour being available elsewhere in the world is surely no shame on us; indeed it is arguably a part of the industrial development cycle. Today, the IDA specifically target high-tech projects and those that offer research and development activities and various other management functions which our skilled and relatively costly labour force can support and carry.

Before finishing this section on the IDA, I would like to comment briefly on one of my important activities in the IDA which had to do with the Export Sales Relief scheme. As already indicated this relief proved to be a major incentive in attracting industry to Ireland, and indeed promoting industry within Ireland. Pat Lalor and myself assisted industrialists in organising themselves to avail of this relief. They would invariably get additional help from their own tax and financial advisers, usually a firm of accountants in Ireland, but the IDA was generally their first contact in this regard. To be eligible for the relief, the operation had to be a manufacturing operation, and the product had to be exported from Ireland. Questions often arose as to whether the operation involved was really a manufacturing one (as opposed to an operation that merely involved repackaging of some sort). A further contentious issue was whether the product to be produced was really a new one—this question might arise in situations where the business was already producing a product, and was now embarking on a new related project. If it could be judged to be a new project and a new product, then a new twenty-year Export Sales Relief period would be available to it.

At an early stage of each project Pat Lalor and I consulted closely with the Revenue Commissioners on these issues. We found them most helpful and positive and they were as anxious as we were in the IDA to make the Export Sales Relief scheme as widely available as possible. Thus it was possible to take a relatively liberal definition of what constituted a manufacturing operation, or a new product or process. We often got help also from colleagues in the accountancy profession in relation to the above issues—a few names that come to mind are: Frank Barrett,[8] Jim Gallagher and Norman Judge. I have very clear recollections of all of these type of discussions and when Pat Lalor would be asked for his views on a question of some significance invariably he would slowly, and deliberately so, start lighting his pipe using matches as if they were going out of fashion. By the time the pipe was lit he was almost sure to have a well thought-out answer to submit.

In the early 1970s, the EEC Agricultural Guarantee and Guidance Fund (better known as FEOGA) provided grant aid in addition to IDA aid to the food processing sector. The preparation of these FEOGA applications to the EEC for grant aid was fairly specialised work and not many people, including the food processors themselves, knew much about them. I felt that it was an area that I could develop an expertise in, and so after spending some three and a half years in the IDA, I decided to leave in late 1972 and undertake, on my own account, the preparation of FEOGA applications, together with IDA and bank applications. A lot of my new work involved me working very closely with the IDA, so I still felt myself to be in some way a part of it.

EEC

As already indicated, this EEC work involved me in the preparation of FEOGA applications in relation to business proposals on behalf of food processing businesses based in Ireland. The dairy co-operatives, the meat processors, the fish processors and some provender mills producing compound feedstuffs were the principal operations eligible for FEOGA aid. FEOGA applications were sent to Brussels via the IDA. In fact the IDA had first to approve the projects for their grant aid and having done so, the IDA would then submit the applications to Brussels. This period of my work life lasted for some nine years, which was by far the longest stint I had ever spent in one job up to that time. Thankfully, I am always interested in new challenges, and my philosophy about work and jobs is to give of one's best for as long as the challenge remains and then move on to pastures new.

The work in the FEOGA area was challenging and pressurised to the extent

---

8. A profile of Frank Barrett can be found in Howard Robinson's book *A History of Accountants in Ireland* (see bibliography).

"Success is getting what you want, happiness is liking what you get."

that applications had to meet certain submission deadlines set by Brussels and the IDA. Furthermore the applications required a great deal of information, not least the preparation of detailed business plans. The work involved a considerable amount of travelling by car as I had to attend on site, invariably all over the country, to discuss the business proposals of the various enterprises. The first person to ask me for help to put together a FEOGA application was that genial general manager of Killeshandra Dairy Co-operative, the late John O'Neill. Very many other clients followed, such as Mitchelstown Dairy Co-operative, North Connacht Farmers and many others in various sectors of the food industry. Effectively, these applications were business plans and it was interesting working with the promoters in putting them together and seeing the different management styles and approaches used by the various enterprises. These were the halcyon days in the agriculture production sector in Ireland and, by the same token, these were also the halcyon days for the food processors due to the greatly increased outputs of raw materials, i.e. milk, beef, lamb, fish and so on. I happened to meet in Ireland on a couple of occasions the Brussels officials who were promoting the FEOGA scheme. They promoted it very enthusiastically and I feel they were very favourably disposed towards Ireland, both at farm level and at processing level. It could be said that the Brussels' motto then for the farming community was "Produce and Intensify."

Sadly there was little thought given then by anybody, including myself, to the possible damage being done to the environment by over-intensification of agriculture; the effects of this just didn't seem to dawn on us then. In any event, as a result of our entry into the EEC and the very favourable stance by Brussels' officials to expanding agricultural output and processing in Ireland (which of course was the big selling point for Ireland joining the EEC), the farmers and the food processors of Ireland never had it so good as in the second half of the 1970s and throughout the 1980s. What a major turnaround we have today in relation to farming in Ireland; there has been, in many areas, a significant reduction in farming intensity and consequently in agricultural output. At least we are beginning to have respect for our environment.

I earned fairly decent fees from my FEOGA work, but I did not take any undue advantage of the fact that expertise in this area was scarce. I happened to be drafting this very part of my book on 23rd August, the birthday of my late wife Beatrice. I want to put on record my grateful thanks to Beatrice who typed all the FEOGA applications for me, in a pre-word processing era, and in doing so gave a huge number of hours to this work without ever complaining. Thank you so much Beatrice; I have no doubt that milk and honey are flowing freely for you in your heavenly abode. I hope we will meet again there.

> *"Happiness is like a butterfly, when pursued is always just beyond your grasp, but which if you will sit down quietly, may alight upon you."*
> — Nathaniel Hawthorne

It was during this FEOGA era (late 1972-81) that Beatrice, myself and family moved house in 1976 from Dublin to Sligo. Sligo was closer to my FEOGA clients, but the country had other attractions which I will return to later.

Part 3

My Wife, Family and Friends, and Later Work Experiences

CHAPTER EIGHT
Married and Family Life in Dublin

I am retracing my steps back some years from the last chapter. As indicated earlier I got married on 1st October, 1966, the day after I handed in my project report to TCD. I married Beatrice Hunt from Gowlane, Doocastle, County Mayo, one of a family of four, the others being Christina, Una and Michael. Her dad, Thomas George, had died some seven years before that. Her mother Bridget was still hale and hearty. Beatrice worked in the Irish Times in Dublin, first in the typing pool, later being promoted to the wages and accounts department and latterly working as personal assistant to the managing director, Major McDowell. Beatrice was living with her aunt and uncle in Cabra and we first met at a Tuairim hop in Dublin in very early 1965. It was love at first sight as far as I was concerned but I think it took Beatrice a bit longer to figure me out. Tuairim, the Irish word for opinion, was a sort of think tank organisation set up in the 1950s, which held lectures and discussions concerning the economy and other problems facing Irish society in those difficult days of high unemployment and emigration. It also published a journal. The late David Thornley of TCD was very active in Tuairim and I am almost certain he was one of its founder members.[9] Law students and probably staff from the UCD law faculty were also active in it as were many others from other universities and other walks of life. Anyway, there was also a social side to Tuairim, including the running of hops (dances in case the term "hop" is an unfamiliar one). The night I met Beatrice, I can distinctly remember saying to myself before going to the hop that at my age of around twenty-eight and, with my exams well in the past, it was high time for me to find a suitable wife. I wasn't five minutes in the dance hall when I spotted my future bride and from then on there was no going back for me.

I think my chances of securing a date with Beatrice were helped by the fact that she was with two other girls that night and I showed a bit of common courtesy and care about arranging a taxi to get them all home after the hop. Once established, our courtship went smoothly and I felt very privileged to be doing a line

---

9. The organisation no longer exists, appearing to have petered out in the 1970s. It is difficult at this remove to ascertain accurate details about it.

with such a fine person. We married after some twenty months. We were married in Beatrice's local Catholic church in Cabra and had our wedding breakfast in the Grand Hotel in Malahide. We had about one hundred and twenty guests at the wedding and, as was the custom then, left that afternoon for our honeymoon in France and Italy. The wedding was a wonderful day and Beatrice looked more beautiful then ever. We were both delighted to be making this important commitment in front of all our relatives and friends. We spent a few days in Paris before going to Sorrento and Capri and then on to Rome. It was a magical two weeks and we enjoyed every minute of it—apart from when I almost got knocked down by a car in the Parisien traffic melée and when we were on a hair-raising taxi ride along the Amalfi coast. We were used to very different standards of driving in Ireland!

After marrying, we lived in Thorncliffe Park, off Orwell Road in Rathgar. My father was generous to me in the matter of purchasing the house outright. The house was not far away from the Irish Management Institute (IMI), to which I had the odd occasion to go on a course. (The Russian Embassy now occupies the IMI premises). We were blessed with a family of five—three girls and two boys, David, Dervila, Conor, Aisling and Ciara. There was also one still-born son in between Aisling and Ciara, which was a great sadness for Beatrice and I, but it made Ciara's subsequent arrival a doubly joyful one. All the children were born within a few hundred yards of our house in Our Lady of Mount Carmel Hospital and delivered under the caring eye of Professor de Valera. Thankfully the childhood days were happy ones and I have many good memories of those times. The children were all active and playful—which often resulted in anxious moments and even a few trips to casualty when they fell off their bikes or hurt themselves in some way; luckily nothing was ever too serious.

We lived in Thorncliffe Park until the summer of 1976, when we moved to Sligo. David and Dervila started school in St. Mary's in Rathmines and Notre Dame in Churchtown respectively while Conor and Aisling went to pre-school in Dublin. As we moved to Sligo in 1976, school started in Sligo for some of the younger ones. Baptisms, Holy Communions and Confirmations were significant events in the family calendar and as the children were close in age (no more than two years separated each child from the next), there were many such happy occasions in relatively quick succession. Beatrice and I took our first alcoholic drink on the day that our first-born, David, was baptised. Thankfully, neither of us ever took to the drink too seriously!

Our third child, Conor, was baptised by Bishop Thomas McGettrick, a second cousin of Beatrice and who was attached to St. Patrick's Missionary Society, Kiltegan, Co. Wicklow. The good bishop made the apt comment that Conor, who was a healthy ten-pound weight at birth, had the head of a bishop; Conor's subsequent career has not (so far!) borne this out. The Society's present Director, Father Kyran Murphy wrote to me about Bishop McGettrick in a note in December 2006 as follows:

> "We make a living by what we get; we make a life by what we give."
> – Winston Churchill

I was with him in Nigeria—a wonderful missionary who did an incredible amount of great work. He set the faith on its firm foundation in Ogoja / Abakaliki—so he is certainly with God and enjoying his reward.

Bishop McGettrick greatly enjoyed his holidays, whenever he took them, back home in Killavil, Ballymote, Co. Sligo. There was nothing he liked better than giving a hand in saving the hay. He was a country man at heart. The Sligo people have always been very supportive of Bishop McGettrick. Even now many years after the Bishop's death, a healthy collection is taken up every August (faithfully organised by Paddy Smith) outside the churches in Sligo city in aid of Bishop McGettrick's leprosy fund. Bishop McGettrick is buried in the country he gave his life to in the diocese of Abakaliki, Nigeria.

Dublin city was still relatively unsophisticated in the late 1960s and early 1970s, and the rearing of young children could be done within certain well-established norms of conduct and behaviour. Children knew what to expect and generally abided thereby—although there was always the possibility of an exception to the rule and the need for some small punishment. Often the threat of suspension of the few pence of pocket money was enough! Beatrice had given up work on our marriage so she looked after the children and the home on a full-time basis, which provided a great deal of stability to our home environment. There were plenty of other young families in the neighbourhood so our children had lots of friends. As the house was in a cul-de-sac, it was a safe place for the children to play and much of their leisure time was spent outside.

We frequently went to Enniscrone for summer holidays in County Sligo, which was Beatrice's family haunt for holidays from her childhood days. It was a great favourite with our children too. There we would meet Beatrice's immediate family, including her mother, Bridget, and some extended family. We continued to go to Enniscrone for several summers after our move to Sligo in 1976. These were great holidays and they reminded me very much of our own family childhood holidays in Bundoran. I must confess that I was a little bold on a couple of occasions during these holidays when I spent somewhat more time fishing than I should have—I hope Beatrice forgives me! However, I often took the two boys with me on these occasions so as well as passing the fishing bug on to them I trust that I was also fulfilling my parental responsibilities—at least that's my excuse!

While living in Dublin we had quite a number of extended family occasions (apart from the formal occasions of christenings, weddings, funerals and so on) as both Beatrice and myself had a lot of relatives living in Dublin. We have many happy memories of these get-togethers. One family we used to meet quite a lot was John Leydon and his daughter and son-in-law, Mary and Barry O'Donnell. John's wife, who was my aunt Nan, had died suddenly some years before that but to me he was always Uncle John. For some reason he had a lot of time for me, and later for Beatrice when she came on the scene. We had a lot of outings with him and frequently Mary and Barry and various other relations would meet up. I have very happy memories of these occasions, as well of course of all our own immediate family outings—we cannot relive them now but it's nice to take time to reflect on them and appreciate our good fortune in having these opportunities for friendships. At these get-togethers when Mary and Barry were able to attend, Barry (a surgeon) would always act the shy and unsure Corkman. However, he was not too shy to pronounce judgment on particular issues or to relate stories, many of which poked fun at politicians as well as his own profession. For instance, he always said that he would drive quickly through certain counties so that he would not be taken to hospital there (referring to the single-surgeon hospitals then the rule in most counties; most now have three surgeons). Critical of political clientelism, he maintained that some politicians would like to see a hospital built in every polling station. And he was fond of recounting the answer the Minister of Health in Kuwait gave him in 1975 when Barry asked if the doctors were happy in Kuwait: "The Minister replied, raising his eyes and his arms to Heaven, 'Alas it is not in the power of Allah the all merciful to make the doctors happy.'"

Barry's father-in-law, John Leydon, was no stranger to the difficulties of administering political decisions having been at one time the Secretary of the Department of Industry and Commerce. John hailed from Arigna where his father almost certainly worked in the coal mining business with my grandfather Michael Layden. Although he moved away from Arigna when he finished secondary school, he retained a deep affection for that part of the country. Throughout his life, he continued to return to visit Arigna and also the Jetty House at Spencer Harbour, County Leitrim (both places are referred to in chapter 1). The Jetty House was a particularly favourite meeting place for our various families. As a young child I have recollections of John Leydon, Nan and Mary coming from Dublin to go to Bundoran on their summer holidays. They would be on their way to or from Bundoran as we were saving hay in what we called the Grove Meadow and they would stop for a chat. Perhaps their biggest draw of all to the country was for the grouse shooting that opened on the 12th August. In my childhood, this was a very big event as the grouse stocks were plentiful. On one of these visits to the Jetty House, John's red setter dog went missing and I happened to find it and my reward was a crisp ten-shilling note which was a lot of money for a child in those days.

> *"The only significance of life on earth consists in helping to establish the kingdom of God. The kingdom of heaven however is within us, it is cultivated and pruned and produces fruit in our own lives, the lives of others and in our world, culture and society."*
> – Leo Tolstoy

John Leydon's Career

I would like to say a little about John Leydon's career as he made a significant contribution to the administration of the Irish state. He started his illustrious career in the British Civil Service in London around 1915 and transferred back to Dublin to the Irish Civil Service in 1923, where he was assigned to the new Department of Finance. His abilities attracted attention from relatively early in his career according to Desmond Roche's extended obituary article, which was published in 1979 after John Leydon's death the previous August. Roche notes that John Leydon was appointed secretary in 1928 to the all-party Economic committee within the Finance Division which by July 1929 "was deadlocked on party lines on the issue of free trade versus protection" (p. 234, quoting Ronan Fanning). It would appear that John Leydon was more in favour of a free trade approach (perhaps highlighting the wisdom of his long term vision), but protectionism seemed to win out at that point. When Fianna Fáil came to power in 1932, Sean Lemass, the Minister for Industry and Commerce, offered John Leydon the position of Secretary of his Department. John Leydon told me himself how he answered, and it went something like this: "It would be a great honour for me to be Secretary, but I would have to be my own man." The Minister replied that that was fine with him; Desmond Roche concurs, noting that Lemass replied "What I want is a man who will show me where I am wrong—the last thing I want is a yes-man" (p. 235). Lemass's reply was, according to Roche, made after John Leydon reminded the Minister of the different views each took on the Economic Committee some years earlier. So began the very formidable Lemass-Leydon partnership; a partnership based on ability and mutual respect and which undoubtedly put its indelible mark on Ireland's economic development.

Although protectionism was the basis of the new government's industrial policy it would appear that John Leydon's inspiration led to the establishment of the "range of state-promoted companies which became so familiar and significant a part of the industrial scene" (Roche, p. 236). These companies included Aer Rianta, Aer Lingus, the Turf Development Board, the Irish Tourist Board, Industrial Alcohol Factories Ltd, the Irish Life Assurance Company and the state-established cement monopoly, Cement Ltd. Later in the 1940s, John Leydon was closely associated with the formation of Irish Shipping Ltd and The Insurance

Corporation of Ireland. John Leydon was a director of many of these companies and often their Chairman. He told me personally that as Chairman he never took a vote at a Directors' meeting. He would always try and get a consensus view agreed rather than have directors take opposite sides. If necessary, he would adjourn the meeting and work in the meantime on getting a consensus view for the next sitting.

The Anglo-Irish Agreement of 1938 which ended the economic war with Britain was, according to Desmond Roche, a political agreement with credit going to the politicians (p. 236), but the Secretaries of the relevant Departments also played a crucial role in the negotiations. He notes that the trade articles of the agreement which Leydon negotiated with senior officials of Britain's then Board of Trade were very favourable to Irish industry as they "allowed the Irish Government to continue protection for Irish industry and at the same time it guaranteed free entry to Britain for Irish industrial goods" (p. 237).

Of course, the full potential of this agreement was not immediately fulfilled as trade rapidly became overshadowed by the 1939–45 world war. During this time, the Department of Industry and Commerce went into limbo to be replaced with the Department of Supplies as all hands were now needed on deck to do what was possible to guarantee and manage supplies of food, raw materials and so on during the hungry war years. A system of rationing was put in place, which was underpinned with a coupon system. These schemes were headed up by John Leydon who administered them fairly and meticulously. He was particularly insistent that there would be no favouritism shown to anyone nor any gifts accepted (Roche, p. 240).

It was generally recognised that John Leydon was one of our most able civil servants ever. Yet he had a certain amount of impatience with official practices that retarded progress and quick action. He believed in quick decision-making once the facts were considered and weighted up. According to Desmond Roche, "he could not understand that there should be any good reasons for procrastination or dilatory handling of business" (p. 239). He believed in good communication and held daily meetings with Lemass and his assistant secretaries Shanagher and Williams as well as weekly conferences attended by the entire upper hierarchy from Minister down to Principal Officers. Principal Officers brought details of any problem encountered to these meetings and a course of action was, if at all possible, decided on the spot.

As might be expected of a man who had such a crucial role in negotiating the Anglo-Irish trade agreement, John Leydon was one of the first civil servants to do extensive overseas travel on public business. Indeed, Roche notes that "to accompany him on an official mission overseas was to make one proud of being Irish, proud too of being a colleague in the service to which he belonged" (p. 243).

John Leydon was an independent thinker and respected that quality in other people and didn't hold it against them even when the view expressed was different to his own. His relationship with Tom Murray, the Assistant Secretary of his department, aptly illustrates this:

> *"Don't ask for the task to be easy. Ask for it to be worth it."*

> Of all Leydon's young men he [Tom Murray] was one who habitually displayed that independence and moral courage so characteristic of Leydon himself. Tom did not hesitate in conference or committee to express, sometimes forcibly, dissent from the line taken by his Secretary—a practice rare enough among senior civil servants who still retain hopes of advancement [...] Leydon responded with a high degree of regard and respect for his young Assistant Secretary, and when an appointment afterwards fell to be made to the Chairmanship of the ESB he recommended Tom in the fullest confidence (Roche, p. 241–242)

On a more personal level, my own memories of Uncle John are of a man who greatly enjoyed the activity of debating on social occasions and who appreciated the opinions of others—as long as they had a sound basis.

In the 1950s he became closely associated with the Irish Management Institute and the Institute of Public Administration of Ireland, although, according to Desmond Roche, he would have preferred that these two bodies be amalgamated so as to avoid duplication of services (p. 244). John Leydon retired from the civil service in 1955 at the age of sixty. Shortly afterwards he became a director of the National Bank and Chairman of the Irish Board in 1956. I have a recollection of him telling me that he had a lot of time for Ian Morrison, who held various positions in the Bank of Ireland Group. I reckon that both of them put their heads together and that they were prime movers in bringing about the restructuring of the Irish banking system, involving several mergers in the 1960s and 1970s.

John Leydon was a religious man and daily Mass was very important to him. He was a recipient of the order of Papal Knight of St. Gregory (an honour conferred on people who have been of particular service to the Catholic Church). Despite his many achievements, he was a modest man and not prone to claiming credit. He worked extremely hard, always acted with the utmost integrity and honesty, and I suspect he always did what he considered to be his duty, despite the consequences. His contribution to society in the formative decades of the new Irish state was very considerable, perhaps unique. Like us all, he had some faults; for my own part, I saw little of these although possibly his work colleagues did—Roche notes that he was not always an easy man to work with, failing to understand that others may sometimes lack his own high level of commitment (p. 241).

He was a serious man, not overly given to humour but very interested in people's personal development. I remember him particularly asking me about the progress of my lectures in UCD and enquiring about the various lecturers I had, including Paddy Lynch with whom he had a close relationship through Aer Lingus. My own

> *"Having a place to go is home, having someone to love is family."*
> – Donna Hedges

children remember him as a kindly, elderly man (he would have been in his late seventies, which seems impossibly old to young children) who seemed to carry an importance beyond his physical stature. John Leydon was, even before age diminished it somewhat, quite a small man. Yet he liked big cars—indeed people used to joke that if you saw a big car with no driver, that would be John Leydon! His favourite car was likely to be an American Dodge; a car that was favoured by many of the Layden family in Arigna, possibly originating from the fact that Dodge lorries were used in the transport of Arigna coal. They were indeed big cars and lorries, distributed at that time by John O'Neill in Dublin, and presumably were valued, not for their size per se, but for the perception that big vehicles were safer than smaller ones. I suspect that it would have been Uncle John's caution rather than ostentation that influenced his choice of car. However, in some ways it was appropriate that his car was out of proportion to his physical stature—his influence and reputation were also deservedly so. I am very honoured but humbled to have known John Leydon so well.

John Leydon.

Our wedding 1st October, 1966

MARRIED AND FAMILY LIFE IN DUBLIN

Group photo with Beatrice's family.

Leading the way

Christening of our first born, David

My brother Joe's wedding

Beatrice with our first two kids

Me trying to be a good daddy

Our five kids, with Ciara on David's lap—'the beauty of innocence'.

All our family in Dublin

Conor and David

Beatrice's sisters, Christina and Una and brother Michael and cousin, Mary Pollock at my son David's wedding to Marina, June 2004.

MARRIED AND FAMILY LIFE IN DUBLIN

At a bankers dinner (probably).

A historical 1937 photo, showing Eamon de Valera, then President of the Executive Council of the Irish Free State greeting Captain Harold E. Gray, Commander of the Pan – American Airways Sikorsky Clipper 3, after it landed at Foynes, County Limerick, on July 6, 1937. Included in the picture are the then Minister for Industry and Commerce, Sean Lemass, and the secretary of that Department, John Leydon. (The foregoing details are extracts from an article written by the late Maxwell Sweeney. Neither the source or date of the article or that of the accompanying photo are known, other than they are press cuttings in the possession of John Leydon's family. They may well be from the Irish Times newspaper, since Maxwell Sweeney worked for that paper in the 1930s.)

CHAPTER NINE

Return to the Country and Other Escapades, and a Stint in Africa

Sligo

A reference to quick decision-making was made in the last chapter. My wife Beatrice and myself put that into practice in relation to our move from Dublin to the country in 1976. We decided in March of that year to move to the country and by July we had moved "lock, stock and barrel" to Sligo town (we now call it a city), having chosen Sligo over Ballina. The beauty of Sligo and the choice of schools won the Sligo vote. When we mentioned the idea of moving to the children they were excited about it, although there were some niggling worries about losing their Dublin friends. Within three months we had sold our Dublin house and had rented a bungalow in Hazelwood (on the outskirts of Sligo town) pending the purchase of a house in Sligo town which we arranged within a year. We had the children (all except Ciara who was just two) duly enrolled in the local national school (Dunally) for the start of the academic year in September 1976. Soon new friends were made and Dublin became a distant memory for them. Overall, the move was a fairly painless exercise.

Why did we make the move to the country? Both Beatrice and I were country people at heart and undoubtedly felt our roots were in the country, and many of our family members were still there. However, the notion of moving to the country was not something we had been thinking about for some time—to the best of my recollection the idea hit us one Saturday morning as we lay in bed in the Spring of 1976. Both of us took to the idea with a spring in our steps. We obviously felt that if we were going to make the move we had to do it before the children got further involved in schooling in Dublin, so time was not on our side. Also practically all of my FEOGA clients were in the country, and a fair few of them were in the north-west. Of course, fishing and shooting were much more accessible to me in the country so I must confess a partiality on that part at least! Perhaps we also envisaged a Dublin with problems looming for the rearing of a family—but I genuinely cannot remember whether we did or not.

In hindsight, I can truthfully say that it was the best decision we ever made and our children, all now in their thirties, agree wholeheartedly. Even now, the three children who are living away from Sligo visit frequently. The attractions of country life, the surf at Strandhill, beautiful scenery, fishing and family ties (they assure me that I am an important factor here!) all lure them back to Sligo. We certainly felt a new freedom in Sligo. As regards my leisure activities, I had fishing and shooting on my doorstep; before this I might have had to drive anything up to two hundred miles each way to participate in these activities. The first September in Sligo, I shot duck within a few hundred yards of our rented house and caught some six salmon in Glencar Lake, for very little fishing effort, within six miles of our house. There was a big snow that first winter and schools were closed for a fortnight. For the children this seemed a fortuitous confirmation of our decision to move to Sligo; they built enormous snowmen in the field behind us and spent hours slipping and sliding on the frozen pond at the end of the field.

From a professional point of view, my FEOGA work transitioned smoothly to our new base in Sligo and Beatrice continued to be generous in making time available to type the applications. It was a great start to our new life, and we felt we were most fortunate and had a lot to be thankful for. We purchased a house in a newly built estate, Rose Hill, just ten minutes walk from the centre of Sligo and moved into that in December 1978. We have lived here very happily ever since, although all of the children have now grown up and acquired their own homes. In 1978, the prospect of adulthood was still a long way off for them and they were delighted with the many friends to be made from the large number of young families surrounding us. Over the summers in particular, the children would disappear "up the back" (the green areas at the back of the estate), returning only at mealtimes. We never had cause to feel concern over this—we always relied on the children to keep an eye on each other. Nowadays, parents are necessarily more vigilant with their children; thankfully at that time, such caution seemed unnecessary and it was the norm for children to have been allowed such freedom.

As the children grew, we had more First Holy Communions and Confirmations as well as outings and holidays, mostly to Enniscrone. Very quickly (or so it seemed to Beatrice and myself), secondary schools were finishing for the older members of the family and they moved on to third-level education. By 1991, even our youngest, Ciara, had left to pursue a graphic design qualification. All the children were frequent visitors but they now had their own, very distinct lives; we were proud and delighted to see our children having developed into adulthood.

"The straight and narrow path is the only one that does not seem to have a traffic problem"

Land Reclamation

Stepping back to our early years in Sligo in the late 1970s, my boyhood and teenage interest in land and farming, which I referred to in chapter 1, began to surface again. I was also aware from my FEOGA work that farming was having a good period in Ireland. So I started to look around for a small farm probably to run, partly at least, as a hobby. But as land reclamation was being pushed at the time with the support of fairly decent grants, I began to look at that possibility. Soon I found myself the owner of seventy acres of heather land on the slopes of the Ox mountains near Dromore West, some twenty-two miles from Sligo town. This land was suitable for reclamation as the layer of bog on top was shallow with gravel and sand beneath, and the impervious iron pan lying immediately beneath the peat, which had to be broken in order to allow for drainage. I engaged a number of contractors to do the various jobs of work such as deep ploughing, burying large boulders, making drains, harrowing, picking stones, rolling, spreading lime and fertilisers, spreading grass seed and the final light harrowing and rolling. It's many the family outing we had to the land picking stones (the two boys were brought on such "outings" more often than the girls), but I think the novelty of this wore off fairly quickly and the lure of a Mars bar each as a reward, bought at a roadside shop on the way home, soon ceased to be a compelling force. Today, I maintain that the boys learnt the virtue of hard work but they assure me that it was child exploitation! At any rate the reclamation work and final seeding was very successfully completed despite some operational problems along the way. Within some two years of buying the land there was a sight to behold, which was seventy acres of baled hay on the side of a mountain. It was technically recognised as a great accomplishment. Looking back at it now I feel somewhat guilty at ravaging nature's lovely heather land which bore a brace of grouse before it was dug up. But I suppose I was doing no more than was being recommended by the Brussels authorities and our farm bodies. The intensification of agriculture that Ireland was experiencing at that time is, I think, something we have cause to regret as we see the loss today of small holdings, traditional varieties and diversity.

I sold the baled hay and had a local expert buy a good stock of ewe sheep and rams to run with them. The first year of sheep farming went very well and I had a good crop of lambs. We genuinely had some nice family outings that summer to see the sheep. Part of such outings would involve moving them from one field to another in order to rotate grazing and one or more of the children would be given the task of counting them as they went through the gate (in order to check that none were missing). At some stage, the count would be lost as the sheep ran through in a pack and the count volunteered was very often the number they thought I needed to hear! At other times there was genuinely hard work, particularly when myself, David and Conor (aged thirteen and ten respectively at the time) spent a few tough days dosing the sheep, but I think we enjoyed it—although the boys may be less inclined to agree! The next winter was going well until very severe weather with hard frost set in for a prolonged period, so that by the following February there was no grass for the sheep to graze on—I have never since seen the countryside so brown. It is very difficult and time-consuming to get sheep that have been used to grazing on grass to feed on anything else and anyway I wasn't free to get so involved, as I had taken up a teaching post in the Regional Technical College, Sligo. So with a heavy heart I sold my very good stock of sheep back to the man that purchased them for me in the first place (Jack Harte). Land without stock wasn't much good to me, so I also sold the land locally. In relation to this project, I want to put on record my sincere thanks to Jack Harte and to his late brother Victor, as well as to Des Harte.

Regional Technical College (RTC), Sligo/Institute of Technology, Sligo

Around 1981 my good friend, Ben Lynch, Director of Education at the Institute of Chartered Accountants in Ireland, mentioned to me that I should try and get a lecturing post at the RTC, Sligo, as it was a very fine organisation. Ben had an involvement with the RTC as it ran some accountancy courses for the Institute. I gave some thought to Ben's suggestion as my FEOGA work was beginning to dry up somewhat and, besides, after nine years of that work, I was ready for a new challenge. Before long I found myself doing part-time lectures in the RTC, Sligo, and within four months (by January 1982) I was hired for a permanent post there. I wish to note my sincere thanks to Ben, and also to Dermot Finan, Head of School of Business and Humanities, who took the risk of taking me on, or more correctly proposing me for interview. I gave up the FEOGA work after this. It was pleasant to be back to conventional paid employment again after a lapse of some nine years. I probably approached my new post with enthusiasm as if it was my first job—I think one always has to do this and of course there is always the learning curve that must be travelled. I greatly enjoyed the teaching experience, the college environment and the students. The subjects I taught were management, enterprise development and accountancy. I was also involved in arranging and overseeing work placements for students as part of their course programme. This was to turn out to be the longest job of my career, lasting for some twenty-one years until my retirement in 2002. However, I took leave of absence for two and a half years to do a stint in Africa (more on this later) and I was also seconded by the college

> *"Nothing costs so little as a few words of recognition."*
> — Father Flanagan

authorities for about eighteen months to act as Financial Controller of the college in the early 1990s.

The Regional Technical Colleges Act was passed into law in 1992, providing for all the RTCs in the country, which up to then were administered through the Vocational Educational Committees (VECs), to be established as independent institutions. This meant that the RTCs had now to undertake management, accounting and various other functions which up to then were performed by the VECs. They also had to engage staff to do so. As a qualified accountant who was already familiar with the college, it made sense for me to be seconded full-time to the position of temporary Financial Controller, pending the recruitment of a permanent appointee at a later stage. The changeover to independence was a very interesting and challenging time for the RTCs. I greatly enjoyed this work and it was a pleasure to work for and with the then Director of the College, Breandan MacConamhna. I want to record my grateful thanks to him and to all the staff I was involved with as we worked very much as a team which made the whole process a much more pleasant one than might otherwise have been the case. Most grateful thanks too to all the VEC staff for their most courteous help in the changeover process. I think I handed over the ship in good shape to the new incumbent, the affable John Cosgrove, who filled the permanent post, together with certain other responsibilities. However, there was the little matter of getting the all clear from the Comptroller and Auditor General (C & A G) before I got my pass back to lecturing freedom.

The C & AG was required to audit the college affairs and report on the financial accounts. At the beginning of the audit he told the Director that he would have to do a very thorough audit as he had heard a rumour that there had been misappropriation of funds at RTC, Sligo. This came as a total shock to the Director as he assumed that I was both honest and reasonably capable of doing what was necessary to avoid this sort of thing happening. I was equally shocked when the Director spoke to me about the matter. However, when I regained my composure I assured him that the systems of internal control that I put in place were pretty watertight and that I would be surprised if misappropriation would have taken place. However we were on tenterhooks for a week or so until the C & AG finished his audit and gave us the all clear, discovering in the meantime that the rumour had no basis. So thankfully I didn't get a P45 and I was back to my old lecturing job after over a year on secondment.

There was a very good work spirit and a feeling of comradeship among all the staff, teaching and otherwise, of the RTC, Sligo, and I felt (as did many others) a sense of pride to be part of an institution that was playing an important role in third level education and in the development of the North West. Perhaps this sense of pride, combined with teamwork, manifested itself at its highest point on those occasions when high-powered delegations from the educational authorities, supplemented with outside business and other personnel, came to the college to evaluate new course proposals the college were putting forward. The vetting undertaken on these occasions was rigorous, and I think this brought the best out in us.

Looking back at the various jobs I undertook over my working life, I would have to say that my period in the RTC/Institute of Technology, Sligo, (all the RTCs became Institutes of Technology in January 1998) particularly my twelve years there after my return from Africa in 1990, stand out as giving me the best job satisfaction of all. Apart from the very congenial staff atmosphere, it was a delight to work with the students and to witness their very good work ethic and the huge respect they showed to their teachers. I have extremely pleasant memories of my students and particularly of the gratitude they showed for what I might have been able to do for them. Judging from them, I think the future of our country is in good hands.

Obviously in the span of more than twenty years of my involvement with the RTC/IT Sligo there were very many changes. Perhaps the most significant of these was the introduction of computers and the difference that they have made to all of our lives. However, my generation did not grow up with computers and their arrival heralded much excitement and indeed consternation (even the occasional difficulty!). I remember when a computer was first installed in the office that I shared with Eamon Fitzpatrick and others. I was attempting to draft my paper for the forthcoming exams on the computer; however, when coffee time came I found myself unable to save the work I had done and was anxious not to lose the little I had so painstakingly completed. The "clever" idea of hanging my overcoat over the monitor while going for my coffee break was my interim solution. I am happy to report that no student hacked in through this somewhat insecure code and that my computer skills have improved somewhat since then!

Today, the Institute of Technology (IT), Sligo, is one of the premier Institutes in the country. IT, Sligo, provides a vast range of courses from Certificates to Diplomas to Degrees, and then to post-graduate Degrees and Doctorates in a wide range of disciplines. These courses are provided through a range of different modes, i.e. fulltime and part-time conventional taught day and evening courses, and distance learning courses which often use advanced computer based learning—in fact I believe the college is at the forefront in online learning. The college also runs tailor-made (bespoke) courses to meet the specific needs of businesses in the region. The college is also involved in both technical and broad based business research, and often works closely with businesses in this regard. The college sees itself as a primary instrument in the promotion of Sligo's Gateway Status to the North West. IT, Sligo, is, I would suggest, a university all but in name. Like the universities, it now confers its own degrees and other qualifications. Its general buildings, class rooms and theatres, library, computer facilities and catering and

> "Gratitude is the flower in the wilderness"
> — Father Flanagan

other amenities are impressive to say the least. Its recently opened all-purpose hall (to accommodate indoor-sports, conferences and so on) ought to be visited. It has a cinder track for athletics as well as football/hurling pitches and has an enviable record in sports. Today the College has some 540 staff members (including part-time and pro rata workers) and about 6,000 students.

Imposing cast of 'Salmon of Knowledge' at the main entrance to the Institute of Technology, Sligo, which no doubt symbolises the ethos of the college! (2007)

View inside the college

"Even the best mountain climbers cannot reach the top unless they have a base camp."

The 'Heavies' —the five brothers in our prime.

A Layden family gathering in our home place in Lecarrow (mid 1970s).

"The little un-remembered acts of kindness and love are the best parts of a person's life."
— William Wordsworth

Beatrice and myself, 2000.

Beatrice and myself at north Antrim coast, 1996.

Daughter Aisling

Beatrice, Aisling and myself at Cliffs of Moher, 1999.

Our family at Christmas (2001)

Some of my family with my sister Imelda

**Paddy's (my brother) family in 1992.
From left: Bernadette, Rory, Maura, Paddy, Roger and Sinead.**

Beatrice with her sisters Christina and Una and cousin Mary Pollock at Fatima (September 2001)

Cousin Sr. Maureen with Imelda and Margaret

A fairly recent gathering of siblings at Margaret's house, including Joe's wife Lily.

Vicky Pallangyo from Tanzania came all the way to see the salmon at the Ridge Pool, Ballina!

In and Out of Africa

In the autumn of 1987 the opportunity presented itself to me to go to Tanzania in East Africa on a two and a half year paid work assignment under an Irish Government aid programme to that country. I had been teaching at the RTC Sligo for over five years then and, despite thoroughly enjoying the work, found my interest being awoken by the advertisement of the post of Technical Advisor to Tanzania's accounting profession. One of my daughters recalls that the post was circulated through the Institute of Chartered Accountants and arrived with the usual mailshot of technical updates, Accountancy Ireland magazine and so on; she even drew my attention to it, suggesting that this would be the perfect job for me. The position was with the Department of Foreign Affairs and was part of Ireland's bilateral aid programme to Tanzania. This aid programme focussed on enabling the recipient country to lead its own development; hence the assignment was a broad-ranging one aimed at upgrading Tanzania's accountancy profession through joining its regulatory accountancy body, the National Board of Accountants and Auditors (NBAA) as a Technical Advisor. NBAA controls the entire accountancy profession in Tanzania (all accountants in Tanzania are certified public accountants; they do not have the multiple professional affiliations that have evolved here) and is based in Dar es Salaam, Tanzania's administrative centre.[10] The aid package also included a modest complement of library books, a printing press and some computers. The assignment covered the period February 1988 to July 1990. Mr David Rowe, a senior Irish accountant mentioned earlier in this book oversaw a number of Irish Government aid programmes in Africa, including this one in Tanzania. David was probably in semi-retirement at that stage, but such a category for David would probably correspond to full work mode for the ordinary person. Both his advice and courtesy were second to none.

This role offered a very interesting new challenge, the opportunity to work abroad and the chance to have my family travel abroad. It also came with a very attractive salary, which was a significant motivating factor at a time when our family were starting third-level education and the Irish economic outlook was still very bleak. I had also turned fifty early in 1987 so perhaps this was some sort of response to a mid-life crisis (although I can't say that I was aware of any such thing!) In any case, I applied for the job, did an interview and was, to my great surprise, offered the position. There was much excitement in the family at the prospect, although lack of knowledge about Tanzania was to be blamed for the initial response of one of the children, which was to jump up and down saying excitedly that "we're all going to Tasmania"!

As it turned out, it was not practical for all of the family to relocate to Tanzania for the duration of the project. The two older children were already

---

10. Dar es Salaam (meaning harbour or abode of peace) was at that time the capital of Tanzania although, since 1996, Dodoma has been designated as the country's official capital.

at college and the next three were all involved in the Intermediate and Leaving Certificate cycles and could not board at their existing schools or easily transfer to other schools. In order to keep our home life as normal as possible, Beatrice and I decided that she would stay in Sligo and I would go to Africa on my own. The holidays were reasonably generous so it would be possible for me to come home twice a year and the whole family could come out for the school and college holidays. Still, the prospect of living away from Beatrice after over twenty years together was very strange and it was with some trepidation that I left Ireland in February 1988. It was a terribly stormy day and the plane from Sligo was cancelled. I had to take the train to Dublin and there was a power cut in Sligo so all the omens seemed negative.

I need not have worried however. Although there were hurdles initially and the changes in climate and living arrangements took some getting used to, I think I can say that this was a truly wonderful experience for all of us. The family's arrival that summer was long-awaited and their visit was truly savoured. Unlike today, there was no email and there was no telephone service in the house I was living in just outside Dar-Es-Salaam. However, I did phone Beatrice every Sunday from a public international telephone exchange. One had to request the international number and then go to a booth when the call was connected—it was a far cry from our modern telecommunications culture; indeed Africa is now one of the biggest growth markets for mobile telephones. It was wonderful to hear beloved voices on the other end of the phone but such telephone calls were somewhat public; hence letters were our most important means of communication. The arrival of a letter from Beatrice, the children or extended family members was always a joyous occasion. Beatrice and I started numbering our letters to each other when we realised that the postal service was sometimes erratic; letter 9 might well arrive before letter 8 for example and one or two letters never arrived at all!

In the absence of family, I completely threw myself into my work and it certainly was an action-packed assignment. I got so absorbed in the work there that I didn't have time to think about my normal job in Sligo; the work in Tanzania became my total focus. The job satisfaction was immense and the variety of work activities truly extensive. But what really gave the feelgood factor about the job was the very high calibre of people I encountered in NBAA. They were highly intelligent and articulate as well as extremely courteous and friendly. They were, as indeed were all the Tanzanians I met, a very patient people. I felt totally at home in NBAA and was unaware that the colour of our skins was different. I feel that I learned a lot more from my NBAA colleagues than they learned from me. However it was a team effort and we did make very good progress on the range of projects that were set down in the aid programme package.

Before going further, I want to say a big thank you (asante sana) to all my friends in Tanzania and also a very big asante sana from my family who were treated most royally during their two summer vacations there. These summers were very special periods in our lives and I find myself somewhat emotional

> *"The way to win respect is to show respect."*
> — Father Flanagan

when I think about them now. Thank you all again. In particular, our safaris to Ngorongoro Crater and other wildlife parks were very memorable and we were thrilled to have had the opportunity to see such magnificent animals roaming free in the crater[11] and on the open plains of Africa.

Before discussing my work in NBAA, I will attempt to give some background information on Tanzania. In giving this brief background, I am indebted to The Annual Business Trade and Investment Guide 2006/2007. Tanzania comprises the country formerly known as Tanganyika and the offshore island of Zanzibar. Tanganyika had a long colonial history with the arrival of the Portugese in 1498. Moving forward, the Germans became involved in 1884 and then in 1919 the League of Nations gave Britain a mandate over Tanganyika. In 1961 Tanganyika got its independence from Britain and became a Republic in 1962 with Julius Nyerere, initially its first Prime Minister and then its first President. Independence was the result of a specific campaign (Julius Nyerere founded the Tanganyika African National Union in 1954 for this purpose) but was also a growing trend in African colonies; from the 1950s to the 1970s, the majority of African countries became independent of their former colonisers and assumed control of their own destiny. Zanzibar, a British protectorate and a sultanate with its mix of Arabic, Indian, Persian, European and African influences, well-known for its famous spice cultivation and trade, got its independence in 1963. In 1964 Tanganyika and Zanzibar merged to become Tanzania under President Nyerere.

Julius Nyerere remained in power until he retired in 1985 of his own accord, unlike many African presidents of the past who were either overthrown or even assassinated. He was replaced by Ali Hassan Mwinyi. In 1992 the Tanzanian constitution was amended to allow for multi-party politics. In 1995 Benjamin Mkapa was chosen as President in Tanzania's first multi-party election and was re-elected for a second term of five years in 2000. The current President of Tanzania is Jakaya Mrisho Kikwete. All the presidents to date have been members of the large CCM[12] party, but some seventeen other parties have emerged since the multi-party system became a reality. Julius Nyerere died in 1999. He was a real father figure in African politics and Tanzanians still have great admiration and affection for him. An appreciation to him written by Charles E. Simmons captures the essence of this great leader:

---

11. One tends to think of craters as relatively small; however, the Ngorongoro crater is some 260 km2.
12. CCM stands for Chama Cha Mapinduzi, which is Kiswahili for Party of the Revolution.

> He was a person of the character of Nelson Mandela, Kwaine Nkrumah and Patrice Lumumba. Africans called him affectionately, 'Mwalimu' or 'Teacher'. He was both a dedicated Catholic and socialist, a humble and simple man who often went back to his dusty remote village and tilled the soil along with family members. When he took office from the British Colonial Governor in 1961, one of his first official acts was to decrease his salary […] From Kilimanjaro to Beijing, and from Lake Victoria to Cairo, simple folk will tell their sons and daughters about a life of devotion to humanity.

Perhaps the Holy Ghost Order can take a bow because I understand Julius Nyerere received some of his education from them!

Tanzania, with its long record of stable government, is today making valiant efforts towards becoming a developed nation of international standing. It has taken many decisions, particularly in the last decade or so, to help it achieve this ambition. Apart from becoming a full democracy, it has liberalised many of its financial, fiscal, legal and ownership conditions so as to become attractive to the foreign investor, as well as indigenous investors. Also a considerable range of tax and other incentives are now available to the investor. It has privatised, and in some cases liquidated, over three hundred of some four hundred of its parastatals (these correspond to state bodies in Ireland). It has tuned up its banking system and it has established a stocks and shares market to facilitate industrialists in raising funds within Tanzania and various foreign banks have established bases in Tanzania. As a member of the East African Community (EAC), Tanzania provides access to a market in excess of ninety million people, and further advantages are provided by its membership of SADC (Southern African Development Community). Furthermore, Tanzania's membership in the group of African, Caribbean and Pacific states (ACP) and its signing of the Cotonou Agreement[13] establishes links and fair trading principles with four hundred and seventy million EU inhabitants.

The coordinating and monitoring of domestic and foreign investment is conducted through the Tanzanian Investment Centre (TIC),[14] which was established in 1990 and has registered some two thousand and seven hundred projects. Tanzania, with a land area of 883,590 sq. kms and 59,000 sq. kms of water, is the largest country in East Africa and has a population of thirty-eight million people, which is projected to grow to a staggering seventy million by 2025. It has two official languages, Kiswahili and English although there are many other indigenous

---

13. The Cotonou Agreement aims to reduce and eventually eradicate poverty while contributing to sustainable development and to the gradual integration of ACP countries into the world economy.
14. For further information, see the TIC website at www.tic.co.tz.

> *[The teacher] "is a dealer in horizons."*
> — Father Flanagan

languages and Arabic is widely spoken in Zanzibar. Its gross domestic product (GDP) is $10.9 billion and its gross national income (GNI) per head of population is some $330 (2004). Although the latter figure is a big improvement on past years, clearly, in the context of the West, Tanzania has a lot of catching up to do. In fact, under Tanzania's Mini-Tiger Plan, GNI is targeted to reach $2,000 in 2025. Annual inflation has fallen from about 33% in 1994 to some 5% in 2005 while the GDP growth rate has risen from 4% in 2000 to 6.8% in 2005.

As regards religious groups, some 45% are Christians, 35% are Muslims and 20% belong to various indigenous religions. Practically all of Zanzibar's population are Muslims. In cultural terms, Tanzania has incredible diversity in terms of tribes and ethnic groups. With more than one hundred and thirty tribes, including of course the graceful semi-nomadic Maasai people, it is one of the most diverse countries in all of Africa.

Agriculture, including fishing, remains the most important sector in Tanzania's GDP, contributing some 46% in 2004. Its major agricultural products include cashew nuts, cotton, coffee, cloves and sisal. Other important sectors in Tanzania are mining and quarrying, manufacturing, electricity and water, construction, tourism, transport, communication, finance and insurance. Its natural precious resources include gold, diamonds, the world famous and unique gemstone, tanzanite, as well as other gemstones. It is also well-supplied with raw materials and power capability, having coal, salt, forestland with hardwoods such as mahogany and camphorwood, hydroelectric and crude oil potential, iron, natural gas and nickel.

However, possibly one of the country's most precious assets is its varied wildlife and wonderful scenery, including the snow-capped Mount Kilimanjaro. Tourism is now the country's fastest growing economic sector.[15] Tanzania has for a long time been aware of the need to protect and conserve its wildlife stocks but now is leveraging the potential to gain from this economically. New hotels are being built through foreign direct investments so that Tanzania is welcoming not only the foreign tourist but also the foreign investor. Thus there is a big welcome (karibu sana) for all. Hopefully, Tanzanians themselves will become more involved in the higher levels of the tourism industry as the hotel sector develops.

I expect that Tanzania is now in a position to compete very successfully in the world market for its share of mobile investment. Obviously, as a developing economy, not everything is ship-shape yet, and I suspect there are some gaps in its infrastructure, but the indications are that good progress is also being made in

---

15. The web site for the Tanzania Tourist Board is www.tanzaniatouristboard.com.

this area. However Ireland developed significantly at a time when its infrastructure lagged behind so it is to be hoped that Tanzania and other African nations can do likewise.

I will now return briefly to the National Board of Accountants and Auditors and my work there. NBAA is the accountancy regulatory body in Tanzania, established by the Auditors and Accountants (Registration) Act (no 33) of 1972 and amended by a later act of 1995. It has a Governing Board and reports to the Ministry of Finance. NBAA's mission is to develop, promote and regulate the accountancy profession in Tanzania, so as to enable its qualified members to render the best professional services to the public, as well as the private sector in Tanzania. The Chairman of the Governing Board is appointed by the President of the United Republic of Tanzania for a term of three years, which may be renewed for a further three years. The other members of the Governing Board are appointed by the Minister for Finance in consultation with the outgoing Board. NBAA members play a vital role in the economic and financial management of the Tanzanian economy. Since its inception in 1972, NBAA has produced, up to 30th June 2006, a total of 15,189 successful candidates at technician, semi and full professional levels of the NBAA examinations. Many of these successful candidates have not, as yet at any rate, been in a position to progress to the final examination stage and thus become a Certified Public Accountant (CPA). Nevertheless, there were at the 30th June 2006, 3490 registered (fully qualified accountants) members on the NBAA's books. However, there is still an acute shortage of qualified professional accountants in Tanzania.

NBAA is operated on rather similar lines to that of the Irish Institute of Chartered Accountants. Indeed, its organisation structure, its examination schemes, its range of various services and its memberships of international accountancy bodies are remarkably similar (thus my previous work experience within the Irish Institute proved particularly useful). It has an Executive Director, and a range of essential committees to run its various services. Like the Irish Institute, the accountant members of NBAA serve on the various committees. Accounting education is mainly provided by various educational colleges or institutes throughout Tanzania. In all, there are twenty-one such educational bodies registered with NBAA. NBAA also produce students' manuals and more of these are currently in course of preparation. Generally, there is still a shortage of library and other educational material for accountants in Tanzania. Any interested donor of such-material would of course be very welcome.[16]

NBAA are also active in the provision of continuing professional education (CPE) for its qualified members. Courses provided therein cover both professional accounting and auditing topics, and also various business topics. In fact during my tenure with NBAA, we ran a course concerning the Responsibilities of Directors

---

16. Further information or contact details can be found on the NBAA web site at www.nbaa-tz.org.

> *"Do you not know my friend, that you owe the first fruits of your heart and voice to God? Run therefore to meet the rising sun so that when the day dawns it may find you ready"*
> — St. Ambrose on Psalm 118 and reproduced from The Glenstal Book of Prayer, p. 64

in the conduct of company affairs. It is interesting to note that it was only in the 1990s that company directors in Ireland began to realise their serious responsibilities in this area. As Tanzania is very keen to attract more foreign investment to its country, it is important that it maintains membership with international accountancy bodies such as IFAC, and this it does. This is particularly relevant in achieving international uniformity in accounting standards. It also appears that independent regulation of the accountancy profession is currently under discussion in Tanzania, perhaps along the lines adopted in Ireland where the membership of the regulatory body has a majority of non-accountants.

In relation to my own work in NBAA from 1988 to 1990, I would like to say that I was involved in a most interesting spread of activities. Nearly the only thing I didn't do was sit the NBAA examinations (possibly I was afraid to do so in case I failed!). In any event, all the diverse activities I was involved in were part of a team effort. Such activities included:

- Restructuring and re-writing the various examination syllabi, which had evolved in response to particular needs rather than being clearly planned
- Discussing with the accountancy educational bodies the provision of student educational needs to underpin the examinations
- Arranging for the compilation and distribution of educational material, including library material
- Correcting examinations and establishing administrative protocols for the setting and correction of examinations
- Preparation of accounting and auditing standards in consultation with international accounting standards
- Provision of a range of short courses and seminars for accountants and members of the business community
- Some work on computerisation
- Attending various committee meetings
- Various day-to-day issues

The above activities are never once-off activities but rather are ongoing and I understand that they are continuing even as I write. My previous work both within the Irish Institute and in the teaching side of the profession was used to its fullest extent in this work.

There are many personnel I should identify individually, both within and outside NBAA, who made my stay in Tanzania so memorable, but in the main I will refrain from doing so because, due to the lapse of time, I would surely fail to remember everyone. I will merely mention four people as follows:

1. The then very able and courteous Executive Director of NBAA, Ludovick Utouh.
2. The then highly respected Chairman of NBAA, Reginald Mengi.
3. William Mamuya who acted as my guide and worked in the same office as me during my stay in Tanzania. I thank him sincerely for his comradeship and tremendous ability.
4. The current Chairman of NBAA, Simon Sayore. It is no surprise to me to find that Mr. Sayore is holding this important post. He was one of the very many able accountants I had the pleasure of encountering while with NBAA.

There were so many other truly great people who were on the staff of the NBAA, and also accountants I met on the various NBAA committees, about who I can only say that I was mightily fortunate to have had the opportunity of encountering them. Asante sana.

I wish also to say a big thank you to the very many courteous and good people and able golfers (I still remember Omari's long drives) I met at the Gymkhana Club. These golf outings at the weekends and my walk on Oyster Bay beach on the way home from work in the evenings meant a great deal to me. Lastly, a big hello and thanks to all my Irish colleagues I met in Tanzania who were working there, representing various organisations, including the Irish Embassy. We have a lot of happy memories of these times and we should surely thank the Tanzanians and the organisations which sent us there. Again I will desist from naming names for fear of overlooking and causing offence. I know no-one will mind if I single out for special mention Katherine O'Dea's wonderful fruit crumbles! The community spirit of the O'Deas and the other Irish working there helped to make home seem nearer.

On safari in Tanzania (Ngorongoro Crater)

Our mode of transport. Conor is the 'pretending' driver.

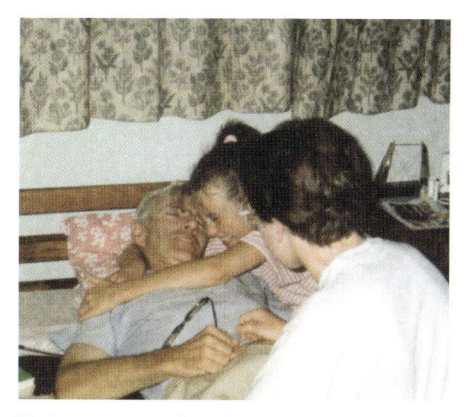

Trying to get a break.

RETURN TO THE COUNTRY AND OTHER ESCAPADES, AND A STINT IN AFRICA

Maasai warriors on the plains at the foot of Mount Kilamanjaro. (Courtesy Finbar O'Reilly/Reuters/Irish Times, November 18, 2006. We did have sightings of these nomadic Maasai warriors.

Two elephants in the wild

A close-up of 'He' who never forgets (Courtesy 'Corporate Tanzania – The Annual Business, Trade and Investment Guide 2006/2007', IMC, Switzerland, 2006). We did actually get very close to an elephant in the wild (not this one), but decided to move on and not take chances!

We got very close to these lions.

Got pretty close to these zebras.

A herd of buffalo.

A Few Comments on Work

Generally all the comments I have made about my various work assignments are very positive from the points of view of my job satisfaction and fulfilment therefrom. However, I do not wish to give the impression that I never encountered problems or disappointments in the work place or that I never made bad decisions in life. We all operate in an environment where imperfect human beings interact with and impact upon one another. Of course I encountered problems and disappointments along the way. The secret, as far as I am concerned, is not to let these problems or disappointments dominate you or hinder you in your performance. You deal with them swiftly as they arise, in the most appropriate and honest and humane manner and then you move on.

Above all, never hold grudges against a work mate or boss (or indeed against anyone for that matter). Holding grudges like this can become a debilitating cancer in your life and blinkers you to life's potential. There is a great sense in practising the old adage "Forgive and Forget," getting on with your work and your life and not dwelling unnecessarily on any hurts that may have come your way. Above all, never set out to get your own back on somebody. In all of this, I think you will often find that people who hurt you or short-changed you in the past can become your staunch friend or supporter in the future, even though that would never have been your objective in the first place. So always look at the big picture.

In the context of my experience of marriage and family life the same kind of comments and advice applies. Marriage and rearing a family is not always a bed of roses—by virtue of our human nature there will always be difficulties and stresses along the way. Surmounting those difficulties together can even increase the love within a marriage and I often wish that people today would make a greater commitment to marriage and be willing to count their blessings rather than their grievances. Of course, this requires work by both partners but offers the very great potential reward of that noble and fulfilling state in life, a committed marriage.

**A high level accountancy conference in Tanzania.
The two white faces are those of Tony O'Dea and myself.**

CHAPTER TEN
Some Conclusions about Achieving Success in Business

This is a very short chapter which touches on a few ideas that might be helpful in the conduct of successful business. I would be presumptuous to suggest that I am an expert in business management. I am not suggesting that at all, but as I have had a lot of exposure in one form or another to the initiation and conduct of businesses (as well as a view of business from the academic side), I am merely listing some conclusions I have come to regarding the operation of a successful business.

1. One's business affairs, both internal and external, should always be conducted with the utmost honesty. Thus untruths should never be told nor unjust dealings done. This implies that a proper code of business ethics is practised. In this way, one is setting the base for loyal staff and loyal customers.
2. Those who are dishonest and don't come straight can find themselves spending a great deal of their time trying to cover their tracks so as not to be caught out. It makes far more sense to concentrate one's efforts on what matters in building up a successful business, and then you can sleep the "sleep of the just" at night.
3. Realise that one's workers are the greatest business asset of all. In fact try to resist referring to them as your workers—you and they are a team. Treat them with respect and dignity and operate an open communications policy with them. Don't expect your workers to do things you would not do yourself. Your own office accommodation should not be unduly luxurious. Lead by example.
4. Within the concept of a team approach, responsibilities must nevertheless be clearly identified. It usually makes for good commitment to get different individuals or teams to lead and champion the various projects or assignments.
5. Know your business and get a good feel for all the areas of the business, particularly those outside your own particular expertise. Any business manager who has not a good understanding of all the aspects of the business is, I believe, at a serious disadvantage.

6. Set out plans for the business, prepare budgets, underpin them with the necessary resources and monitor performance on a timely basis. Even if your budgets are not being met, the budgeting discipline is important, for it gives you a baseline for taking corrective action and pushes you to properly get to know the business environment you are working in.
7. In planning a new business venture, carry out the necessary research under all the usual headings i.e. marketing, technical, personnel, financial, and so on. Develop as realistic a business plan as is possible. While one should be rigorous with the research in these areas, it is necessary to balance research details with the time factor. For instance, waiting until 100% accurate research details become available in three years' time for a project that should start in one year's time may not be of any use—the opportunities the project was offering may have been lost by then. Furthermore, people tend to lose interest where the research period is unduly long and thus good potential projects are never realised. Thus a relative quick investment decision on the basis of say 80% accurate information might well be the best option. Make up for the other 20% by close monitoring of the project, once operations start. In any case, I do not think there is such a thing as 100% accurate research information. There is always a risk with new projects, but close monitoring after commencement enables you to make timely decisions about the direction of the project.
8. Be committed to your business and have staying power. This is particularly important for new businesses. However, recognise defeat if it is staring you in the face and cut your losses and end honourably.
9. Know the capabilities of your fellow business promoters, managers and staff. Don't just assume, possibly because of the status of a person, that he or she has all the necessary skills to perform his or her task in the business. Do a proper inventory of training needs of all concerned and then attend to these needs. It could well be that you, the promoter or a high-ranking manager needs training, just as much as others in the organisation.
10. Be aware of capitalising on short term or opportunistic gains to the possible detriment of the long term future of the business.
11. Be a person of your word, be reliable, adhere to commitments, keep appointments and be on time.
12. Give credit to others for achievements, rather than take credit yourself.
13. Be humble. Humility is not necessarily a recognition of inadequacy, but rather a recognition of your dependence on others.

> *"To err is human, to forgive divine."*
> — Rudyard Kipling

Of course many of these statements apply to life in general and not merely to business. I conclude this chapter with a most apt statement on leadership made by a well-known Redemptorist priest, Father Peter Byrne C.Ss.R. Fr. Byrne suggests that a good leader "is not one who shows off his skills and strengths to others but one who reveals to people their own riches. So I was enriched and humbled by what people taught me" (p. 45).

*"Lord keep us from getting so involved in life
that we forget why you gave us life."*
— Mark Link S. J.

"There is no pillow so soft as a clear conscience."

*"It is not the mountains ahead that wear you out.
It's the grain of sand in your shoe."*

"Don't be afraid to go out on a limb. That is where the fruit is."

Part 4

The Arigna Industrial Revolution from 1600s to the Present

CHAPTER ELEVEN
The Arigna Coal Mining Industry and the Earlier Ironworks

Overview of Iron and Coal mining

While Arigna is generally well known for its coalmining activities, it is not so well known for its ironworks. Yet there were major ironwork activities in the general Arigna and surrounding areas going back as far as the 1600s when a significant ironworks operated at Creevelea, County Leitrim, ten miles north-west of Arigna. There were also ironworks located at Arigna itself and at Drumshanbo (which was just a few miles away) and Ballinamore (some twenty miles distant). These operations were promoted by foreign industrialists, usually British, and sometimes very large numbers of workers were employed in these operations, usually brought from the UK and elsewhere. The output of these various ironworks was often, from a business point of view, unsatisfactory and many of them appear to have closed before reaching their potential. The Creevelea ironworks was a significant operation but was destroyed in the 1641 Rising, as indeed were many others. It was later reopened.

Many of the ironworks that still remained open in the nineteenth century were dogged with bad management, including frequent changes of management, and fraud and misappropriation of funds in some cases. One such case led to a major inquiry in the House of Commons in London. At times perhaps poor market prices for iron ore were the problem. However a major problem, particularly in the later ironworks which used coal to fire the blast furnaces is that proper research of the coal deposits available in the general Arigna area was not carried out and there were exaggerated claims of the quantities of coal available, particularly that relating to the thickness of the coal seams. I suspect too, that the promoters, though probably of notable status, were to an extent gullible by allowing themselves to be carried away by the promotional hype surrounding the huge potential iron mining in the area offered the investor. Thus it would appear that they failed to properly research the operational details of mining in the Arigna area.

Furthermore, the apparently common practice of bringing in and planting foreign workers who would be un-accustomed to the local scene may well have contributed to the poor performance of these operations. Perhaps I could quote again from *A History of Accountants in Ireland* by H. W. Robinson: "The nineteenth century in Britain, and to a lesser extent in Ireland, was a period of wild speculation, of failures and crashes, of booms and crises, of embezzlements and frauds" (p. 32). Robinson suggests that Irish business failures "were in the main the result of mis-management and misfortune" (p. 34) and it appears that this was the case in relation to the ironworks in Arigna and surrounding areas.

All the local ironworks up to the late 1700s used timber as a fuel to fire the furnaces. In fact the timber was converted to charcoal first. But by the late 1700s all the forests in the area had been cut down and used up. So a new fuel had to be found. Turf was initially tried, but not very successfully. It was at this point that coal was first mined in the Arigna area to fire the iron furnaces. Perhaps another extract from Dr. Robinson's *History* is apt and serves to illustrate the cost of operating such iron furnaces:

> With the invention of the steam engine and the use of coal in place of charcoal, the iron industry, in particular, expanded rapidly in England, so that by the beginning of the nineteen century it was by no means uncommon to find up to five hundred men employed in a single works. By 1833, one quarter of the cost of bar iron consisted of interest on capital and when times were bad it was necessary to sell iron at a price that would do little more that cover prime cost" (p. 145-46).

The ironworks at Creevelea used coal in their latter stages and the ironworks at Drumshanbo also used coal to fire the furnaces. However, the attention switched from Drumshanbo to Arigna in the late 1700s where a significant ironworks was established using locally mined coal to fire the furnaces. The indications are that it wasn't very successful. Later follow-up efforts in the early 1800s didn't stand the test of time either. By the mid-1800s, the production of iron ore ceased for good in Arigna but it appears to have continued at Creevelea until about 1900.

I might add that Arigna and the surrounding areas attracted an incredible amount of interest among the investment public (usually the landlords and their colleagues from abroad) from the early 1600s to the early 1800s. Not all of this interest manifested itself in actual projects, but much of it did; however such projects appear not to have been very successful.

The modern era of coal mining in Arigna, as an industry in its own right, unrelated to iron smelting, commenced in the second half of the 1800s. This time it was local promoters in the main who were involved, the most prominent of which was Michael Layden. He was my grandfather. There were some other local promoters as well, and in addition, it is likely that small amounts of coal were mined by several individuals for many years before that, probably mostly at easily accessible outcrop points. Also around the same time, the Arigna Mining Company,

> *"From one who loves, wounds are well intentioned;*
> *from one who hates, kisses are ominous."*
>
> — Proverb 27: 6

promoted by the Earl of Kingston, got involved in coal mining in Arigna. It had a shaky start and almost collapsed, but then it traded quite successfully until it closed down in the late 1920s due to losing a court case. Coal mining in Arigna continued at a significant level all through the 1900s and right up to 1990 when all the mines in Arigna, including Bencroy mine on Slieve-an-Ierin (which translates as Iron Mountain), closed down when the local Electricity Supply Board (ESB) power generating station ceased to take any more coal supplies, pending its closure a couple of years later. Anyway, all the good quality coal had essentially been mined at this time but it had been hoped that the ESB would build a new power station that would use the vast quantities of low grade crow coal available in both the Arigna and Slieve-an-Ierin mountains. This was not to be.

Regarding quantities of coal produced in Arigna, it was only in the 1900s and particularly from the 1930s and 40s onwards up to 1990, that very significant quantities were produced. For instance annual output rose in these years to some 60,000 imperial tons of coal compared to some 12,000 tons in the late 1800s. The Arigna coal gained special significance during the Second World War because of shortages of imported fuels and it was purchased by various state companies, such as the Railways and others. The Arigna coalmining industry gave significant employment for up to three or four hundred people for many years at a time when off-farm jobs were extremely scarce.

All that remains of mining in Arigna now is a mining museum "The Arigna Mining Experience," which actually replicates typical coal mining operations in a real underground mining shaft. It attracts a very considerable numbers of visitors, and offers a stunning view of Lough Allen and the surrounding areas. There are, however, other successful businesses operating in Arigna today which relate to energy production or mining/quarrying. These include the production of smokeless coal briquettes (using imported coal), wind farms and the quarrying and production of decorative stone.

Iron Works Promoted by Sir Charles Coote and by Others

The ironworks were, as already mentioned, typically owned and operated by British industrialists. Sir Charles Coote was one such and *The History of County Leitrim, Part 2, 1691 to Modern Times* gives an interesting insight into the extent of his property and influence:

> Sir Charles Coote who built the fortified town of Jamestown and was richly endowed with land in Leitrim and Roscommon in the Plantation of Leitrim 1621 established a number of mining operations in the county, at Ballinamore, Drumshanbo, and here at Creevelea. These were destroyed during the Rebellion of 1641 but were restarted about 1695 after peace had been restored following the Williamite wars. Much iron smelting was carried out in this period but the huge volume of wood needed for the blast furnaces gradually denuded the forests so that by the 1760s all operations had closed down. (Dr. R.J. Quinn, p. 49-50)

Incidentally, Sir Charles also established iron works at Arigna, but the above history only concerns county Leitrim. Quinn goes on to state that none of the almost 3,000 men working for Sir Charles in the various locations were Irish, having come from England and Holland. In later years many Scottish miners came to work in Creevelea (p. 51). Although the ironworks at Creevelea are now long closed, the iron from these works has been used in public structures such as the Ha'penny Bridge in Dublin and the original Tay Bridge in Scotland. Quinn even notes that some of the cannons used in the Crimean War were made from Creevelea iron (p. 51).

Dr. Quinn informs us that the iron works at Creevelea were re-established for a second time in 1852 by a Scotch company and in doing so they constructed two blast furnaces and also roasting and cooking kilns. While the venture appeared to be successful for a short period, the company went bankrupt in 1854. He further explains that this

> was not due to any inferior quality of the iron but to external factors, possibly the long distance involved in carting coal to the furnaces. In the 1860's the Works under new management commenced operations again, this time using peat as a source of power. This did not prove satisfactory, however, and coal was again used. By 1872 the works were again idle, this time due to the fall in the price of iron. Twenty–five years later the Peat Charcoal Fuel and Iron Company of Ireland Ltd., Creevelea, Co. Leitrim, was established on the site (1896), £40,000 having been spent on the modernisation of the plant. Despite all this the huge foundry was again idle by 1900 and so the almost untouched orebody still awaits a new mining entrepreneur. (p. 50)

The final but sad comment by Dr Quinn on the Creevelea operation is that the iron works were demolished by explosives during World War 2 and the materials used for road surfacing (p. 50). However, there was starting to be some local involvement in the iron business and Quinn observes that "A family of O'Reilly, (Thomas, Patrick and Andrew) worked the smelting works at Furnace Hill, Drumshanbo, until they moved to the Arigna valley" (p. 51) and also that a local

> "Love is patient; love is kind; it is not envious or boastful or arrogant or rude. It does not insist on its own way; it is not irritable or resentful; it does not rejoice in wrongdoing, but rejoices in the truth. It bears all things, believes all things, hopes all things, endures all things."
> — 1 Corinthians 13:4–7

entrepreneur, Patrick Reynolds, "managed the Drumshanbo works for a time" (p.51). I will deal with the O'Reilly operation in more detail presently.

The Arigna Scene

Writing in 1964, under the title *The Arigna Valley*, the author P. J. Flanagan throws a lot of light on the various mining ventures in Arigna and surrounding areas in the past several centuries. He makes an initial observation that a visitor to the area "may pass quite unaware of the long and important mining history of the Arigna Valley" (p. 20). Continuing, he states:

> Lough Allen divides what is known as the "Connaught Mineral Field." On the western side of the lake is the historic Arigna valley, to the east, Slieve-an-Ierin or 'Iron Mountain'. Despite the fact that the latter area is said to be richer in minerals, very little activity has taken place there and I shall have little to say about it. On the other hand, the Arigna side has been worked almost with imagination. [...] The iron deposits have been worked as far back as the 15th century, and mines were still in operation in the 1600s. In his *Ireland's Natural History*, Boate mentions the iron-mines operated by Sir Charles Coote in Leitrim and Roscommon [...] It is probable that Coote's works were on the site of the present Arigna village; he lived at Cootehall, not very far away. He also had works at Creevelea, in the townland of Gowlaun, near Drumkeerin; this is another place of interest, though not strictly in the Arigna valley. [...] Coote also had works at Drumshanbo and Ballinamore. All these works were destroyed in the rebellion of 1641, and the first phase came to an end. (p. 20)

Interestingly, Flanagan casts some light on Coote's lack of employment of the Irish stating that "on no account were Irishmen to be employed, lest they should learn the secrets of the iron industry" (p. 20).

Rev. Joseph Meehan, C.C., in his 1906 paper confirms that Sir Charles Coote's ironworks at Arigna and Creevelea were both burned down by the insurgents in

1641. However, in regard to employing only English and Dutch (which incidentally he numbered at 2,500 or 2,600), he cited the reason for this exclusion of Irish (quoting Boote's National History of Ireland) as being because "the natives were then considered the most barbarous natives of the whole earth and as having no skills in any of these things" (p. 129). I wonder would these plants have been burned down if these so-called natives, probably starving with hunger, were employed instead of foreigners (I am not of course condoning the destruction of the plants). I suggest also that what these natives lacked in skills (which could in any case be remedied by training) might have been more than made up by their knowledge of the local scene. Furthermore, they could probably have been employed at wages significantly less than those paid to the foreign workers. It would appear from the literature of later years that houses were built for at least some of the foreign workers, thus adding further to the running costs of these operations. In addition, management salaries appear to have been very extravagant, judging from information given by Isaac Weld's 1832 publication The Statistical Survey of the County of Roscommon. Weld indicates that the annual salary of the chief manager of the Arigna ironworks in the early 1800s was £500, while the furnace manager received £273, and a watchman at the colliery received £18 for the year (p. 53). So the chief manager got a salary of almost twenty-eight times that of the watchman. It is also quite likely that he had a fine house provided for him. Some sources also suggest that these foreign workers, possibly including management, didn't always behave themselves and that some developed an undue liking for the local brew!

P. J. Flanagan's article notes that all the plants destroyed in the 1641 rebellion had been re-opened before the end of the 1600s. Again, we can see that the iron from these plants was not merely used locally but was a key material in enabling world trade; he observes that "the works of Patrick Reynolds at Drumshanbo are said to have produced the iron used in the first ship built at Limerick for the East India Company" (p. 20). However, he also notes that the "indiscriminate use of timber finally led to supplies running out" leading to the closure of the Drumshanbo works in 1765 and the Creevelea works in 1768" (p. 21). Around this time, coal began to be considered as a furnace fuel and Flanagan notes that "a family named O'Reilly began to make their name in local history. They are said to have worked in Furnace Hill [Drumshanbo plant] using coal from Seitenaskeagh [in Arigna] and [...] iron ore from Slieve-an-Ierin" (p. 21). Unfortunately, their operation was not to last and ceased after "a boat loaded with iron ore foundered off Cormongan townland [a shoreline of Lough Allen]" (p. 21).

Others now began to consider using coal, which P. J. Flanagan notes was first discovered on Altagowlan, a part of the Arigna coalfield which was then (1765) known as Mounterkenny[17] (p. 21). The landowner, a Mr. Jones, worked the coal for a time; indeed the "colliery was thought of such importance that a Parliamentary

---

17. This area was probably about two miles west of Lough Allen

> *"The person who lacks purpose will never go far or do much."*
> — Father Flanagan

grant was voted to aid the making of roads to it, but as so often happened, nothing was done and the colliery was abandoned" (Flanagan, P.J., p. 21). However, it is clear that the prospect of coal attracted much interest, both in its own right and as a fuel for further iron works. There was plenty of coal available at Aughabehy (part of the Arigna coalfields) and

> before 1800, the land owner (or "royalty owner") Colonel Thomas Tenison worked it [...] Further down the same side of the Valley, the Rover colliery of the Archbishop of Tuam started production [...] After the O'Reillys left Furnace Hill they embarked on a venture which was to prove financially fatal to themselves, but was to be responsible for much of the railway construction of the area; this was the erection about 1788 of the Arigna Iron Works. There were three O'Reilly brothers, and between them they built the works, spending much money in the process. Compared with earlier works, these were on a really massive scale, and it is easily understandable that the promoters were in deep financial waters before long. They approached the Irish Parliament for a grant of £10,000; an investigating committee sent in two favourable reports, but no money was given. The O'Reillys then contacted the famous Dublin banking firm of Latouche; the bankers made an advance, which proved insufficient, and then made a second one. The money was used, but too late, and the O'Reillys became bankrupt in 1793. (Flanagan, P.J., p. 21)

According to P. J. Flanagan, there were various other manoeuvres to keep the plant open but they were of no avail, and thus the Arigna Iron Works closed down in 1798, just ten years after its opening. The works were put up for sale by the Court of Chancery. The article continues:

> Despite his bank investing of £10,000, Peter Latouche was apparently very interested. When the Chancery sale came up, he hurried away with "the opinion that money alone was wanting to render the concern most profitable". So for £25,000, he bought the Arigna Iron Works, this was, I think, about 1804-5. But sad to relate, Latouche was no more successful than the O'Reillys, and gave up in despair about 1808. Isaac Weld states that Latouche ceased his efforts "after considerable expenditure of money and various trials under new and different managers". Griffith strongly criticised the latter point, saying that the frequent change of management "tended more than any other cause to accelerate the fail-

ure of the undertaking", as each man tended to throw out everything done before him, and then introduce his own plans. There is a telling story about Latouche and Arigna. He was showing a friend around the gardens of his beautiful estate [...] in Co. Wicklow. He paused before an iron gate and said [...] "That gate, Sir cost me £80,000, for it is the only thing I ever got out of the Arigna Iron Works in return for all my money expended there!" (Flanagan, P.J. p. 22)

P. J. Flanagan quotes from two nineteenth-century sources, Isaac Weld and Richard Griffith. I will also be drawing further on these authors in order to supply contemporary accounts of the story of Arigna mining. It may be apparent that the story is not always an easy one to tell, but hopefully the corroboration from various authors will help to supply context and authenticity. We can be sure of at least one thing, that the Arigna story is an incredible story of start-ups, of closures, of fortunes lost, of hopes dashed and of business promoters and financiers (people whom one would expect to know better) making apparently very bad business decisions. We have probably touched on several of the possible reasons for the many failures, but you may wish to draw your own conclusions about them. Anyway, the story continues.

Earlier, I made reference to promotional hype—specifically there was huge promotional hype concerning the mining potential that Arigna and Slieve-an-Ierin offered. It was assumed that all that was needed to make a fortune was to amass a pool of money to invest therein, and this was now possible through the formation of joint stock companies, by virtue of enabling legislation which had been passed in parliament. In this regard, Isaac Weld's 1832 publication supplies a useful account.

> The discovery of coal in so many parts of these mountains, naturally gave rise to hope, not only amongst the immediate proprietors of the soil, but throughout the country in general. No rigorous investigations into the thickness or extent of the seams appear however to have been deemed necessary; but that which had been seen was eagerly assumed as an earnest of the rich masses which remained hidden in the bowels of the earth. Industry and capital alone were supposed to be wanting, to add largely to the increase of national wealth. The importance of collieries to manufacturers was dwelt upon with zeal, and became a frequent subject of discussion in the Irish parliament. New laws were passed to facilitate the opening of roads to the mouths of the coal pits. An extensive water communication was also to be provided for the transmission of these ideal mineral treasures; and the river Shannon, which ran so immediately in the vicinity of the district, was forthwith to be rendered navigable in every part of its course, and made the channel of commerce through a vast extent of inland country. Thus, in the fond expectation of enthusiasts of the day, Ireland was to become independent of Great

> *"In the happiness brought to others, our own happiness is reflected."*
> — Father Flanagan

> Britain for her supply of coals; manufacturers were to spring up; and, as a necessary consequence, wealth was to follow in their train, and be diffused throughout a smiling land. The sequel will show how much delusion there has been on the subject. (p. 35–36)

Weld also makes reference to the survey of the Connaught coal district carried out by Mr Richard Griffith and published in 1818 about ten years after the Arigna iron works closed down.

> The future prosperity of the Connaught coal district [...] may be said to depend entirely upon the produce of the bed No.12,[18] (called the three foot coal), which though of moderate thichness, is fortunately of great extent. Its quality as fuel for domestic purposes is excellent, and if used for smelting iron, it is amongst the best in the empire. The thickness of this coal is rarely less than three feet four inches." (Weld, p. 41-42, quoting from Griffith) [19]

According to Weld, Mr. Griffith calculated a coal reserve of thirty million tons (incorporating both the Arigna and Slieve-an-Ierin mountains), enough to last for 500 years on the basis of 50,000 tons being used annually in the country and an additional 10,000 tons being used in the iron works (p. 42). Unfortunately, the large scale availability of three-foot seams of good quality coal did not turn out to be a reality. Typically, the seam was closer to eighteen inches, and even then, faults developed in the seams. In relation to Griffith's assessment of the coal seams, Weld states:

> But, as I have already explained, there is apparently an error in the statement as to the extent and the thickness of the principal bed of coal, numbered 12, in his table of the stratification; attributable, I believe, to the Aughabehey and Rover pits not having being accessible, at the period of his visit; and to the erroneous information having been communicated to him on the subject, by persons who ought to have known better". (p. 41)

---

18. This bed No.12 consists of the Aughabehy and Rover collieries.
19. I have been unable to obtain a copy of Griffith's survey and hence have had to rely on Weld's and other references to it.

It might be noted that, according to "Some Notes on Leitrim Industry", written by Patrick Flanagan[20] in 1970, a three-foot seam of coal was found: "it was in Leitrim that the Arigna valley's main (three foot) seam of coal was first discovered on the lands of Mr. Jones in 1765" (p. 421). However, such a seam was certainly less extensive than originally thought. At any rate, arising from Griffith's report, investment interest in Arigna quickly followed, and according to Weld, three companies showed interest: the Arigna Coal and Iron Company; the Irish Mining Company; and the Hibernian Mining Company. When these "all joint stock companies with large capitals and intelligent and enterprising agents, had entered into the field, and the country on the confines of Lough Allen, at once became the theatre of activity and industry" (Weld, p. 43). The Arigna Coal and Iron Company "obtained possession of the old works, and the collieries attached to them on the south side of the river" [the works operated by the O'Reillys and later by Latouche], while "the other two companies began their operations in the mountains on the north side of the Arigna river" (p. 43–44).

Weld tells us that the Hibernian Mining Company did not proceed with mining after carrying out trials as to the thickness of the coal seams, which they found to be disappointing (p. 44). The Irish Mining Company did proceed to mine coal at Tullynaha, where the coal was raised up a shaft from the coal bed by means of a steam engine and later by a manually operated winding system, when the steam engine broke down. It is probable that this pit was worked for some decades, possibly into the 1850s, by the Irish Mining Company before operations ceased (p. 44–46). Some people appear to be of the view that this is the pit that became known generally as the Engine Pit, but my cousin Brendan Layden is certain that The Engine Pit was located at Knockateean, just a short distance up from the Colliery House. As a youngster walking the mountains during the grouse shooting, that was also my understanding. However, Brendan surmised that any pit with a vertical shaft which was worked by a steam engine or other powered source, would likely have been referred to as an engine pit.

As already indicated, the Arigna Coal and Iron Company took possession of the Arigna iron works and collieries attached to them, (incidentally the correct name of the company would appear to be the Arigna Iron and Coal Mining Company). They did so in the Winter of 1824–25, according to Weld, who says he visited the area in the Spring of 1825. He goes on to state:

> The buildings and offices, confined for the most part to an extensive yard, were then undergoing repairs; a mining agent, Captain Vivian, presided over the whole; and engineers, smiths, fire master, masons,

---

20. This Patrick Flanagan and P. J. Flanagan, (author of The Arigna Valley) are one and the same person. As he used initials for one publication and his first name for the other, I have (in order to distinguish the two publications) given the specific name used in each publication when referring to them.

> "To my God a heart of flame; to my fellow man a heart of love, and to myself a heart of steel."
> — St. Augustine

miners, &c., all Englishmen, skilled in the business of their respective departments, were actively employed; and all, according to the usual habits of Englishmen, had contrived to make themselves comfortable, in the first place. It was like a little colony in a new country; and it was really pleasurable to behold the contrast which their several dwellings, from the good housewifery of their families, afforded to the ordinary habits of the people of the surrounding wild districts. But ardent spirits, *the liquid devil*, in the emphatic language of the late Dean Kirwan, had already begun to exercise a baneful influence over the conduct of many of the people, and those not the lowest; whiskey was too cheap to be resisted, and those who should have set better example, were amongst the first to succumb.

An immense heap of iron stone had been collected, at that time, near the furnace; but there was no provision of coal equal to smelting it. (p. 47–48)

So it would appear that there was no shortage of the iron raw material, but the real problem appears to have been the inability to mine efficiently and effectively the relatively thin seams of coal, which were contained in sometimes difficult mining environments. The English were almost certainly unfamiliar with such thin seams and working conditions. Incidentally, the iron stone was readily available in Arigna, particularly in the bed of the Arigna river and where it outcropped, without any need of mining it. Had iron smelting become a big venture in the 1800s, then it is likely that open-cast mining of the stone, would have been undertaken. From a review of the literature, it would appear that the Arigna iron stone was generally considered to be of high quality with the iron stone being approximately 35% pure iron.

Weld states that he visited Arigna again in the autumn of 1830 and found that the "furnace became gobbed" and inoperable; it appeared that the flowing iron and furnace had become fused (p. 48). Thus over a period of seven years in "this great and promising mining district" with an outlay by the mining company which was estimated at over £50,000, "the whole produce of iron […] did not amount to 300 tons" (p. 50). This suggests that the ability of the company to smelt iron could be called into question. Weld also states that in 1826 there was "a complete change at the board, and in the management of the company" (p. 50).

P. J. Flanagan largely concurs with Weld's account and gives further information on the board's attempts to control the operation:

> As a result of the initial scandal, the new board became worried, and even doubted the value of the property they had acquired. So they asked Mr. J. A. Twigg of Chesterfield to make a complete survey and report; for this we should be grateful to them. Twigg's report published in London in 1827, contained some interesting recommendations: (I) to complete the adit at Aughabehy, begun by the O'Reillys; (II) to build coke-yards near the mouth of the adit; (III) to build a railway from the coke-yard to the works. The directors, unusually for those who receive reports, lost no time in implementing Twigg's suggestions, but they also adopted a bad habit of earlier years—they changed managers a few times. (p. 27)

While the company did not reap the benefits of these investments, at least future generations of coal miners would benefit from the railway system built from Aughabehy to the works at Arigna, as by 1920 a railway line would connect to the existing public railway station at Mount Allen some two miles away. In this matter, P.J. Flanagan points out that Griffith in his report on the Connaught coal district, had recommended similar action twelve years previously. He notes that by February 1832, this railway line, which measured 5,500 yards, was completed (p. 27–28).

It is interesting to note, according to Weld, that Mr Twigg reported that on "reaching Arigna [...] I did not find that any previous trials had effectually been made, for proving either the quantity or quality of the coal mines, within the coal district leased to the company" (p. 51). This somewhat devalues the survey done by Griffith which had identified such huge potential. Joseph Meehan's 1907 article on the Connacht Mineral Area gives further detail both on Griffith's survey and on the Arigna Iron and Coal Mining Company:

> In 1818 he [Mr.Griffith] brought out a book entitled *Geological and Mining Survey of the Connaught Coal District* [...] Mr. (or Sir Richard) Griffith was, at the time he published the work, Inspector-General of His Majesty's Royal Mines in Ireland, and Mining Engineer to the Dublin Society [...] Arigna, a south-eastern corner of the Connacht Mineral Area, has been celebrated for iron manufacture since the first time iron was made in Ireland. "I have great confidence in narrating that there is no situation in the empire", wrote the mining authority just mentioned, "in which cast-iron can be manufactured at a cheaper rate or of superior quality" (Survey p. 62). At Drumshambo, on the southern shore of Lough Allen, the last charcoal-heated furnace in Ireland went out in 1765 for want of fuel—the immense Leitrim woods had given out. And at the same spot, too, coal converted into coke was first used in this country to smelt ore. There alone, in fact (Creevelea, also in the

> *[Are we too busy to pray?] "It is possible to offer fervent prayer even while walking in public or strolling along, or seated in your shop...while buying or selling...or even cooking."*
> — St. John Chrysostom

Connacht Area, excepted), has it ever been used for this purpose. The Drumshambo coke furnace was built in 1788 [...] John Grieve, in a valuable Report on the Arigna Iron Works, written in May 1800, states that 'the works are on an extensive scale, and well executed'. They consisted of a blast furnace 44 feet high, an excellent boring mill, a foundry, two cupolas, a complete set of 'potting-shops, patterns and warehouses', a forge with a refining hearth, air-furnaces for puddling, etc., etc., and a 'mumbling hammer of about three tons weight' (p. 135–36).

And in addition to all these—which may be called technical buildings and contrivances—there were, as Grieve testifies, 'very many good houses for the workmen and excellent houses for the managers'. (p. 137)

No doubt this array of works could compare favourably with any such works then existent in England or Scotland. We are not, therefore, surprised that, as testified by Mr. Whitworth, Drumshambo iron had gained quite a reputation before the end of the eighteenth century. The works were erected and owned by three brothers of the not un-Irish name of O'Reilly. They had learned mining engineering in France, and they had introduced into Ireland in the manufacture of the metal all the refinements in use on the Continent. Limerick then possessed shipbuilding yards, and it is on record that the first ship built there for the East India Company was fitted out and fastened with iron manufactured by O'Reilly Brothers. The iron was conveyed down the Shannon from Drumshambo. 'The pig-iron which was made at Arigna' wrote John Grieve, of Edinburgh, in his valuable Report 'was excellent for castings, and it ran into as fine goods as any pig-iron in England'. When refined it was highly prized by the old smiths (p. 137).

Meehan goes on to question what caused the breakdown of this flourishing industry. It cites the main cause as "transit facilities" in transporting coal from "an inaccessible place on the Brahlieve [Arigna] mountain, two good Irish miles away… on the backs of packed horses" (p. 137). Adding "bad management and the wildest speculation on the London Stock Exchange" to these transport costs meant, in Meehan's evaluation, that "only a miracle could keep it going" (p. 141). In fact, he suggests that it is a wonder that the Arigna Iron Company lasted as long as it did (a period of eighteen years from 1818 to 1836.

House of Commons Inquiry

Perhaps not surprisingly, the Arigna Iron and Coal Mining Company was making news in London around this time, but not for the right reasons. A select Committee was appointed by the House of Commons to "inquire into the Origin, Management, and present State" of the company (p. 3). The Committee published its report on the 3rd April, 1827, a copy of which I have seen and from which I am quoting from. The report, inter alia, gave attention to three main areas:

- To the title and also the advantages of the Arigna property, as set forth in the Prospectuses of November and December 1824.
- To a fraudulent traffic in the shares of the company's stock, alleged to have been carried on to a great extent very soon after the company was established.
- To the division of the £15,000 among certain of the persons concerned in forming the company. (p. 11)

Regarding the first of these, the report states:

> Of the title and advantages of the Arigna property, the Prospectuses issued by the promoters of the company in November and December 1824, exhibited a very attractive representation. The property was stated to abound in excellent coal, iron-ore, and other minerals; its command also of good roads and other acquired facilities were strongly set forth (p. 11).

In relation to the second issue, the fraudulent traffic in shares, the following are some brief extracts from the report:

> No list of original shareholders has ever been produced to the Committee; no such list is now in existence among the documents of the company (p. 14).

> The dazzling effect of the names of persons of station and eminence associated in the undertaking, seems to have produced results which, even at that period of epidemic speculation, could scarcely have been anticipated. The premium on the shares exceeded £20, and was at one period enhanced to £26 (p. 14).

The third subject under consideration was "the division of £15,000, part of the purchase-money paid by the company for the Arigna property, among certain persons through whose influence the company was formed" (p. 15). It seems that this £15,000 represented three-fifths of the purchase money of £25,000 paid for the mines and other property, and the question at issue concerned the propriety of hav-

> *"No one is too good to perform whatever is required of him."*
> — Father Flanagan

ing this £15,000 appropriated to certain individuals and done so in a secret manner which was unknown to the members of the company in general (p. 15–16).

As this was an inquiry and not a court case, there were no verdicts issued. Those who were accused did defend, or perhaps tried to defend, themselves before the Committee. At the very least, I would have to conclude there wasn't much evidence of professional ethics being practised. Similar behaviour today would find itself open to charges of misrepresentation, insider trading, and failure to impose arms-length principles on transactions between the company and those who managed it; the perpetrators would be liable to severe penalties!

The closure of the Arigna Iron and Coal Mining Company finally in 1838 brought to an end iron mining and smelting in Arigna. Before moving on to what P. J. Flanagan calls the modern age of coal mining in the Arigna valley, perhaps a few other titbits of interest might be noted.

The Lough Allen-Lough Gill Connection

P. J. Flanagan refers to an ambitious scheme to connect Lough Allen with Lough Gill by canal and hence to Sligo port, so that timber from American ships could find its way (presumably by barge) to Lough Allen and from there be floated down the Shannon, serving various towns on the way. However, the plan was dropped on the basis of being too expensive because of the many locks needed. However, a railway was proposed in its place and so on August 3rd 1846, the Sligo and Shannon Railway Act was passed with the company having a capital of £100,000 in shares and £26,000 in loans. However, that was as far as the scheme proceeded and in 1849 the company was placed before the Master in Chancery for winding-up. (p. 30–31)

Fawcett, Buchan and Spencer Harbour Collieries

Patrick Flanagan in "Some Notes on Leitrim Industry" notes that in the 1850s James Fawcett owned "a dozen townlands in the parish of Inishmagrath, near the north-west corner of Lough Allen [...] The total area was just short of 1,000 acres" (p. 41). Included in these townlands were Seltanaskeagh (a mining region on the Arigna mountains) and Gubb and Lecarrow, the two townlands that made up the farm of some one hundred acres, on which I grew up on as a youngster, and already referred to in chapter 1. According to Patrick Flanagan, these three townlands plus others, including Gowlaun where the Creevelea Iron Works was located, were leased to a Patrick Buchan, who was involved in mining (p. 411). He gives this account:

> On his holding in Seltanaskeagh were located "workmen's houses" for the miners which he employed winning coal from his pits there [...] His lease of the Seltanaskeagh mines appears to have expired in 1872/3 whereupon Henry Fawcett & Company Limited recommenced operations as from May 1873. These were the "Spencer Harbour Collieries" which were provided by Fawcett with a "wire tramway" (aerial rope) from the pits down the mountain to the road leading to Lough Allen at Spencer Harbour in the townland of Gubb. (Flanagan, Patrick, p. 411)

All of these territories are very close to my upbringing, but my family, including older members of my extended family, were not very aware of the involvement in coalmining by the Fawcett family (our family farm was brought from a Fawcett, presumably a descendent). We were surprised to learn that there was an aerial rope way from the pit on the mountain to the road near Spencer Harbour, a distance of some three miles. Perhaps, the ropeway worked on gravity rather than being mechanically driven (which method was very unlikely to have been developed at that time). If it was a gravity flow system, presumably full buckets descending from the mountain wound up the empty buckets simultaneously. However, despite our surprise at there being an aerial rope, I must relate that the field at the outskirts of our farm along the main road was called "the tramway field," so perhaps this is confirmation of the wire tramway referred to by Patrick Flanagan.

Spencer Harbour Clay Works

Patrick Flanagan goes on to talk about the "Lough Allen Clay Works Limited" which I can only assume are the clay works at Spencer Harbour (as mentioned in chapter 1), and around whose high brick chimney we played as children. The chimney, I am glad to say, still stands erect today although it appears that the works were short-lived. Associated with the coal in the region were deposits of fire clay which gave very fine bricks and which appear to have been worked from Buchan's time onwards, if not earlier, and it was this resource which resulted in the setting up of the clay works in the mid-1870s. As it will be noted there is a considerable degree of mystery about this concern which burst on the scene about 1873 and just as dramatically disappeared less than a decade later. One rather improbable reason was advanced in 1923 by Major Lefroy, who also commented on the setting up of the works:

> One of the late chief engineers of Guinness' who left Guinness' with £40,000, went up to Lough Allen and at the extreme end started a brick and tile works. He left it there and left all his money there because the (Lough Allen) canal, even in those days, was worse than in our day. Certainly, the canal was far from perfect but if the works were as good as

> "Work as if you don't need the money. Love as if you were never hurt."

> the owner claimed in 1881 it is unlikely that they would have been abandoned six months later. Indeed, he stated that the works were only just finished and that there was "every prospect of an increasing trade.".
>
> The managing director of the 'Lough Allen Clay Company', as it was also described, was George Arthur Waller, who also worked boats of his own between Lough Allen and Limerick. (p. 411–12)

Although short-lived, the clay works appear to have been successful, with its products being distributed throughout the country, according to Patrick Flanagan's account. Again it is notable that the manager was not a local one.

> Waller maintained that the clay works had been "brought to such a success" that there was a backlog of orders and that additional capital and boats were necessary. There was "every description of clay" at Lough Allen including some fine white clay suitable for pottery which however, was not made. But virtually everything else was—fire bricks, sewerage and drainage pipes, bricks, tiles and moulded plaster-of-paris goods. The manager was "a first-rate Staffordshire man" who despatched boatloads of sewerage pipes for such places as Woodford, Killaloe, Galway and Roscommon, and "high-class fire bricks" to Dublin for such customers as the Alliance Gas Company, Guinness' Brewery and Roe's Distillery. (Flanagan, Patrick, p. 413)

So the clay works at Spencer Harbour on the shores of beautiful Lough Allen is yet another story of highs and lows following in relatively quick succession. What a pity!

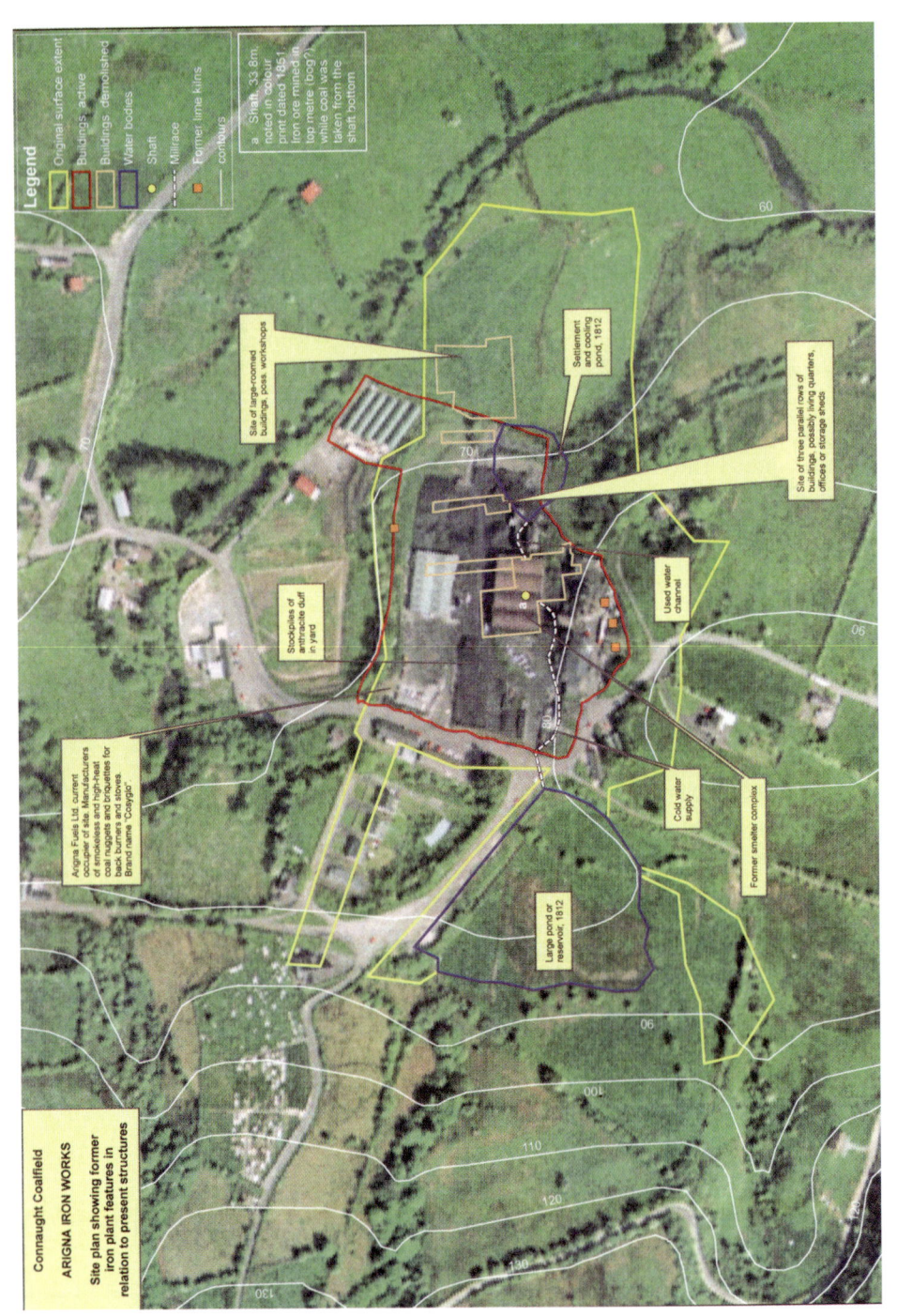

Ordnance Survey Map showing location of Arigna Iron Works, which is basically the present site of the Arigna Fuels briquette plant. Note the date 1812 on the map. (Courtesy: Ordnance Survey Ireland Permit No. 8427 / Ordinance Survey Ireland and Government of Ireland)

130   THE ARIGNA INDUSTRIAL REVOLUTION FROM 1600S TO   THE PRESENT

Modern Age of Coal Mining in Arigna

P. J. Flanagan notes that the modern age of mining began in the Arigna Valley in 1888. After the earlier fiascos, this was a much more organised phase:

> From that year, mining has been carried on almost without interruption and in this time too, most of the railway development has taken place. What especially marked out 1888 was the incorporation of the Arigna Mining Company, formed by some directors of the newly opened Cavan, Leitrim & Roscommon Light Railway, for the purpose of supplying the railway with cheap coal. The Chairman of both concerns was the Earl of Kingston who, as descendant of Col. Tenison, owned the extensive coal royalties on both sides of the river. The formation of the company was a very credible move, but was to be the cause of local feeling running very high against the directors. The charge was that they were interested only in the mining company, which was a private concern; the more productive it was, the greater their financial return. The railway, on the other hand, had its dividends guaranteed by the ratepayers, and so far as the shareholders were concerned, it did not matter how badly the line was run—they got their money anyway. In fact, this allegation was untrue, but the question is too involved to deal with here. (p. 32)
>
> At about the same time, the Layden family began mining in the Valley. They have been responsible for much of the development of the area, and their name is synonymous with coal-production in Arigna. Whereas they did well from the beginning, the Mining Company had a much more difficult time. There was trouble from the start, and after a short time the entire mine at Aughabehy was offered to a creditor in satisfaction of a debt of £83! The offer was refused, foolishly as it turned out; before very long the company's fortunes rose, and for years they paid a 5% dividend. In addition they paid two bonuses, of 50% each of the original capital (about £3,000). (p. 32)

In "Some Notes on Leitrim Industry," Flanagan notes that the mine which had been established to extract the three foot seam of coal found on Mr. Jones' land in 1765 had been abandoned before 1800 (p. 421). It was many years later before further mining commenced:

> A trial pit for coal was made in Tullycorka by Michael McTiernan in 1873 but was abandoned in that year. Michael Layden mined from 1884 onwards in Tullymurray (also called Tullymorrow) and he also worked the Knockatean coal from the late 1870s onwards. This last townland was one of the more important coal mining locations in Leitrim. Trials

for coal were made by Patrick Walsh in 1873; Patrick Rynn worked the coal 1876-8 and Michael Layden from about 1879 on. Michael Keaveny worked it there in 1881-2, by which time there were at least eight pits. Seltanaskeagh, another important place, has been discussed earlier. (p. 421)

Knockatean differed from most other places in the Arigna region in that much of the mining was by shafts instead of the more usual adits (p. 421)

The understanding of the Layden family today, is that Michael Layden commenced his coal mining in Arigna in the 1870s and thus this concurs with the above references. The Knockateean (spelled with an extra 'e' in keeping with the spelling in Michael Layden's Will) area would have been mined in several places, including the so-called Engine Pit, which Michael Layden definitely worked. Generally, most other pits in the Arigna area, outside Knockateean, had horizontal entrances or adits into the face of the mountain, rather than vertical shafts, as already indicated by Flanagan. It is our view also, that Michael Layden worked the Lugmore pit at a very early stage in his mining career—in fact it could well have been his first pit to work. The Lugmore pit was located some two miles north of the engine pit and is part of the Seltanaskeagh region, previously referred to above where, according to Flanagan, Fawcett & Company Limited and Spencer Harbour Collieries mined. The mine at Tullymurray worked by Michael Layden, as referred to above by Flanagan, was the original "Spionkop" mine, called after a battle in the Boer war.

P. J. Flanagan notes that "elsewhere in the Valley in the early 1900s mining was in progress in several places. In almost every case there was a tramway system of fairly standard type" (p. 32). The tramway system referred to, consisted of a set of rails laid at some two feet apart from the shaft entrance to the coal face. In some of the bigger pits there were double tramways. The rolling stock consisted of hutches on to which the coal was shovelled at the coal face and the hutches were normally drawn out with a steel winding rope, turned by diesel or electric power.

During the early 1900s, there were, as related by Flanagan, many efforts made and schemes put forward to extend the Cavan and Leitrim Railway (C&LR) from its terminus at Mount Allen to Arigna village, a distance of less than two miles, and further up the valley to the Aughabehy pit. There were various setbacks but the Great War changed the situation and renewed efforts resulted in the Board of Works' approval, so that construction of the line was commenced in 1918 and finished and passed by the inspectors on February 17, 1920. The line from Mount Allen to Arigna village served the area well for the transport of coal for some thirty-five years, while the extension to Aughabehy was only used for some eleven years to 1931, as the Earl of Kingston's Arigna Mining Company had gone out of business and the Aughabehy mine closed (p. 33–34). Regarding the Arigna Mining

> "Consider the tortoise. He only makes progress when he sticks his neck out."

Company ceasing business and the closure of the extension railway to Aughabehy, Flanagan cites two reasons:

> The first oddly enough, was the formation of the Great Southern Railways in 1925, absorbing most Irish railways, including the C. & L. This meant the end of the mutually profitable contract between the Mining Co. and the C. & L., as the G.S.R.—on paper at any rate—found it more convenient to import Welsh coal in bulk for all its lines. The other factor was a long and tedious dispute with the Laydens. Legal action, over what might be called "territorial rights," was taken by the Mining Co. in 1924, finishing in the Supreme Court in Dec., 1929. The final judgment was against the Mining Co., and they decided to go into voluntary liquidation and turn over all their mining royalties to the Laydens in lieu of costs etc. (p. 34–35)

> Accordingly, the Laydens moved into Aughabehy colliery, and before long had taken out the remaining coal; thus in 1931, after nearly 150 years, Aughabehy was worked for the last time. (p. 35)

Carting coal by horse and cart from the pits was always a difficult task in Arigna, so in the early 1930s the Laydens erected an aerial ropeway from the Arigna railway station to three pits in which they were then mining. These were Derreenavoggy, some eight hundred yards away overlooking the station, and where mining was commenced by them in 1924; Rover, some one and a half miles north of the station and where mining was commenced by them in 1916; and Rockhill, some two miles beyond and south of Derreenavoggy in the Kilronan direction, where mining was commenced by them in 1930. Buckets capable of taking about half a ton of coal travelled on this ropeway using electric power produced by a diesel generator. This was before the rural electrification era but, when that era arrived, the ropeway was duly driven by electricity from the Electricity Supply Board. The ropeway from the Rover pit connected to Derreenavoggy and so did the ropeway from Rockhill. Thus the output from the three pits used the common ropeway from Derreenavoggy to the Arigna station. At the station, the full buckets were tipped into the awaiting train wagons, and from there it was possible for the wagons to join up with the national rail system. The building and operation of the aerial ropeway was quite a technical feat in those days. The ropeway served the mines very well for over forty years into the 1970s. However, the ropeway from Rover to Derreenavoggy, a length of less than a mile, became redundant in the late 1930s when the pit became fully worked out (Rover was the oldest pit in the

Arigna valley). By the 1970s, mining was also taking place at some other pits and transport by lorry was then possible.

The Iron Man

The next big technical development in Arigna mining was the introduction of mechanical coal cutters at the coal face in the early 1940s. The affectionate name for this coal cutter was "the iron man." These cutters helped to reduce the drudgery of mining coal with hand picks and (later) air picks, and they greatly assisted in increasing the output of coal. Mining in Arigna got a particular boost during the war years, because of scarcity of alternative fuel supplies. Particularly, our national railways were keen to secure supplies of Arigna coal to fire their steam engine trains. Other important national customers at that time were the Irish Sugar Company, the Electricity Supply Board and Cement Ltd.

New Era

In the aftermath of the war in the late 40s and early 50s, market prospects for Arigna coal were beginning to dim because of new sources of energy and new technologies, such as the replacement of the steam engine by electric power. The implications for the local economy of Arigna and for employment arising from a significant reduction in mining activities could have been very serious, because there was virtually no other industrial employment available in the area. Fortunately, the Government of the day decided that the Electricity Supply Board (ESB) should build, close to Arigna, a fifteen-megawatt electricity generating station which would be powered with Arigna coal. This generating station, which was expected to have a thirty-year useful life, commenced operations in 1958 and closed in 1992. It ceased to take supplies of coal from 1990 onwards and used up its stock piles of coal until it closed. The station purchased in the order of 45,000 to 50,000 tons of coal and slack annually from the various Arigna mines, including some from the Bencroy mine in Slieve-an-Ierin. This annual tonnage would have reduced somewhat in the latter years. This consumption of coal guaranteed the viability of the mines during this period. In addition to sales of coal to the ESB during this period, there would have been some 10,000 to 20,000 tons of coal or slack sold to other customers (this was somewhat less in the 1980s as reserves of good coal began to run low).

Thus by 1990, virtually all the good quality coal in Arigna had been mined, but there were vast reserves of a lower grade coal, called crow coal, both in the Arigna mountains and in Slieve-an-Ierin mountains, if only a use could be found for it. Thus in the 1980s, there was a great expectation in the Arigna area that the ESB would build a new power station capable of burning this lower grade crow coal. A great deal of research and development was being done by a number of parties, including the ESB, to devise an appropriate process to burn the crow coal. A fluidised bed system was accepted as suitable. This system was based on burning coal on a suspended bed of air to give good combustion conditions, based on the three 'Ts': time (particles exposed to high temperatures); temperature; and turbulence (mixing of particles in the air). Ambitious plans, based on new mining approaches, were being envisaged by the local coal miners to mine large quantities of the crow coal for the this new 45 megawatt power station. Alas, however, the Government and the ESB decided not to go ahead with the new station. As might be expected, this decision came as a shock to the local community. Thus with the reserves of good quality coal exhausted, the long era of mining in Arigna came to an end in 1990.

Some Reflections

Coal mining was certainly not easy work and there was always personal danger attached to it. Thankfully over the very many years of mining in Arigna, there were very few serious accidents or deaths. Miners were on the whole very careful once they entered the mine, because they knew the dangers involved, such as falling rock, or whatever. The widespread practice of saying a prayer at a statue of Our Lady or a picture of the Sacred Heart at the entrance to the mine helps to put the potential danger into context. Great credit is due to the Arigna miners for their courage, their work ethic, their loyalty to the job, and last but definitely not least the dexterity they demonstrated in hewing coal in difficult conditions and from thin coal seams, which English and Scottish miners would probably totally disregard as worthwhile. Perhaps the reader might allow me indulge in a little nostalgia in turning to that lovely poem by local poet Johnny Gallagher.

The Miner of Nineteen-Thirty-Two
by Johnny Gallagher

(This is a story of a man who went into the pit when he was 13 years of age
and spent all his lifetime in Derreenavoggy Pit)

On a pleasure trip to Derreenavoggy Pit, an old miner there I found
I asked him walk with me and talk, of his years spent underground.
"Ah" he says "the pit—tis time I quit, my age I won't tell you,
But to tell you the truth, I was a hardy youth Back in Nineteen-Thirty-Two."

"Year in year out, my daily rout was to Derreenavoggy Pit.
I proudly strode the long straight road, as my little lamp I lit.
With a pick and a wedge and a four pound sledge, to do the job I do.
Four bob a day, it was my pay, Back in Nineteen –Thirty –Two."

"When I'd reach the gob, I'd start my job, my kit bag I'd leave down.
I'd have to chance and turn a branch and put in a leg and crown.
Lying on my side, I'd cut it wide, while the water t' would soak through.
Conditions then tested men, Back in Nineteen-Thirty-Two."

"I'd be at my ease, down on my knees, shovelling coal and slate.
I got many a shock from the bottom rock, as I used my number eight.
A hole I'd drill and stem and fill, all jobs I used to do.
Roads I'd brush and hutches push, Back in Nineteen-Thirty-Two."

"Then near the slope, the haulage rope, we always kept in action.
Seeing buckets slide down the mountainside was Arigna's main attraction.
Our transport all was very small—and lorries very few.
You'd never see a JCB, Back in Nineteen-Thirty-Two."

"Oh Arigna gay, it's many a day since first I saw your light.
Though I'd some hard times down in your mines, still I loved you day and night.
From the grand Cross Alts to Bothans Cross, the Bothin, the Horseshoe,
To me remain the very same as they did, Back in Thirty-Two."

"Our great chance to see, in Nineteen-Sixty-Three, we got our own lounge Bar.
We can have our wine in our leisure time and we haven't to travel far.
'Tis in that joint I enjoy a pint when my working day is through.
Sure 'twas a shame we hadn't the same, Back in Nineteen-Thirty-Two."

"On the Sabbath day in me own old aul way, I praise Gods Holy Will,
Before the Shrine that'll last all time, at our church here on Chapel Hill.
And at the graveyard there, I say a fervent prayer, for the great men that I knew,
That kept their place near the face with me, Back in Thirty-Two."

Myself and him, we then went in, to Arigna's Grand Saloon.
Where we joined the throng, in dance and song and the Minstrals played the tune.
He joined the fun and he drank beer and rum and he sang the Foggy Dew.
And proud I am to have met that man, That Miner of Thirty-Two.

Thanks to Johnny Gallagher and the men who inspired his poem. The accompanying map shows the locations in Arigna and surrounding areas in which significant coal mining took place in the past couple hundred of years. It also indicates

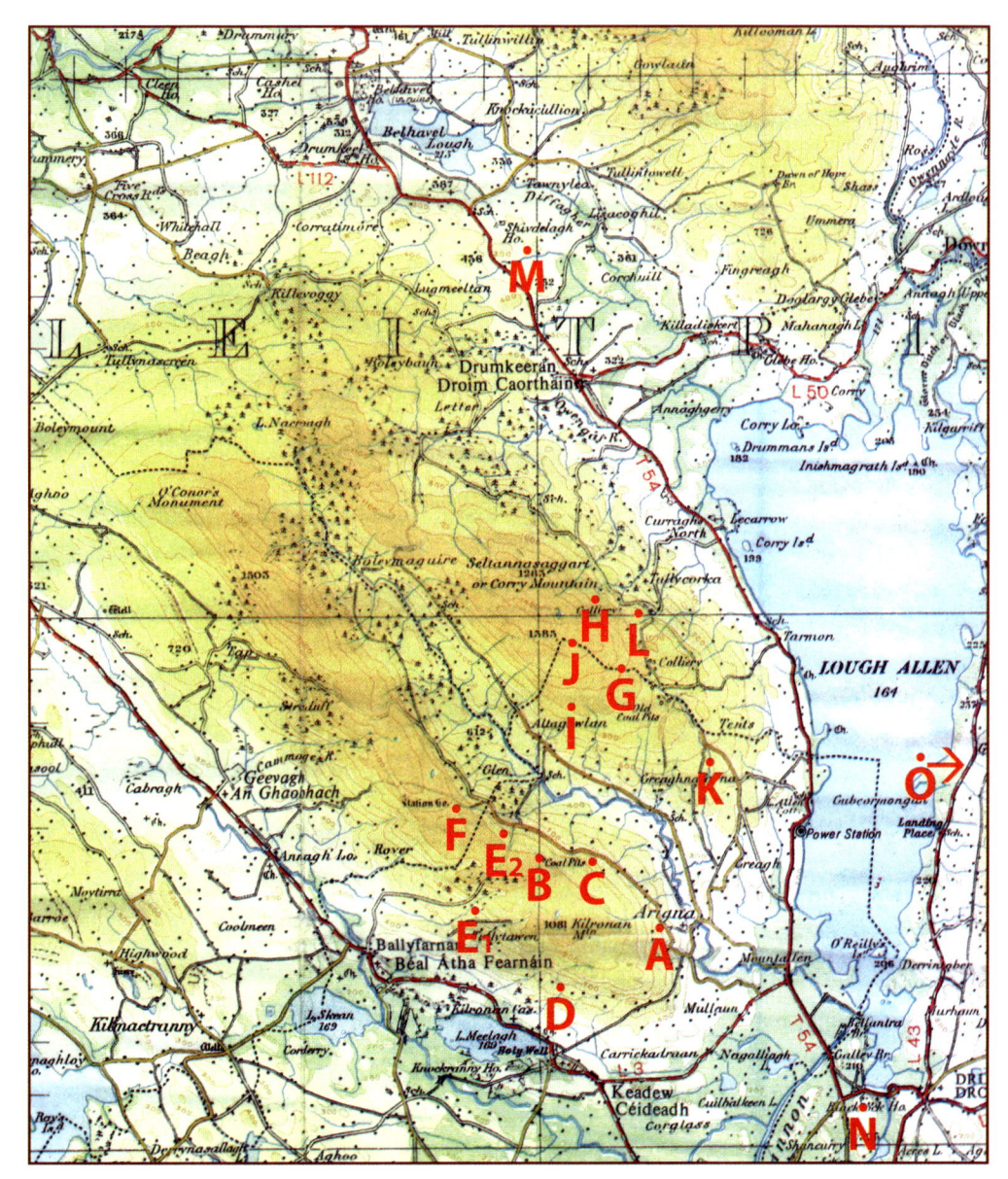

LEGEND. A – Derreenavoggy pit (overlooking Arigna village, the site of the earlier iron works), worked by the Laydens from 1924 onwards; **B** – Aughabehy pit, worked by the Earl of Kingston's Arigna Mining Company, and by others before that. Closed 1931; **C** – Rover mines worked by Laydens from 1916 onwards, and also by various other operators; **D** – Rockhill pit where mining was commenced by the Laydens in 1930; **E1 and E2** (same coal seam) – Mine worked by Flynn and Lehany in latter decades, and before that by Broderick and Ryan, and earlier by Lynn and others; **F** – Denis Flynn's present quarrying and production of decorative stone; **G** – Engine pit (vertical shaft worked by steam engine) in Knockateean. Possibly the first pit worked by Michael Layden in the 1870s; **H** – Lugmore pit. This pit was also worked by Michael Layden in the 1870s or thereabouts. It is possible that other locals worked there also; **I** – Greatnalough - this is the site of Lynch's pit and later known as Spion Kop; **J** – Tullymurray pit – this was the originals Spion Kop. Worked by Michael Layden in the 1880s and by others; **K** – Seltinaveeny pit – originally worked by the Dohertys; **L** – Seltanaskeagh pit – originally worked by the Fawcett family; **M** – Site of Creevalea Iron Works; **N** – Furnace Hill, Drumshanbo, location of early iron works; **O** – Bencroy coal mine in Slieve-an-Ierin, worked by Paddy Wynne and earlier by Tom Cull.

the locations of the various iron and other works which were undertaken since the 1600s.

Quite a few local families and individuals have been involved in coal mining in Arigna, although some were involved in a relatively small way. All those that I am aware of are listed hereunder in alphabetical order:

> Bruens, Broderick & Ryan, Christies, Daly, Doherty, Flynn and Lehany, Greene, Grogans, Laydens, Lynchs, Lynns, McDermott Roe, McTiernan, Noones.

I might add that in several places throughout the Arigna coal mining areas, individual land owners would often hew out a little coal for their own use, usually where it outcropped at the end of a slope, but sometimes they would have dug holes to find it.

To complete the picture of personnel involved in coal mining in the general locality, I would add the name of Tom Cull who mined in the moderate size Bencroy colliery at Gubnaveagh on the Slieve-an-Eirin mountain in the 1920s, and which was later taken over by Paddy Wynne who worked the mine until it closed in 1990. I would like to finish this chapter by alluding to a conversation I had with Owen McManus of Arigna and to the making and use of culm balls in Arigna.

Interview with Owen McManus and Some Background on Michael Layden

I met Owen McManus in his house in Arigna, not far away from the old Aughabehy mine, on 1st May, 2007. At the age of 90 when I met him, Owen was born in 1916 and is one of the oldest inhabitants of the Arigna valley. It was a pleasure to hear him muse over his many years of life. His memory was impeccable and I might add that he certainly didn't look his age. The well known J. P. McManus is his nephew.

Owen worked in various mines in the area for thirty-eight years and at the coal face. He ran a small farm and took time off mining to work the farm. This was a typical practice for a lot of the miners in Arigna. There was a mutual understanding between the mine owners and the miners in this regard. Owen said the miners were paid fortnightly and that a typical wage for the two weeks was £3—"you'd think you were a millionaire", Owen said. He started work in the mines in 1935. He said the "work was tough but the day was short when you got in on it," and he indicated that the miners were happy with their lot and that there was good craic.

One reason that I wanted to interview a very senior member of the Arigna valley, such as Owen McManus, was to collect some information on my grandfather, Michael Layden, who started coal mining in the 1870s. Unfortunately, Owen was not able to help me in this regard as he was born in the same year as my grandfather

> *"It is said that there is none so blind as those who say they can see."*

died (1916). However, Owen knew my grandfather's six sons who became mining proprietors on their father's death. They are listed in chapter 1 and included my Uncle Michael, better known as Mick, who became the general manager and worked very hard, and my father, Patrick, who attended to administrative matters, in addition to his teaching job. My other four uncles were also all involved in the mines and Owen knew all of these six Layden brothers, as he did the next generation of Laydens (my cousins and brothers) who continued the mining tradition from the late 1940s and early 1950s. A comment that Owen made about my father was that "he was a great man to have a few good cattle at the fair."

Seeing that Owen wasn't able to fill me in on my grandfather Michael Layden, I will take the opportunity to summarise what I have been able to find out through our family and extended family members. Michael Layden was born in 1853, one of a family of seven and reared on a small farm in Arigna. He emigrated at a relatively young age to Scotland where we understand he worked in the coal mines there and it is likely that he returned in his early 20s to start mining in Arigna, no doubt armed with mining skills. Incidentally, some eighty years later his grandson Miceal would likewise go to Scotland to gain mining experience, except that grandson Miceal had a professional engineering qualification behind him. It appears that Michael established a very successful coal mining operation in Arigna, while being the bread winner for a very large family of twelve. They lived in a two storey house which was known as the Colliery House. Whether this was the house of his father or not, we don't know for sure. He died in 1916 at the age of 63. His last Will and Testament is attached as an appendix and it makes for interesting reading. I suggest there is a nice human touch to be detected in his will. I conclude that he was a very solid citizen and a man of great dexterity and probably of ingenuity.

Returning to my meeting with Owen McManus, having finished our serious discussions, Owen recited the Story of Knock shrine and sang the last verse. He then told me that he remembered well the year (1940) when St. Patrick's Day (17th March) and Palm Sunday (Sunday before Easter Sunday) fell on the same day. He assured me that it would be 2040 before that would happen again. So you young people take note! I remember clearly my father telling us in school as to what determines the date of Easter Sunday—it is the first Sunday after the first full moon after the spring equinox.

Owen had another bit of surprising information for me—it was that both May Day (1st May) and Christmas Day (25th December) always fall on the same day of the week in any particular year. Thus in 2006 both these days fell on a Monday, while in 2007 both are scheduled to fall on Tuesdays, and so on. His last puzzle for me was "The piper, his wife, a fiddler and his mother all slept in three beds but no two slept together. How was this so?" I shall leave the reader to puzzle over this.

Culm Balls

In talking about culm balls, we are not referring to ammunition for combat purposes, but rather about home produced fuel. Culm balls were much used in Arigna and surrounding areas as fire fuel in the first half of the last century, and possibly up to the late 1960s. They may well have been produced in the 1800s as well. They were also produced for local use in other parts of the country, particularly in the Castlecomer region of Kilkenny and the Ballingarry region of Tipperary, as evidenced by Michael J. Conry's beautiful book Dancing the Culm, which also has a fine chapter on the use of culm as a domestic fuel in the Arigna area. It will be noted that both Castlecomer and Ballingarry had coal mining activities in their respective regions. Personally, I have a clear recollection of our family using culm balls and I am also pretty certain that I participated in their making. This poem gives a sense both of the culm and of the social life of the times:

> Arigna coal and culm, we always kept in store
> We brought it down from Leyden's[21] pit, a place that's called Lugmore,
> We mixed the daub and culm, t'would burn the whole night long,
> The neighbours came in rambling, you'd be sure to hear a song
> John Gallagher (quoted in Conry, p. 204)

My recollection of making culm balls accords with this poem; we mixed coal slack (culm) with daub dug from the ground (of which there was no shortage in Leitrim) and we added water and, after a good mixing, we made balls of it with our hands about the size of a large orange. The daub was used as a binder. They gave out tremendous heat and lasted for hours and hours. However, according to Conry, washing soda was often added to help in the binding process, which he indicated also improved the burning quality of the culm. He also indicated that in some instances cow dung was added and perhaps peat mould as well. Anyway, whatever the mixture consisted of, it was, according to Conry trampled on by foot and well mixed before balls were made by hand (p. 228–29). He also said that blue daub was better than yellow daub "because it was more clayey [...] and secondly because the yellow daub was inclined to contain more stones, which in the words of a Cloone observer 'could smash the mugs and plates on the dresser'" (p. 227).

---

21. Although this appears to refer to the Layden mining operations, Leyden is a variant of the surname which is widespread throughout county Leitrim.

CHAPTER TWELVE
Arigna Today

While farming and other normal activities continue today in Arigna, together with some small enterprises, the four main activities taking place there are:

- A mining museum, The Arigna Mining Experience
- A smokeless fuel briquette plant
- Wind mill operations
- Quarrying and decorative stone production

The Arigna Mining Experience

When coal mining ceased in Arigna in 1990, the resilient people of Arigna did not sit back and quickly established a task force to consider what alternative activities and employment opportunities might be organised in the area. Various different bodies were set up, some of which were linked with national schemes while others were specific to the area. The Arigna Community Development Company (ACDC) was established and, among other activities, organised a number of FÁS training courses. Through the efforts of ACDC, the Arigna Leader Company (forming part of the national Leader body)[22] was established as a lending and support agency for potential new enterprises in the Arigna area. In addition, the Arigna Enterprise Fund was established to provide funding for new enterprises to replace the jobs lost due to closure of the mines and the power station. The funding included repayable loan assistance from the ESB. The Arigna Enterprise Centre was also established to provide a location for new business start-ups, effectively acting as a business incubation centre.

Various members of the local community, including ex-miners and some of the mine owners, were actively involved in the above organisations. Mary Robinson,

---

22. The Leader programme is an EU-funded programme to support rural development. It has operated under various phases: Leader I (until 1994), Leader II (1994-1999), and Leader+ (2000-2006).

then President of Ireland, was invited to Arigna in 1991 and the focal point of her visit was a very impressive exhibition in the Arigna community hall of artefacts, mementos and photographs relating to mining in the area, going back for several hundreds of years. President Robinson came again to Arigna on August 5th, 1992 to officially open the Arigna Enterprise Centre.

The 1991 exhibition attended by President Robinson was the springboard that led to the eventual establishment and opening in April 2003 of the Arigna mining museum, the Arigna Mining Experience. However, a lot of hard work was undertaken before this opening became a reality, including the preparation of a feasibility study and business plan and the procurement of approval from the Department of the Marine and Natural Resources for partial funding for the project. At the same time, funding from private sources, from both home and abroad, as well as from Leader and from the Arigna Enterprise Fund was also secured. An old mine overlooking Arigna village was acquired for a consideration of one euro. Actual physical work on the site and underground, including roadways and new buildings started in 2001 and finished in time for the official opening on the April 23rd, 2003 in the presence of a large gathering of local people and invited guests. The whole exercise was truly a great example of community effort in action.

The museum building, which is meant to replicate the shape of the slack heap (which was known as a "bing" of slack or culm) just above it at Derreenavoggy pit, houses various artefacts relating to mining, including iron mining, together with an impressive array of photographs and also samples of the coal that was mined in the past. There is also a coffee shop and a souvenir shop, as well as a screening space where visitors can watch a film explaining the mining history of the area and the specific underground mining operations.[23] The views from the museum of Arigna and of Lough Allen out in front and below are wonderful. However, the real treat is the conducted tour on foot by ex-miners of the underground mine which takes some forty minutes. Here the visitor can see mining as it took place in Arigna closely replicated and will almost certainly be amazed and taken aback at the tough working conditions the miners endured. The miners hewed coal from narrow seams beneath huge strata of rock, which were supported with wooden pillars to avoid rock falls when the coal was being taken out from beneath. The visitor who watches the film and does the tour can really get an insight into what coal mining was like in Arigna and the different job tasks involved. A very brief overview of the main mining tasks is given on the following page.

---

23. Further information on the museum can be found on their website (www.arignaminingexperience.ie) or by contacting them at 071-9646466.

Main Mining Tasks

The standard practice on entering the mine was to say a prayer at the Sacred Heart picture or at Our Lady's statue as one passed by same, because the dangerous nature of the work was always present in one's mind. The main mining tasks or job categories involved were:

- *Cutter:* The cutter cut the coal out from beneath the rock with a hand pick up to the 1940s. The hand pick was replaced then with mechanical coal cutters, locally referred to as the iron man. However there would still be some need for the hand pick. Further help came later with the introduction of pneumatic air picks, particularly in dealing with rock boring and removal. The cutter also shovelled the coal out to the drawer, doing so after he had six to eight cwts[24] of coal cut, enough to fill a hutch.
- *Shoveler:* The shoveler was a new position that arose when the mechanical coal cutters came on the scene. He shovelled the coal cut by these mechanical coal cutters out to the drawers.
- *Drawer:* The drawer filled the hutches with the coal and despatched them to the pit head on the tramway, usually operated mechanically.
- *Brusher:* The brusher, with the use of explosives, blasted the rock in order to prepare for the extension of the coal face for the next day's working, usually advancing one yard a day. It involved the use of pneumatic drills (when they became available in the 1960s), or sledges and hand tools in the earlier years, to bore holes in the rock in which were inserted gelignite. When all the explosives were inserted tight in the various borings and the fuses connected (stemming this was called), the immediate area was vacated by the miners and the brusher lit the fuses which sent off the explosives, thus blasting the rock. Then the debris had to be removed, i.e. brushed.

The visitor can only marvel at the great men that the Arigna miners were, working in such cramped and very often wet conditions with the impending danger of a rock fall, or occasionally foul air or gases, or inadequate air. The old carbide lamp, with its naked flame, worn on the miner's helmet was always an early detector of bad or insufficient air. I certainly remember these being used in my childhood and I understand their use continued up to the late 1970s.[25] Carbide itself (or calcium carbide to use its correct name) produces, when water is added, what is scientifi-

---

24. A cwt is an imperial weight abbreviation for a hundredweight (which was actually 112 pounds in weight or about fifty-one kilograms).
25. For a description of the carbide lamp and its operation, see www.sip.ie/sip019B/carbide/carbide.htm.

cally known as an exothermic reaction, i.e. it produces heat—and of course light, which was what the miners needed. As schoolchildren (but away from school in our own possibly misspent time), I can recall that we conducted what one might call extra-curricular scientific experiments with the carbide that was so easily available to us. One would take a can that had a lid on it and make a small hole in the can's base. Then one would place a piece of carbide inside the can, wet it by spitting on it and then replace the lid of the can tightly. A lighted match would then be pushed into the hole in the base of the can, resulting in a mini-explosion which would cause the lid to fly off. We found this to be great entertainment. Thankfully, I don't think we ever came to any serious harm through such (presumably) forbidden scientific endeavours. I do recall on one occasion that I singed my eyebrows due to the flame coming back out the hole instead of blowing the lid off. Perhaps I had the lid on too tight; in any case I'm sure that I learned something from the incident!

Staff at Museum

There are thirteen people currently employed at the museum. Five of them are included in my photograph below together with the museum's Chairman, Seamus Rynn. From left to right, they are Seamus Rynn, Valerie Stenson, Bernie Coggins, Maurice Cullen, Michael Flynn and Seamus Lehany. Other staff who are missing from the photograph are Peter McNiff, Michael Joe McLoughlin, Leo Wynne, Margaret Gaffney, Grainne Cullen, Veronique Barry, Mia McCrann and Orla Guighan.

Aerial rope from Derreenavoggy to siding at Arigna coalworks /railway station.

A closer view of the aerial rope. A full bucket is descending towards the siding, while an empty bucket is on its way back to Derreenavoggy. Note the train wagons in the picture. (These pictures relate to early 1950s)

Carting coal / slack with horse and cart from an Arigna coal mine in 1933. (Courtesy: Father F. M. Browne, SJ, Collection / Irish Picture Library)

The shaft of the Arigna coal mine on the Roscommon/Leitrim border, 1889. (Courtesy: Leland Lewis Duncan Collection/Irish Picture Library)

Empty coal hutches on way into the mine and filled coal hutches on the way out. (Date late 1940s).

Miner with pneumatic drill at the coal face shortly before the mines closed in 1990. (Courtesy Derek Speirs)

Shovelling coal at coal face on to hutch, 1990. (Courtesy Derek Speirs)

Drawing out a full hutch of coal, 1990. (Courtesy Derek Speirs)

Miners emerging into daylight again after their day's work, 1990. (Courtesy Derek Speirs)

The late Michael Rynn after his day's work in the mine, 1990. (Courtesy Derek Speirs)

Eugene McPartland epitomises the 'man' the miner was, 1990. (Courtesy Derek Speirs)

J.P. McManus with his uncle Owen McManus at the opening of the Arigna Mining Museum in April 2003.

Where does coal come from?

I would like to conclude this section by giving a brief explanation of what coal is and how it is formed. The Oxford Dictionary tells us that coal is "a hard black or blackish rock, mainly carbonised plant matter, found in underground seams and used as a fuel." A more in-depth explanation helps us understand the long and complex process involved in the carbonisation of plant matter:

> Coal is a fossil fuel created from the remains of plants that lived and died about 100 to 400 million years ago when parts of the earth were covered with huge swampy forests. Coal is classified as a non renewable energy source because it takes millions of years to form. [...] Millions of years ago, dead plant matter fell into the swampy water and over the years, a thick layer of dead plants lay decaying at the bottom of the swamps. Over time, the surface and climate of the earth changed, and more water and dirt washed in, halting the decay process. The weight of the top layers of water and dirt packed down the lower layers of plant matter. Under heat and pressure, this plant matter underwent chemical and physical changes, pushing out oxygen and leaving rich hydrocarbon deposits. What once had been plants gradually turned into coal.[26]

Thus when we burn coal, we are actually releasing energy that has been stored in plants. The energy that the plants originally obtained from sunlight and stored in plant form is finally, when coal is burned, converted back into energy in the form of heat.

Smokeless Fuel Briquettes

In the early 1980s the Laydens, and particularly my first cousin Brendan Layden Snr., started to carry out research into the production of smokeless and low-smoke fuel briquettes in Arigna, using as a basic raw material both Arigna coal slack and that obtained from elsewhere, particularly from Northern Ireland. While there was not a great deal of public discussion in the 1980s about the use of environmental friendly fuels, nevertheless the signs were there that changes in attitudes about the use of smokey fuels would be forthcoming.

A company called Arigna Fuels Limited was established in 1984 in order to pursue the briquette venture. After considerable research, including enlisting help from sources outside Ireland and visiting briquette plants abroad, a modern computerised briquetting plant was chosen and subsequently installed at Arigna.

---

26. This explanation was obtained from www.need.org/needpdf/infobook_activities/SecInfo/CoalS.pdf.

Commercial production and trading commenced in 1990. However, to arrive at this stage required the following technical areas to be investigated and decisions taken thereon:

- *Coal selection and preparation requirements:* There were several different coal raw materials that could be used, so it was necessary to select a combination that would produce a good briquette.
- *Binder selection and preparation:* There were a range of different binders available, such as bitumen, starch, or resins so it was necessary to choose between these and obtain suitable equipment.
- *Coal and binder mixing:* It is essential that the separate streams of coal and binder be metered to obtain the appropriate mix and quality.
- *Conditioning:* This concerns the conditioning of the coal and binder mix with steam in the pug mill (see diagram) and its subsequent cooling in the screw cooler (see diagram) to the correct temperature for the next operation (pressing).
- *Pressing:* This moulds the product into the briquette shapes required. Apart from the briquette shapes to be chosen, there were various technical factors to be considered.
- *Cooling and storage:* This was a relatively straightforward matter of moving the briquettes by conveyor belt, allowing them to cool and then storing them.
- *Bagging and Palletising:* This was a relatively minor matter, requiring only the identification of suitable plant and installing it at the most efficient location for onward distribution.

In subsequent years various alterations and additions were made to the original plant, the most important of which was the installation of a large oven in which to cook or cure the briquettes in order to render them smokeless, or low in smoke, depending on the different market requirements. The type of raw materials used in the first place will also impact on the smoke content. A diagram of the Arigna Briquette Plant is given overleaf. The oven is not included.

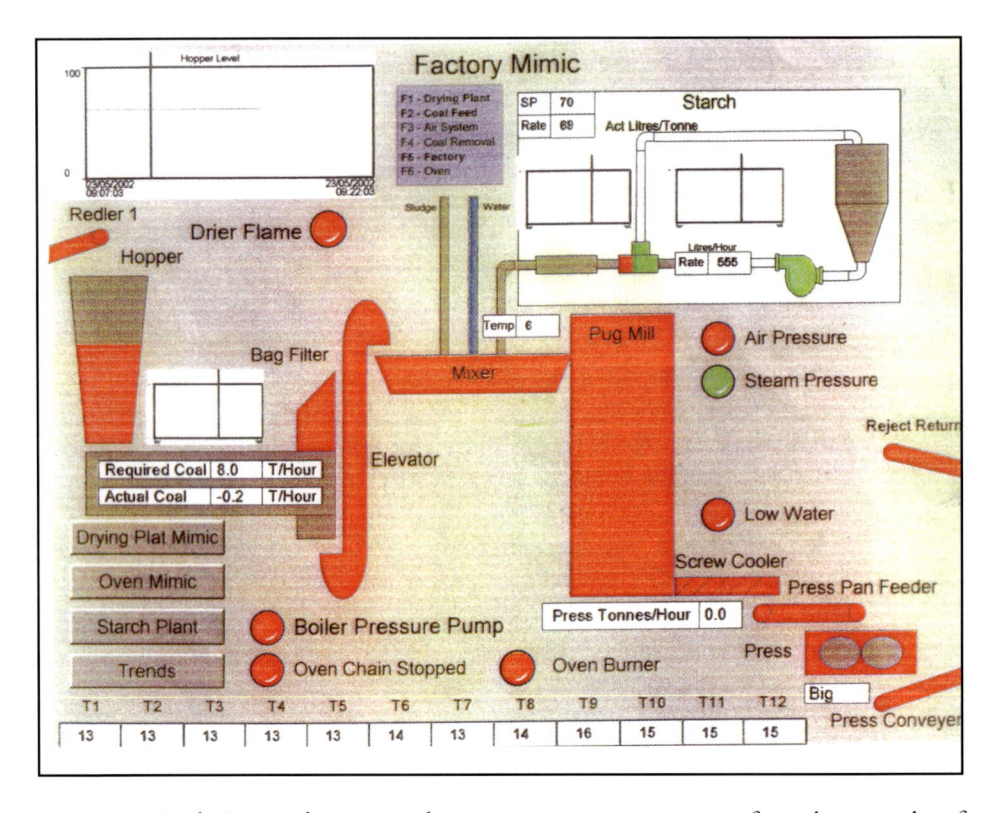

Arigna Fuels Limited now produces some 60,000 tonnes of product yearly of which some 80% is sold on the Irish market and some 20% exported to Northern Ireland, U. K. and some to mainland Europe. The following different briquette products are produced by the company:[27]

- Cosyglo. A premium environmentally friendly fuel designed for open fires. Available in smokeless and low smoke versions.
- Ecobrite. A quality smokeless fuel for cooking and other closed appliances.
- Ecobrite Extra. A premium fuel specially designed for Aga or range cookers and glass fronted appliances.
- Bord Na Móna Firepak. A convenient fire consisting of an ovoid designed to burn for 3 or 4 hours.

There are two basic shapes and sizes of briquette available. The Cosyglo briquette is shaped somewhat like a hen's egg but is about twice the size of a large egg. The other briquettes are smaller and squarer in shape. The photographs on the next page are of the product packaging used to supply the various products.

---

27. For further information, please refer to the company's web site, www.arignafuels.ie

Arigna Fuels Limited employs some fifty people and is managed by Peter Layden and his two brothers Brendan and David, all sons of Brendan Layden Snr. They represent the fourth generation of Laydens involved in Arigna enterprises. The company operates an active research and development programme in order to ensure that such an enterprise will remain viable and can keep up with technical and environmental developments. The plant is located approximately on the site of the old Arigna iron works.

Windmills

The Laydens became interested in windmills in the 1980s, particularly the late Miceal Layden. His son Michael worked in the windmill area for a time in the USA and Michael's sister Sheila also became actively involved in the windmills, particularly after her father's death in 1994. Other members of their family as well as the extended Layden families (including Brendan Layden's family) also became involved.

The establishment of windmills in Ireland has been a very difficult task up to now, largely because of the lack of active Government support for windmills and the lack of facilitation by the Electricity Supply Board (ESB) in connecting wind-generated electricity to the National Grid. However, as I write it would appear that, in the present climate of concern about global warming, both the Government and the ESB are now disposed to dealing with the problems militating against wind power generation. There can also be problems in securing planning permission for the erection of wind turbines. But perhaps general attitudes are also changing here, so that planning difficulties may lessen.

Notwithstanding the difficulties of the past in developing windmills, the Laydens succeeded in helping two outside investors to set up windmill farms in Arigna. They did this by providing these investors with two serviced sites with full planning permissions. Then in more recent years, they established two windmill farms in their own right in Arigna. All the windmill farms are thankfully working very well. All the wind farms are placed on the top of the Arigna and nearby mountains, some of them on sites under which coal was mined in the past. This development is an index of our changing world as we move from carbon-heavy energy sources to renewable ones.

Erection of turbine completed

Wind turbine under construction

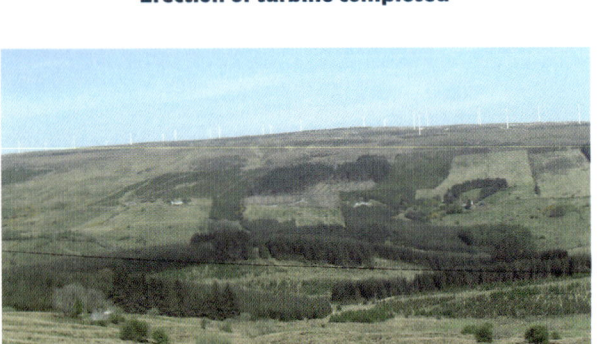

A distant view of wind farms in Arigna

Quarrying and Production of Decorative Stone

Denis Flynn took over in 1977 the running of the coalmining operation carried on by Flynn and Lehany, which group included Mick Flynn (Denis's father), Tommie Flynn and Joe Lehany. This coal mining business ceased in 1990 in common with the other coal mines in the area. Denis Flynn also set about finding an alternative business activity and, in 1993, he set up his new business of quarrying and production of decorative stone. This quarry is near the site of the old coal mine he previously worked (this old coal mine is marked on the Arigna area map on page 137). The company is called Hillstreet Quarries Ltd and trades under the name of Glenview.[28]

---

28. For further information on the company, see their website at www.glenviewworld.com.

The present day operation of the company is very significant, employing sixty-two people. The quarrying of the stone is, as would be expected, done by the opencast method and the principal operations involved are quarrying and crushing. The principal products produced are various sandstone products, chippings and associated products. The company's promotional literature show these products to be most decorative and varying in colour, sizes and contours, and, in the case of the sandstone, with a very smooth finish, as if they were polished. The accompanying photograph is of the company's products as displayed in the company's office. Unfortunately the photography does not do justice to the products. The company also produces specially graded washed sand, particularly suitable for children's play areas as well as building products, such as concrete mix, drainage chippings, builder's sand and paving sand. The sandstone and chippings have many uses, such as driveways, parking areas, paths, garden features, water features, and so on. All of the company's products are supplied throughout Ireland and some are also exported to the UK market.

Coal being mined by opencast from coal seam at base of quarry.

A view of the quarry works

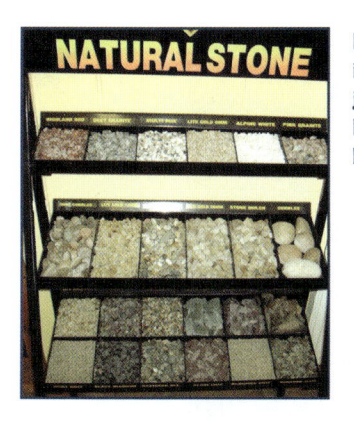

Display of decorative stone products in office (This image does not do justice to the products – the company has a very attractive range of A4 brochures)

ARIGNA TODAY

Conclusion on Arigna

So it can be truthfully said that Arigna did not lie down under the traces when coal mining ceased in 1990. It is clear that energy and mining activity is on-going in Arigna on several fronts. In addition, there are a number of individual or small business operations in place, such as rearing of goats and production of goat's cheese, organic pig production, mushroom production, and so on. Nor is coal production fully extinct in Arigna; at the base of the rock that Denis Flynn quarries lies a seam of coal which is excavated by JCB (by Sean Greene) and sold to Quinn Cement as a raw material used in cement making. Old habits do indeed die hard!

I have very much enjoyed sharing this story with you. However, it is time now to say a big thanks to all involved in the continuing story of Arigna and move on to my next section.

A view from the Mining Museum – Lough Allen in the background

A view of Arigna Fuels briquette plant

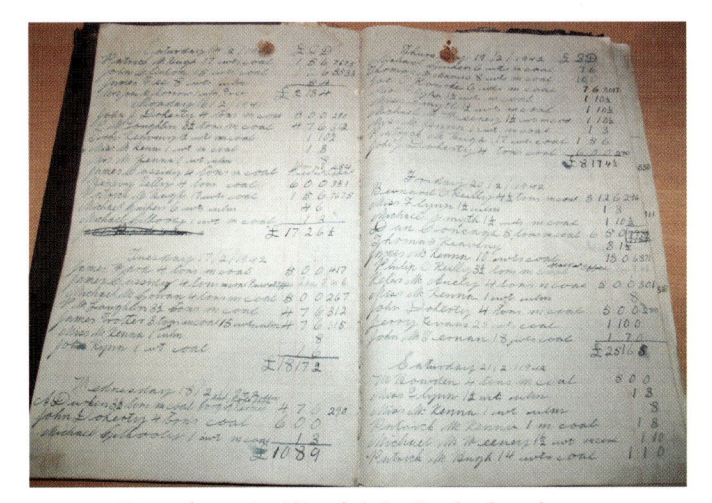

Pages from the Mines' Sales Book, dated 1942

Part 5

The World of Angling

CHAPTER THIRTEEN
Gone Fishing: A Healthy and Absorbing Hobby

Preamble

I cannot think of a healthier and more absorbing hobby than fishing, particularly when one considers the expansive world that fishing can lead one into. Fishing is not just about catching fish; there are many other angles to it, not least that of gaining an insight into the entire water element of our environment that is the home of the fish and all the factors that can impact for good or bad on that home. Thus an accomplished angler will not only be adept at catching fish, but will have a thorough understanding of the life cycle of the fish species that he or she pursues as well as a thorough knowledge of all the environmental and other factors that can affect the fish's existence and development.

These same factors can very often impact on many other aspects of our general environment. So the accomplished angler is, in my view, also an accomplished and sensitive environmentalist, a true guardian of planet earth. The state or condition of the watery world of fish is invariably a barometer for the state of our environment in general. Thus when a learned angler raises concerns about pollution or other factors adversely impacting on fisheries, his or her views should be accorded careful consideration. It is now obvious that humankind has seriously interfered with nature's processes, and we must now take remedial steps to put things right.

The angler is, in my opinion, privileged to have the opportunity of engaging with fish and their watery world. A panorama of fascinations lie in store for him or her, particularly for those who are willing to investigate a little below the surface. Perhaps the greatest fascination of all is with the life cycle of the Atlantic salmon, known as the King of Fish. Think of this King being hatched out in a gravel bed, in a tiny mountain stream in the dead of winter, and as a two or three year old juvenile migrating possibly thousands of miles out to sea to feed off the coasts of Greenland, the Faeroe islands, or wherever, and returning later as an adult salmon from the wide expanse of sea to spawn in that same gravel, in that same tiny mountain stream, thus repeating a very specific pattern through an incredible homing instinct to continue the life cycle of the species. Think also of all the obstacles, both manmade and natural, confronting the salmon on both its outward journey and its return, including the fascinating spectacle of salmon jumping over waterfalls of maybe up to eleven or twelve feet high.

Perhaps equally fascinating is the life cycle of another anadromous fish (i.e. one which lives in both fresh water and sea water), the fresh water eel which hatches out in the Sargasso Sea, and after some three or four years of juvenile life there, the young eel (called an elver) migrates up our rivers to mature as an adult eel in fresh water, and in due course it will set out to spawn in the Sargasso Sea. Thus the fresh water stage and the sea water stage of the salmon and the eel are opposite to one another.

Further regarding fascination with watery worlds, think of a river or stream in the dead of winter when nature appears to be asleep or dead; yet in the gravel and under stones one will discover a whole new world of insect life, which fish and also birds are dependent on for food while farmers and horticulturists need them for the pollination of their crops. Clearly our environment is a very complex and inter-related system, thus interference or destruction of any of the subsystems can have disastrous effects. Thus the angler who takes the trouble to understand and be sensitive to the watery world of his or her prey is a very important member of society. The genuine and committed angler truly appreciates and respects nature and is fascinated with life cycles, be they fish, insects or even plants and flowers. The cycles of the seasons, the type of weather, the direction of the winds and the temperatures are all of interest to the angler. So the complete angler is first and foremost a naturalist. Actual fishing comes afterwards. Of course, Our Lord had a very special place for fishermen. I like very much the sign which appears on a fishing hut on the river Slaney and which is reproduced by Peter O'Reilly in his beautiful book Flyfishing in Ireland: "The Gods do not deduct from man's allotted span the hours spent in fishing."

Perhaps the greatest thing about angling is its ability to totally absorb the interest and concentration of the angler while in the act of fishing—all worries and distractions just disappear. The authors Purnell, Yates and Dawn in their book *The Concise Encyclopedia of Fishing* made reference to Izaak Walton's views on fishing as follows:

> Izaak Walton (1593–1683), regarded by many as the father of fresh water fishing, once likened angling to poetry. Perhaps he was referring to its qualities of relaxation, or of inspiration, or of its ability to inspire passion and obsession. Yet in the same book, *The Compleat Angler*, he observed that angling is like mathematics, in that it can never be fully learned. Both analogies are as true today as when he penned them long ago in the seventeenth century. (p. 6)

In all, I submit that the world of angling is an expansive world.

> "We may say of angling, as Dr Botheler said of strawberries, 'Doubtless God could have made a better berry, but doubtless God never did'; and so, if I might be judge," God never did make a more calm, quiet, innocent recreation than angling.
>
> — Izaak Walton

In the remainder of this chapter, I will give an overview of game, coarse and sea angling. In a book of this nature, it is not possible to give more than a cursory treatment of game, coarse and sea angling, even if I was competent to do so. I will treat game angling in greater detail than either coarse or sea angling because I have more experience in this area. However, I have engaged in both coarse and sea angling and it was in coarse angling on the shores of Lough Allen that I first took to the waters some two-thirds of a century ago. Notwithstanding the above constraints, I hope I will have a good deal of helpful comment to make on angling types, methods, techniques and tackle to use.

Game Angling

When we talk about game angling, we are basically talking about fishing for trout and salmon. When I refer to salmon in this book, I am talking about the majestic Atlantic salmon and not other species, such as Pacific salmon, found in other parts of the world. The basic trout species in Ireland are the native brown trout and the non-native rainbow trout (which are usually artificially stocked in certain restricted waters). We also have sea trout (sometimes referred to as white trout) in most river systems which connect to the sea. Essentially, the sea trout is a brown trout that goes to sea to feed, usually feeding close to the coast line. However, it is not fully clear whether or not there are some biological differences between the brown trout and the sea trout. There are also a few other trout varieties found in some specific waters in Ireland, such as the gillaroo, sonaghan and ferox. These latter types could loosely be said to be strains of brown trout.

The habits of the sea trout and the salmon are rather similar and both species have suffered significant declines in recent decades, due possibly to the adverse environmental effects of salmon farming off our coasts, as well as various other factors.

Life Cycles of Trout (brown trout & sea trout) and Salmon

Both trout and salmon spawn in late autumn or winter, typically November to January, with December being the prime month. Spawning takes places in streams and rivers, frequently high up in the headwaters. The spawning process for both the trout and the salmon is basically the same. The female (hen) fish digs a redd, i.e. a saucer-shaped hole, in the gravel in relatively shallow flowing water at the "flow out" of a pool by turning on its side and flapping with its tail and body, thereby creating a suction that dislodges the gravel several inches downstream. During this process, the male (cock) protects the redd and the female from other fish intruders. When the redd is deep enough, say six inches or more, the male and female come alongside over the redd and the female lays some eggs (ova), and immediately the male fertilises them with a deposit of its milt (sperm). Then the female moves upstream for some inches and digs another (continuous) hole in the gravel and the gravel so dislodged covers the eggs previously laid.

The process of laying eggs and fertilisation is repeated several times until the female has laid all her eggs. The female will usually cover the last deposit of her eggs with fist size stones, if available, as well as with gravel. The whole spawning operation is thought to take up to twelve hours, or more, but water conditions can have a bearing on this. Many years ago, farmers used to capture salmon from the spawning redds and feed them to their pigs. Sometimes due to scarcity of food, they might chance eating the salmon themselves, but it was regarded as dangerous to eat and anyway the quality of the flesh would be soft and make for very poor eating. Poaching salmon off the redds is now a serious criminal offence. Brown trout and sea trout normally spawn several times during their lives, while the majority of salmon spawn only once, although some do spawn a second and very occasionally a third time.

Brown trout live their entire lives in their river or freshwater lake system. Their growth and size depends on the feeding available. In rich limestone waters, they may grow to ten pounds or more, but typically they would range from one to three pounds, together with a range of smaller fish. The rich limestone waters would, assuming there is no pollution, produce a rich array of fly and insect life for the fish to feed on and thus they grow quickly. The opposite would normally be the case in non-limestone and acid-type waters, where food availability for the fish would be low and accordingly brown trout generally remain small.

However, it is these latter types of waters that normally accommodate sea trout and salmon – perhaps in the genetic formation of these fish in the past, the poor fresh water feeding forced them to migrate to sea and feed there. Both sea trout and salmon migrate to sea after their juvenile stage in fresh water. The sea trout will normally feed near to their native river and close to the coast line, where sand eels would be their principal food. The salmon, on the other hand, may travel long distances to feed off the coasts of Greenland, the Faeroe Islands and elsewhere. Their diet at sea will be varied and includes crustaceans, sand eels and various small fish. Water temperatures apparently have a significant effect on the abundance and availability of the salmon's food.

While the sea trout will normally return to its native river every year, and sometimes twice in the one year, salmon will stay at sea for at least one full year,

A completed salmon redd. Note the fist sized stones placed in the centre of the redd. ☞

A cock salmon (note its reddish hue typical of cock salmon after several months in the fresh water) on the spawning grounds / beds. ☞

Another salmon, barely discernible, on the spawning grounds. The disturbance in the water is either a hen salmon digging / cutting a redd, or it could be a cock salmon chasing away an intruding fellow cock. (Note: It is important not to disturb salmon when spawning.) ☞

There are a pair of spawning salmon on the redd on the far side of the picture, but they are barely discernible. On the near side and to the upper left, there is a large hen salmon on her side cutting her redd—only the tail half of her is visible. ☞

On the near side of the picture a cock salmon is discernible on the redd. The hen salmon which is darker in colour is slightly above him but is not discernible. Another cock salmon was constantly intruding from behind and at one stage got far as the hen and snapped at it. Boys will be boys! ☞

GONE FISHING: A HEALTHY AND ABSORBING HOBBY

and some will stay for two, three or perhaps four years. I describe below the various stages in the life cycle of a salmon.

The Salmon's Life Cycle and Homing Instinct

Juvenile Stages

- Eyed ova: The fertilised ova in the gravel.
- Alevin: The hatched-out ova with a food sac attached, still in gravel.
- Fry: The former alevin now emerges from gravel after the food sac has been depleted, some three to four months after the eggs were laid.
- Parr: The fry has now grown into a small fish (perhaps up to a finger in length) with distinctive thumb marks along its flanks.
- Smolt: After a sudden biological change occurs, colouration of the fish changes from a dark grey to bright silver and the juvenile salmon has a compelling impulse to migrate quickly to its feeding grounds in the sea. Typically, the juvenile is some six inches long at this stage and is two to three years old.

Adult Stages

- Grilse: After one year at sea, many salmon will return to their native rivers to spawn, at which stage they are known as one sea winter (1SW) salmon or more normally as grilse. Their typical weight would be four to six pounds. They usually enter their native rivers in summer or early Autumn.
- Spring Salmon: This is a salmon which has spent two or more years at sea before returning to spawn. If it returns after two years it is known as a two sea winter (2SW) salmon; a three sea winter (3SW) salmon if it returns after three years, and so on. These fish are sometimes referred to as multi sea winter (MSW) salmon. They can weigh anything from eight pounds to twenty pounds, or more. It is obvious therefore that salmon grow enormously fast at sea, as they can avail of a rich and plentiful diet there. However, in recent years there is growing concern in fishery circles about a possible diminution in the availability of this rich and plentiful diet, which may be due to directly related man-made causes, such as over-fishing of the fish sub-species that salmon feed on, as well as more indirect climate change factors.
- Typically, spring salmon enter their native rivers in the springtime (hence their name), but some enter in the summer and autumn also. When spring salmon and grilse enter the river they have a beautiful silvery blue colouration along their flanks and their bellies are a brilliant white. After some time in the fresh water, this beautiful colouration darkens

greatly and the male salmon will take on a reddish hue and develop a kype (a fleshy hook) in its lower jaw. The flesh of the salmon softens and loses its attractive flavour as it matures towards the spawning stage.

- Kelt or Spent salmon: A salmon after spawning is called a "kelt" or a "spent." Their natural urge is to return to the sea after spawning but sometimes, perhaps in order to recover their strength, this return may be delayed for a period of up to two or three months. During this period they turn very silvery again, and the novice angler fishing in February, March and sometimes April, could well believe that he or she has caught a fresh-run salmon. Typically the salmon will be thin and elongated. Kelts must by law be released safely back to the water and, in any case, would make for bad eating. Quite a few of the kelts die in the fresh water on their way back to the sea. The amazing thing is that salmon do not eat in fresh water, and sometimes a full year could elapse from the time that an adult salmon enters the river in early spring and departs as a kelt in the following spring. During this time it lives off the rich fats it built up during its voracious feeding at sea.

The ability of the salmon to home back to its native river is yet another amazing characteristic of the salmon. Having possibly travelled thousands of miles in the sea since it left as a smolt, it can now return to its native country and then pick out its own river from possibly among hundreds of rivers. I like to think of this amazing feat of salmon as an example of one of the many great features of nature provided for by our Creator. Sutterby & Greenhalgh, authors of Atlantic Salmon – an illustrated natural history, make reference to three possible methods that humans can use to find their way, i.e. orienteering, navigation and piloting or homing, and contemplate salmon doing likewise. The authors note that this process for salmon "is unconscious; it is instinctive or automatic. The salmon does not 'make a decision'. It does not think or analyse and then decide the direction to take. Which is why its migrations are so wonderful" (p. 74).

This suggests to me that salmon have a built-in radar that is capable of automatically taking cognisance of all the physical and other environmental characteristics it encounters, and it would appear that one of these characteristics would definitely be the smell or taste of the river, as well as the particular part of that river, in which the salmon was hatched (p. 78). To spot salmon eagerly returning from the sea, with reproduction in mind, and entering their native river and surging upstream, sometimes in relatively low water conditions but perhaps in the sure expectation of impending rain and flood conditions, is a sight to behold and is surely another of the wonders of the world and of nature. No wonder the Atlantic Salmon is called the King of Fish. Surely the salmon deserves our utmost respect, and we must not do anything, through either over-fishing or damage to our environment, that would interfere with this true barometer of how well or otherwise we humans are managing planet earth.

Garavogue River, Sligo. A good spot for a salmon.

Drumcliffe sea pools in low/medium water

Drumcliffe sea pools in high water

Glencar Lake – dark threatening clouds

> "Keep us from getting so involved in pursuing the things money can buy, that we lose the things money can't buy."
>
> Mark Link S.J.

Glencar Lake – Diffreen bay near Glencar Waterfall

View from parking area at Glencar Waterfall

Glencar Waterfall, Co. Leitrim

Joe's pool, Ballisodare River.

Ballisodare River in high water.

Estuary at Easkey River

The Cathedral beat, Moy River, Ballina.

A 33 lbs salmon caught commercially by Plunkett McCann in Aughris Bay, Sligo, in 2006, on display in the Beach Bar, Aughris. It is wonderful to know that salmon of this size are still running.

A lively Owenduff fish of some 10lbs surges up river from under the footbridge (requiring some tricky manoeuvres).

The same fish getting its freedom.

Success for each of us on the Owenduff River, Co. Mayo

Dervila proves that women are better fishers than men.

GONE FISHING: A HEALTHY AND ABSORBING HOBBY

A quiet lamb on the banks of the Owenduff

A beautiful specimen for David on the Owenduff

Beaching a fish in a confined area on the Owenduff

A neat hand tailing operation follows

Well bent into a good fish in Barretts pool, Owenduff

Near the source of the Owenduff River

Conor beaching a good fish (This becomes a habit with him)

His assistant lends a hand

His assistant passes the test

GONE FISHING: A HEALTHY AND ABSORBING HOBBY

High water over the Rock weir, Owenduff

A look down river in the high water

Admiring Padraic's salmon

An upper beat on the Owenduff River

High up on the Gweebarra River, Doocharry, Co. Donegal

Gweebarra River again

Morrison's pool, Delphi Fishery (Courtesy Peter Mantle)

A nice setting at Delphi (Courtesy Peter Mantle)

Action at the Rock pool, Delphi (Courtesy Peter Mantle)

GONE FISHING: A HEALTHY AND ABSORBING HOBBY

A very good fish from Sligo waters (probably from Easkey River)

Late evening fishing at Glencar

'Lord of the Falls' – a painting by Maurice Meade, Sligo, depicting salmon ascending the Ballisodare Falls with the statue of Christ in the nearby cemetery overseeing their progress – perhaps a reminder to us humans that we too must push on in life under the protection of our Saviour!

> "O the gallant fisher's life,
> It is the best of any:
> 'Tis full of pleasure, void of strife,
> And 'tis beloved by many.
> Other joys are but toys
> Only this, lawful is;
> For our skill breeds no ill
> But content and pleasure."
>
> — Izaak Walton

The Art of Catching Trout or Salmon

There are three main methods of fishing for trout or salmon:

- Fly fishing
- Spinning with lures
- Bait fishing

Fly Fishing

Fly fishing is generally regarded as the most sporting and satisfying method of catching fish from an angler's point of view. It is probably also the most skilful method of fishing, in that the angler is using his or her prowess to deceive the fish in its own watery environment with tools and tackle that are more testing for the angler than those used in the other methods of fishing.

Fly fishing can be divided into:

- Wet fly fishing
- Dry fly fishing
- Dapping with natural flies

Wet Fly Fishing.

Wet fly fishing implies fishing with one or more artificial flies (normally not exceeding three flies) which sink in the water and are made to move in the water, either by the current or by the angler, and sometimes by both, thus mimicking natural insects / flies at their various life cycle stages. Thus an appreciation of entomology, i.e. the study of insects or flies, including their various life cycle stages, can greatly add to the enjoyment of fishing as well as to the success in catching fish. For instance, the duck fly normally hatch out from the beds of lakes or rivers in March and April, olives start to hatch out in April and continue for several months, the May fly hatches out in May, and then later on, various sedges, including the famous green peter, hatch out, as do grasshoppers, daddy long legs and so on. Then each of these insects or flies have their own particular life cycle, typically ranging from the larva (grub) stage, pupa stage (half way development) and the final imago or dun stage (complete fly).

Some flies, particularly the May fly (often called the "green drake") have an additional final stage called the spinner stage, where the green drakes leave the water and fly to the bushes, later leaving the bushes to fly and spin in the air. At this point the flies have turned grey/black and the males and females mate. Following this, the females return to the water to deposit their eggs, thus continuing the renewal of the species before their own death which quickly follows while the male also dies, possibly on land. Generally it takes two years for the May fly to develop and hatch out but it lives typically for just two days. What a sobering thought!

In any event, the successful fly angler will normally fish with artificial flies which not alone replicate the natural flies on or underneath the water, but also the particular life stage that the fly is at. All of this may seem complicated, but the would-be angler should not be put off by this apparent science. It is all much simpler than it sounds and, anyway, any worthwhile tackle shop assistant should be able to offer advice as to what flies to fish at any particular time of the year. Otherwise take advice from a competent angler with who you are familiar. For those who wish to go deeper into the subject, I suggest that you acquire a good book on the subject, and in this regard I don't think you can do better than securing a copy of Fly Fishing in Ireland by Peter O'Reilly, already referred to earlier in the chapter. I would add that I know of no more a competent and knowledgeable angler than Peter O'Reilly. He has written several other books pertaining to angling in Ireland; a useful one on the subject of flies is his Trout & Salmon Flies of Ireland. A little later, I will deal briefly with the actual gear and tackle as well as the movements and actions involved in fishing.

Dry Fly Fishing.

Basically everything I have said above in relation to insect or fly life applies also to dry fly fishing. The only real difference is that in dry fly fishing the artificial fly, normally only one fly rather than two or three, is fished dry, that is afloat on the water surface, thus mimicking the final dun or spinner stage of the natural fly. Normally the angler does not move or work the fly, as in wet fly fishing. Dry fly fishing is sometimes regarded as the purest and most skilful form of fly fishing,

> "It gives me a deep comforting sense that 'things seen are temporal and things unseen are eternal'."
> Helen Keller – a gifted blind author

particularly in the context of trying to fool a big trout to take an artificial fly for a natural fly in relatively calm water conditions, in full view to the trout. Fishing the spinner stage of the May fly (known as spent fishing as the May fly is spent and about to die) can be a deadly way to catch big trout, assuming one can get the right fishing conditions. Many of the fly categories can be successfully fished dry.

Dapping with natural flies

Dapping with natural flies resembles dry fly fishing, in that fish are pursued at the final dun stage of the fly on the water surface. However, instead of using an artificial fly the actual natural fly is used, by mounting it on a hook and dapping it on the water's surface, generally using a long light rod with light "blow" line attached so that the wind will extend the fly out from the angler. Thus casting with the rod is not required. Dapping is usually done from a boat and, although not requiring a great degree of skill, can be very rewarding way of catching big trout. Your heart can beat faster, or perhaps miss a beat, when that big trout appears in front of your eyes to accept your offering. It is important to give the trout some time to go down with the fly, before tightening or striking. A pre-requisite for dapping is the ability to collect the natural flies on the bushes, grass, or wherever. The May fly, daddy long legs and the grass hopper would be favourite dapping flies.

The foregoing comments on wet fly, dry fly and dapping apply mainly to trout fishing, both in lake and river environments. While all three methods of fishing can also catch salmon, generally most fly fishing for salmon in Ireland falls into the category of wet fly fishing, when one or more flies are fished with movement under the water surface, be it on a river or lake. However, with lake fishing the bob fly, i.e. the fly nearest to the rod tip, is often fished through the surface and cutting the water, and this can often entice a take, be it salmon or trout. To a certain extent, this method is mimicking dry fly fishing. The other flies would fish under the water.

An interesting point about fly fishing for salmon is that salmon do not feed at all when in fresh water; thus the various stages of fly life cycles should be of little consequence to salmon. This begs the question as to why a salmon will take a fly, or any other lure for that matter, in fresh water. There are various theories on this subject, such as the "aggression/protective" theory and the "memory reflex" theory. The first one suggests that the salmon in protecting its territory will attack whatever may be encroaching on its territory, while the second theory would claim that the fly or lure coming into the vision of the salmon gives the salmon a memory recall of its feeding days at sea and so it will attack the fly and in the process get hooked. Possibly, both these theories have relevance, but I can assure you that salmon don't attack near as much as most anglers would like them to! Various other environmental factors, such as weather conditions, the length that salmon are in the fresh water (salmon take better when they enter fresh from the sea), can have a big bearing on the salmon's willingness to accept an offering from an angler.

Gear and Tackle

The basic tools of the trade for the fly angler are fly rods, fly reels, fly lines, leaders or casts and a range of artificial flies. I will deal with these in turn.

Fly Rods.

Today virtually all fly rods are made from carbon fibre (or some derivation thereof) primarily due to the relative lightness of this material compared to the greenheart[29] used in the distant past and the split cane and tubular steel used more recently. However, rods made of split cane are still available and their manufacture is regarded as a highly skilled craft. The casting ability of carbon rods has been developed to a high degree. Fly rods generally come in two, three or four pieces, so to assemble the rod the pieces are fitted together through the use of ferrules. The rod will normally have a cork handle or butt to which a fly reel is fitted. The rod tapers progressively from the thick butt to the narrow point, so as to facilitate handling and casting. It has metal rings throughout its length, through which line from the fly reel is threaded.

The choice and variation in fly rods today is immense, particularly in relation to the length and strength of rods and in types of rod actions, all this depending on the type of fishing intended. Rods can vary in length from typically eight feet to sixteen feet or more. The shorter rods up to ten or eleven feet would normally be used for trout fishing, while the longer and more powerful rods would generally be used for salmon fishing. However, the more powerful ten and eleven feet rods can also be successfully used for salmon fishing.

Fly rods are rated on the international AFTM[30] scale. This scale basically indicates the strength and power of the rod. Thus a rod with an AFTM 12 rating would indicate a very powerful and strong rod suitable for salmon fishing in dif-

---

29. Greenheart (scientifically known as *Chlorocardium rodiei*) is a very strong evergreen wood, so strong that it is used in extreme marine applications; for example the *Endurance* ship on which Tom Crean journeyed to the Antarctic on the Shacketon expedition was sheathed in greenheart to protect the ship of being crushed by ice when moving through or frozen into the Antarctic ice packs.
30. This stands for the Association of Fishing Tackle Manufacturers.

> *"Doubt not but angling will prove to be, like virtue, a reward to itself."*
> — Izaak Walton

ficult fishing conditions, whereas an AFTM 6 rod would be a very much less powerful rod suitable for more delicate trout fishing conditions. This rating scale also indicates the fly line that suits the rod; this is important as the rod should be matched with the correct fly line in order to get the proper weight balance for casting purposes. Thus fly lines are rated precisely on the same AFTM scale – in fact the rating was originally introduced to identify the fly line weights and the rods were then rated on the basis of the line weights that suited them.

The other very important feature of fly rods is that of the rod "actions.". Rods come in a range of different actions, which have got to do with their casting types and abilities. Rod actions could be categorised into soft, medium and stiff. Typically the actions that are now identified on rod promotions are "mid to tip" actions and "tip" actions, and possibly "butt to tip" actions although I have not noticed any of the latter lately.

The butt to tip action is one where the whole rod from butt to tip bends when you cast or swing the rod. I term this a soft rod and it can be very attractive and easy to fish with, provided the fishing conditions are not too testing. This type of rod enables a lot of the strain in casting to be transferred (or absorbed) from the angler to the rod. Also when you are playing a strong fish you can feel its movement right down to the butt and you can afford to bend the rod in the fish to a great extent because of the soft and somewhat whippy action of the rod. It is a type of rod I am very fond of, but I feel that they are harder and harder to come by today. However, the mid to tip action rod which is readily available is probably a good compromise.

At the other end of the spectrum are the tip action rods. These are meant for long and precise casting, possibly in trying fishing conditions. Everything about tip action, in my opinion, is opposite to what I said about the butt to tip action, and based on my little experience of these tip action rods, I just don't like them. I find they are not much pleasure to fish with, but I emphasise that my experience of them is limited, and no doubt they have their uses.

The mid to tip rod is normally sufficiently forgiving to overcome the drawbacks of the tip action rods and allow for a reasonable share of the characteristics of the more soft butt to tip action to be achieved. However, I remember reading an article in some fishing magazine in the not too distant past where the author complained fairly stringently about the inaccurate descriptions being used in promotional literature to describe rods, particularly their actions. So if you a buying a rod, test it for its suitability to you, and if you are new to angling I suggest you consider a soft action rod, rather than a stiff tip action one.

Fly reels and fly lines.

Fly reels are compact and smooth winding and unwinding devices with tension, which holds the fly line plus backing (light line). This backing enables one to play a running fish that has taken all the fly line off the reel. Reels vary in size and width and, of course, weight. The smaller capacity reels would cater for the light trout lines and rods, while the larger capacity reels would generally cater for the heavier salmon lines and rods. The technical characteristics of reel tensions (which give the angler a certain control over the paying out and retrieving of line) vary from reel to reel.

Fly lines, in addition to being rated on the AFTM scale, which typically range from 4 to 12 (the higher rating signifying a heavier line), can be categorised under further headings, as follows:

- *Density:* These include floating, intermediate, sinking, sink tip and shooting head lines. Floating lines, as the name suggests, float on the water surface. Intermediate lines will sink a little in the water, while sinking lines will sink more. Sink tip lines have a sinking line of some three metres in front attached to a floating line behind. Shooting heads are rather heavy special purpose lines of some ten to twelve metres in length which are attached to some thirty metres of narrow profile running line. The shooting head itself can be floating, intermediate or sinking. These lines are usually used with big salmon rods on big rivers where extra distance in casting is desirable.

    Normally, floating lines are used in summer wet fly fishing (both trout and salmon) and for dry fly fishing for trout. Intermediate lines would also be frequently used for summer wet fly fishing, but some people would also use them for spring and autumn fishing. Sinking lines would normally be used for spring wet fly fishing and possibly also for autumn fishing.

- *Profile:* Fly lines come in different profiles, mainly double tapered (DT) and weight forward (WF). A double tapered line can be fished from either end, in that the end attached to the backing on the reel drum can be reversed. In this way one can get many extra years fishing from the line. So the line could be said to be in two identical halves, although sometimes the profile of each half is somewhat different so as to give one more choice. The profile of each half is such that the line is thicker (the diameter is wider) at the mid point of the line and progressively narrows towards the end or point of the line. The weight forward line, on the other hand, can only be fished in one way as the reel end of the line is flat and not suitable for casting. The forward part of the line is rather similar in profile to that of a doubled tapered line except the weight in the forward portion is more pronounced. A weight forward line is often used to achieve longer casts. However, double tapered lines are often easier to cast.

> *"Idle time not idly spent."*
> — Sir Henry Wooton

- *Leader:* A leader, sometimes called a cast, is a monofilament line of some three yards long which is attached to the fly line. The leader may be of varying breaking strains depending on what fish one is pursuing and the conditions one is fishing in. So if you are fishing for salmon in a big river with a strong flow of water, you might fish twenty pound breaking strain (BS), whereas you might fish a six pound BS for trout in normal conditions. The question of balance always applies; thus a big salmon rod will be accompanied with a heavy fly line and normally with a heavy leader, and vice versa for a light trout rod. To the other end of the leader is attached the fly one wishes to fish. Sometimes up to three flies can be mounted on the leader, one at the point and the others at distances back from the point. Again the size of the fly tends to balance with the rod, fly line and leader.

Artificial Flies.

Flies have already been referred to and particularly artificial trout flies which are intended to imitate the natural insects and flies at their various stages of life that trout typically feed on. Unlike trout flies, salmon flies do not imitate natural insects or flies, however, the popular salmon shrimp fly (of which there are many varieties) does partly at least imitate some of the crustaceans which the salmon encounters while feeding at sea. In any event, there is a huge range of both trout and salmon flies available on the market.

If you are really enthusiastic, you could buy a fly tying kit, take some lessons in fly tying and tie your own flies, perhaps using patterns from a well recognised fly tier. In this regard, you could well consider the patterns and tying instructions contained in Peter O'Reilly's book *Trout and Salmon Flies of Ireland*. Fly tying can be an absorbing pastime and perhaps gives one an opportunity to get further involved in the study of nature. While most trout flies are mounted on conventional single hooks, salmon flies come in many different hook and body types, such as single hook, double (twin) hook, treble hook, tube flies with plastic, aluminium or copper bodies and lastly waddingtons, which is a type of a solid metal tube fly. A huge range of materials are used in making up flies such as bird feathers, animal hair, animal fur and others, both natural and synthetics.

There is a numbering system to identify fly hook sizes, typically ranging from 1 to 15, whereby the bigger the number the smaller the hook and vice versa. So the very tiny no. 15 hook would be used for delicate trout fishing, while the big no. 1 hook would be identified with salmon fishing in heavy waters.

Knots and Casting

We are almost ready to go fly fishing. However, two important items remain, a knowledge of the knots used by the angler in making up tackle and a knowledge of, and proficiency in, casting a fly rod. As regards the knots, please refer to the Appendix on Fishing for an explanation of the essential knots required, together with some photographs thereof. The Appendix also explains some of the different casting methods. I recommend that all newcomers to fly angling should make a proper effort to become proficient in casting—it will greatly add to one's enjoyment of the sport, as well as to your safety and that of others.

There is a skill involved in casting but it can be acquired fairly quickly, and particularly if one avails of instruction from a professional fly caster or even an angling colleague, complimented perhaps with instruction from a book (hopefully my notes in the Appendix will be of some help) and/or a video or DVD on casting. By way of introduction, I comment very briefly here on some different casting methods.

The standard fly cast used by most anglers is the overhead cast, whereby the angler brings the fly rod, with a determined but controlled movement, over his/her head, and a little behind the head, allowing the line to straighten out behind but not fall to the ground. After a split second pause, one casts the rod forward which brings the line, to which the leader and fly are attached, straight out in front and some feet above the water surface. Stopping the rod's movement at that point allows the line and fly to drop gently onto the water. On large rivers where heavy rods and tackle are used, the overhead cast can be tiring and in these situations, spey casting (both single and double spey casting) will often be used. However, spey casting is often used on smaller rivers too where there are bushes or other obstructions that prevent the angler from undertaking overhead casting. As an alternative in these situations, roll casting can be used. These methods are explained in the Appendix.

Going Fishing

Hopefully, the would-be fly angler reading this book is not totally confused at this stage. So let's go fishing and try to simplify matters by assuming you want to fish the fly for summer salmon in a medium-sized river where typically the salmon weigh from 3 lbs to 10 lbs. I would advise as follows:

- Procure a 10 or 11 foot fly rod with a butt to tip action, or failing this, a mid to tip action, where the action is not too stiff nor too whippy, and with an AFTM rating of 7 or 8. If necessary seek advice from an angling colleague or a fish tackle shop assistant.
- Mount a medium capacity fly reel to the rod, whose weight suits, i.e. balances, the rod.

> *"The fact is that nothing earthly can fill the void in the human heart."*
> — Father Flanagan

- Procure a doubled tapered (DT) intermediate fly line with AFTM rating of 7 or 8. Also procure about 100 yards of backing line – join one end of this to the reel inner centre and wind it on to the reel. Join the fly line to the other end of the backing line and wind it on to the reel.
- Assemble the rod, threading the fly line through the rings of the rod. Attach about 3 yards of monofilament nylon line of 10 to 12 pound breaking strain to the line. See the Appendix for the various knots required.
- Procure about one dozen salmon flies for a start. You can add more later on. We fishers collect far too many flies. Consider the following patterns: Gary Dog, Silver Wilkinson, shrimp fly and Green Peter. (While the Green Peter is a trout fly, it is also a most productive salmon fly). You could choose these flies in singles, doubles or trebles, or in all three, except the Green Peter which would normally be a single hook. If using singles, perhaps choose sizes 6 and 8, if doubles, 8 and 10 and if trebles, 10 and 12. The height of water will partly determine size of fly. If the water is very high, bigger flies than those listed here may be required.
- Having arrived at the river and having seen the height and condition of the water, you can now choose a suitable fly size to suit the level of the water. As regards the pattern, that's up to you. I am partial to all the four patterns listed above. Should the water be coloured after a flood, it is likely to be unproductive to fish the fly until the colour clears. Anyway choose the fly and tie it to the point of the leader. Many river salmon anglers fish two flies on the leader, I usually only fish one fly.
- Don your waders, fishing coat, hat, and anything else you consider appropriate. Strictly for safety purposes, all anglers should wear glasses to protect their eyes against the chance of the fly hook lodging therein during casting. You might wish to bring a landing net to land your fish, I normally don't bother, provided the waters I am fishing have shallows and shingle which make it possible to beach a fish.
- Start fishing the pools, starting at the top of each pool, by casting your fly across the pool but perhaps slightly down at an angle. Let the current take your fly down with it but at the same time draw in (i.e. retrieve) the line so as to keep reasonably good movement of the fly in the water. Keep the rod tip low, until it is time to make the next cast. Move down a yard or so and make the next cast and repeat the process until you have fished to the end of the pool. Then move on to next pool.
- If you hook a salmon, keep a gentle to solid strain on the fish but you must not hold the fish too tight – let it run when it wants to do so, but

- keep an appropriate strain on at all times. Sometimes it is useful to move up and down the pool with the fish. When the fish tires, it will come to the surface and it is time to think of bringing it ashore, but be careful and do not force the fish too much. Let's hope you bring home the silver, or at least land it.
- Do not forget the important matter of procuring your state salmon licence and tags, which are normally available in tackle shops. Depending on what waters you plan to fish, it may also be necessary to procure permission and pay far a fishing permit. If you catch a salmon (or a large sea trout) and retain it, you must insert one of the tags through its gills as soon as you have landed and killed it. The fish is killed by holding it still on the bank and giving it a sharp, quick blow at the back of its head with a "priest"[31] or a stone. You should always do this before removing the hook as the salmon that you have worked so hard to get may leap or wriggle back to the river once you leave your rod down and the tension slackens. It would be a shame to lose a fish at such a late stage. It is also important to dispatch the fish quickly and humanely.
- If you are operating catch and release (i.e. if state and local fishery regulations[32] require this or if this is your own preference), it is recommended that you play the fish fairly hard and quickly tire it out, as this is less detrimental to the fish than a prolonged playing exercise. Ideally, use an appropriate dehooking pliers to extract the hook while the fish is still in the water, if possible without handling the fish. Many fisheries recommend that barbless hooks be used if you are fishing on a catch and release basis.

Enjoy yourself and hopefully you will have what we anglers use as a good luck wish to each other, "Tight Lines!"

Spinning with Lures

Spinning for trout and salmon with artificial lures, such as devons, spoons and so on, is generally more straightforward than fly fishing. It is relatively easy for a novice angler to become fairly accomplished in spinning. Generally the gear involved

---

31. The priest is a short thick implement, perhaps six inches long and slightly heavier at one end. It looks not unlike a section of a wooden broom handle although you can get metal ones also. It presumably got its name from the practice of using it to administer the "last rites" to the fish.

32. At different times of year and in different districts, the state fishing regulations may require total catch and release or allow a certain limited number of salmon or large trout to be retained in a particular period. At the moment, an angler with an annual licence may retain ten fish for the year but there are also daily limits and regional restrictions so anglers must check the regulations carefully.

> *"Into the dish the idler dips his hand but is too tired to bring it back to his mouth."*
> — Proverb 26:15

comprises a two piece rod of some nine foot in length, and a spinning reel loaded with monofilament line of some 10lbs breaking strain or possibly more, depending on the fish you plan to pursue and the type of fishing environment involved. You also need a selection of spinning lures. To prepare the gear, you assemble the rod, fit the spinning reel in the reel holder at the rod butt, thread the monofilament line through the rings and then attach the spinning lure of your choice to the monofilament. To keep the monofilament from kinking due to the spinning lure, a swivel is inserted about 18 inches back from the lure.

The spinning reel used generally is what is known as a fixed spool reel. It has a completely different mechanism to that of a fly reel, and also the rod casting technique is quite different to fly casting. There is a bale arm or clip on the spinning reel, which when released allows the line (to which has been attached a lure which has weight in it) to run off the reel, if at the same time the rod is thrust or cast forward in the direction of the water that you wish to fish. The casting technique is very simple as the weight of the lure really pulls the line off the reel. Thus a simple overhead or side cast or thrust forward is sufficient. When the lure drops in the water out in front of the angler, possibly fifty yards or more out in the water, the angler starts to wind the reel and immediately the bale arm automatically closes and the lure is wound in and hopefully a fish will make a grab for the lure.

Spinning can be undertaken either in lakes or rivers and either from the shore, bank or boat, as indeed fly fishing can. The method of spinning used for game fishing, coarse fishing or sea fishing is essentially the same although different spinning lures might be used, and the weight, strength and length of rods may vary. Reels and lines may also vary, depending on the quarry being pursued and the territory being fished. Spinning for salmon on a big river with a strong flow of water would obviously require much heavier and stronger gear and tackle than that spinning for trout in a small river. Likewise, beach casting in the sea requires strong gear and tackle.

Perhaps the real skill in spinning is knowing at what speed to wind in the spinning lure and being able to get a trade-off between letting the lure sink low enough in the water to get down to the fish yet not so low as to get snagged on the bottom (thereby running the risk of losing the lure). If one is spinning for salmon on a sizable river, generally the angler will cast straight across (but perhaps slightly down at an angle) the river and allow the lure to sink for a moment before starting to wind, but if there is a good flow of water, you would normally allow the current to take the lure around in an arc, while possibly winding in very slowly at the same time. At the end of the arc, the winding speed would be increased.

The point of the rod would normally be kept low near the water's surface but lifted gradually at the end of the wind or retrieve. In some ways, the same fishing tactics are adopted in fly fishing for salmon as in spinning for them, in so far as the movement of the fly and lure is concerned. Like the fly fisher, the spinning angler will move down river a yard or two for the next cast. It should be noted that some waters do not allow spinning, or perhaps any other form of angling other than fly fishing.

Bait Fishing

Bait fishing for game fish, such as trout and salmon, normally involves fishing with natural bait such as worms, maggots and so on. For instance, the black head worm, found in gardens and elsewhere, and which is firm and strong is a great favourite for salmon fishing. Natural (dead) prawns or shrimps are sometimes used as bait instead of worms. However, this method of fishing is banned in many places.

The gear used in bait fishing is essentially the same as that used for spinning, except that worms or other bait take the place of spinning lures. So if worm fishing for salmon in a medium sized river, you will mount your spinning rod and reel in the normal way, thread the monofilament line through the rod rings, attach a bare single hook, perhaps a size 6, and mount one or two black head worms thereon. A piece of lead or other weight may be attached to the line a foot or more back from the hook to give weight to enable a cast to be made and particularly to weigh the bait down in the water, so that it moves down with the current close to or perhaps on the river bed, where the salmon are lying.

The ideal location for this type of fishing is where there is a relatively strong current going through a good holding pool for fish. What applies to bait fishing for salmon applies equally to bait fishing for trout. Should the current not be sufficiently strong to move the bait downstream, then a float may be attached to the line a yard or so back from the bait, or more precisely at a distance that allows the bait to fish along the bed of the river. As children fishing for trout, we used corks from whiskey or stout bottles as floats; nowadays there are very fancy floats available, including those that automatically adjust to the depth of water being fished.

The main skill in bait fishing is probably that of developing a sensitivity as to how to effectively move the bait along the river bed and then to react appropriately when you get a "take". Most salmon worm anglers give a taking salmon a lot of time and even let the fish move away for several yards with the worm in its mouth, before tightening on the fish. Fly fishers would find it hard to get used to this. With both fly fishing and spinning for trout and salmon, the angler moves fairly fast along the river (because if a take is going to come, it usually happens on first sighting by the fish of the fly or spinning lure); however, in worm fishing the angler moves much slower, because a trout or salmon may accept a bait offering after having seen it several times.

> "The distance is nothing. It is the first step that is difficult."

Coarse Angling

The designation "coarse" does not refer to the method of fishing; indeed coarse fishing today involves the use of highly sophisticated fishing gear, equipment and techniques on the part of many of its participants. Rather the word coarse came about historically to describe the species of fish being pursued, which were regarded as coarse or lower-class fish from an edible point of view, and which were more likely to be pursued by poor people who retained all fish caught for their consumption. Most coarse anglers today return the fish alive to the water. The main species of coarse fish include bream, roach, rudd, dace, carp, perch, chub, tench, barbel, zander and pike. However, pike are often now regarded as a game fish, partly because it can be caught by specially designed flies and indeed by ordinary flies—I have caught a number of pike in the Garavogue and Bonet rivers, while fishing for salmon.

The main method of fishing used for coarse fish is bait fishing, using a variety of baits such as worms, maggots from rotten meat, bread, luncheon meat and various other offerings. However some of the fish species can be caught by spinning artificial lures, particularly perch and pike. The general gear and tackle already identified for spinning and bait fishing apply also for coarse fishing, except this has been added to greatly by those who might be described as professional coarse anglers. Basically however, the worm fishing methods for salmon and trout outlined previously, apply to bait fishing for coarse fish.

But the comparison almost immediately stops there in that instead of using the standard spinning rods and other gear, a whole range of specialist and usually very expensive rods and other gear have been developed to cater for coarse fishing, particularly in trying fishing conditions, such as low water or bright sunny conditions. This specialist gear enables a sensitivity to be brought to bear on the fishing so that success can be achieved even in very unfavourable fishing conditions. The accomplished coarse angler will attempt to deceive his or her quarry in conditions that favour the quarry not being deceived. Thus very delicate and sensitive tactics are adopted, such as very light lines, tiny small hooks, lack of water disturbance through sensitive fishing and light tackle, and so on.

Some of the specialist rods on the market for coarse angling include float rods, leger rods and the pole rod. The float rods may be up to 15 feet long and specially designed, often with a very sensitive top piece, and are used to fish with a float. The long rod helps to give more control to the angler, particularly if fishing in clear spots between weeds or lily pads. The leger rods, typically up to 12 feet in length, are used for bottom fishing without floats and do not have to be as sensitive as the float rods. The pole is a very specialist and indeed expensive rod, although trout and salmon anglers would probably not regard it as a rod as casting is not required. The pole comes in sections made up of very light carbon or similar material, which are assembled at the water's edge, and as many sections added as is necessary to fish specific and precise locations, perhaps under hanging bushes on the far side of the river, pond or wherever. These rods do not have reels or conventional lines. Instead the top section of the pole has a short elastic line attached to it, to which is mounted the hook and bait. If a fish is caught it has to be played on this very short line and the rod is disassembled section by section in order to land the fish.

The float and leger rods mentioned above often use the standard spinning reels mentioned for trout and salmon fishing, but sometimes more sophisticated centre-pin and multiplier reels are also used. Indeed, the latter reels are sometimes used for salmon fishing also. The other accessories used in coarse fishing, particularly hooks, floats and monofilament lines, are highly developed and sophisticated. A huge range of them exists to cater for all conceivable fishing conditions and to enable the angler to balance sensitivity with durability. Thus light and sensitive gear and tackle must not only permit fish to be caught in trying fishing conditions, such as low water and sunny conditions, but they must be strong enough to withstand the strain encountered in playing relatively big fish.

The popularity attached to coarse fishing has been greatly enhanced by the numerous match fishing competitions held in Ireland, the UK and further afield. These matches are generally very big business events in tourism terms, with competitors competing from many countries with substantial prize monies or other rewards on offer. All fish caught in these events are temporarily retained in keep nets, then weighed and released back to the water. It is these competitions that brought about the very high level of sophistication in gear and tackle.

For further study of coarse fishing, I would recommend that you would procure an appropriate book and/or instructional video or DVD. One such book that I can recommend is one referred to earlier by Purnell, Yates and Dawn, *The Concise Encyclopedia of Fishing*, which has a substantial section on coarse fishing.

Sea Angling

Sea angling offers an exciting and a varied array of fishing opportunities and fishing environments. These can vary from the straightforward spinning for mackerel from a pier to beach casting with fairly powerful rods and from cliff fishing to a varied range of boat fishing methods. The fishing environment is very different to that of inland fishing by virtue of the moving tides and the unpredictability of the sea. While safety issues feature in all types of fishing, they are particularly pertinent in sea fishing.

> *"Autumn is over but the idler does not plough,*
> *at harvest time he looks—nothing there!"*
> — Proverb 20:4

Spinning of lures and bait fishing would be the main methods of angling used in the sea, but the methods and bait used would generally be different to that already discussed. Fly fishing for certain species such as mackerel, sea trout and bass is now gaining momentum. Generally, it could be said that sea fishing is more challenging and more unpredictable than inland fishing because of the constantly changing seas and movement of fish, with the possible exception of mackerel fishing during the hot summer months. Possible species of sea fish include cod, plaice, whiting, sole, halibut, turbot, brill, pollock, ling, mackerel, mullet, wrasse, dogfish, conger eel, silver eel, skates, rays, small sharks, bass and sea trout.

The basic gear and tackle used comprises spinning rods of various lengths and strengths and sturdy boat fishing rods, standard and heavy duty spinning reels, heavy duty multiplier reels, monofilament or braided lines of varying strengths, a variety of hooks for baiting and a range of spinning lures, often specially designed for sea fishing. Rigs or wire traces are frequently attached to the end of the fishing line, where heavy fish or those with sharp teeth (who may cut the line) are the quarry. The bait or lure is then attached to this trace. The trace may have lead attached to it in order to keep the bait or lure low in the water or on the sea bed. Some special spinning baits which work on the surface of the water are also used for certain fish species. Special flies have been designed, particularly for bass and sea trout, which can normally be used with standard fly fishing gear. Be aware that salt water can corrode reels, particularly if they contain metal, a problem that one will not encounter in fresh water angling.

Normally sea fishing rods would not exceed twelve feet and many would be shorter. The beach caster would typically be twelve feet long and strong, because it has to be capable of casting the bait a long distance and a weight is invariably attached to the bait to keep it working on the sand. Also the rod must be capable of playing a fish in a strong moving tide. Typically the shorter but very sturdy rods of 8 to 10 feet would be used for boat fishing, such as fishing over wrecks, or uptiding and downtiding. Cramped space on boats makes these shorter rods a necessity. Boat rods need to be sturdy to be able to haul heavy fish from the bottom, such as (small) sharks, skate, conger eels and so on.

A very large range of baits are used which are mounted normally on a single strong large hook. These baits include lugworm, ragworm and sand eels, all of which are found in the mud or sand on the sea coasts. Small squid and mackerel pieces are also very popular baits as are peeler crabs. All these baits would usually be fished on the sea bottom either from the shore or from a boat, so weights would generally be attached to them. If spinning is your choice, then in addition to some of the fresh water spinning lures which will do fine in the sea as well, there are many specialised sea spinning lures, such as imitation rubber sand eels and many other rubber or metal imitations. There are also a variety of feathered lures and many novice sea anglers will be familiar with the rig of feathered hooks for mackerel fishing. Visit any good tackle shop and you are certain to see an incredible array of imitation and other spinning lures for sea fishing, possibly even including those used for tuna fishing.

Fishing locations at sea include piers, breakwaters, beaches, rocks and cliffs, all of which are fished from land, while boat fishing can be done from small boats, particularly over reefs and sandbanks and inshore areas, and from large boats to more distant locations, including over sunken boat wrecks. In most coastal towns around Ireland, it is possible for groups of up to about twelve people to charter fully equipped fishing boats, complete with skipper and fishing gear, tackle, lures and baits, for a day's fishing at sea. Often it will be possible to join a party where one or more vacancies are available. This can be a very convenient way of getting introduced to sea fishing and learning about what is involved; as the boats are required to comply with all relevant safety regulations, it is also a safer way to learn. Such trips can be very good fun and afford a great opportunity to learn about and respect the sea. For those who wish to learn more about sea fishing, you might consult an appropriate book, such as *The Concise Encyclopedia of Fishing* by Purnell, Yates and Dawn already mentioned, or watch an appropriate video or DVD.

For some people, sea angling has much greater appeal than any other form of angling. This is probably due to the attractive, varied and expansive environment one encounters on the sea, where surprises are always on the cards. Such surprises could include the sighting of big mammals and varied bird life, and possibly catching big fish. But the pleasantness and feeling of liberation on being out on the sea on a balmy summer's day, or even fishing from the coastline in such conditions, is possibly the number one attraction of sea fishing. However, don't allow the attraction of sea angling to lead you to neglect safety factors; always be aware of general water safety factors (including moving tides), ideally don't go sea fishing on your own and always inform somebody at home when going sea fishing.

Happy Days!

CHAPTER FOURTEEN
The Atlantic Salmon and Salmon Angling: The Author's Passion

Whilst a reasonable amount has been written about salmon and salmon angling in the previous chapter, I wish to return to the subject in this chapter, partly to remind ourselves of the majestic nature of the Atlantic salmon, but also to consider some further aspects on the subject, as well as relating some of my own experiences, for what these may be worth.

Let me start by stating that, in my experience, it doesn't matter how many salmon one may have caught over the years, every decent-sized salmon that one hooks stimulates a rush of adrenalin and excitement which I suggest is beyond compare. Above all, one will want to safely land the salmon, after whatever struggle is involved, notwithstanding that in some instances you may return the fish fully alive to the water. Ideally in such situations one will endeavour not to take the fish out of the water at any stage, even when removing the hook.

Why is the excitement so great and what is the achievement? Perhaps it is the opportunity to get a close look at yet another majestic anadromous creature which possibly has travelled thousands of miles in the sea and has come home again to its native river. Perhaps it is to add one more salmon to one's catch statistics. We salmon anglers are not vain and we would never gloat over our ability to catch salmon – or would we? This begs the question: is catching salmon related to ability and skill or good luck, or perhaps both? I would suggest that there is an element of both, but ability and skill are dominant.

Regarding the thrill of hooking and landing a salmon, the thrill can vary between one salmon and another. For instance the first salmon in a new season in springtime is very special and one is made to feel good (in fact very good) to be alive for yet another season, and I invariably thank God for this. To catch a salmon in a pool or part of a lake that you never caught one in before, even though you have often fished there, is also special. To catch a salmon in new waters which you never fished before can be very poignant. To catch one's first ever salmon is possibly indescribable in terms of the rush of adrenalin. I have seen it in the faces of my own family members and in others. Size of salmon and the condition of the fish does of course have a bearing on the level of excitement. To catch a fresh-run

15 pound salmon straight in from the sea in mint condition certainly raises the excitement stakes.

Specifically, the salmon that each year give me the ultimate pleasure in catching are the few spring salmon that I usually (unfortunately not always) succeed in catching in the Drumcliffe/Glencar system in Sligo/Leitrim, the Garavogue river in Sligo and the Owenduff river in Mayo. Generally March, April and May are the prime months for spring salmon, weighing typically from 8 to 12 pounds. The Ballisodare Fishery is a particularly prolific fishery with very good runs of both spring and summer salmon, and I normally have my share of luck there. For summer and autumn salmon, Easkey river is very popular and has lovely fly water, where typically the fish range from 4 to 6 pounds, but with bigger fish on offer. Over the years, I have caught many salmon there but managed to catch two salmon that weighed some 14 pounds each. An attractive feature of the Easkey river is that one can stand (or even sit in one's car) at the estuary mouth below Easkey village and, if your luck is in, watch salmon run in from the sea over the relative shallow fords and upriver, usually hastily as their instinct is to move close to their spawning grounds. With a combination of luck and skill, you might even get one or more to accept your fly!

As regards personal experiences, perhaps I can quote a comment that one of my sons made to me some thirty years ago when he was a youngster: "Dad it became very routine after a while." He was commenting on the apparent ease with which I caught six spring salmon on the fly, five in one pool, over a two hour period of fishing, on the Owenduff river in Mayo. As the line from the Van Morrison song goes "There will be Days Like This," but not many I can assure you! In later years that same son encountered a rather similar experience of catching six sizable salmon in one day's fishing. The five salmon that I caught in the one pool in that episode was when fishing from a high bank. I could see the salmon clearly rising to the fly and many of them rose three times before they took the fly. There was one salmon that rose to my fly nine times but I failed to catch it, perhaps thankfully in the interest of the conversation of the species. In passing, I might note that my children tell me that I remember the exact details of every salmon I caught such as where I was fishing, the fly I was using, how the salmon played; in fact they suggest that I have a better memory for these things than I have for certain other things that may be more important. There may indeed be some truth in this!

I kept all of those six salmon and the thought of releasing some of these fish (or perhaps ceasing to fish) never crossed my mind – catch and release was never heard of then. As I get older and hopefully wiser, my respect for the Atlantic salmon increases and so does my concern for the continuation of the species in abundance. Thankfully today, we have all become much more attuned to the conservation of our salmon stocks, but I must be honest and say that I would never agree with total catch and release – I think there must be a balance between retention of fish and releasing them. Otherwise, I don't think I would bother fishing for salmon.

> *"It is playing safe that we create a world of utmost insecurity."*
> — Dag Hammarskjold

I am happy to report that I have passed my enthusiasm for fishing onto most of my children and as a family we very much enjoy an annual fishing holiday in Mayo. Those who are slightly less enthusiastic about fishing itself love the peace, solitude and long walks that the pleasant environment affords and they always enjoy the vicarious excitement of the fishing triumphs of their siblings (and indeed of their father!). In recent years, my two sons and myself have gone on fishing trips to Norway on two occasions and we really enjoyed the opportunity and challenge of fishing on very different and much bigger rivers than we have been used to. However, it is hard to beat Ireland for fishing. No matter where one fishes, anticipation is always a factor.

Conservation, Management and Development Issues

Thankfully, there now appears to be a genuine realisation among all the participants in the salmon industry in Ireland that it is vital that we take steps to ensure the proper conservation, management and development of our salmon stocks, with the view to bringing these stocks back to a level of abundance. Abundance of salmon will not alone benefit each and all of the parties involved directly in the industry such as anglers, fishery owners, tackle shops, hotels and guest houses and other angling tourist earners, commercial netsmen and fish processors, but the state will reap significant benefits. The greatest state benefit that I see deriving from an abundance of salmon is that a flagship status will be conferred on Ireland, giving the image of a clean unpolluted land where nature is allowed to run its course and where there is an environmental sensitivity that ensures that Ireland is truly green.

If this image can be genuinely attained, as I believe it can, then we must all work to attain it as the benefits to the state will be immense in terms of earnings from all tourist sections, not just angling, and indeed from international mobile business interests. However, there are many benefits over and above that of the economy as we work to preserve our environment and our angling heritage as well as the hospitality that Ireland has rightly been famous for in the past. With the Green Party now participating in Government and with all elements in the general environmental area and those involved in fisheries playing their part, one has got to be optimistic about the future of the salmon and of our environment. Every one of us (and that means "I") has a role to play.

In the context of the conservation of our salmon, the decision by the Government last year to end drift netting for salmon was, in my view, a very wise one. Unfortunately this decision should have been taken thirty years ago at a time when there were huge runs of salmon, some 90% of which were captured by drift netters before they reached the rivers to spawn. Drift net licences were given out somewhat indiscriminately in the 1960s and 1970s without consideration for the consequences. This should not have happened and, from the point of view of managing salmon stocks, drift netting is not a natural or sensible way to exploit salmon. However, I do feel for the genuine drift netter who has salmon fishing in their blood and are now denied this fishing in the future. Unfortunately, there is no ecologically sustainable way back to such netting.

However, I would recommend that drift netters be given the chance to get involved in an alternative method of commercial salmon fishing, such as salmon ranching. I believe that salmon ranching has great potential in Ireland and would strongly recommend that the relevant state bodies should pursue with vigour the development of salmon ranching. The concept involved in salmon ranching is fairly simple. It involves the release of young hatchery-reared salmon (smolts) in the mouths of small rivers or streams which do not at present support wild salmon or support them in only negligible quantities and capturing all the returning fish commercially. An angling facility could also be built downstream of the netting area. Salmon processing and smoking facilities could also be developed alongside each ranching station or perhaps strategically located to accommodate two or more stations. I feel sure that existing salmon processors would be very interested.

The young smolts would not be reared at each ranching station, but rather would be reared centrally as is presently done in the supply of smolts to salmon farms. Indeed, salmon farmers should also be encouraged to go into salmon ranching, which would be environmentally much more acceptable than their present operations (for research in this regard, see the next section on the Delphi/Erriff experiments). The ranched salmon also would be a far superior product to the farmed salmon, since the salmon would feed naturally at sea as a wild salmon. Interestingly, the ranched salmon develop a homing instinct for the river into which they are released (provided that they remain there for a few weeks) so, like the wild salmon, they experience the urge to spawn and thus return to their "native" river. The main obstacle that impeded the development of a salmon ranching industry in this country up to now was the drift netting for salmon, as most of the returning ranched salmon would have been caught by drift netters, thus rendering the business unviable for the ranchers. Now that this is no longer the case, I believe that we should move without delay on this new exciting enterprise.

I am also heartened to have read recently that there is an EU proposal whereby all fish catches at sea must be landed at recognised ports. This would mean that catches can be inspected on land, so that any illegally caught fish, including salmon, can with much greater ease be spotted, and thus controlled, than is the position as of now. This would also enable the spotting of accidentally caught salmon smolts in herring and mackerel nets, which may provide useful information as to salmon migration patterns and enable better conservation.

> *"When we are at our lowest, God is closest."*

Ireland has wonderful salmon fisheries and I believe that, with more hands-on involvement by all the stakeholders in the industry in the development and management of these fisheries, it can become the prime salmon angling destination in the world. I feel, however, that we have had far too much of a top-down approach to the management and the development of our salmon fisheries at far too high a cost. Local angling clubs, fishery owners and anglers themselves, who have been the custodians of our fisheries for centuries and who have often given their services free of charge have largely been ignored in the last several years. Anglers, I believe, now feel a sense of alienation and the fraternal and community spirit that dominated local fisheries has been severely dented.

I suggest that the powers that be and the angling confraternity put their heads and hearts together in a new co-operative approach to the management and development of our inland fisheries. Hopefully in the process, the climate of bureaucracy that has emerged in recent years will dissipate and a genuine enthusiasm for the development of new worthwhile projects will emerge from all parties. In this situation, it should be possible to explore ways for the control of fishing in a manner that is friendly and yet effective, in all of which the over-riding atmosphere will be one of mutual co-operation and respect. After all, angling is meant to be pleasurable.

It behoves all anglers to always act with propriety, particularly on the river bank, and no angler should ever put to the test, through improper conduct, the common bond of comradeship that exists between them. Anglers are a privileged people because of their close connection with nature and the quarry they pursue; with such privilege comes an obligation to nature and to others, including the owners of the land through which the anglers pass. Finally, I would make a plea for the involvement in fishing by more young people, particularly in this age of so many unhelpful distractions for them. The authorities have been relatively active in this area, but more needs to be done by them and by fishing clubs and so on.

The Delphi/Erriff Experiments on the Impact of Salmon Farming

Both the Delphi fishery in Mayo and the Erriff fishery in Galway, have both wild and ranched salmon.[33] As the ranched salmon are identified by means of micro-

---

33. The Erriff fishery has mainly wild salmon with only a relatively limited stock of ranched salmon, possibly to enable research into the species.

chip and are also all captured at the end of each season,[34] this allows the fisheries to collect substantial information on the salmon smolts and the returning adult salmon. Since 2005, both fisheries have been collecting data on the effect of sea lice on wild or hatchery salmon. Sea lice are fish parasites which can be lethal to young salmon and trout. They are often found in very high concentrations around salmon farms and can infect the wild juvenile salmon and trout population as they migrate past these farms.

A report in the *Delphi Fishery News 2007* explained that in 2005 the hatchery-reared smolts in the Erriff river were separated into two groups while in 2006 the same was done for the Delphi smolts. One group in each year was treated with Slice (an anti-sea lice preparation administered with food) while the second group was left untreated. The report gives the results for both fisheries as follows:

> The results from the Erriff releases in 2005 are extremely worrying, with an implied destruction of over 90% of all wild salmon smolts from that river. About 5,000 treated and 5,000 untreated smolts were released. According to the Marine Institute's official report, 37 adult salmon were recovered in 2006 from the treated group, but from the untreated group just 2 adults were recovered.
>
> The 2006 Delphi releases look set to prove [...] significant. With the two smolt groups having been differentially tagged and branded, the 2007 rod catches indicate that the treated group survived many times better than the untreated group.

Both sets of smolts migrate past the salmon farm in Killary Harbour and the experiment appears to corroborate the findings of the late Dr Graham Shaw, who studied the Killary lice situation in earlier years and concluded that "even 'low' levels of ovigerous (egg-bearing) lice on the farm in the spring – just 0.3 per fish – can have serious negative impacts on wild smolts." The Delphi report notes that the sea lice levels on the Killary farm during April 2006 (the time of the Delphi smolt migration) "were catastrophically high at nearly 20 times the limit laid down in the farm's licence." Unsurprisingly, the report concludes that there "is now hard evidence to show that lice from salmon farms are destroying Ireland's wild salmon as well as sea trout."

While these experiments may still be at a preliminary stage, they nevertheless look to be pretty conclusive and certainly they uphold the long-held worst suspicions of many people about the detrimental affects of salmon farms on our wild salmon, and on our sea trout. There are further issues (environmental and otherwise) with salmon farming and it has been the subject of much controversy. I would suggest that it needs to be the subject of much more serious official consid-

---

34. This is to prevent inter-breeding with the wild salmon stocks.

> "The first men that our Saviour dear
> Did choose to wait upon him here
> Blest fishers were; and fish the last
> Food was, that he on earth did taste;
> I therefore strive to follow those
> Whom He to follow Him hath chose."
>
> — Izaak Walton

eration. One positive move would be to have salmon farmers replace their farming activities with ranching.

Appendix on Fishing

Finally, I refer interested readers to the Appendix on Fishing which provides explanatory notes on the following topics:

- A Few Hints that Might Help You Find a Salmon
- Some Knots Used in Making up Fishing Tackle
- Casting a Fly Rod:
    - Overhead Cast
    - Roll Cast
    - Single Spey Cast
    - Double Spey Cast
- Safety Matters

David plays a big fish on the Gaula River in Central Norway

He proudly holds up his 25.5lbs beauty

Enjoying the moment

Fishing the Guala River some 50 kilometers from river mouth

'Showing off' the overhead cast on the Suldal River in Southern Norway

Part 6

Our Footprints on the Physical Environment

CHAPTER FIFTEEN
Environmental Issues

I was going to leave this chapter out of the book because I have no special expertise on the environment over and above what I learned from exposure to fishing and some farming. On reflection I decided to include it because caring for the environment is the responsibility of all of us; as such it is part of life which this book is largely about. I draw in this chapter on expert source material rather than on my own experience – however, my own experience has convinced me that our lack of respect for and our careless treatment of our environment have had a seriously adverse effect on it.

There appears, at least on the surface, to be quite a dramatic change for the better in the recent past in the public attitude towards respect for the environment. The result of this is that many people probably now feel that they have a moral, as well as often a legal, responsibility to protect the environment for future generations. For this to be effective, everybody must be converted not only to this way of thinking but to the habit of acting accordingly. Unfortunately, we have been far too slow to recognise the serious harm our modern way of living has being doing to the environment. For a long time many people seem to have regarded the scenario of global warming as being over-hyped and paid only lip-service to environmental issues, believing them to be a minority interest. I believe that recently, there has been a sea-change in such attitudes, partly attributable to Al Gore's 2006 film *An Inconvenient Truth*. I, for one, certainly believe Al Gore's global warning to be well founded and suggest that the film should be obligatory viewing for all and I have summarised below what seem to me to be some of the more serious environmental developments outlined in this film.

The levels of carbon dioxide (CO_2) in the earth's atmosphere have continued to rise since 1958 (according to research referred to in the film). Although some may dispute the link between higher CO_2 and higher temperatures, Al Gore notes that measuring the CO_2 levels in ice, which can give us thousands of years of data, shows a direct correlation between increasing CO_2 levels and higher temperatures as well as proving that today's CO_2 levels are much higher than at anytime in the past. Hence, the increasing CO_2 levels in the earth's atmosphere will cause temperatures to rise.

These increasing temperatures will cause ice caps and glaciers to melt and Al Gore referred to several examples of reduced glaciers and snow coverings, including the reduced snow cap on Mount Kilimanjaro (which I was privileged to view from a plane). At the present rate of reduction, this snow cap, the original discovery of which astounded explorers who had originally dismissed tales of a snow-capped mountain so close to the equator as mere myth,[35] could be gone within a mere ten years. Many snow caps are however, significantly larger than Mount Kilimanjaro's one and Al Gore pointed out that the permafrost (i.e. sub-soil that has been frozen since the end of the last ice age 11,000 years ago) of the polar ice caps is melting causing the ice caps to collapse along with the buildings that have been built thereon. This melting ice will cause sea levels to increase and much of the world's land will disappear as a result; he gave Greenland as an example of a country that will be substantially affected.

Increasing temperatures will not only cause a change in sea levels, it will change life as we know it. Al Gore suggests that a one degree change in temperature at the Equator would be equivalent to a twelve degree change at the North Pole. Obviously such a change is very significant and the film speculates that this will affect our seasons, impact on insect and bird life, and bring the prospect of new human diseases appearing. Evaporation of water from the soil will obviously increase as a result of global warming, thus giving rise to more problems in growing crops. Water temperatures will rise along with air temperatures and Al Gore points out that rising ocean temperature will cause more storms, tornadoes, typhoons and hurricanes as wind velocity increases with warm temperatures. Global warming, he indicated, would bring more precipitation (rainfall) but paradoxically it would also cause more drought, partly because global warming relocates precipitation. For instance, Lake Chad in Darfur has almost dried up.

At the end of the film Mr Gore referred to the fact that the "inconvenient truth" that is the scientific evidence of global warming is often manipulated by those whom it does not suit to acknowledge this truth because of vested economic interests, fears of potential job losses and so on. However, he suggests that many of the steps we can take to deal with global warming will bring new employment and opportunities so that it is not necessarily a question of having to choose between the economy and planet earth. We have, he said, the potential to develop and use environmentally friendly technologies to replace old technologies. The technologies we use are a matter of choice and we should choose (and indeed continue to develop) the highest standard from an environmental point of view. He notes that the automobile industry in the United States works to environmental standards that are lower than those used in China.

---

35. Mount Kilimanjaro, at a height of 5,895 metres, is often shrouded in cloud for days or weeks at a time and the snow-capped summit is completely obscured from view. Hence, early explorers doubted native tales of its existence until they saw it with their own eyes on one of its brief appearances from the mist.

> *"He has sent me to bring the good news to the poor, to proclaim liberty to captives and to the blind new sight, to set the downtrodden free."*
> — Luke 4:18

Mr Gore finishes the film by asking "Are you ready to change the way you live?" It appears to me that this question is one that we must all take on board in every aspect of our lives—as workers, as owners or users of homes, other property and cars, as managers of businesses, as managers of county and borough councils, as politicians, as consumers, as tourists, as leisure users and as disposers of waste. No doubt, this is not an exhaustive list of the areas in which we must take action. Certainly, we must not say to ourselves that "what I do, or don't do, doesn't matter." Of course it matters, and one multiplied by millions matters greatly. Governments, including our own, have of course very special responsibilities in this whole area. One has I believe reason to be optimistic that our present Government will act decisively to deal with the problems of climate change, not just at national level, but at local level and at the level of certain state bodies. Furthermore, the members of Government should themselves show the way forward for individual action.

Despite all the warnings about global warming, there are still those who say there is no basis for the concern being expressed. I happened to read a newspaper article recently where the writer was suggesting that we had no need to worry about climate change, as the changes in climatic conditions now taking place are simply due to natural cyclical phenomena. However, the writer did not convince me and I was pleased therefore to have the opportunity shortly afterwards to read an offering on the same subject from a scientist that I have the highest regard for, that is Professor William Reville, Associate Professor of Biochemistry and Public Awareness of Science Officer at University College Cork. Professor Reville is a columnist with the *Irish Times* and had an article in that newspaper on climate change and related matters on August 9th, 2007. The editorial of the same day supported the Professor's remarks.

Professor Reville's article concentrates on the fourth report[36] published in February 2007 report from the Inter-governmental Panel on Climate Control (IPCC) and the argument that global warming (a matter which itself is not in dispute) is not caused by human activities. The IPCC report, he suggests "removes any lingering doubt on the latter point" reporting that "it is 'very likely' (i.e. the probability is more than 90 per cent), that global warming is caused by human

---

36. Professor Reville notes that the IPCC was formed in 1988 to assess scientific information on climate change and that the current report is the fourth report (the first three reports were in 1990, 1995 and 2001 respectively) issued by the IPCC since its formation.

activities, primarily from the burning of fossil fuel." Some of the damage done by greenhouse gases is irreversible and even if greenhouse gas emission was stopped now, "the world would continue to warm somewhat"; however, this is not a reason for inaction and he reminds us that it is still possible to "do something about the longer -term effects of this problem, but, we had better get cracking on this right away or we will bequeath an awful problem to our children."

The evidence of the IPCC reports is, according to Professor Reville, "overwhelming." Firstly, the world is definitely warming; the 2001 report estimated a warming trend of between 0.40 and 0.80 degrees from 1901 to 2000 while the 2007 report updates the estimate to between 0.56 and 0.92 degrees for the period from 1906 to 2005. Secondly, this warming is clearly accelerating as demonstrated by the rise in the estimate in the 2007 report, a trend confirmed by estimates that suggest that "the bulk of 20th-century warming occurred in the last 50 years."[37] Further supporting this is the statement in the 2007 report that 11 of the past 12 years are the warmest since 1850, when reliable records began; Professor Reville suggests that "the odds of such warm sequential years happening by chance are miniscule."

As regards the argument that global warming is unrelated to human and industrial activity, the IPCC report is unequivocal. Professor Reville reports that it concludes that around 90% of global warming is the result of human emissions of greenhouse gases with just 10% related to changes in solar activity. Concentrations of carbon dioxide, methane and nitrous oxide, which had remained stable in the earth's atmosphere for 19,000 years, started to increase rapidly around the year 1800 and carbon dioxide levels today are 35 per cent greater than pre-industrial levels. In order to arrive at these conclusions, the IPCC (according to Professor Reville) "reviewed all studies of changes in positive and negative radiative forces (influences that cause the world's climate to grow warmer or colder) over the past 200 years" and found the greatest warming forces to be the long-lived greenhouse gases (carbon dioxide, methane, nitrous oxide and halocarbons) with carbon dioxide by far the most significant of these forces.

The IPCC report, like Al Gore's film, found this warming world to be showing many symptoms. Professor Reville notes that these include rising sea levels (between 2.4 and 3.8mm per year since 1978), decreasing ice in the Artic Sea (which shows a reduction of between 2.1% and 3.3% per decade since 1978), decreased spring snow cover in northern mid-latitudes, shrunken glaciers and ice sheets, and increased rainfall in several major regions (including northern Europe) while rainfall has decreased elsewhere (including across South Africa). Surmising as to how global warming will affect Europe, Professor Reville suggests that likely consequences are flash flooding in inland areas, health threatening heat waves and wildfires in Southern Europe (with associated water shortages and difficul-

---

37. Professor Reville notes that the estimate for the 1956–2005 period alone is 0.50 to 0.80 degrees.

> *"I am the vessel. The draft is God's. And God is the thirsty one."*
> — Dag Hammarskjold

ties in crop production), lower rainfall, the spread of new infectious diseases (like malaria), and flooding of low-lying areas. He believes that "some or all of these" changes will arrive by 2080 and concludes that "if temperature increase is not slowed, it will overwhelm us."

Ireland cannot escape the consequences of such global warming. In fact the Environmental Protection Agency report *Key Meteorological Indications of Climate Change in Ireland* (written by Dr. John Sweeney and Dr. Laura McElwain and launched on August 29th, 2007) concludes that Ireland warmed up by 0.42 degrees per decade between 1980 and 2004. This is almost twice the level of the average global increase.

Concern about global warming appears to be accelerating rapidly. Francis Jacobs, head of the EU Parliament Office in Dublin has stated that "the United Nations believes climate change is a big a threat as global war."[38] Meanwhile the government strategy document produced in April 2007 asserted that "reducing greenhouse gases is a global priority and requires committed international action and cooperation" and commits itself to "contribute fully" to the achievement of targets that have been set at EU level (*National Climate Change Strategy 2007-2012*, p. 4). I believe it is important in this regard that Ireland does not merely rate itself against other countries or justify its failure to meet targets by pointing out that others have similarly failed;[39] rather we must all cooperate in order to meet (and ideally exceed) our targets. In the context of international cooperation and the fact that climate change is no respecter of borders, it has been noted that "Africa produces less pollution than any other continent but is most at risk from climate change – and is the least equipped to deal with it" (Frank McDonald (Environmental Editor), *Irish Times*, November 18th, 2006).

However, we must remind ourselves that, as environmental author, Mark Lynas, has pointed out, the trend of global warming is reversible. Interviewed by Brian O'Connell, Mark Lynas has suggested that if we fail to act "temperatures could rise by 6 degrees this century" (*Irish Times*, March 17th, 2007). Mark Lynas spells out in his interview the potentially catastrophic implications each degree increase in temperature which, he suggests are as follows:

---

38. Mr. Jacobs was speaking at the Institute of Technology, Sligo, as reported in the Sligo Champion newspaper of 9th May, 2007
39. I refer here to the Taoiseach's statement that "we are also committed to a reduction of 30% by 2020 *provided that other developed countries undertake comparable reductions and the more advanced developing countries make a contribution in line with their capabilities*" (emphasis added, *National Climate Change Strategy 2007-2012*, p. 4).

- + 2 Degrees Coral reefs almost extinct
- + 3 Degrees Rainforest turns to desert
- + 4 Degrees Melting ice caps displaces millions
- + 5 Degrees Sea levels rise by five metres
- + 6 Degrees Most of life is exterminated

With such a scenario before us, it is imperative that we act now. Some have suggested that the use of petrol and diesel should be replaced with biofuels; others, such as George Monbiot, have argued that biofuels are not a solution. He suggests that "oil produced from plants set up competition for food between cars and people," a situation where people and the environment will be the losers, and goes on to argue that "biodiesel from palm oil causes 10 times as much climate change as diesel" (quoted from "Motor News" section, *Irish Times*, April 11th, 2007).

Perhaps biofuels are not the way forward, but I am not competent to make a judgement thereon. The important issue, which is very clear to me, is that the rate at which we are consuming fossil fuels is not sustainable and no alternative fuel appears to be readily available. Thus we all have to take steps to seriously reduce our carbon footprints, starting now. This can only be done by being aware of the consequences of everyday activities—driving to the supermarket, buying food which has been transported from overseas, being careless about energy usage—and changing our behaviour accordingly.

The need to adapt our behaviour for environmental reasons has become a political issue, indeed the high profile of the Green Party in recent years is a direct result of greater public concern with this issue. As Trevor Sargent noted at the 2007 Green Party Conference, "stopping climate change was a matter of basic human rights [...] We don't inherit the earth from our parents. We borrow it from our children". (*Irish Times*, 26 February, 2007). A similar sentiment was expressed by Professor William Reville in his article "Persuading ourselves that it's not too late to save the planet" and he goes on to consider the difficult issue of motivating people to take action:

> If we do nothing these awful consequences will not kick in next year, they will gradually develop over decades, but come they will and our children will certainly inherit them. The only sane reaction to this situation is to make reduction of greenhouse gas emissions a top priority both at Government and individual citizen level. But, the reality is that while we hear much concern expressed about global warming, that seems to be largely theoretical and is not being translated into gut-level feelings that would motivate effective action. There is a big job to be done to motivate people to take this action on climate change [...] For me, the thought of bequeathing a sick planet to our children is the single biggest factor motivating me to take some action on climate change.
>
> (*Irish Times*, 13 September, 2007)

> "The only wisdom that we can hope to acquire is the wisdom of humility."
> — T.S. Eliot

I believe that Professor William Reville in the above and earlier writings has analysed the climate change issues in a most competent and logical manner. His conclusion that the Government and individual citizens must make the "reduction of greenhouse gas emissions a top priority" cannot, I submit, be disputed. So let us all start **now** to take the appropriate steps, even though some may be uncomfortable for us.

A blazing skyline at sunset

Keem Bay, Achill

High up at the 'look out' point over Keem Bay

Benbulben in all its glory

Glencar Lake

A beach vista of Benbulben

Benbulben from another angle

ENVIRONMENTAL ISSUES

Snow capped Benbulben

A beautiful winter scene along the Diffreen River, Co. Leitrim

Making the most of the snow

Another beautiful winter scene along the Drumcliffe River, Sligo

Part 7

Religion and Spirituality as Part of a Full Life

Preamble to Part 7

As a layman this is a somewhat difficult part of the book for me to write. You might well say that I have no qualifications to write on this subject, and in any event you might wonder why there should be a section on religion and spirituality in a book given over mostly to the more tangible things of life. If I was writing this book as a younger person, it is almost certain this section would not appear. It is as I grow older that I realise more potently the folly and the emptiness of living a life without a genuine religious and spiritual dimension. I always tried, within my many limitations, to practice my catholic faith and be a decent Christian, but I think now that I was often shallow in my commitment thereto. The material dimensions of life probably always attracted me, and possibly unduly so, and also I was probably less sensitive to the concerns and plight of others than I should have been as a genuine Christian. Possibly this realisation is all part of maturing, a process that I truly believe continues throughout our entire lives. I thank God that I have had the opportunity of growing older, and hopefully wiser, because not everybody gets this opportunity. Personally, I would have liked to have started this maturing process much earlier in life.

I have another reason for having a section on religion and spirituality in the book, and that is my concern at the apparent large scale falling-off in religious practices today, particularly among young adults and middle aged people. Possibly as a consequence, or partly so, of this falling-off in religious practices, there has been a very big increase in societal problems, such as the break-down of the family, over-indulgence in alcohol, drug taking, road deaths, suicide, and so on. Possibly these problems have arisen because of our new-found wealth as a nation and as individuals. I am certainly not decrying our new-found wealth, but I suggest we could use it and manage it much better in many instances. I feel a more genuine religious and spiritual dimension to our lives would give us more balance as individuals and thus help us to live more satisfying lives and be better citizens. Hence the title for this part of the book "Religion and Spirituality as Part of a Full Life."

You might be glad to hear that I won't personally be pontificating very much (although I do express some strong opinions) in what follows as I rely mainly on the writings and comments of others. These writings are ones that I have found particularly relevant in my own life's journey; perhaps you may also find them to be so.

CHAPTER SIXTEEN
The Material Dimension of Life, False Gods and Problem Issues

I think I am genuinely thankful that I am gone past the stage of raising a family, because doing so today is very difficult. Despite our wealth, the high cost of housing and the high cost of living is placing great financial strains on family life. Alongside this, the ever expanding horizons of children and teenagers for goods, services and freedom, makes the job of parenting very difficult indeed. The typical family situation today is frequently one where both parents are out working, possibly commuting long distances and often stressed-out when they get home, while children are spending much of the time on their own with free access to television and the internet (which are often in their own bedrooms) and sometimes loose parental control in regard to their socialising habits.

If I seem negative about today's younger generation, please forgive me; I think of young people as our hope for the future and feel that parenting is accordingly a most important responsibility, providing that bedrock for the future. Although I know of many parents doing a wonderful job of raising their children in today's more challenging environment, it seems to me that this is by no means universal. It would appear that many children's desires for goods and services must be met "now," so that the notion of earning them through apprenticeship or work is gone. I suggest that many of our children have very little to look forward to in life because they are exposed to so much at an early age. Their zest for life may even be affected by this. As a society, we surely need to consider the long-term implications of how today's consumerist environment may affect our children's development.

In addition to this, many families do not have time, or are not prepared to make time, for religion in their lives. Thus they fail to realise the immense satisfaction and fulfilment that a spiritual dimension to life can bring. Instead, in many cases, satisfaction and fulfilment is sought in false gods such as alcohol, drugs, sex, and so on. Our alarming high rates of suicide, road death, murder, and family breakdown is not something we can be proud of as a nation or as individuals. I think we must urgently take stock of where all of this is leading us to and get back to basics.

With regard to valuing the basics, the person I probably admire most of all for doing this is the late Father Edward Joseph Flanagan of Boys Town fame Nebraska, USA (a short section is devoted to Boys Town later on in the book). Father Flanagan was a native of Ballymoe, county Roscommon and a past pupil of Summerhill College, Sligo. A man who apparently had the ear of several American Presidents, he was a great visionary who, over ninety years ago, appeared to have been able to conceptualise precisely the problems facing youth, parents and the family problems which seem more current than ever in today's world. The following are some quotes from Father Flanagan's extensive writings:

- There are no bad boys. There is only bad environment, bad training, bad example, bad thinking.
- When parents fail to do their job, when they allow their children to run the streets [...] then the parents and not the children are the delinquents.
- Youth needs the force of good and attractive examples ... they are apt imitators. They may be easily led to follow where they cannot be driven.
- A life without discipline is like a ship without a rudder ...
- Nothing costs so little as a few words of recognition.
- Youth who have not been loved and protected are not likely to love others and protect the rights of others.
- Without religious faith there can be no lasting enthusiasm. Man cannot lift himself by tugging at his own bootstraps.
- Without God at the beginning, there can only be confusion at the end.
- No boy's education is complete until he has been taught to accept nothing from life except what he can win with his own hands. We all must work. We all have some job to do.
- The fact is that nothing earthly can fill the void in the human heart.
- Our young people are our greatest wealth. Give them a chance and they will give a good account of themselves.

(Quotes courtesy of Girls and Boys Town Hall of History, Omaha, Nebraska)

There is widespread concern about the problems we are experiencing in society today and I am by no means alone in linking some of these problems to the lack of religion in everyday life. A January 2007 *Sunday Tribune* poll found that 79% of Irish people agreed with a statement (originally made by Archbishop Sean Brady in an interview with the *Irish Times*) that there is "a growing coarseness and aggression" in Irish society (Quinn David, "Huge Majority").[40] David Quinn notes that the poll's results indicate that "concern about growing coarseness and aggression cuts across the rural-urban divide, different socio-economic groups as well as age groups" (ibid.). Archbishop Brady suggested that such coarseness and aggression

---

40. David Quinn, writing for the Irish Catholic, was reporting on Archbishop Brady's original interview with the Irish Times and the subsequent Sunday Tribune poll conducted after that interview.

> *"He who rejects discipline despises his own self;*
> *he who listens to correction wins discernment."*
>
> — Proverb 15:32

was evident "on the roads, in drinking, the increase in sexualisation of children at an earlier age, stress, excess generally" and has a "dehumanising" effect (ibid.). He cited the RTE show *Podge and Rodge* as "symbolic of an Ireland that is becoming more crass and vulgar" and said that there was "very deep concern, particularly by parents, about where we are going morally and spiritually" (ibid.). Moreover, he asserted that there was a link between the increased coarseness and aggression and "increased secularisation and the marginalisation of religion" (ibid.).

Such trends are also seen, not just in everyday life, but in the celebration of what used to be religious festivals. Father Vincent Twomey, Emeritus Professor of Moral Theology at St. Patrick's College, Maynooth recently lamented the way we celebrate St. Patrick's Day:

> In an increasing secularised and vulgarised country, 'Paddy's Week' is descending into an excuse for mindless alcohol-fuelled revelry. Must it be so? [...] It is time to reclaim St. Patrick's Day as a church festival, one that should have a special ecumenical perspective, since all Christians in Ireland trace the origins of their faith back to Patrick.
>
> (McGarry, Patsy, March 13th, 2007)[41]

A similar trend may be seen in our celebrations of Christmas where the material and consumerist aspects of the giving season often seem to eclipse the joyous religious commemoration of Christ's birth.

However, it is not only our religious leaders that are publicly voicing their concern about the effects of secularisation. In a speech given at Dublin Castle when launching a major new initiative that will for the first time see structured dialogue between the State and Churches, faith communities and non-confessional bodies, the Taoiseach, Bertie Ahern made the following contribution to the secularisaton debate:

> There is a form of aggressive secularism which would have the State and State institutions ignore the importance of the religious dimension. They argue that the State and public policy should become intolerant of religious belief and preference and confine it, at best, to the purely

---

41. Patsy McGarry, *Irish Times* Religious Affairs Correspondent, was reporting in that paper on Fr. Twomey's article in the then current edition of the *Word* magazine, of which Fr Twomey is editor.

private and personal, without rights or a role within the public domain. The illiberal voices harm democracy by denying a crucial dimension of the dignity of every person and their rights to live out their spiritual code within a framework of lawful practice, which is respectful of the dignity and rights of all citizens.

(reported by David Quinn in the *Irish Catholic*, March 1st, 2007)

I suggest that the foregoing comments by the Taoiseach are very significant and I hope they can be welcomed by all our citizens.

CHAPTER SEVENTEEN
The God Dimension and the Relevance of Religion and Spirituality

From time immemorial, numerous people have tried to prove that there is no God and no need to pay homage to a superior being. They all seemed to have failed to do so – there was always the problem of satisfactorily explaining how the world began, which leads to the question: Was there a prime mover and a grand designer? Perhaps the most well-known intervention to this debate in recent times was Richard Dawkins' book, *The God Delusion* (2006). Mr Dawkins, as is evident from his title, argues against the existence of God and got widespread media attention in his attempt to promote the claims and statements made in his book. I was particularly pleased to find that the highly respected *Irish Times* columnist (on science, religion and other subjects) Professor William Reville of University College Cork, who I referred to earlier in this book, was ready and willing to supply the other side of the argument.

Professor Reville characterises Dawkins as a "proselytising atheist and scientist […who] can brilliantly explain complex scientific concepts to a general audience" but laments that, in *The God Delusion*, Dawkins only "displays this ability in patches […and] all too often he lapses into cynical rhetorical dismissal of his adversary" (*Irish Times*, Jan 4th, 2007). Although, Professor Reville notes, Dawkins holds the position of Oxford University Professor of the Public Understanding of Science his opposition to religion is a matter of personal opinion rather than the official stance of science on this matter. According to Professor Reville, other equally eminent scientists have opposite opinions and he gives the example of Harvard evolutionary biologist Stephen Jay Gould who argues that "science and religion operate out of 'non overlapping magisteria' and that science has nothing to say about religion" (ibid.). Similarly, Francis Collins, who is leading the American venture to sequence the human genome is a devout Christian whose book, *The Language of God*, explains that religion and science can be entirely compatible. Interestingly, Collins' book was published in the same year as Dawkins but got significantly less publicity; like Al Gore's film, it may contain what for many is an inconvenient truth.

According to Professor Reville, approximately 40% of scientists believe in God, some of whom "are the most famous who ever lived, which naturally irritates the hell out of Dawkins" (*Irish Times*, Jan 4th, 2007). Albert Einstein is a case in point; Professor Reville notes that although "Dawkins goes to considerable lengths to convince us that Einstein was really an atheist who used poetic language," Einstein's position appeared "to hover between deism and pantheism"[42] (ibid.). Dawkins is, Professor Reville suggests, at his worst when dismissing pre-modern proofs of God's existence, being "ignorantly contemptuous of St. Thomas Aquinas and St. Anselm" (ibid.). Thomas Aquinas (1225–1274) used reason to argue for God's existence, conceiving of a being "who created a world with its own ordering and processes," a development that "prepared the ground for the development of the natural sciences in the later Middle Ages" (ibid.). St. Anselm (1033-1109) famously argued for the existence of God in 1078, stating that "it is possible to conceive of a being greater than whom nothing can be conceived. Such a being must therefore exist since existence is greater than non-existence" (ibid.). This is an argument which has challenged philosophers for centuries yet Dawkins dismisses it out of hand.

Dawkins is critical of the many excesses of fundamentalism (from suicide bombers to creationism) and, as Professor Reville points out, although "all moderate religious people would agree with him here" this is hardly a justification for rejecting all religion (*Irish Times*, Jan 4th, 2007). Professor Reville contends that Dawkins' reasoning (that moderate religion makes the world 'safe' for extreme religion by endorsing faith) is wrong and would, if applied generally, result in us getting "rid of many good things because of the extreme behaviour of the few"; he suggests that applying a similar logic to science would, on the basis that science has given the world nuclear and biological weapons, result in the clearly nonsensical decision to abolish science entirely (ibid.). Professor Reville concludes that the "best weapon to use against fundamentalism is moderate religion" and that "Dawkins only distracts moderate religion from its task" (ibid.). He suggests that Dawkins might better apply his talents to "the new secular religion of political correctness (PC) which has silently taken over public life in recent decades?" (ibid.).

As one might expect, Professor Reville has given a very comprehensive rebuttal to Professor Dawkin's *The God Delusion*, and in the process has given us very good theology as to the existence of God. Professor Reville's reference to political correctness (PC) is most noteworthy. I personally consider political correctness to be a cancer in our society today, eating away at practically every value system and traditional cultural norm we have, or had. If this trend continues, soon we will not be able to stand for anything and we will become a baseless society.

In the debate over the existence of God and the argument that evolution disproves such existence, Pope Benedict's new book *Creation and Evolution* has made a useful contribution to the debate. In his book the Pope has been somewhat

---

42. Deism is a belief in the existence of a supreme being based on reason and personal experience, while pantheism is the belief that God is identifiable with the forces of nature.

> *"Lord I commend my past to your mercy, my future to your providence, and my present to your love."*
> — St. Padre Pio's prayer

critical of evolutionary theory suggesting that it is "not a complete, scientifically verified theory" (quoted by Derek Scally, *Irish Times*, April 12th, 2007). He suggests that it is "in large part not experimentally verifiable because we cannot bring 10,000 generations into a laboratory" which leaves "considerable gaps in experimental verification […] as a result of the incredible timeframe which the theory addresses" (ibid.). According to Derek Scally, the Pope "dismissed the idea of 'nature' or 'evolution' as an active subject in itself" arguing that "evolutionary progression […] suggested a pre-evolutionary "creative rationality" or God" (ibid.).

Such creative rationality makes sense when we consider the vast differences between humankind and the animal kingdom. In this regard, I quote the unpublished comments of a learned friend of mine from Sligo, Frank Murphy, concerning what differentiates humans from animals:

> Man has a dual nature, animal and spiritual. It is because of his spiritual nature that we call him human. The animal nature is motivated by instinct; the spiritual by logic and reason. The two natures, each having a distinct motivation, can sometimes be in conflict, so the harmony of the human being requires that each be subjected to an element of discipline. Instinct is innate and therefore difficult to change, but the spiritual nature has tremendous capacity for development.
>
> One of the problems of today's society is that we are losing our capacity to think. We are too inclined to accept what we receive from the mass media without critical analysis. We have introduced through our schools, programmes which suggest that 'all actions should be guided by feelings'. Even a cursory examination would suggest otherwise. Feelings are subjective emotions and may derive from instinct rather than from logic and reason.
>
> We see every day greater examples of man's inhumanity to man, such as in the increase in violent crime. If we fail to develop our spiritual nature, our animal nature will dominate and we will end up with the law of the jungle, which is the survival of the fittest.

I would like to add to Frank Murphy's most competent comments, that we humans have the ability to smile whereas animals do not. What a pity that we don't smile more; a smile can make a huge difference to the day of both the receiver and the giver! Incidentally, I understand that research has shown that religious people are happier in life than those who are not religious. Perhaps it is that they are less likely to seek excessive happiness in material things that can never really satisfy, and can never provide a basis for the permanent smile or inner happiness that is associated with a deep faith.

It has been suggested that when we are well off materially there is a tendency to feel independent of God and religion, and the Cross of Christ becomes irrelevant. Perhaps, in this regard we should not ignore Luke's Gospel:

> There was once a rich man who, having had a good harvest from his land, thought to himself, "What am I to do? I have not enough room to store my crops". Then he said, "This is what I will do: I will pull down my barns and build bigger ones, and store all my grain and goods in them, and I will say to my soul: My soul, you have plenty of good things laid by for many years to come; take things easy, eat, drink, have a good time". But God said to him, "Fool! This very night the demand will be made for your soul; and this hoard of yours, whose will it be then?"
> (Luke, 12: 13-21)

Obviously, we have to be concerned with the material things of life also, and we would be expected to make wise decisions in relation to our financial and material affairs and those of our dependents. It is a question of getting the balance right, i.e. the balance between the spiritual dimension and the material dimension. Work is generally thought of only in its material dimension. If we only could remember that work done and offered up in the right frame of mind, no matter how exalted or humble the work may be, can be a most powerful prayer and spiritual exercise. The notion of service to those around us comes into play here, as indeed does service to God. Unfortunately, we so often fail to think of these dimensions of work.

World Religious Adherence

Although it seems to be the case that religious adherence is in decline in Ireland and generally so in Europe as well, this is by no means a global trend. Richard Whelan[43] notes that although Irish and European trends might lead one to believe that worldwide "faith is wilting in the face of modernity and rational scepticism" but on the contrary "in the rest of the world religious belief and practice is flourishing" (*Irish Catholic*, March 1st, 2007). Whelan notes that the percentage of the world's population affiliated to one of the four main religions (Catholicism, Protestantism, Islam, or Hinduism) rose from 50% at the start of the 20th century to almost 64% at the start of the 21st century. He reports that it is estimated "that this

---

43. Richard Whelan is the author of *Al-Qaedaism: The Threat to Islam, The Threat to the World*, published in 2005.

> *"Man cannot live without joy; therefore when he is deprived of true spiritual joy, it is necessary that he become addicted to carnal pleasures."*
> — St. Thomas Aquinas

figure will be close to 70% by 2025" and further points out that as these statistics omit other religions, actual religious observance is significantly higher than the figures reported (ibid.). He cites the World Values Survey (which surveys sample populations throughout 85% of the world) as confirming that religious belief is growing, a finding confirmed by the research of Ronald Inglehart and Pippa Norris (ibid.).[44] Richard Whelan concludes that these finding have two implications:

> First, what is happening currently in the EU in general, and in Ireland in particular, is not the norm in religious observance and is likely to be reversed. Second the dimly understood need for an "other" dimension in all our lives, beyond that of secular modernity, "retail therapy" or our growing drug dependence, becomes more evident and necessary by the day.
>
> (*Irish Catholic*, March 1st, 2007)

Religious Freedom in Ireland

Apart from the Taoiseach's comments (see previous chapter) on aggressive secularism, other public figures have also made welcome statements on the need for religious freedom. One such figure is Martin Mansergh[45] who in February 2007 "stoutly defended the principle of religious freedom" in a Seanad exchange (*Irish Catholic* editorial, March 1st, 2007). As both a politician and a member of a minority religion (the Church of Ireland), he is well-placed to understand the complex intersection between the personal and the public in matters of religion. The *Irish Catholic* editorial noted the significance of his position:

> If he was a catholic he could easily, although certainly wrongly, be accused of wanting to restore the Catholic Church to its former 'special position' in Irish life. But as a member of the Church of Ireland, he cannot be so accused. In fact, as such he will be particularly sensitive to the needs of minority groups, and to why minority groups are best

---

44. Inglehart and Norris are the authors of *Sacred and Secular: Politics and Religion Worldwide* published by Cambridge University Press in 2004.
45. Martin Mansergh is now a TD, having been elected in May 2007; he was, at the time of the comments reported here, a senator.

protected in a pluralist society, one that respects all points of view.

But he is also very aware that a genuinely pluralist, liberal society, must respect religious freedom. Religious freedom means, among other things, allowing faith-based organisations to operate according to their ethos within the confines of a liberal Constitution.

As Senator Mansergh argued in the Seanad last week, this means not forcing Church-run adoption agencies to consider gay couples as prospective adoptive parents. It also means not forcing Church-run crises pregnancy agencies such as Cura to compromise their ethos by having to hand out contact details for organisations that will provide phone numbers of abortion clinics.

The Progressive Democrat's 2007 annual conference also discussed the issue of religious freedom. The then Tánaiste and Minister for Justice, Michael McDowell, told delegates that, as a liberal republican party, they should "honour and respect religious practice and conviction [...and] deal with the Churches as partners in social action, not as usurpers of some kind of liberal, secular republican view of society" (quoted by Michael Kelly, *The Irish Catholic*, February 22nd, 2007). He also referred to the key role of "the family, school and faith community [...in] social cohesion and imparting values" (ibid.). Michael Kelly points out that these comments represented something of a turnaround for a party which adopted an extremely secular line when it was founded in 1986 and indicated "that the PDs now want a more friendly relationship with the Church" (ibid.).

The *Irish Catholic* columnist David Quinn,[46] who addressed the PD conference, suggested that the decline of religion and family were linked to Ireland's social problems and advised them that "your party must have a very carefully worked out family policy [...] cognisant of the fact that there are still very good, very rational reasons, for supporting marriage above all, while not neglecting any family in need" (quoted by Michael Kelly, *The Irish Catholic*, February 22nd, 2007). He further advised them that the party needed "a new attitude towards the Church, a word I use in the broadest sense" and that there was "no necessary clash between this ambition, and Progressive Democrat ideology" (ibid.).

The PDs have long been thought of as a party with a primarily economic agenda. Perhaps their softening attitude towards the Church is the start of a more general acknowledgement that religion is an important part of our lives. Bishop Donal Murray has recently pointed out the dangers of a secularised society:[47]

---

46. David Quinn is also Director of the Iona Institute, a non-governmental organisation dedicated to the strengthening of civil society through making the case for marriage and religious practice.
47. Bishop Donal Murray is the Bishop of Limerick and was addressing a conference on Europe and Religion held in Dublin in 2007.

> *"A glad heart is excellent medicine,
> a spirit depressed wastes the bones away."*
> — Proverb 17:22

> A secularised society comes to think of itself more as a State, or an economy, or a legislative and administrative framework than a community of persons. Because there is no common attention to the fundamental questions of the meaning and purpose of human life, the criteria of success and failure and the goals of social life become divorced from the genuine growth of human relationships and of human persons.
> (reported in the *Irish Catholic*, May 24th 2007, p. 7)

Bishop Murray suggests that Irish Christians, rather than becoming demoralised by society's relegation of faith to a position of little importance, should seek to cultivate a feeling of belonging "to a vibrant, supportive community with, a mission, a community which cannot regard its faith as a, mere private possession" (p. 7). He suggests that today's challenge is that of St. Paul and hopes that Ireland can play a role in responding to this challenge:

> 'Do not be conformed to this world but be transformed by the renewal of your mind that you prove what is the will of God, what is good and acceptable and perfect'. That is the challenge of religious identity in Europe. Perhaps Ireland will have a leading role in responding to the challenge—that is up to us—but I hope that we will at least participate creatively in the essential process of giving a soul to twenty-first century Europe. (p. 7)

Pope Benedict XVI

Perhaps it is fitting to finish this chapter with comments from Pope Benedict XVI, as reported in the February 2007 issue of the *Alive* newspaper. One of the themes of his address was that obedience to God's law increases rather than limits people's freedom and happiness. He stated that "the moral law which God gave us has the aim not of oppressing us but of freeing us from evil and of making us happy," arguing that "without God man is lost" while the exclusion of religion from social life, far from providing freedom, "undermines the very foundations of life together" (p.3).

The Pope pointed out that secularity has come to mean "a total separation between State and Church, with the Church having no right to intervene in questions concerning the life and behaviour of citizens," promoting an a-religious approach to life and leaving no place for God. He has suggested that this view of secularity be replaced with one which respects *both* "the legitimate autonomy of earthly affairs" and the place of "God and his moral law, Christ and his Church" (p.3). He argues that hostility towards expressions of religion in public institutions is a "degenerated form of secularity" and insists that Christians and their representatives should not be prevented from pronouncing "on the moral problems that today face the conscience of all human beings, especially legislators" (p.3). Rather than have this regarded as undue interference in State matters, it should be seen as "the affirmation and the defence of those values that give meaning to people's lives and safeguard their dignity" (p.3). The Church's role is to proclaim the truth and the good news. Pope Benedict has made many apt utterances in his short pontificate to-date and the foregoing are surely further examples thereof.

CHAPTER EIGHTEEN
Some Deeper Reflections on Religious Practices

Much of this chapter will be based on extracts from *Bible Alive*, a monthly magazine published in the UK and which has a wide circulation around the world, including Ireland.[48] It is a great favourite with a wide cross-section of people, containing daily reflections on one or more of the Scripture readings for each day of the month and sometimes commentary on saints whose feast day it may be. In addition, two to three feature articles are included in each monthly issue, often dealing with the heroic deeds of various people, lives lived in the service of others or faith conversions. The daily reflections are useful both for those who want to reflect further on their readings of the Bible and for those who might find reading the Bible difficult.

One group who find *Bible Alive* to be of particular use are prisoners and the November 2006 issue had a feature article on this topic. The editor noted that "through the generosity of our readers over the last ten years we have been sending *Bible Alive*, Bibles, books and other Christian resources to encourage prisoners in their faith" and had been greatly impressed with the prisoner's responses. In the context of rehabilitation, the editor reminds us that it is not only prisoners who need to be converted:

> The gospel is about transformation, change, conversion, new life and being a new creation. The road of conversion is one we are all called to walk—we are all sinners, we are all beggars, we all need God's mercy.

The prisoner's testimonials attest to the comfort that God's mercy offers and some of them refer to the daily reflections, which must surely offer hope in their difficult lives. I have quoted some of these testimonials as follows:

> *Bible Alive* has made a massive difference to my life, and given me great comfort which I have not had for a lot of years even before I came to prison.

---

48. *Bible Alive* can be purchased in Ireland, from Bible Alive, PO Box 10, Navan, Co. Meath. At the time of writing, the annual subscription is €28.95.

Being newly introduced to the love of our Lord I am finding reading *Bible Alive* very eye-opening and fulfilling. The love of our Lord for me has been of great comfort to me in troubled times.

I would like to thank all those who make it possible for us young people to receive copies of *Bible Alive*. It is good for us here in the prison to realise that we are not forgotten by others while we are in prison. I am very grateful to Bible Alive.

I know the Lord wants to help me rebuild my life. The Lord helps me with the problems I face and incur because of my behaviour and attitude. *Bible Alive* is a very big part of my spiritual life.

Bible Alive means a lot to me because it gives me strength to carry on each day and I like to read it from day to day.

I find that reading *Bible Alive* when I have a down spell often lifts me and puts our little personal issues in perspective.

Bible Alive gives me encouragement and support during a very difficult time in my life.

For the remainder of this section, I have taken extracts from particular daily reflections in *Bible Alive* (and occasionally other publications) that I have found particularly useful. I have grouped these by theme so that the reader can dip in and out of them as they wish. Daily reflections are referenced by date only, appropriate details are given for other articles.

A. God's Love for Us

Out of love and humility the Son of God became a man in the person of Jesus. It is hard, if not impossible, to find an analogy to unpack the significance of the incarnation. C. S. Lewis considered that it was rather like one of us becoming a slug to redeem and save all slugs – not a very flattering analogy, one has to admit! However, what is clear is that at the heart of the Blessed Trinity is overwhelming love, revealed in Jesus who 'did not consider equality with God a thing to be grasped, but emptied himself, taking the form of a servant, being born in the likeness of men' (Philippians 2: 6-7)

November 7th, 2006

For him [Paul] the gospel is deeply rooted in God's love, mercy and kindness. We could never earn or deserve salvation: it is pure gift. And as if this weren't enough, we have also received another gift—perhaps the greatest gift of all—the Holy Spirit (Titus 3: 5). St. Paul had a gospel vision—do you?

November 15th, 2006

Do you ever have bad days?

Well, join the human race because, of course, we all have bad days and things often don't seem to go right! The question is: What is the Christian response to these ordinary, very human situations?

We deal with life's difficulties by reminding ourselves of the most amazing and life-changing truth which St. John brings to our attention today: 'How great is the love the Father has lavished on us, that we should be called children of God! And that is what we are! (3:1 NIV)

'God loves each of us as if there were only one of us'. (St. Augustine)

January 3rd, 2007

The Parable of the Prodigal Son is a masterpiece and offers us a profound and life-changing insight into the heart of God the Father.

March 10th, 2007

B. Faith

Paul's faith in Christ gave him a blessing and grace which is actually available to us all. His faith in Christ opened up to him the secret of being content in whatever situation he faced. 'I have learned the secret of facing plenty and hunger, abundance and want' (Philippians 2: 12)

Today we celebrate the memorial of St. Martin of Tours, a man who like Paul had learnt the secret of being content in any and all situations

November 11th, 2006

How would you define faith? How about this definition: 'Now faith is the assurance of things hoped for, the conviction of things not seen' (Hebrews 11, verse 1).This may seem to kick against the seeing-is-believing philosophy of our day, but does it in actual fact? We don't see electricity but we believe in it; we don't see the cash in the hole in the wall but we believe it's there; we don't see radio waves but we can hear the sound they produce.

[…] faith is a gift. This is not to say that our reason does not have an important part to play – the beauty of the created world testifies to the design of the good Creator. Even scientists are forced to admit that there is a creative design to the universe

January 27th, 2007

We should cherish the gift of faith. If you have it, you are blessed. If you don't yet have it but would like to, all you need to do is ask God who gives generously to all without finding fault.

February 12th, 2007

The wonderful thing about the Christian faith is that we believe in the resurrection of the body and the soul. As St. Paul explains very beautifully in 1 Corinthians 15: 42-44, there will be a bodily resurrection: 'What is sown is perishable, what is raised is imperishable …'

The transfiguration of Jesus, about which we read in today's Gospel, is a promise that one day our own bodies will shine with the radiant beauty of Christ. It provides us, if you like, with a glimpse of heaven, where our raised bodies will be infused and radiated with God's life, beauty and holiness.

February 17th, 2007

Faith is the currency of the kingdom of God. We need faith to enter it and we need faith to live in it. We must always resist the notion, however, that faith is unreasonable or unrealistic – it is not. Faith works alongside our reason, and so reason informs faith and faith purifies reason.

God created us with free will – we can choose to believe in Jesus or reject him. To remain indifferent to Jesus is to reject him. There is no neutral ground.

March 30th, 2007

C. Salvation

Reflecting on the gift of salvation St. Margaret Mary Alacoque wrote: We cannot be saved without a struggle, for this life is a continual warfare. But be of good courage, do not be disheartened or troubled about your faults, but always try to draw from them a sense of your need of God and his mercy which must never be absent from your heart.

November 15th, 2006

Life is one long temptation. We all have different weaknesses, different Achilles heels, but no one is immune from the onslaught of being tempted to sin, to give way and fall. It can be any number of things …

We should turn our temptations on their head by thinking differently about them. Instead of seeing them as opportunities for sin, we should view them as moments of grace. They are sent not to weaken us but to strengthen us.

February 25th, 2007

D. Pilgrims

We are pilgrims, we are on our way to our Father's house, we are passing through this world on our way to the next. Our life is a brief moment when compared with eternity.

January 2nd, 2007

E. The Meaning of Life

What is life all about? What really is its meaning, its essence and its purpose? These are huge questions, but they need to be answered because otherwise life is meaningless, without purpose and consequently futile.

As St. Paul says, if life and faith are meaningless and futile: 'Let us eat and drink for tomorrow we die' (1 Cor. 15:32). Indeed, many people base their lives on this overriding philosophy. We need to be clear that the gospel offers a robust and unambiguous message that life is not futile or meaningless but finds its purpose, dignity and destiny not in a philosophy, or a way of life, or an ethic, but in a person – and this person is Jesus Christ our Lord, the Son of God, the Second Person of the Blessed Trinity, the God-Man, our Saviour.

January 6th, 2007

F. Jesus is the Key

Jesus is the key, meaning and purpose of human existence. […] Jesus is the answer to every question! He is the purpose, meaning and essence of human life. In Jesus salvation is brought within our reach – only the eternal son of God could redeem and save us

January 9th, 2007

At his hour, at the cross, Jesus transformed everything and his death and resurrection gave birth to the new wine of the new humanity [gospel reading today was about Cana and changing water into wine]. The human race was born again and we drank the wine from the cup of the new covenant in the Eucharist sealed in his blood.

January 14th, 2007

We can harbour ways of thinking about Jesus which suggest that it was somehow easy for him. Hebrews corrects this false impression by bringing us in touch with the interior struggle the Lord must have engaged in moment by moment in order not to sin. He had to pray to his Father for the grace to resist temptation because he was tempted in every way that we are but did not sin (Hebrews 5, verses

7-10). Jesus had to offer up loud cries and prayers to his father – we certainly see this in the Garden of Gethsemane, but in fact the Lord lived like this every day. If he had succumbed, if he had just given into one angry, rebellious or selfish thought, our salvation would have been lost. This must have been a real possibility, which is why the best and only response is to pray.

January 15th, 2007

For St. Luke Jesus' ministry began when he visited the synagogue in his home town of Nazareth. He read to the congregation … The passage Jesus read was Isaiah 61:1-2, which speaks about one on whom the Spirit of the Lord would rest, who would be anointed and who would proclaim the 'good news'. For St. Luke the 'good news' was freedom for the prisoner, sight to the blind, release for the oppressed and a declaration of the Lord's blessing and favour.

Luke saw in Jesus the 'ministry of inclusion' and his message constantly challenges us to reach out to just such people because the good news is that all are cherished children of God.

January 21st, 2007

The Church has one fundamental question to ask every single human being and that question is: who do you say Jesus is? The answer to this question is vital because in Jesus we have God's definitive answer for the human race. Jesus is the way, the truth and the life; he is the resurrection and the life; and he is the gateway from death into eternal life.

January 28th, 2007

To ignore Jesus is to ignore eternal life.

May 5th, 2007

Jesus is the only name through which we may be saved (Acts 4: 12).

May 15th, 2007

G. Death and Heaven

'Every action of yours, every thought, should be those of one who expects to die before the day is out. Death would have no great terrors for you if you had a quiet conscience … Then why not keep clear of sin instead of running away from death? If you aren't fit to face death today, it's very unlikely you will be tomorrow' (St. Thomas a Kempis).

March 19th, 2007

Death is a fact of life […] Death is the great leveller – no one is exempt.

> "There is a gentle breeze if we can catch it, which blows all the time to help us on our journey through life to our destination. That breeze is the Holy Spirit. But the wind cannot be caught or used unless the sail is hoisted, and the hoisting is our task."
> — Cardinal Basil Hume

Evangelical atheists such as Richard Dawkins and Stephen Hawkins believe that the goal of human life is to pass on our DNA and then die! […] The philosopher Bertrand Russell believed that life was a journey into oblivion and wrote rather depressingly: 'There is darkness without and when I die there will be darkness within. There is no splendour, no vastness, anywhere; only triviality, for a moment and then darkness'. The converted atheist C.S. Lewis, in contrast, wrote amusingly about an atheist's epithet: 'Here lies an atheist all dressed up but with nowhere to go, I bet he wishes that were so'.

We can however, by God's grace, approach death with faith, hope and love. For us death is not the end; it is, in fact, the beginning and the gateway into life and life to the full.

'Life is to live in such a way that we are not afraid to die. Everything seems to me to pass so quickly … that we must concentrate our thoughts on how to die rather than how to live'. (St. Teresa of Avila)

January 10th, 2007

On the issue of how marriage and family life is transformed after death and in heavenly life, Fr. Raniero Cantalamessa, OFM, who is the preacher to the Vatican offers some very useful and comforting reflections.

> Does the death of a husband or wife, which brings about the legal end of marriage, also bring with it the total end of communion between the two persons? Does something of that bond which so strongly united the two persons on earth remain in heaven, or will all be forgotten once we have crossed the threshold into eternal life?
>
> Jesus' opponents present Jesus with the unlikely case of a woman who was successively the wife of seven brothers, asking him whose wife she would be after the resurrection. Jesus answered: "When they rise from the dead they will neither marry or be given in marriage but will be like angels in heaven" (verse. 35) [Luke 20].
>
> Interpreting this saying of Jesus wrongly, some have claimed that marriage will have no follow-up in heaven. But with his reply Jesus is rejecting the caricature the Sadducees presented of heaven, as if it were

going to be a simple continuation of the earthly relation of the spouses. Jesus does not exclude the possibility that they might rediscover in God the bond that united them on earth.

According to this vision, marriage does not come to a complete end at death but is transfigured, spiritualized, freed from the limits that mark life on earth, as also the ties between parents and children or between friends will not be forgotten. In a preface for the dead the liturgy proclaims: 'Life is transformed, not taken away'. Even marriage, which is part of life, will be transfigured, not nullified. But what about those who have had a negative experience of earthly marriage, an experience of misunderstanding and suffering?

Should not this idea that the marital bond will not break at death be for them, rather than a consolation, a reason for fear? No, for in the passage from time to eternity the good remains and evil falls away. The love that united them, perhaps only for a brief time, remains; defects, misunderstandings, suffering that they inflicted on each other, will fall away.

This very suffering, accepted with faith, will be transformed into glory. Many spouses will experience true love for each other only when they will be reunited "in God", and with this love there will be the joy and fullness of the union that they did not know on earth. In God all will be understood, all will be excused, all will be forgiven.

November 24th, 2007

H. Rest and the Sabbath Day

Today consider this important idea: God wants you to enjoy his rest [...]

To be what? To be still, be quiet, be peaceful, be relaxed and be at rest. Something about modern living today seems to work against what God wants. It's as if there is a conspiracy of haste.

The noise of life shuts out the gentle voice of God who speaks to us in the silence of our hearts.

The importance of rest is revealed in the fact that God rested after creating the world (Hebrews 4, verse 4). The Hebrew and Christian traditions have interpreted this as a sign of the importance of the Sabbath rest – so flaunted and ignored by our consumer-driven, 24/7 society. The promise of rest anticipates our eternal rest in Christ.

The wonderful truth the writer of Hebrews wants us to grasp is that we can know and enjoy God's rest today, right now.

God's rest involves us in a lively and engaging participation in the truths of our faith.

Proclaim the following truths today and you will know God's rest:

"Easter is God's refusal that anyone should be left for dead."

God loves me; God sent his Son to die for me; I have the Holy Spirit living inside of me; God wants me to know joy and peace.

January 12th, 2007

I. Prayer and the Eucharist

We can know God, converse with him and hear him speak to us – in prayer, through reading his word and supremely when we receive him in the Eucharist. God is not remote, distant and removed, but closer to us than water is to a fish or than the air we breathe. The Eucharist is a foretaste of the banquet of heaven at which we will rejoice and celebrate the victory of the new covenant for all eternity [the new covenant sealed in the blood of Christ].

January 19th, 2007

There's nothing so great, my children, as the Eucharist. If you were to put all the good actions in the world against a Communion well made, it would be like a grain of dust against a mountain" (St. John Vianney)

Article on The Eucharist, January 2007, p.52

Our bodies flag, get weary and grow tired if they are not fed. The same is true of our souls – they too need to be fed and nourished. The ache in the human heart can only be filled by being nourished on the Eucharist. The Eucharist is the greatest source of nourishment and food we have.

The miracle of the feeding of the four thousand pointed to the miracle we can experience in our lives every day—the miracle of the Eucharist.

February 10th, 2007

J. Be Yourself

'Don't wish to be anything but what you are, and try to do that perfectly' (St. Francais de Sales).

January 24th, 2007

K. Humility and Respect

St. Augustine wrote: 'Do you wish to rise? Begin by descending. Do you plan a tower that will pierce the clouds? First lay the foundation of humility'. St. John Chrysostom reflected: 'Let us with great diligence implant in our souls the mother of all things that are good – I mean humility'. To be humble does not mean you have to hate yourself or put yourself down. The truly humble actually have a very positive sense of their own dignity and worth – it is this that makes them humble. Our dignity is grounded in the truth that we are created, loved and redeemed by God. The humble point to God, saying: Not to us, not to us, O Lord, but to thy name be glory.

February 8th, 2007

I would like to add that humility is a recognition of our dependence on God and on others for what we are and have – 'there go I but for the grace of God'.

Truly Christian people have a deep respect for every human being, and for all that pertains to human life. That respect should be reflected in our speech. We should speak graciously and courteously to everyone – the salesperson, the bus driver, the bin collector, the derelict. We should speak candidly but respectfully of birth and sex, of life and death. Speech is communication, but communication does not end when we have spoken. Others speak too and we should listen. As we should speak with truth and respect, we should listen with care.

Redemptorist Communications's Sunday Mass bulletin for May 27th, 2007

L. Embracing the Cross and Denying the Self

The message of the gospel will always be at its heart a proclamation of the cross, embracing self-denial, and the gospel paradox will always be true that to save your life you have to lose it. This fundamental principle of our faith raises some penetrating but valuable questions: What will it mean for me today to die to myself? How can I take up my cross?

What is certain is that today we will be invited to die. Every day we are invited to lay down our life in one way or another.

February 16th, 2007

The only way to really know what love is, is to study, pray and reflect on the life of Jesus. He is love and he showed us how to love.

Most of us won't be asked to lay down our lives literally as a martyr; however, there is a daily laying down of our lives to which we are called. This sacrifice is more to do with small things than with grandiose gestures—love is lived out in the nitty-gritty of daily life.

St. Therese of Lisieux once said: 'Love is the vocation that includes all others'.

January 5th, 2007

> *"I believe in the surprises of the Holy Spirit."*
> — Cardinal Leo Suenens

M. God's Mercy

The truth is that nobody is beyond redemption – this is the scandal of our faith. Jesus had a heart for sinners and so should we, because we like them are sinners.

'Our sins are nothing but a grain of sand alongside the great mountain of the mercy of God' (St. John Vianney)

February 24th, 2007

When we sin or fall we are always very surprised, but God is not – he knows we are sinners. In one sense, if one can put it like this, it's not sin that is the problem: it's the fact that we don't turn to God to deal with it.

Padre Pio, who spent many, many hours hearing confessions, said: 'Remember the sinner who is sorry for his sins is closer to God than the just man who boosts of his good works'.

On Good Friday we commemorate the single event which conquered sin once and for all – on the cross Jesus made himself an anvil and on this anvil he hammered out our sins.

'God will not deny his mercy to anyone. Heaven and earth may change, but God's mercy will never be exhausted' (Sr. Faustina Kowalska).

March 28th, 2007

N. Evangelisation of Culture

The following extracts are taken from the *Bible Alive* review of and quotes from Dr Dudley Plunkett's book *Saving Secular Society* published by Alive Publishing:

> A recurrent theme of Pope John Paul II's writings was the need for Christians to make their own contribution to a new evangelization and to the 'evangelization of culture'. There has been a widespread response to the new evangelization, but less so to the rather more opaque injunction to evangelize culture.
>
> "The evangelization of culture must show that in today's Europe too it is possible to live the Gospel fully as a path which gives meaning to existence" (Ecclesia in Europa).

Secular society is facing great uncertainties and challenges, whether we are thinking of values in everyday life, ethics in political and scientific decision-making, criteria for beauty in the arts and art criticism, or integrity in broadcasting [...]

I start from the view that contemporary secular culture needs to be looked at with fresh eyes. In speaking of culture I am referring to the whole way of life, values and understandings of a community or society, not only its most refined intellectual, scientific, literary or artistic achievements, and it appears to me from my own observation and experience that a sceptical or satirical mentality is choking the life out of our culture. The media make a virtue out of negativity, by claiming to be the voice of rationality, legitimate criticism and cultural freedom. Science exalts itself by claiming autonomy from ethical principles, in the attitude of 'if it can be done then let it be done' in a comic mimicry of the Creator, and many blindly accept science's authority, which becomes a kind of pied piper leading us all we, or they, know not where.

Why should we place any hope in Christian faith, especially if this is a post-Christian age? I believe that a new spiritual awareness is dawning in Western society. We have seen it in the strength of religious belief in the United States, the interest in religion among some of the most intelligent of the young, and in the moral authority exercised by Pope John Paul II who outfaced vilification and held tenaciously to transcendent principles and values. It would be a disaster if a way forward existed that continued to be rejected because of old prejudices.

The invitation here is to look again at the wisdom and truths of Christian faith: that Jesus Ghrist is God, that he lived on earth and preached a message that will never pass away, that he accepted death by crucifixion to make a new life possible for all humanity, and that he rose from death into a heavenly glory that he desires all people to share.

Easter 2007 issue

O. True Testimony

Today we celebrate the feast of St. Mark who stands with his three brother apostles as one of the four Evangelists. Concerning the witness of the Gospels Pope John Paul II wrote: 'What we receive from them is a vision of faith based on precise historical testimony: a true testimony which the Gospels, despite their complex redaction and primary catechetical purpose, pass on to us in an entirely trustworthy way' (Novo millennio inuente 17).

St. Mark's Gospel begins with a very clear proclamation of Christian faith. St. Mark immediately proclaims Jesus as 'Christ' and 'Son of God' and leaves us in no doubt that his primary purpose is to affirm and proclaim this truth.

> *"I never have any difficulty in miracles, since I experienced the miracle of a change in my own heart."*
> — St. Augustine

St. Mark's Gospel is a wonderful evangelistic tool: many have been converted to Christ by reading it from cover to cover.

April 25th, 2007

P. Searching?

Whatever the age, culture, civilization or nation, people are always searching for God.

January 7th, 2007

Q. The Holy Spirit

We always have to remember that the early Church was made up of ordinary men and women. St. John Vianney said: 'Those who are led by the Holy Spirit have true ideas: that is why so many ignorant people are wiser than the learned. The Holy Spirit is light and strength'.

May 2nd, 2007

R. Anger

Anger is an interesting if not complex area of human living!

For him [Jesus] anger is serious – really serious, because unless it is righteous (and let's face it, righteous anger is rare) we are harming both ourselves and the person (or persons) who has hurt us. In effect, and this is where Jesus' teaching gets radical, the Lord is comparing anger to murder … for Jesus there is 'murder of the heart' just as there is 'adultery of the heart'.

The truth is that our society and culture is bringing forth new forms of anger and rage: road rage, air rage, rage at the hospital A & E Department and rage in the home – to mention just a few.

'Lord Jesus […] Grant me the grace to be slow to anger and not let the sun go down when I am still angry – lead me rather to repentance and salvation'.

March 2nd, 2007

The foregoing are just brief extracts, which do not do justice to the full texts of the rich statements and commentary relevant to our Christian faith and the living thereof, contained in Bible Alive over a six-month period. What a wonderful insight they give us, and a recipe for living! I will finish this chapter by making some comments on the Mass and some comments on the encouraging signs coming through from the youth movement.

The Mass

The Mass, which is now often referred to as the Eucharist, is the most powerful of all acts of worship. As Vatican II declared it is "the source and summit of the Christian life." Why is this so? There are a number of interrelated reasons but they all revolve around Jesus Christ, true God and true man. God came on earth, taking on human flesh, to bring salvation to the human race in the most difficult manner possible, i.e. death on a cross. God could have chosen any number of easy ways to save us, but he did not. He chose the hardest way possible, because he wanted to show his infinite love for us. Jesus' life on earth always focussed on his death on the cross, it wasn't just because of a bad decision by Pontius Pilate. The Mass is a presentation of Jesus' life on earth, but particularly it re-presents his passion, death and resurrection. At the Last Supper, our Saviour Jesus Christ instituted the Eucharistic sacrifice of his Body and Blood, i.e. The Mass.

> Now as they were eating, Jesus took some bread, and when he had said the blessing he broke it and gave it to his disciples. 'Take it and eat', he said 'this is my body'. Then he took a cup, and when he had returned thanks he gave it to them. 'Drink all of you from this', 'for this is my blood, the blood of the covenant, which is to be poured out for many for the forgiveness of sins.' (Matthew 26: 26–28).

At the Last Supper Jesus foresaw his sacrificial death on Calvary on Good Friday when he physically gave his body and blood in death on a cross. Thus the consecrated bread and wine would truly, both sacramentally and sacrificially, be the real body and blood of Jesus. Jesus' resurrection from the dead on Easter Sunday proved the authenticity of his Last Supper actions and proved also that he was God as well as man.

When we attend at Mass, we share in Jesus' whole life, but particularly in the Last Supper, Good Friday and Easter Sunday events. Just imagine that at Mass we become part of all the happenings that took place over 2,000 years ago. What's more, the whole heavenly kingdom joins us at each Mass. St. John of the Cross is reputed to have said words along the following lines:

> The Mass is the most sacred action on earth; it is the sacrament that joins us here and now with Christ's sacrifice in heaven; here heaven and earth meet as in no other circumstance, and will continue to do so until Christ comes again to bring us into the fullness of God's presence.

> "*In vain the mocker looks for wisdom, knowledge comes easy to the discerning man.*"
> — Proverb 14: 6

So to be present at Mass is an awesome experience, or at least that is what it should be. Unfortunately and sadly, most of us fail to appreciate the significance of the Mass. No wonder St. John Vianney is supposed to have said that "if we really understood the Mass, we would die of joy." St. Thomas Aquinas, the great theologian and philosopher, received a great revelation after celebrating Mass on 6th December, 1273, which led him to say that "all he had written was mere straw compared to the glory and splendour of God." It is understood that he wrote no more after this revelation.

Surely we must try to advance our awareness and appreciation of the Mass and attend it with greater reverence. Do people who miss Sunday Mass realise what they are missing? I somehow doubt it. Those that say Mass is boring obviously don't realise the significance of the event either! Some people possibly have the notion that the Mass we celebrate today was something the Church just made up over the centuries, but this is not so. St. Justin Martyr writing around the year 150 AD described the Mass as it was then celebrated —essentially the Mass was identical in structure then to the Mass we celebrate today. Perhaps there are some people who do not believe in the Real Presence, i.e. that Jesus' real body and blood are present under the species of bread and wine. Jesus who is God said so and I believe. Jesus didn't come on earth to deceive us.

For those that need convincing about the Real Presence, perhaps what is referred to as the Eucharistic Miracle of Lanciano (an Italian town on the Adriatic Sea) might help. This reputed miracle was brought to my notice fairly recently by Mary Kelly of Sligo, who some two years ago was part of an Irish pilgrimage, led by an Irish priest, to various pilgrimage sites in Italy. Mary gave me a brochure on the Lanciano miracle which she picked up in the Church of St. Legontian, the location of the reputed miracle. She also saw the reliquary containing the coagulated flesh and blood. Mary has absolutely no doubt about the authenticity of this event. The following is an extract from the brochure:

> This wondrous event took place in the 8th century AD in the little Church of St. Legontian, as a divine response to a Basilian monk's doubt about Jesus' Real Presence in the Eucharist. During Holy Mass, after the twofold consecration, the host was changed into live Flesh and the wine was changed into live Blood, which coagulated into five globules, irregular and different in shape and size.

It was the doubting Basilian monk who was celebrating the Mass. According to the brochure, various ecclesiastical investigations have been conducted, including scientific analyses as recently as 1970–71, "conducted with absolute and unquestionable scientific precision" which "sustained the following conclusions":

- The Flesh is real Flesh. The Blood is real Blood
- The Flesh and the Blood belong to the human species
- The Flesh consists of the muscular tissue of the heart

The flesh and blood also have the same blood type (AB) and the brochure comments on their remarkably well-preserved condition:

> The preservation of the Flesh and of the Blood which were left in their natural state for twelve centuries and exposed to the action of atmospheric and biological agents remains an extraordinary phenomenon.

In conclusion, the brochure states that "it may be said that science, when called upon to testify, has given a certain and thorough response as regards the authenticity of the Eucharistic Miracle of Lanciano." Incidentally, an amazing piece of information given on one web site (www.michaeljournal.org/eucharist3.htm) is that the five globules contained in the reliquary, when weighed either separately or together weigh the same, i.e. 15.85 grams. The Catholic Church teaches that Jesus is really and totally present in either the whole consecrated host or a fragment of it.

Pope Benedict has recently reminded us that "for every Christian generation, the Eucharist is the indispensable nourishment that sustains them as they cross the desert of this world" (as reported by Paul Keenan on June 14th, 2007). When asked if it is a sin to miss Sunday Mass, Father Peter Byrne C.Ss.R., answers as follows:

> There are wars raging in about 30 countries; people die daily in needless violence with consequent misery and grief to families; thousands of unborn children are at risk of never being allowed to live, to take their first step, utter their first word; every minute children die of starvation; sickness is rampant in the world; every Mass is a Healing Mass; are you content to lie in bed while Jesus comes on the altar to raise a healing hand over our beautiful but wounded world? Have you no feeling for the children and adults that could live if you joined the Mass through which Jesus heals, brings life, love and peace on Earth?
> Do not ask about missing Mass on Sunday; ask rather how you can attend daily Mass. (*The Power to Heal*, p. 56)

Eucharistic Adoration is effectively a continuation of the Mass and the above mentioned booklet, *The Power to Heal*, is about special Eucharistic Adoration services which Father Peter Byrne holds throughout Ireland, and in many countries in the world. The stories told in this booklet of the many healings (really miracles as

> "The longest journey is the journey inward."
> — Dag Hammarskjold

they appear to me) when people are blessed with the Sacred Host (as consecrated at Mass) during these Eucharistic Healing Missions, are extremely compelling. One particular story is about an expectant mother who had been told, before attending the Mission, that the child she was carrying would be deformed and she was planning to have an abortion. After coming to the Mission she decided against having an abortion and subsequently gave birth to a perfectly healthy child. If you are sceptical about the Real Presence, I would strongly recommend you buy this little booklet which can be read in an hour or two although, for me at least, the contents are too good to rush through the pages. If your faith needs a boost, and surely we all fall into this category, then I equally recommend this read to you.

Jesus never forces himself upon us. He respects our freedom. *The Power to Heal* gives a wonderful account of how we can open ourselves to Him:

> A famous painting by Holman Hunt shows Christ with a lantern in his hand knocking on a door. Someone told the artist that the door has no handle. "It has a handle" he replied, "but it is on the inside". Open the door of your heart to Christ. (p. 64)

The Youth Movement

Whatever disturbing signs there may be about the falling off in religious practices, there are also many very encouraging signs and particularly among younger people. I know of many young people in Sligo, such as the Youth Prayer Group (some of their members are now in their 30s) who would put so-called elders like myself to shame. They are surely the religious hope of the future. These types of prayer groups are multiplied all over the country and indeed throughout the world. These world-wide youth prayer groups or movements find a common expression in the much publicised World Youth Congresses, the next one which is to be held in Sydney in August 2008. Pope Benedict is building up a great relationship with the young people, and no doubt the 2008 Congress will be a very special occasion for him. In fact, for Pope Benedict, the ability to truly celebrate is related to one's faith in God's existence. An article in the January 2007 edition of Alive reported his remarks on this subject:

> Speaking without notes to the bishops of Switzerland, he [Pope] recalled a remark by the German atheist philosopher Nietzsche, that human beings can celebrate only if God does not exist. "That is absurd" said

Benedict. "It's only if God exists and touches us that there can be true festive celebration. And we know that these feasts of faith open people's hearts wide." [...] The Pope had a special word for people who seek meditation outside the Church because they do not find a spiritual dimension in Christianity. "We must show them once again not only that this spiritual dimension exists but that it is the source of all things," he said. That meant promoting schools of prayer and prayer groups "where it is possible to learn personal prayer in all its dimensions." ("Only believers know how to really party says Pope," p. 1–2)

The same newspaper reported encouraging signs of a return to religion among young people in Holland, suggesting that "a new generation of young people who are not governed by anti-Catholic prejudice are the hope of the Church in Holland" ("Young People are Hope of the Church in Holland," p. 2). It was reported that a small but very committed number of people were discovering faith during the World Youth Days while a "growing number of Catholic families, often with the support of new ecclesial movements were [...] offering a faith environment to their children" (p. 2). This was also seen as a positive sign that diocesan practice and the Church in Rome were offering a consistent message and providing clear direction in today's world (p. 2).

Although not directly relating to the youth, I would like to finish this chapter of the book by briefly referring to an article by Father Joe Kavanagh, O.P., who reminds us that "winter always yields to springtime [...] and the darkness has its dawn." The Church has had its problems but Father Kavanagh saw these disturbing times as signs of "a God breaking in on a neat and tidy system, they are signs of hope; and the vulnerability that is all around is nothing less than a call" from God to share in his experience of earthly pain and suffering.

Coincidentally, I happened to hear Father Kavanagh speak a most beautiful homily in Sligo recently on a very simple theme, but yet, as he said, it is the "Big Story" of our lives, i.e. God's unspeakable mercy and love for each of us. We are God's pride and joy in this most beautiful world that he created, but sadly we so often fail to grasp the impact of this big story, and instead we allow our own small stories of sin or otherwise (important though they may be) to blot out the central big story, according to Father Kavanagh. Father Kavanagh referred to St. Augustine's attempt to figure out how the good thief who hung alongside Jesus on Calvary, and who would have done an awful lot of bad deeds in his life, could have been granted a straight passage to paradise by Jesus, without any time in purgatory to cleanse his bad deeds. The big story of God's infinite love must be the answer, which the thief saw in Jesus' eyes when he turned to him, connected to the thief's own genuine sorrow. Incidentally, Father Kavanagh drew the concept of the big story from the great story teller from the Blasket Islands, Tomás Ó Criomhthain, who gave up story-telling when the radio and newspapers arrived with all their little stories and, as he said, "drove the big story out of my head."

CHAPTER NINETEEN
Family and Other Issues for Society

This chapter briefly considers the following topics:

- The Family as the Basic Unit of Society
- The Sacredness of Life
- Learning from the Girls and Boys Town Model, USA
- Where Now as a Society?

The Family as the Basic Unit of Society

I think it is correct to say that the traditional family of mother and father and their children has been the edifice upon which strong communities and nations have been built in the past. It now appears that there may be some serious cracks beginning to appear in this edifice with many new family types appearing. It is not for me to pass judgement on these new family types, particularly when so many parents (in different family types) put so much effort into creating a secure and loving environment for their children. However, I ask two questions: Firstly, do children not have the basic right to be brought up in a secure environment where they have a mother and a father and, more often than not, one or more siblings to relate to as they develop as young people? Secondly, are we morally or even legally entitled to coldly decide to raise children where the traditional natural environment is not present?

It seems to me that we must consider possible limitations on children's ability to develop as fully rounded human beings if they are not raised in the traditional manner. What will be the implications for these children as they grow up and what will be the implications for society in general? These issues seem to me to require serious consideration. As Father Flanagan of Boys Town said many years ago: "Parenthood is the most sacred office, endowed with the highest responsible duties ever given to man or woman." Are we as individuals, as a people and as a nation ensuring that these responsible duties of parenthood can and are properly exercised? The many serious problems we have in society today suggest to me that we might not be measuring up very well in the parenthood stakes.

Incidentally, marriage is a natural institution which emerged at the dawn of creation. But it is not purely a human institution. God is the author of marriage, having made both man and woman in his own likeness and "this is why a man leaves his father and mother and joins himself to his wife, and they become one body" (Genesis 2: 24). This matter comes up again in the New Testament:

> He [Jesus] answered, 'Have you not read that the creator from the beginning made them male and female and that he said: This is why a man must leave father and mother, and cling to his wife, and the two become one body? They are no longer two, therefore, but one body. So then, what God has united, man must not divide.' (Matthew 19: 4–6)

Unfortunately, situations arise where man does divide what God has united and it appears that this may often be detrimental to the children of these marriages. David Quinn, who addressed the 2007 Catholic Youth Conference in All Hallows College, Dublin, on the theme of the threat to marriage, was reported to be appalled that there was no debate whatsoever going on about the growing crisis, despite the massive emotional distress experienced by the couples and the often "devastating" effects on children.

> Stressing that there are many exceptions, he said, "children from divorced families, for example, tend to fare worse in school, are more likely to suffer from depression, are more likely to abuse drugs and alcohol, are more likely to drop out of school, and are more likely to suffer later marital breakdown themselves."
> (reported in *Alive!* July/August 2007, p. 1)

Mr Quinn suggested that marriage should not only be thought of as a relationship between two people which should end if the love dies but rather should be seen as "a social institution designed for the welfare and protection of children" (ibid. p. 2). He argues that love is not necessarily a constant and may wax and wane over the course of married life. Mr Quinn also highlighted the damage caused by cohabitation and suggested that cohabitation is, in the long term, bad for children because so many cohabiting couples split up. He is reported as seeing the roots and the solution to the problem of marital breakdown as follows:

> At the root of the problem is a complete overemphasis on the importance of personal freedom and a phobia about commitment. Yet research shows that "making the right commitments and sticking to them is the way to happiness", he said. Instead of this, there is a new type of sexual

> •
> *"If you have nothing good to say about somebody, say nothing at all."*
> •

repression today, one which "represses the commitment and the impulse towards children that comes with sex."
(Reported in *Alive!* July/August 2007, p. 2)

However, we should be careful not to overstate marriage problems in Ireland. Bishop Willie Walsh is President of Accord (a Catholic Church agency involved in marriage preparation, counselling and in school programmes) and his article on a recent marriage survey suggests that it "presents an encouraging picture [... of] the wellbeing of marriage" (*Irish Times*, April 24th, 2007). Bishop Walsh states that Accord has worked with 150,000 clients in the previous three years through its various programmes. The agency's commissioned survey of over 700 couples focussed on the first seven years of marriage and Bishop believes that its results provide "a timely antidote to a creeping trend towards presenting the lifelong loving relationship which is marriage as being in something tending towards terminal decay" (ibid.). The Bishop notes that media reporting has tended to focus on the negative aspects, such as the recent census results showing an increase of 70 per cent in divorce rates. Such reporting ignores the fact that Ireland was coming from a situation with a very low divorce rate; the Bishop notes that "Ireland continues to have one of the lowest divorce rates in the western world" (ibid.). Furthermore, there is a rising trend in the numbers of marriages as well as the marriage rate itself;[49] Bishop Walsh sees this as indicating "with absolute clarity that couples view their marriage as a life long commitment only to be broken in extreme circumstances" (ibid.).

Not only do couples regard marriage as a serious commitment, but the research indicates very high levels of satisfaction within it. Bishop Walsh reports that:

> 77 per cent [of those surveyed] are very happy with their marriage and 86 percent would recommend marriage to another couple. It is refreshing to observe that two-thirds of couples feel their relationship has strengthened since they married, with the main benefits for them being love, fulfilment, family security and companionship. [...]

---

49. Bishop Walsh's article is based on the Accord survey and marriage figures. Official state statistics maintained by the Central Statistics Office (CSO) largely confirm this trend. From 1997 to 2006, the number of marriages has increased every year except for 2003; it showed a small decline but the rising trend was restored in 2004 when the marriage figure was greater than 2002. Over the same period, the marriage rate rose from a low of 4.3 per thousand of the total population in 1997 to a high of 5.2 in 2002; it has remained at either 5.1 or 5.2 for every year between 2002 and 2006. Figures are not yet available for 2007. See CSO website at www.cso.ie/statistics/bthsdths-marriages.htm.

> 98 per cent of couples interviewed would marry the same person again, while only 7 per cent had thought about separation or divorce.
> (*Irish Times*, April 24th, 2007).

These encouraging statistics should not be taken to imply that there are never difficulties of any sort; of course there are and Bishop Walsh reports that "parenting undoubtedly presents the biggest challenge" (ibid.), possibly due to the fact that it becomes harder for the couple to get time out for themselves. In this respect, Bishop Walsh notes that "only three in ten of those couples married seven years managed to take time out together once a week or more" (ibid.).

Unsurprisingly, given the change in social attitudes, the survey shows that cohabitation before marriage is becoming more common. Bishop Walsh suggests that modern couples see cohabitation "as a form of deferred marriage, driven perhaps by economic circumstances, price of houses and cost of weddings as much as anything else" (ibid.). Interestingly, just 25% of couples described themselves as not being at all religious while "the majority claimed to be 'moderately religious' and attended religious services either regularly or occasionally" (ibid.). Bishop Walsh notes that these figures indicate that the decline in religious practice among young couples is less extreme than is sometimes suggested.[50]

The Bishop concludes that "Ireland is unique in Europe in its commitment in our Constitution to guard with special care the institution of marriage, on which the family is founded" and suggests that "loving families [...] contribute significantly to the wellbeing of our whole society" (ibid.).

Carl O'Brien, Social Affairs Correspondent with the Irish Times also reported on the Accord survey. In addition to noting those trends already discussed above, he commented that the survey's findings accorded with a number of other studies in the US and Britain which "show that married people are more satisfied with their lives than their non-married peers" and furthermore are "more likely to live longer and report lower levels of depression and have a higher standard of health" (*Irish Times*, April 24th, 2007). He noted that the high satisfaction within marriage may well have been affected by the fact that the Accord survey excluded people in previous marriages as well as non-married people in committed relationships and cohabiting couples who choose not to marry. Furthermore, he suggests that the likelihood of positive responses would be increased by "the age-old problem of persuading people to reveal their true feelings about deeply personal issues to a stranger who arrives on their doorstep with a clipboard" (ibid.). Nonetheless he concludes that the census figures reveal that, despite the rising divorce rate, "marriage is firmly back in fashion" with an increase of 7.6% in the number of

---

50. This survey was of married couples; hence long-term unmarried couples (who may well have a lower rate of religious affiliation) are excluded. Thus, the survey's reported rate of religious sentiment may not represent the religious sentiment of the general population.

> *"Come to me all you who labour and are overburdened,*
> *and I will give you rest ...*
> *Yes my yoke is easy and my burden light."*
> — Matthew 11:28–30

marriages over the previous four years. The popularity of marriage was borne out by the 2006 census results reported for Sligo:

> There are 6,961 husband and wife couples with children of any age, with 487 cohabiting couples in the same category. There are 1,797 lone mothers with children of any age and 296 lone fathers with kids.
> (Reported by Paul Deering, *Sligo Champion*, June 20th, 2007)

However, it is also clear from the number of lone mothers and fathers that there is a significant amount of marriage and relationship breakdown.

In the context of marriage breakdown, it might be surmised that the financial pressures facing many couples today together with the lack of quality family time that can result when both partners must work full-time are contributory factors. In this regard, recent remarks by Bishop Christopher Jones, Bishop of Elphin, are relevant.

> [Bishop Jones] said that in the recent Irish general election campaign he had never heard a politician speak about the family. The focus had been on the economy and on health and education services. [...] Indeed in recent years a minister for finance created tax initiatives specifically geared to attracting both parents of young children into the world of work. It was good for the economy but not for young children or for their future as citizens of our country. The big appeal during the election was for more investment in crèches and pre-schools so that parents could be out at work all day. He referred to a recent report which disclosed that in 2006 Irish taxpayers paid 25 million euro to keep 54 children in detention – "€500,000 per child." After publication of this report there had been appeals to the Government to invest more money in the family at an early stage, which would "generate huge dividends in terms of ensuring healthier and happier families and therefore healthier and happier adults". He added: "Surely the Government should introduce tax incentives that would encourage at least one parent to remain at home with babies and young children".
> (Reported by Patry McGarry, *Irish Times*, August 6th, 2007)

Such views, although often not popular in today's so-called liberal society, are not only held by the clergy. Eva Herman, one of Germany's top television broadcasters, has been vocal in her advocacy of the mother's role within the home. Her two books, *The Eva Principle: Towards a New Femininity* (2006) and *Dear Eva Herman* (2007) have been both remarkably popular and controversial. A report in *Alive!* notes that her 2007 book "caused a new outpouring of feminist rage with claims that mothers not staying at home with their children is leading to family breakdown and 'a soulless society'" (July/August 2007, p. 6). In her 2006 book, which sold over 100,000 copies in ten days, Eva expressed regret for her three divorces, condemned abortion while drawing attention to the trauma it causes to the women who undergo abortion, and rejected the idea that women should prioritise their careers over their family. The report notes her contention that emancipation, career success and self-fulfilment do not compensate for the "radical" goals of motherhood, home-maker and wife. "Let's say it loud", she wrote, "we women overburdened ourselves, we allowed ourselves to be too easily seduced by career opportunities" (p. 6).

Although Ireland's increasing birthrate (which has been higher in the period from 2002-2006 than at any time since 1992) might lead one to believe that family life is becoming a priority again, such families are not—particularly for those under 30—founded on the institution of marriage. A report by Paul Keenan, based on CSO figures released during 2007, noted that "almost 60 percent of women under the age of 30 in Ireland are having their children outside marriage with this figure rising to 78 per cent among 20 to 24 year olds" ("Over half of births to under-30s outside marriage," p. 5). He also notes that almost half of all births are to women under 30 and suggests that the high incidence of births outside marriage in this under-30 cohort "is still something of a surprise and is rarely highlighted" (p. 5). The combination of these two statistics means that just over a third of all births in the State are outside marriage. In contrast to the younger age group, the vast majority of births to women over 30 are within marriage; Keenan observes that, in 2006, only 18% of births to 30–34 year olds and 14% of births to 35-39 year olds were outside marriage. Obviously, not all births outside marriage are to lone parents and Keenan suggests that "an unknown, but certainly high number, are to cohabiting couples" and further notes "that the teenage mother is something of a myth," as births to teenagers are just 3% of all births and 10% of those outside marriage. Thus the challenge for today's Church, and indeed for all of today's society, is to make marriage relevant to those for whom it is no longer regarded as a necessary part of family life.

In November 2007, *Alive!* published an article entitled "Review lists ten damaging effects of cohabitation." The article mainly dealt with US findings on cohabitation and I reproduce the article below in full largely without comment (apart from footnotes contextualising some of the statistics), except to say that these findings disturbed me. I am genuinely sorry if this article should upset any of my readers; I know that my attitude to this subject is not a fashionable one but I felt that the article was an important one. In the context of an apparently widely held opinion in Ireland that living together before marriage is beneficial, this US research on the effects of

> "Lord help me to live for something, lest I die for nothing."
> — A favourite quote of Canon Niall Ahern

cohabitation is somewhat worrying. Obviously, social and other factors may differ between the US and Ireland and the US author may be concentrating only on one side of the argument; nonetheless it gives food for thought.

> In a recent *Irish Times* survey 74% of women said that it was "a good idea for couples to live together for a period of time before they decide to marry."
>
> No reasons were given for this view, but the September issue of the US Catholic journal, *New Oxford Review*, carried a review of research of the ill-effects of cohabitation
>
> Dr A Patrick Schneider II began with Chuck Colson's remark that "cohabitation is training for divorce," then listed "Ten Facts" from the research. He reported that in the US:
>
> 1. Cohabitation is now 11 times as common as it was in the 1960s.[51]
> 2. Only one-sixth of cohabiting couples are together after three years; one in ten survives five or more years.[52]
> 3. The divorce rate of those who cohabit prior to marriage is nearly double (39% vs. 21%) that of couples who did not cohabit.
> 4. Women often end up with the responsibilities of marriage—particularly when there are children—without the legal protection, and contribute 70% of the couple's income.
> 5. The rate of sexually transmitted diseases among cohabiting couples is six times higher than among married women. Cohabiting men are four times more likely to be unfaithful than husbands.
> 6. Marriages preceded by cohabitation are more prone to drug and alcohol problems. Depression is three times more likely in cohabitating couples than among married couples.
> 7. Cohabitors who never marry have 78% less wealth than the continuously married.[53]

---

51. This is not in itself an ill-effect, merely a statistic. Yet the nine points listed after it may make it so.
52. If cohabiting is used as a "test run" for marriage, it could also be argued that cohabitation works to prevent those who are not suitable marriage partners from getting married in the first instance. Not everyone, however, would agree with this logic; indeed, point 3 above may potentially contradict it.
53. Wealth may be affected by tax laws, which typically favour married couples over non-married ones.

8. Compared to children of married parents, children aged 12–17 with cohabiting parents are six times more likely to have emotional and behavioural problems and are more likely to be expelled from school. The poverty rate among children of cohabiting couples is five times the rate of children in married households. They also have fewer grandparents, aunts, uncles, and cousins; the family tree is pruned.
9. In the US 3 out of 4 children involved in criminal activity were from cohabiting homes. 70% of juveniles in state-run institutions are from fatherless homes.
10. Rates of serious abuse of children are lowest in intact families; 6 times higher in stepfamilies; 20 times higher in cohabiting biological-parent families; and 33 times higher when the mother is cohabiting with a boyfriend who is not the father.

Compared to a married woman, a cohabiting woman is 3 times more likely to experience physical aggression, and 9 times more likely to be murdered.[54] The review with references is available online.[55]

(*Alive!* November 2007, p.6)

The Sacredness of Life

According to Biblical tradition the Ten Commandments were written by God and given to Moses on Mount Sinai in the form of two stone tablets. Accounts of this can be found in the Old Testament Books of Exodus and Deuteronomy. Unfortunately, many people today are not very familiar with the Ten Commandments, including the Fifth Commandment 'You shall Not Kill'. It would seem reasonable to assume that this Commandment applies to all stages of life, from conception in the womb until natural death and all the stages in between. Thus on this basis, there are many issues that confront us, such as abortion, embryo stem cell research and experimentation, suicide, murder, gangland killings, unjust wars, deaths from starvation or other causes due to deliberate Government action or inaction, deaths on the road due to undue care, including excessive speed and driving under the influence of alcohol or drugs, and euthanasia.

On an examination of conscience concerning these issues, neither Ireland nor many other countries are performing very well. In fact in several of these areas we in Ireland are performing very poorly, and I feel we have much to be ashamed

---

54. With regard to the abuse of either women or children, it may be that married women are less inclined to report such abuse. Hence, the actual difference may be less significant than suggested above.
55. The full text of Dr Schneider's article, which gives more detailed statistics and full source references is available on www.lifesite.net/ldn/2007/oct/07100902.html.

> "What a desolation life would be without the Eucharist!"
> – Edel Quinn

of. As individuals, as communities and as a nation we have a lot of work to do to enhance our respect for life and to take action to see this respect through. Perhaps I might offer some questions for the reader to consider in relation to the sacredness of life:

- Is anyone ever entitled to make a decision to purposely kill a baby in the womb no matter at what stage of life the baby is at? Is the baby not entitled to a start in life, just as I and you were given? How many great people, born as a seemingly helpless baby, perhaps even with disabilities and whose life could have been easily terminated without fuss, made tremendous contributions to humankind thereafter? Think of the awful trauma and guilt and even depression that mothers who abort their babies often suffer in later life. "Before I formed you in the womb I knew you" (Jeremiah 1: 5).
- Do we question ourselves sufficiently, as parents or guardians of the young, about our possible shortcomings in our parenting? Is our parenting backed up with appropriate example from us? Do we instil in our young people a sound religious ethos, including a respect for other people and respect for life? Do we ever consider that possible shortcomings in these areas could be the cause of unsavoury social behaviour, including serious alcohol and drug abuse, together with other evils, such as needless killings, road deaths and suicides?
- Is the so-called liberal agenda really attractive when we consider its possible downsides?
- Why do medical researchers and scientists continue to experiment with human embryos leading to their destruction, when adult stem cell research and experimentation, which involves no loss of life, offers great potential for medical science and has no ethical problems?
- While the Crisis Pregnancy Agency (CPA) does great work in assisting women with crisis pregnancies, one might ask why does a state agency, as the CPA is, operating in a country whose constitution guarantees that it will defend and vindicate the right to life of the unborn, deem it appropriate to facilitate abortion through the provision of information thereon. This question is all the more pertinent bearing in mind that the CPA was set up "to address the issue of crisis pregnancy in Ireland through", inter alia, "a reduction in the number of women with crisis pregnancies who opt for abortion by offering services and supports which make other options more attractive" (www.crisispregnancies.ie/about.html).

- Is it time for all of us individually, for all organs of society and interest groups, and for all our politicians to act more honestly and openly in matters concerning the good of society? Thankfully, we have had some good examples of this from our politicians of late, but much remains to be done.

Perhaps, I could finish this section by quoting briefly from the Message for the World Day of Peace, 1st January, 2007, by Pope Benedict XVI. Quoting from St. Augustine, the Pope said: "God created us without our aid; but he did not choose to save us without our aid". Consequently, the Pope went on to say that "all human beings have the duty to cultivate an awareness of this twofold aspect of gift and task".

Learning from the Girls and Boys Town Model, USA

I had the privilege of visiting Father Edward Joseph Flanagan's Girls and Boys Town home in Omaha, Nebraska, USA in July, 2007, as part of a delegation from the Diocese of Elphin, headed by the Bishop of Elphin, Dr. Christopher Jones. Father Flanagan (1886–1948) was born in Ballymoe, Co. Roscommon, in the Diocese of Elphin, attended Summerhill College in Sligo, became a priest with great difficulty because of ill health, and eventually as a young priest and against all the odds (including resistance from within his own ranks), set up his first Boys Town home in Omaha in 1917. The rest we might well say is history. This remarkable man, who died from a heart attack in Berlin, Germany in 1948, while on active service in his cause for young people, was a visionary of the first order and left a wonderful legacy to humankind. The Boys Town model (now renamed "Girls and Boys Town") is now widespread throughout the US and has applications in various countries throughout the world.

The basic mission of Girls and Boys Town is the rehabilitation of young girls and boys from broken homes, those who are homeless, those who suffer from alcohol or substance abuse, abused children, and so on. The US Government applauded the work of Father Flanagan and his organisation, and indeed commissioned him to undertake a number of assignments abroad, particularly after World War Two, in the general area of child care and rehabilitation. Father Flanagan was working on one of those assignments at the time of his death.

As stated, I was privileged to be part of the delegation to Girls and Boys Town in July 2007. I had studied a good deal about Father Flanagan and in fact was involved with others in writing a booklet on him in 2006. Like many others, I developed a huge respect for him and for his extraordinarily advanced philosophies for dealing with troubled children. However, it wasn't until I visited Girls and Boys Town with my colleagues and saw at first hand the operation on the ground, talked to various people running the Omaha Girls and Boys Town campus, met graduates of the campus going back for more than fifty years (and heard

> "Prayer is the movement of the Holy Spirit in the human heart through which God reaches out and embraces human beings. It is a duet of love in which the action of the Spirit inspires and sustains us in the darkness of faith. It is an inward call from Christ who dwells within the depths of the human soul, and who longs to be known and loved here. It is the exciting adventure of the search for God's presence and the endless joy of rejoicing in it when it is found."
>
> — The Glenstal Book of Prayer, p11

them speak so proudly of their alma mater) and had various presentations on the work of Girls and Boys Town not only in the base campus of Omaha but throughout its vast organisation, that I began to realise the enormity of Father Flanagan's achievements.

As a result of our trip, I think we were probably all asking ourselves as to how we might replicate the work of Girls and Boys Town in Ireland, not necessarily by setting up Girls and Boys Town campuses in Ireland, but by learning from their various work programmes and adopting or adapting them, as appropriate, in our health services, prison and reform services, and so on. While the main focus of Girls and Boys Town programmes may appear to be concerned with the rehabilitation needs of young people, to me there is much more to their programmes in that they give a great insight into how to manage the development of young people, ideally so that they don't get into trouble in the first place. Thus I list briefly below some of the specifics of the Girls and Boys Town care and rehabilitation programmes.

- Girls and Boys Town admits girls and boys in the age group 10 to 17 years who have experienced one or more of these problems: chronic school behaviour problems, aggressive behaviour, a pattern of disruptive placement, a history of psychiatric problems, pre-delinquent or delinquent behaviour, a history of drug or alcohol abuse or physical or sexual victimization. Typically, the girls and boys spend eighteen months on campus.
- Prior to admission to campus, each youth undergoes a thorough assessment process which includes an individual psychological or psychiatric evaluation, a social history and an assessment of intellectual functioning. Further assessments are made on arrival on campus, many of these are also on-going while on campus. These include suicide probability assessment; a problem behaviour assessment under the Achenback checklist; psychiatric assessment; substance abuse screening or inventory; writing skills assessment; nutritional assessment; and various others.

- The Omaha campus has the capacity to cater for over 500 girls and boys, housed in seventy residential homes.
- The basic Girls and Boys Town model is family based, whereby the boys and girls, at eight to a house, are housed in family style, non-institutional and non-bureaucratic environment with a host husband and wife acting as father and mother, and also an assistant to help out with the work. The system replicates as closely as possible a normal family environment. Individual and family rights are respected at all times. At no time are mechanical restraints, seclusion, or isolation used. Positive interventions and the least restrictive methods of treatment are hallmarks of Girls and Boys Town model. Privilege restrictions occur as a last resort and are continuously monitored for appropriateness. However, there are standard procedures in place for the operation and conduct of each family or house, and also for monitoring the outcomes of the children, and in certain respects the outcomes of the host parents. The monitoring system includes the use of a Points Card for each girl and boy where points are awarded for good behaviour and deducted for bad behaviour. The children participate in house work, including the cooking of meals, dealing with laundry, hygiene, and so on.
- The campus operates all year round education for the children, but with half-day schools in summer months. The year-round school is used to make up for the fact that those admitted to campus are usually very much behind in their level of education. The educational programme provided is most comprehensive. Apart from the standard school subjects which are duly covered, special emphasis is placed on raising the reading ability of the children, as this is considered crucial for their future prospects. Mathematics is also given a high priority. Other programmes provided, include:
    1. Youth Employment Programme that simulates the process of real world employment seeking: preparing job applications, doing interviews etc.
    2. Senior Planning activities, which include a curriculum to help prepare the graduating youth to develop appropriate competences.
    3. An aftercare programme which affords the youth the opportunity to secure scholarships for advanced study and training.
- The girls and boys also receive training in several of the standard trades and also engage in some farm work. They also receive basic training for the Army.
- An absolute requirement of the Girls and Boys Town model is that all girls and boys on campus must participate in religious activities, normally of their choice. Research carried out has shown that by having a spiritual dimension, the treatment programmes show enhanced positive results, such as a drop in aggression, drop in suicide attempts, and so

on. Incidentally, Girls and Boys Town is non-denominational and of course is non-racial, and was so when Father Flanagan set up his first home in 1917, at a time when racial segregation would have been much in evidence.
- Sport is also a very big aspect of the Girls and Boys Town model. The facilities for practically all types of sports, including athletics, are of a very high standard.
- When girls and boys graduate from the campus, they usually go to one of three destinations: further education, work or back to their homes.
- Apart from the various programmes already mentioned above, the campus also provides counselling and treatment programmes as appropriate. These include individual and group counselling or therapy services, substance abuse education, substance abuse treatment and a youth rights programme.
- In addition to the above on-campus standard residential programmes, there are other programmes provided, such as:
  1. Common Sense Parenting workshops for parents who wish to improve their parenting skills.
  2. Respite and Assessment Home for the temporary housing and assessment of children with acute behavioural problems
  3. Emergency Shelter Service to help abused, neglected, runaway and troubled youths and their families resolve crises. There is also the Family Preservation and Family Centred Services which provide intensive in-home treatment for families in crisis.

It is probably very evident to the reader, that the Girls and Boys Town model for the rehabilitation, care and development of young people in their care is very genuinely a totally holistic approach.

For me, the highlights of our visit to Girls and Boys Town campus, Omaha, Nebraska, in July 2007, were:

- Meeting graduates from Girls and Boys Town, some going back to Father Flanagan's days, and many in the decades which followed, witnessing at first hand the pride these people had in their alma mater and witnessing also their success in life. Without Father Flanagan's home, many of these people may not have made a success of their lives.
- Partaking in an evening meal in one of the family residences with eight boys from different parts of America and one who had connections with Kenya, together with their host mother and father and assistant. The boys behaviour and self-confidence clearly demonstrated how successful the Girls and Boys Town model is in practice.
- The beautiful layout of the Girls and Boys Town campus with copious mature trees and green belts and a lake, with an extensive array of build-

ings, including churches, Hall of History, Visitor Centre, trades centre, sports centre, educational facilities, residential houses and many more. The campus still has the original house which Father Flanagan occupied as his residence and office for most of his tenure at Boys Town (as it was then called). Also much of the original Overlook farm, on which the campus was built, is still retained by Girls and Boys Town, and the girls and boys still do some of the farm work. As might be expected, the campus is a popular tourist stop as it is steeped in history and has very interesting memorabilia.

- The sophisticated and professional nature of the Girls and Boys Town programmes of care and education and the competence of the people behind these programmes were most impressive.
- The extreme kindness and hospitality shown to us by all the staff at Girls and Boys Town and by the many graduates we met (who were on campus for their bi-annual convention) as well as the great pleasure and joy they expressed to us as visitors from Father Flanagan's ancestral homeland.
- Bishop Christopher Jones' keynote address to the Alumni Convention Banquet on the Saturday evening and his homily the next morning to a packed church when he was chief celebrant at the Sunday Mass, made one feel very proud to be Irish and particularly to hail from Father Flanagan's ancestral diocese. Bishop Jones' birth place and that of Father Flanagan are within ten miles of one another in county Roscommon.

I conclude this section by giving the reflections written by a sample of six girls and boys graduating from Girls and Boys Town campus in Omaha in 2007. The reflections were written by the girls and boys themselves. All names appearing in the reflections have been excluded.

> Before I came, I was a little girl living a life of abuse, unhealthy relationships and pain. I was raised and taught all the wrong things in life. I was not brought up in a loving or stable home. I thought love was being severely beaten so you could learn your lesson. The more pain I received showed how much you were loved. I chose to deal with all of this with alcohol and drugs. Before I came, I was a lost child. You have given me an opportunity to live in a real family home. You took me into your heart. My Family-Teachers [...] taught me so much about life. They even taught me to love myself so that I could love others well. They taught me to control my hatred and anger to show other emotions and to be a stronger person. Thank you Girls and Boys Town.

> When I came I was a scared boy. I was in a gang. We hurt others and they hurt us. I was afraid someone would kill my mom. I always wanted

to be alone. I kept my distance from all others. When I came to Girls and Boys Town, I knew I was ready. I didn't want to have friends back home in… who only wanted to sell drugs and shoot people for the fun of it. You have made me to grow up into a good man. I no longer skip school, hang around with the wrong people, treat girls with no respect and all those bad things. I don't need to do that anymore. What I need to do is to continue what I am doing now at Girls and Boys Town. Thank you from my heart.

Before I came, I drank constantly at the age of 15. My mom died a year before I came. I was having a hard time dealing with her loss. I had moved five times in two years prior to coming here. No one could handle me. I was a depressed, angry person. I was mad at my mom. I found it hard to find peace with God and my family, who didn't want to deal with me. I was on the same road my family was – the road to alcoholism. When I came, I was so used to moving that I thought it was just another move. I fit right in and the girls in my home and Family-Teachers made me feel welcome. I was determined to leave within a year. It was hard for me to accept feedback. I came in the summer and I couldn't understand why these people all went to summer school. This place has done wonders for me. I never would have gotten through it if it were not for Girls and Boys Town. I have become an awesome and modest young lady. I have obtained a family. I have two parents for the first time in my life. I have become a better person. I never thought this was possible. I am going on to nursing school. This is because Girls and Boys Town believes in me and pushes me to excel.

Before I came, I knew all that I wanted was money. I knew my mom didn't have any money for a boy like me and there was no sense asking her. She kept telling me that you will get money if you go to school, but I didn't see too many people in school who had money either. There were people who were half the age of my mom getting money selling drugs. The gangs were there, so I was with them. When I came I didn't want to change. Nobody told me about a point card or having to go to church. At first, I tried to scrape by until my 12 to 18 months was over. I did start to like school a little bit. It also felt good not to be selling drugs for the green. I started to work out – but I was still trying to go home. Something happened. I decided to stay. I know that I would not have graduated if I wasn't here at Father Flanagan's. I learned here how to survive better than I ever learned to survive on the streets. When I came, I hung out with the wrong crowd and was looking for love and happiness in all the wrong places. I was a dropout and didn't care what anyone thought about me. When I came, I was lost and didn't know what to do. I cried every day on the phone with my mom telling her this place couldn't change me. I was wrong. It did change me. I gave this place a try and they really helped me tremendously reach my goals when others told me that I never could. You have helped me get a good education. You have given me a chance to learn more about life. You have helped me learn what a real family lives like. You have helped with building a better relationship with my family and helped me control my anger.

Before I came, I was angry at everything. I didn't know right from wrong. I never had a chance to find out. When I came, I thought Girls and Boys Town was going to be a jail for bad boys. Then I found out it is not a jail, it is a home. I did not want to be here my first month because I did not open up and let my hurts out. I didn't want anyone to tell me what to do. I grew up without a father, so I didn't know anything about morality. Wow ... I have changed. What you have done is something very special to me. You have given me the chance to find out how good it is to go to high school, to earn a diploma, to make friends, to go to church and to get a job. Thank you Girls and Boys Town.

Many of us have met at least one person who had the world handed to them by their mom and dad. I am not one to pass judgment but in my opinion that's just asking for trouble. For example, here is a parent who really doesn't know how to parent. Mom and dad give their daughter whatever she wants and call it good. They later find out she is very promiscuous and into drugs and alcohol. Giving their daughter everything she desired and not leading her on a structured way set her up for disaster. That is my story. I tested the waters to see how much I could get away with and how often, and soon nobody cared. It was way too late until I came here to Girls and Boys Town.

I referred earlier on to the highlights of our visit to Girls and Boys Town but perhaps the real highlights and delights come from reading the foregoing reflections of the 2007 graduates. They surely speak volumes for the efficacy of the youth nurturing model put into practice by Father Flanagan.

Where Now as a Society?

When I initially drafted the outline for the chapters for this book, I included the above heading. While writing the other chapters, I sort of got cold feet about writing this chapter, on the basis that it would be presumptuous of me to make predictions about our future. Just at that point, whether by providence or otherwise, I read the editorial in the *Sligo Champion* newspaper of 8th August 2007. There I saw the chapter I would have wished to write, if I had the ability to do so. With the kind permission of the *Sligo Champion* I reproduce the editorial in full. I also wish to express my gratitude to the Archbishop of Tuam, Dr. Michael Neary, whose address on Reek Sunday on the summit of Croagh Patrick gave rise to the Sligo Champion editorial.

Sligo Champion Editorial, "Where we're going"

The Archbishop of Tuam, Dr. Michael Neary, could hardly have chosen a more appropriate place than Croagh Patrick for some timely comments he made on modern Irish society. Preaching to pilgrims on Reek Sunday, he encouraged the nation to slow down the pace of life, and 'taking a lesson from the old mountain', to put aside a moment to reflect and wonder at the beauty of the earth and the value of true friends.

On any other day, Dr. Neary's comments might have gone relatively unnoticed, but what he said rang very true and bears repetition and contemplation as the greedy cult of the Celtic Tiger becomes ever more all-devouring.

He declared that society had rushed the earth in an age when the seasons were struggling for their own identity. The lands were ravished for greed and even some crops were now genetically modified for quicker profit. The forests had been stripped for paper and our own waste had polluted the seas.

We lived in the age of the instant, where there was no joy in the anticipation and no time to value the achievement. Hotels had already advertised the 'sparkle they can put into Christmas'. They advertised for Christmas as children were returning to school after their summer holiday, and they then drew attention to summer breaks even before Christmas night. The sacredness of now, 'the sacrament of the present moment' had been forgotten.

Too many young people in their journey through life had come to believe that giving up on life was more attractive than the living of it. Perhaps our greatest fault lay in our robbing our children of their childhood. These were the precious irreplaceable years of play, discovery, wonder and imagination. Too often now, video games stole playtime away, while imagination gave way to the special effects of the latest film offering, and the unreal world of the soap opera gate-crashed their innocent exploration of life. Style and fashion could push aside the mystery and beauty of their First Holy Communion day and, all too soon, they were dragged into adolescence before their primary school days had ended. Sadly, even in our education system the joy of learning could be lost in extensive testing.

Today also, there was the perception of the child as consumer by advertising agents, who introduced them to computer games and chat rooms designed to entice them to more challenging and sophisticated levels, often conscripting them into hysteria of style wars and more frightening possibilities. With these precious years of childhood rushed into adolescence came the peer pressure to take up alcohol and more sinister levels of drug dependence.

Dr. Neary's comments may be regarded by the modern generation as 'uncool', conservative, old-fashioned and out of character with the new Ireland, but nonetheless, they are absolutely on the mark. Increasingly, church leaders—Dr. Christopher Jones, Bishop of Elphin among them—have been rightly warning against the direction Irish society is going, and it's fair to say that more and more people are taking on board what they have to say.

For beneath all the glitz and glamour and falsity of Irish society, there is a feeling of unease, a sub-conscious that all is not well despite our new-found wealth. Many ordinary people are beginning to anticipate where we are going as a society, and what they see ahead leaves them with a feeling of disquiet. In an age of insatiable consumerism, we are in danger of breeding a generation fuelled by greed, selfishness, over-indulgence and a disregard for what might be termed the traditional decencies of Irish life.

Good neighbourliness seems to be on the decline. Many people do not know who lives next door—nor have they any wish to. Amidst vast housing estates, there is isolation, poverty, loneliness, depression and a host of social ills. A new phrase has been coined—'the Valley of the Tinted Windows'. Teen suicides, particularly among young men, are on the increase, drug abuse is rampant, our national alcohol problem is among the worst in the world, street violence is frightening, the murder rate has soared, gang crime is appalling and everywhere there is disregard for the rights of others.

Against this background, Dr. Neary's remarks are important. At the very least, they may force us into stopping short and taking stock of where we stand as individuals and as a nation. And in the process, we may be troubled by what we discover.

(*Sligo Champion* August 8th, 2007, p. 8)

I again express my grateful thanks to Dr. Neary and the Sligo Champion and my sincere hope that the spirit and memory of Father Flanagan can help us in the rediscovery and repatriation of ourselves and of our society.

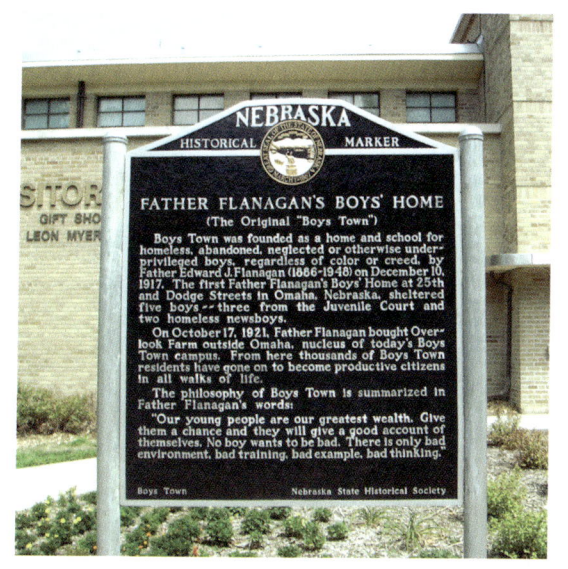

A historical plaque encompassing the story of Father Flanagan

The Symbol of Girls and Boys Town: 'He ain't heavy, Father, he's my brother'

Group photograph of delegation from Diocese of Elphin to Girls and Boys Town Home in Omaha, Nebraska, USA in July 2007, with Father Boes, Director of the Home. The group poses at the memorial statue of Father Edward Joseph Flanagan, founder of the Home in 1917. For much of his life, Father Flanagan resided and had his office in the house behind the memorial. It is now a much visited museum.

> "When one door of happiness closes another opens.
> But often we look so long at the closed door
> that we do not see the one that has opened to us."
> — Helen Keller

> "The worst loneliness is not to be comfortable with yourself."
> — Mark Twain

> "Don't be afraid to go out on a limb. That is where the fruit is."

> "A young person should never be made to feel
> that no great thing is expected of him."
> — Father Flanagan

Part 8

The End Game

CHAPTER TWENTY
Conclusions on Life

I hope people reading this book will get something worthwhile from it, and get some small share of the pleasure that I got from writing it. I can categorically say that I had immense pleasure in compiling this book, despite whatever problems may have faced me along the way – not least the fact that such a major writing assignment was new to me.[56] But I believe that in life we must always be prepared "to plough new furrows." The greatest pleasure I got was the revival of old memories of people (including deceased family and relatives), things and events, many of which I had totally forgotten about, or thought I had, but they were still there in the sub-conscious and, when recalled, came out vividly. I believe that memories help to put life into perspective, and that is surely important for all of us. I am truly grateful that the Good Lord spared me so that I had the opportunity to so write this book. I am very grateful to my family and all the people who gave me encouragement in undertaking the assignment. I am especially grateful to my late wife, Beatrice, to whom the book is dedicated, and who was the real inspiration behind the project. Thank you Beatrice for being such a great wife to me and mother to our children, and I ask your forgiveness for my shortcomings in life.

My book has basically been about all the things that are part of one's life. When I set out the framework for the book on my 70th birthday, I wondered what should be contained in this last chapter. The fact that I was moving into my autumn years probably focussed my mind on looking back on the things I could have done better in life, particularly my relationships with the various people in my life, which, in the rush of life, I didn't always attend to as well as I might have. In any event, by coincidence or otherwise, just about that time one of my sons gave me a book he had just read, *Tuesdays with Morrie* by Mitch Albom. I connected straight away with this book and found it had the material that I would like to have in this concluding chapter. *Tuesdays with Morrie* is a true story and recounts interviews (which took place on Tuesdays) between an aging and sick American Professor Morrie (Morris) Schwartz, and the author, Mitch

---

56. Thanks in particular to my daughter, Dervila, for her invaluable help in editing the book.

Albom, one of his ex-students. It is an inspiring read which I would recommend to anyone.

It is probably presumptuous and pretentious of me to claim that many of the philosophies and views on the meaning of life expressed by the Professor in the book coincided with mine, but at the very least they struck a close chord with me. So with grateful thanks to Mitch Albom and the late Professor Morrie, I list hereunder, as largely reflecting my own conclusions on life, just some of the very many statements made by the Professor.

- Learn to forgive yourself and to forgive others (p. 18).
- The way you get meaning into your life is to devote yourself to loving others, devote yourself to your community around you, and devote yourself to creating something that gives you purpose and meaning (p. 43).
- The most important thing in life is to learn how to give out love, and to let it come in (p. 52).
- Once you learn how to die, you learn how to live (p. 82).
- If you don't have the support and love and caring and concern that you get from a family, you don't have much at all (p. 91).
- Aging is not just decay, you know. It's growth (p. 118).
- The truth is, part of me is every age (p. 120).
- We put our values in the wrong things. And it leads to very disillusioned lives (p. 123-24).
- Wherever I went in my life, I met people wanting to gobble up something new. Gobble up a new car. Gobble up a new piece of property. […] You know how I always interpreted that? These were people so hungry for love that they were accepting substitutes. […] You can't substitute material things for love or for gentleness or for tenderness or for a sense of comradeship (p. 125).
- There's a big confusion in this country over what we want versus what we need (p. 126).
- But giving to other people is what makes me feel alive. Not my car or my house (p. 128).
- And love is how you stay alive, even after you have gone (p. 133).
- People haven't found meaning in their lives, so they are running all the time looking for it (p. 136).
- [Talking about marriage] If you don't respect the other person, you're gonna have a lot of trouble. If you don't know how to compromise, you're gonna have a lot of trouble. If you can't talk openly about what goes on between you, you're gonna have a lot of trouble. And if you don't have a common set of values in life, you're gonna have a lot of trouble (p. 149).

> *"Every actions of yours, every thought, should be those of one who expects to die before the day is out"*.
> — St. Thomas a Kempis

- The problem, Mitch, is that we don't believe we are as much alike as we are. Whites and blacks, Catholics and Protestants, men and women … But believe me, when you are dying you see it is true. We all have the same beginning—birth—and we all have the same end—death. So how different can we be? (p. 156–57).
- Be compassionate […] and take responsibility for each other. If we only learned those lessons, this would be so much better a place (p. 163).
- Love each other or die (p. 163).
- I am bargaining with Him up there now. I'm asking Him, "Do I get to be one of the angels?" (p. 163).
- Forgive yourself before you die. Then forgive others (p.164).
- There is no point in keeping vengeance or stubbornness […] These things I so regret in my life. Pride. Vanity. Why do we do the things we do? (p.164).
- Forgive yourself. Forgive others. Don't wait, Mitch. Not everyone gets the time I'm getting. Not everyone is so lucky (p. 167).
- I mourn my dwindling time, but I cherish the chance it gives me to make things right (p. 167).
- Death ends a life, not a relationship (p. 174).
- Love is when you are as concerned about someone else's situation as you are about your own (p. 178).

The last two statements above were made by the Professor on the 13th Tuesday of his meeting with Mitch. Mitch called to the Professor's home for their final meeting on the 14th Tuesday. Shortly afterwards, the Professor departed this life. Mitch concludes that Professor Morrie had taught him, above all that "there is no such thing as 'too late' in life. He was changing until the day he said good-bye" (p. 190). I fully concur with this. Thank you Mitch. Thank You Professor Morrie.

My own advice is that life always has its problems, but one must work through these problems as best as one can and do not let them overcome you. Deal with them with honesty and with integrity. The comments which I made at the end of chapter 9 relating to work, marriage and family are very much in keeping with this approach. In fact they are also very much my conclusions on life and the reader might wish to refer back to them now in such a context. Professor Morrie has given us a lot of very sound advice to help us on our way in life. I might add that we should never allow ourselves to be fooled by the apparent ease by which other people often seem to be able to live their lives—we can be sure that they too have many problems to contend with. Finally, remember that alcohol, drugs, or loose living will never solve life's problems.

Reader, thank you for journeying with me! I hope we remain friends!

Prophets Of A Future Not Our Own

It helps now and then to step back and take a long view.
The Kingdom is not only beyond our efforts,
it is beyond our vision.

We accomplish in our lifetime only a fraction
of the magnificent enterprise that is God's work.
Nothing we do is complete, which is another way of
saying that the kingdom always lies beyond us.
No statement says all that could be said.
No prayer fully expresses our faith. No confession
brings perfection, no pastoral visit brings wholeness.
No program accomplishes the Church's mission.
No set of goals and objectives include everything.

This is what we are about. We plant the seeds that one
day will grow. We water the seeds already planted
knowing that they hold future promise.
We lay foundations that will need further development.
We provide yeast that produces effects
far beyond our capabilities.

We cannot do everything, and there is a sense of
liberation in realizing this.
This enables us to do something, and to do it very well.
It may be incomplete, but it is a beginning,
a step along the way, an opportunity for the Lord's
grace to enter and do the rest.
We may never see the end results, but that is the
difference between the master builder and the worker.

We are workers, not master builders, ministers, not
messiahs. We are prophets of a future not our own.

— **Archbishop Oscar Romero, http://www.larynandjanel.com/important_
documents/prophets_of_a_future_not_our_own_oscar_romero.html**

Appendices

Appendix 1
Last Will and Testament of Michael Layden (deceased), dated October 23rd, 1916

Probate.

IN THE HIGH COURT OF JUSTICE IN IRELAND.
KING'S BENCH DIVISION (Probate)

The Principal Registry.

BE IT KNOWN that on the 12th day of January 1917 the last Will a copy of which, signed by the Registrar, is hereunto annexed of Michael Layden late of Knockitawn in the County of Leitrim Farmer and Colliery Proprietor deceased, who died on or about the 25th day of November 1916 at 39 Upper Mount Street, Dublin, was proved and registered in the Principal Registry of the said Division and that the Administration of the personal Estate of the said Deceased was granted by the aforesaid Court to Patrick Layden, School Teacher and Michael Layden Farmer, both of Knockitawn aforesaid, sons of deceased, the executors named in the said Will they having been first sworn faithfully to administer the same.

And it is hereby certified that an Affidavit for Inland Revenue has been delivered wherein it is shewn that the gross value of the personal estate of the said Deceased within the United Kingdom (exclusive of what the deceased may have been possessed of or entitled to as a Trustee and not beneficially) amounts to £3188. 6. 8. for the purpose of Estate Duty.

And that it appears by a Receipt signed by an Inland Revenue Officer on the said Affidavit that £90.14. 11 for Estate Duty and interest thereon has been paid the duty being charged thereon at the rate of £3. per cent.

Henry C. Warren. (Seal)
Registrar.

Extracted by J. A. Kiernan, Solicitor.

PROBATE ENGROSSMENT.

This is the last Will and Testament of me Michael Layden of Knockateean and Spencer Harbour in the County of Leitrim Farmer and Colliery Proprietor.

I hereby revoke all Wills and Testamentary instruments heretofore by me made. I appoint Patrick Layden of Spencer Harbour School Teacher in County Leitrim and Michael Layden Jur. of Spencer Harbour Farm Labourer to be the Executors of this my Will I direct my Executors to pay my just debts and Funeral and Testamentary expenses.

I give and bequeath my farm of land and house in Knockateean to my eldest son John Layden for his own use but if there be no issue the farm and House is to go to some of his two brothers James Layden or Peter Layden. I also bequeath to my wife my freehold house and land in Gub during her lifetime but she is to have no claim on it afterwards I also allow my daughter Bridget to have the free use of the front half of my house in Gub during her mothers lifetime if she wishes to live in it by herself and some more of the family her brothers and sisters I also wish to state that my house in Gub is intended for all my family to live there during their lifetime if they so wish and that no member of the family will have a greater claim on it than another member I also bequeath my farm in Drumasuane for the use and accommodation of all my family during their lifetime with equal rights to all but if anyone of my family gets married, they must then leave the premises if the majority of the other parts of the family so wishes I also bequeath £2500 that I have invested in the War Loan to my family when the Government pays it back to be divided in equal shares between 12 of them I also direct that the interest paid half yearly on £2500 War Loan shall be paid into the General Acount to maintain the house and clother the children I also make over all my coal mines in Roscommon and Leitrim to my sons to work for the use of the houses and a General account of the profits kept and divide them fairly.

WITNESS my hand this twenty third 23rd day of October 1916.

(Testator to sign here)   MICHAEL LAYDEN --------------------------

Signed by the above named Testator as his last Will in the presence of us both being present at the same time who in his presence and in the presence of each other have hereunto subscribed our names as witnesses.

Witnesses to sign here with   )
their address and occupation.)   Michael McWeeny   Farmer.
)   Spencer Harbour.
)
)   John Layden , Farm Labourer,
                                              Curglass.

Henry C. Warren.
    Regr.

I certify that the foregoing engrossment to be a true copy of original Will and that same contains 5 folios of 90 words each.

James A. Kiernan Solicitor, Ballinamore.

Appendix 2
Beatrice Layden's Favourite Prayer and Some Poems

Beatrice's Favourite Prayer

Mother of Hope, Star of the Sea,
sure consolation of a Pilgrim people,
guide our steps on our journey through life,
so that we may walk along paths of
peace and harmony,
of progress, justice and freedom.

Reconcile Brothers and Sisters,
may hatred and rancour disappear,
may divisions and barriers be overcome,
may rifts be closed and wounds be healed,
may Christ be our peace,
may his pardon renew our hearts
today and always.

Sometimes a sudden thought or memory
Brings on the flow of tears
But the tears we shed are tears of love
From all those treasured years.

When we think of you, we feel your closeness
And your spirit in our heart
How fortunate and blessed we are
You really never did depart

Each day we continue to talk to you
And keep your spirit ablaze
And ask your advice and tell you things
Throughout our waking days
For within us you will always live
So there is no need to fear
So on with life with happy smiles
As you'd want it, Beatrice dear

(23/08/03

Poem from Aisling in memory of her Mum's first birthday after her death on 23 May, 2003:)

Poems by Beatrice Layden:

Horizons

I see a sparrow lone and dry
I think of how he is born to fly
So unlike us and yet the same
In the universal mind of man.

What greater context can we have
Than to see all nature as one soul
Our common life, our common goal
All so mortal, so forlorn.

One shared pathway we must tread
Sure companions doubt and dread
Yet our thoughts must rise o'er these
And learn to soar amongst the trees.

Like the sparrow too we can try
To lift our glances to the sky
Horizons then unbounded be
Uncluttered by mortality.

Bedtime

A happy gurgle bounce and kick
Goodnight, my darling, snuggle in
A yawn, a sigh with droopy eyes
So goes to sleep a happy child.

Total dependence, constant care
These I must accept, provide
And lavish all my love and care
On this completely helpless child.

At the other end of life
The same conditions will prevail
Old, infirm, perhaps insane
Yet needing love and care.

Death

Vision recedes and grows more dim
Speech grows thicker, coldness creeps
The icy fingers of death's chill
Slowly taking a soul in thrall.

Oh that some miracle divine
Could give me back the one I love
Aged, deaf, contrary yet
A Mother, friend and comforter.

But I must bow my head and pray.
Accept what cannot now be changed.
There is no more that can be done.
The day is o'er the race is run.

Life

I have no new words to speak
No prime thoughts to wake the soul
Repetition, endless, deadly dull,
Dark, dank, deaf and dismally dour.

Expression rises to the top
Utterance release then somehow Peace
A miracle or so it seems
As the uniqueness of each thought is bared.

Totally inadequate, prosaic verse
Cannot reveal the separate niche
Of each and every human being
Cannot compare to one caress.

One groove for each to fill or fail
Only you can fill the void
Of loneliness and ease the pain
Of other's self-inflicted grief.

Appendix 3
Reflections on Life by Max Ehrmann and Marianne Williamson

"Desiderata" by Max Ehrmann (1872–1945)

This prose poem offers some very sound advice for living in today's world.

Go placidly amid the noise and haste,
and remember what peace there may be in silence.
As far as possible, without surrender,
be on good terms with all persons.
Speak your truth quietly and clearly;
and listen to others,
even the dull and the ignorant;
they too, have their story.

Avoid loud and aggressive persons;
they are vexatious to the spirit.
If you compare yourself with others,
you may become vain and bitter;
for always, there will be greater and
lesser persons than yourself.
Enjoy your achievements as well as your plans.

Keep interested in your own career, however humble;
it is real possession in changing fortunes of time.
Exercise caution in your business affairs,
for the world is full of trickery.
But let this not blind you to what virtue there is;
many persons strive for high ideals
and everywhere, life is full of heroism.

Be yourself!
Especially, do not feign affection.
Neither be cynical about love –
for in the face of all aridity and disenchantment,
it is as perennial as the grass.

Take kindly the counsel of the years,
gracefully surrendering the things of youth.
Nurture strength of spirit to shield you in sudden misfortune.

But do not distress yourself with dark imaginings.
Many fears are born of fatigue and loneliness.
Beyond a wholesome discipline,
be gentle with yourself.

You are a child of the universe,
no less than the trees and the stars;
you have a right to be here.
And whether or not it is clear to you,
no doubt the universe is unfolding as it should.

Therefore be at peace with God,
whatever you conceive Him to be,
and whatever your labors and aspirations,
in the noisy confusion of life, keep peace with your soul.

With all its sham, drudgery, and broken dreams,
it is still a beautiful world.
Be cheerful.
Strive to be happy.

"Our Deepest Fear" by Marianne Williamson

This reflection, often incorrectly attributed to Nelson Mandela, suggests that the only thing that limits us is our fear; if we can overcome this, we can truly fulfil our potential in every sense.

Our deepest fear is not that we are inadequate.
Our deepest fear is that
we are powerful beyond measure.
It is our light, not our darkness, that most
frightens us.
We ask ourselves, who am I to be brilliant,
gorgeous, talented and fabulous?
Actually, who are you *not* to be?
You are a child of God.
Your playing small does not serve the world.
There's nothing enlightened about
shrinking so that other people
won't feel insecure around you.
We are all meant to shine, as children do.
We were born to make manifest
the Glory of God that is within us.
It's not just in some of us: it's in everyone.
And as we let our own light shine,
We unconsciously give other people
permission to do the same.
As we are liberated from our own fear,
our presence automatically liberates others.

(Source: *A Return to Love*, by Marianne Williamson)

Appendix 4
Fishing

(A) A Few Hints that Might Help You Find a Salmon:

1. Move on Briskly.

If a salmon is going to take a fly or a spinning bait, it will usually take it straight away on first seeing the fly or lure. However, this is not necessarily the case with the worm. Thus when fly fishing or spinning, fish the waters relatively fast and use your available fishing time to fish as much water as is possible, consistent of course with pleasurable relaxed exercise. If you rise a salmon and it doesn't take, hold back from casting again for half a minute or more and then try again. Some salmon will rise several times, particularly salmon fresh in from the sea, before taking the fly. Pause briefly between casts. Sometimes changing the fly to a different size or pattern may work. If after about a dozen casts spaced out, and assuming the fish has stopped rising to your fly, move on so as not to pester the fish and thus put it off the take. I have rarely if ever caught a salmon through pestering it. If you can, come back later in the day and try again. I reckon a rising or taking fish remains in that mood for some time. So a cast over it the next day or several days later could produce results.

Incidentally, another important reason for moving along briskly on the river bank is to facilitate other anglers who may be coming behind you fishing the same waters. It is selfish and unsporting to hog a fishing spot for an undue length of time.

2. Avoid Undue False Casts.

Some anglers seem to develop the habit of making false casts as preparation to making a really good and possibly long cast. As a rule, I would suggest that false casting is a waste of both energy and fishing time. Very often the first (false) cast, particularly with overhead casting, would have been the best cast, had you directed your mind accordingly. You don't need to be told that you won't catch a fish in the air – the fly must be in the water! (It is reputed that many years ago, an experienced angler in the west of Ireland (perhaps it was the late Mick Kelly), when asked as to what fly fished best in that location, answered "the fly that's in the water"). Getting back to casting, occasionally it could be necessary to make one false overhead cast in order to get one's line into fishing position, particularly when you have retrieved the line and fly very close to you. However, a better bet normally in these situations is to give a short roll cast to straighten the line out in front of you in preparation for the next cast (see casting techniques later). It should be noted that in dry fly fishing, false casts are often used to dry the fly in the air before making the next fly presentation.

3. Tread Lightly and Out of Sight.

If fishing a river try to avoid heavy steps that could cause vibrations, which fish can pick up very easily. Also try and avoid making yourself visible to the fish, particularly where you are on a high bank overlooking the river. Perhaps step back from the river and increase the length of your casts. Fish can see you more easily when the water surface is calm.

4. Be Confident and Fish Carefully.

Always fish with confidence. I like to think that anglers are positive people by nature. Anyway, fishing with confidence seems to help in catching fish, strange though this may appear. Perhaps this is because when you are confident you are also fishing with care and attention and possibly skilfully as well. Occasionally pure luck can get you a fish, but one needs more than luck to get consistent results over the long period.

5. Square Casting and Working the Fly.

Generally I like to cast my fly straight across (square) the river towards the bank opposite me, rather than diagonally down river which is the normal fishing convention. Furthermore, I start working (i.e. retrieving or pulling in line) my fly very soon after it drops on the water, rather than leave the retrieve to the end when the fly has drifted down and around on my side of the river. I have found the square casting and the constant working of the fly to be particularly useful when the river is fairly wide and somewhat slow moving. However, I do cast diagonally down river as well, and I often have such a cast on the water on my side of the river before casting squarely across.

Incidentally, I am not a supporter of fishing a floating line for salmon, even in summer months. I normally fish an intermediate / slow sinking line in summer, and a standard sinking line, or a sink–tip line in spring up to around mid May. Perhaps, fishing with sinking lines explains the logic behind square casts and (fairly) fast retrieves, in that the fly is deeper in the water than with a floating line, and thus the fly can be worked faster over longer distances of water, without coming to the surface, thereby better mimicking the movement of juvenile fish or insects that might be the target of one's quarry. However, I cannot be sure that my method of fishing will catch more fish or not, compared to the more conventional methods. In any event, I would not have made the above comments about my methods of fishing, were it not for the fact that around the time of writing this section of the book, I happened to read an article by Phil Fairchild in the July 2007 issue of Trout and Salmon magazine. Mr Fairchild offers some observations as to what determines success and failure in angling, i.e. in catching salmon. The following are some extracts from the article:

> What I think marks out those fisherman whom I know to be consistently successful is that they tend to do things differently.
>
> There is a common tendency to fish like an automaton: decent cast at 45 degrees, initial upstream mend [to put your line up river of the path of your fly] and then let the fly swim round to the dangle, leave for a few seconds and then strip back fast prior to taking a couple of paces down stream and casting again. We do it because the great and the good have told us that this is how it has been done for years.
>
> The key to my technique is simply speed. I fish my fly with movement even in fast streams.[…]
>
> I tend to fish some sort of sinking line more than most. Very little of my year round fishing will be with a floating line, and if I do use one, there will inevitably be a sinking tip attached.
>
> The other key requirement is that I need the fly to fish from splashdown […]
>
> Stealth and gentle presentation are essential.
>
> Inherent in fishing the fly fast is that I will tend to cast square much more often than the norm. I am really not interested in the concept of dead-drift fishing; I want the fly to be moving so that the angry or nosy is compelled to investigate. In a crude way, my style is about the "induced take". I want the fly to appear in the fish's window, as near to the fish as possible, and then to take it away, forcing the fish to investigate with the only method available – i.e. to grab it.
>
> I am convinced that the other great advantage of the technique of the moving fly is that we feel and register many more takes than when we let the fly fish unaided. The other great advantage of fishing the fly actively is that I am certain you will successfully hook many more of the fish that take in the last few yards of each cast.
>
> The joy of fishing for salmon is that the longer we go on, the more we realise how little we know.

I fully concur with the last sentence, and not just in relation to salmon fishing but in all aspects of life!

6. Backing Up.

I find backing up a pool can often bring success. The conventional way is to fish a pool downstream and I will normally do this on my first visit to the pool. Later and particularly when I return to the pool after being down river, I would normally opt to fish the pool from the tail upwards to the flow-in, fishing squarely and working my fly fairly fast. I don't actually back up the pool; rather I walk up the pool (sometimes sideways) and cast squarely in the same way as if I was fishing down the pool. Sometimes instead, or even in addition, to hand retrieving the line, I will walk a couple of yards (up river) drawing in line with the rod point thus keeping plenty of movement in the fly. The concept of backing up is well established and the theory is that when backing up the fly appears suddenly in the fish's vision and due to territorial aggression, or otherwise, the fish is induced to attack the fly. Unfortunately, they don't attack the fly as frequently as we might like.

Fish normally face upstream against the flow, so that when fishing downstream in the conventional manner the fish has an opportunity to see the fly swimming in its window of vision perhaps several yards above it before it reaches the fish, so that the surprise element is lost. Incidentally, this a further reason for fishing a pool fast, when fishing down in the conventional manner (i.e. so as to enhance the likelihood of surprise). I find that relatively big wide pools are more suitable to backing-up. A practical reason for backing up a pool on your return from down river is that it eliminates your walking to the top of the pool. Of course if there are others fishing the pool down you would not normally fish it upwards until they are finished.

7. Getting a 'kink' out of your cast (or leader).

Often due to a wind knot which you have undone you may get a kink in your cast that you wish to straighten out. Simply wet the kink area and then rub it (with a hand on each side of the kink to give torque) a few times on the cork handle of your rod and the kink will disappear. If you are worried about marking the cork handle you could just rub the kink on the rubber of your wader.

(B) Some Knots Used in Making Up Fly Fishing Tackle

The notes which follow provide the minimum information necessary for a novice angler to set up his or her tackle. Thus only a few essential knots are described, but these are the ones that I have used successfully for years.

1. The Turle Knot.

This knot is used to tie the fly to the monofilament leader or cast.

a) Thread the leader end through the eye of the fly for about three inches.
b) Make a loop with a double wind at the end of the leader, i.e. in front of the fly (fly is behind the loop).
c) Tuck the leader, lying immediately behind the loop, in through the loop and form a new loop which you hold tight between the thumb and forefinger.
d) Pull on the leader and the old loop tightens and becomes a base knot for the new loop.
e) Let the fly now drop through the loop.
f) Then pull the loop tight at the base of the eye of the fly.

Note: A salmon fly has an upward eye, while a trout fly has a downward eye (this is demonstrated later). When dropping the fly through the loop, a salmon fly will be dropped through the loop from underneath the loop, while a trout fly will be dropped through the top of the loop.

2. Blood Knot.

The blood knot, which is sometimes referred to as a half-blood knot, is particularly useful for attaching the monofilament leader to tube fly hooks, and also for attaching monofilament line to hooks and lures used in bait fishing and spinning. It can also be used for attaching both salmon and trout flies to the monofilament leader, but as the knot can twist on the eye of the hook, the fly may not always swim straight, although normally remaining secure. So for this reason I prefer the turle knot as above.

To tie a blood knot:

a) Thread the monofilament line through the eye of the hook for about three inches.
b) Make a minimum of four, but possibly five or six, twists of the monofilament end around the core monofilament.
c) Then thread end of monofilament line through loop forming at the eye of the hook.
d) Pull tight.

3. Tucked Blood Knot.

This is really an adapted version of the blood knot, whereby the end of the monofilament line is threaded back through the encompassing loop.

4. Double Blood Knot.

This knot is ideal for tying two pieces of monofilament line together, and particularly when you want to put a dropper on your leader for a second fly, which requires you to cut the leader in two.

To tie a double blood knot:

a) Cross the two cut ends of the monofilament line to be joined. If you are making a dropper then leave one end long enough for this purpose, say eight inches. This end should always be the part of your leader nearest the fly line.
b) Using the same principle as for the blood knot in 2 above, make four to six twists of each end of the monofilament and tuck through cross loop at centre in opposite directions (this involves two separate consecutive movements).
c) Place both hands on monofilament leader on each side of the knot you have assembled, and pull both hands tight. Now the ends should be standing out in opposite directions and the long one of these will be the dropper.

5. Making Leader Loop and attaching Fly Line to Leader Loop.

a) An ordinary loop with a single knot, or a double knot if you prefer, may be used to make a loop on your leader to which the fly line is attached.
b) To attach the fly line to the leader loop just made, make a single knot at the very end of your fly line and pull the knot very tight, perhaps with the aid of a light pliers.
c) Thread the fly line end through the leader loop from underneath the loop. Twist the fly line once around the loop and through the corner loop between the fly line and leader loop. Keep this in place between your thumb and forefinger and pull the fly line fairly tight. Then pull fly line and leader tight.

During fishing you should check the knot now and again, particularly when a new fly line is being used that may not be supple and thus may tend to undo the knot.

6. Undoing Fly line from Leader Loop.

Simply hold the fly line end between the thumb and forefinger and push the leader loop towards the thumb and forefinger and the attachment comes apart. Never cut the end of the line off (unless of course it is frayed), as fly lines are generally tapered and you could affect the balance of the line by cutting a piece off.

Some fly lines now have loops attached to them; if so the procedures at 5 and 6 won't apply.

Always test your various knots after making them and then occasionally while fishing to ensure they are all in order. I normally tie all the foregoing knots using dark maxima monofilament line and I find they work very well. Other monofilaments may have different properties so I cannot speak about their efficacy with the above knots.

Sample of salmon flies: Row 1—Single hooks; Row 2—Double hooks; Row 3—Treble hooks; Row 4—Tube flies (hooks as desired to be inserted)

Sample of wet trout flies: Row 1—Green Peters; Row 2—Two Bibios & one Dunkeld; Row 3—Two Black Pennells and one Zulu; Row 4—Butchers; Row 5—March Brown; Row 6—Hare's Ears; Row 7—Greenwells Glory.

Notes: All flies in the first three rows are very effective salmon flies as well as trout flies (both brown trout and sea trout). I remember one time catching four spring salmon of about 11lbs each on a size 8 single hook Green Peter in the month of May over a two hour period in the Owenduff—pure slaughter!. The Butchers at the fourth row are good for sea trout as well as brown trout. The flies at Rows 5, 6 and 7 were our favourite flies for brown trout in the 'good old days' on the Arigna, Yellow and Erwin's Rivers.

Sample of dry flies – mostly Mayflies

Spinning lures

APPENDIX 4 291

Fly reels

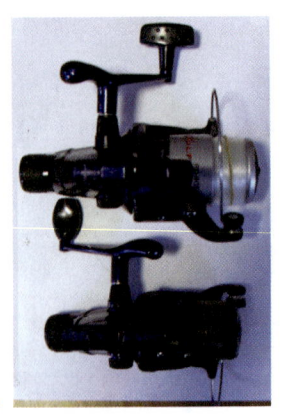

Spinning reels

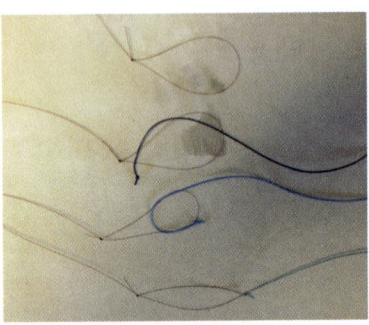

Putting loop on leader and attaching loop to flyline

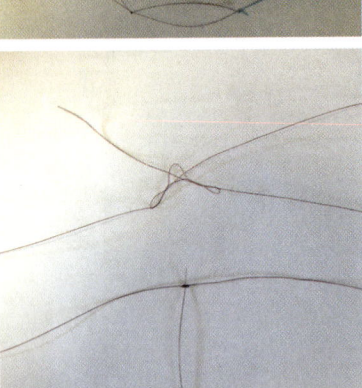

Putting dropper on leader (cast) using the full blood kn

Salmon fly with upward eye and trout fly with downward eye

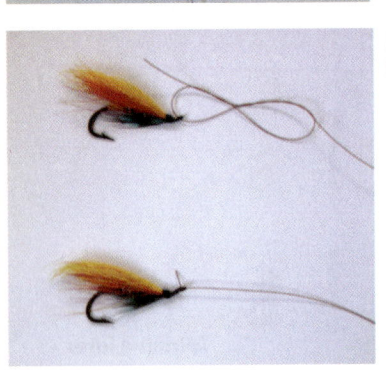

Making the half blood knot

Making the turle knot

292   APPENDICES

(C) Casting a Fly Rod

Overhead Casting.

The standard cast used by most fly anglers fishing the typical small and medium sized rivers in Ireland is the overhead cast. As the name of the cast suggests, the rod is positively raised over one's head causing the line and leader to become airborne above your head and behind, and then with a thrust forward of the rod, the line and leader projects out in front of you and alights on the water. The following are the basic rules for overhead casting:

- The rod can be held with either one or two hands, depending on whether a single-handed or a double-handed rod is being used. For convenience we will assume for the moment that a single-handed rod is being used. Hold the butt of the rod firmly, but not too tightly, with your right hand (if you are right-handed) and with your thumb on top and all four fingers gripping the butt just above the reel holder. Regard the rod butt and your forearm as moving together in one piece – this helps to prevent too much wrist action in your back and forward casts, giving you better control of your casting movements.
- Start the overhead cast by lifting the line, leader and fly (initially a learner should use cotton wool instead of a fly in the interests of safety) off the water with the rod tip close to the water. With decisiveness, but not too fast, make a backward and upward swing of the rod over your head and stop the back-swing a bit beyond the perpendicular, say at the 12.30 to 1 o'clock position. Pause for a split second to let the line and leader straighten out behind you but do not allow them to touch the ground. This pause is important because it allows the line to load the rod for the forward cast. Then with decisiveness, but again not too fast, make a forward cast of the rod and stop for a second or two at about 10 o'clock to give time for the line and leader to propel forward, and then you can drop your rod tip closer to the water. This pause helps the line, leader and fly to drop onto the water without fuss or causing a splash. My father's tip long ago for dropping the line and fly gently on the water was to imagine the water level to be three feet higher than it actually was and then drop the line and fly on that imaginary level, which should result in a gentle landing on the real water surface below.
- After some experience of casting, the above individual movements may tend to merge together. However, every now and again it is good to remind oneself of the individual stages involved.
- If you are using a double-handed rod, then the left weaker hand (if you are right-handed) will hold the butt of the rod below the reel holder, and both hands will work the rod.

- While the back cast should, in theory, start with the rod tip close to the water, as indicated above, in practice I normally start it at about 10 o'clock. This is because when finishing the retrieve of line on my previous cast I usually lift the rod tip to about 10 o'clock and then start my next cast. But to make the next cast easier, you could flick the line out in front of you with a miniature roll cast and then drop your rod tip in readiness for the overhead cast.
- A further important point concerns the control of your line during casting. Thus when starting your overhead cast, and assuming you are using a single-handed rod, hold the line (since perhaps several yards of line will be hanging loose from the reel as a result of your previous retrieve of line) with your left free hand and do not release the line until you reach about 11 o'clock on your forward cast. If you are using a double handed rod, then hold the line under the forefinger of your right upper hand and release also at about 11 o'clock.

Other hints on overhead casting:

1. When undertaking the overhead cast I like to lift my hand(s) fairly high over my head so as to enhance line trajectory and also, for safety purposes, to keep the fly well airborne.
2. Instead of making the backward and forward cast directly over your head, you could choose to go in an arc slightly left or right of your body. You might particularly want to do this for safety reasons when a strong wind is blowing that might cause the fly to go astray and hook yourself. Thus with a strong wind blowing from your left to right, then casting in an arc somewhat right of you should keep the fly well clear of your body. With a right to left strong wind, you could cast on your left side. Thus in this situation, and assuming you are right-handed, you will be bringing your right hand over your left shoulder. Incidentally, whether there is a strong wind blowing or not, I often find myself casting in an arc which is somewhat right or left of my body.

Roll Casting.

A roll cast starts at the end of the retrieve of line from your previous cast without pause, by lifting the rod tip high and moving it relatively slowly (no backward cast involved) in an arc to your side and bringing it back as far as about 2 o'clock. The fly and some line remains in the water out in front of you. The rod pointed high behind you and the line hanging from the rod tip gives a shape of a D loop. The important thing, however, is that as soon you have brought the rod back to the 2 o'clock position, you make a determined forward thrust of the rod out to the 10 o'clock position in the direction you wish the fly to fish. Generally, unless you have a strong wind in your favour, you will not get great distances with this cast.

However, it can be very convenient when there are bushes or other obstructions behind you that prevents you undertaking overhead casts.

Single Spey and Double Spey Casting.

The simple roll cast, just described, whereby you bring rod and line to your side, making a D loop and then trusting the rod forward, is the basic ingredient for all spey casts. Spey casting is very efficient from the point of view of the fisher's energy use compared to overhead casting, particularly when you are using long rods of 13 or 14 feet or more. It is also safer (you are less likely to hook yourself or somebody behind you) provided the cast is properly made, since the fly is never supposed to leave the water. Spey casting is particularly suitable where there are obstructions behind that prevent overhead casting. While spey casting is quite appropriate with single-handed rods, it is more normally associated with double-handed fishing on fairly large rivers.

The Commanding Hand:

When fishing down left bank[57] of river with single spey cast, the right hand is always on top, i.e. up on the butt of the rod, while the left hand will be placed at the very end of the butt. Thus the right hand is the commanding hand. This is the case regardless of whether one is naturally left-handed or right-handed. The reverse is the case when fishing down the right bank, i.e. the left hand is on top and this is the commanding hand (notwithstanding that you may be right handed).

The situation differs when using a double spey cast. When fishing down the left bank with double spey cast, the left hand is on top in command. The reverse is the case when fishing down the right bank, i.e. the right hand is on top.

In summary, in single spey casting the opposite hand to river bank is on top, while in double spey casting, the same hand as the river bank is on top.

Stance and grip:

Adopt a fairly wide stance with feet apart and with opposite foot forward, pointing in direction you wish to cast in, to that of commanding hand (i.e. right hand on top, then left foot forward). Move body weight from back foot to front foot when casting forward. Do the opposite weight movement when casting backward. Do not sway the body unduly.

---

57. The left bank means the bank of river on your left side as you look down the river in the direction of the flow of water. Thus the right bank is on your right side as you look down the river.

To hold a double-handed rod:

Hold the commanding (upper) hand, which can be either right or left, at the point where the rod with reel on it balances, i.e. the fulcrum. Hold the other hand at the very butt of the rod. When casting backwards or forwards, or even flicking line to your side, both hands should work in opposite directions, i.e. one hand pushes out while the other hand pulls in, and this will make the rod spring operate fully and greatly ease the effort the fisher has to make (see relevant reference below under 'Making a single spey cast').

Influence of the Wind on Choice of Single or Double Spey Cast:

Wind can determine whether you use a single spey or a double spey cast. Assume you are fishing downstream and there is a strong wind blowing upstream, then use a single spey cast. However, if the wind is blowing downstream, use a double spey cast. (This is for safety as well as for angling effectiveness). If wind is light, one could use either method, and it is likely that single spey would be used since there are less movements in it, but it often depends on one's preferences.

Making a single spey cast:

At the end of the previous cast, lift the rod tip up to about 11 o'clock and this will also lift some of the line off the water (at this stage you will probably have retrieved quite a bit of line which will be lying at your feet), then flick a loop of line to your upper side with a sweep of the rod in a relatively low trajectory bringing the tip of the rod a little behind you and with a loop of line further behind (but the fly and a good length of line still remains out in the water in front of you). Then with a positive cast forward, cast the rod pointing upwards which will flick the line out into the fishing position in the river, stop momentarily at 10 o'clock as usual. As you make the final cast or flick, the top hand is pushing the rod out while the bottom is pulling the butt into your body. Don't forget about your stance.

To summarise, the single spey has three movements:

1. Lift to 11 o'clock
2. Draw rod and line to upper shoulder in low trajectory, placing a loop of line behind you
3. Final forward cast

Making a double spey cast:

Start exactly as with single spey cast bringing rod tip to 11 o'clock, then bring rod around to your upper shoulder and a little behind in a relatively low trajectory, then dump line in a loop out in front of you with a forward but positive movement of the rod, then draw back rod in a relatively low trajectory to your lower shoulder and also a loop of line, then finally launch forward quickly with your rod pointing upwards to get your line into fishing position in the river, stopping briefly at 10 o'clock.

In summary, the double spey has five movements compared to the single spey's three:

1. Lift rod to 11 o'clock
2. Draw rod and line to upper shoulder in low trajectory
3. Dump line out in river in front of you
4. Draw back rod and line to lower shoulder
5. Quick forward cast of rod putting line out into fishing position

All of these movements are executed fairly quickly.

Further Instruction:

Single spey and double spey casting are complicated and you would be well advised to take instruction from a recognised fishing instructor and/or view an appropriate video or DVD. I recently viewed quite a good video by Michael Evans on *Spey casting and Salmon Fishing –Volume 1* as well as a useful DVD by Jim Vincent, Simon Gawesworth and Leif Stavmo on *International Spey Casting*. I also remember some ten years ago viewing a video on *Overhead Casting* by Michael Evans.

(D) Angling Safety Matters

Angling, like so many other things we do in life, calls for an awareness of safety matters. The following are just some safety precautions the angler should take:

1. When casting, be aware of touching overhead power lines.
2. When overhead casting, be aware of hooking people or animals behind you.
3. Be aware of hooking yourself or other fishers.
4. Wear glasses to protect your eyes from being hooked. Head gear that protects your head and ears ought to be considered, particularly in windy conditions when control of one's fishing is more difficult.
5. Wear a life jacket always when fishing from a boat, or on a river bank where the water is deep and dangerous were you to trip and fall in, or where a bank edge could cave in.
6. When you get tired after a long day's fishing, your fishing can deteriorate and carelessness could more easily lead to accidents. Better call it a day until another occasion.
7. Be careful when wading in water, particularly in fast flowing or deep water. Also be wary of the terrain under one's feet – slippery stones can easily result in a ducking. Life jackets should be worn in these situations.
8. Perhaps let somebody know when you go fishing in case some accident should occur. Certainly this should apply when going sea fishing.
9. Don't leave debris of any description behind you on the river bank or lake shore. This includes monofilament line and hooks that could cause serious harm to birds and animals.
10. Make sure that you have public liability insurance. I understand most household policies have such insurance, but it would be wise to check.

Bibliography

Books, Magazines and Newspapers

Albom, Mitch. *Tuesdays with Morrie.* London, Time Warner Books, 1997.
Alive (monthly newspaper published in Dublin). Uncredited reports on:
    "Only believers know how to really party says Pope." January 2007, p.1–2..
    "Pope upholds important role of religion in society." February 2007.
    "Young people are hope of church in Holland." January 2007.
    "Major debate on marriage needed, for sake of children." July/August 2007, p.1-2.
    "Mother's place is in home, says German newscaster." July/August 2007, p.6..
    "Review lists ten damaging effects of cohabitation." November 2007.
Benedict, Pope XVI. "Message for World Day of Peace." Rome: Vatican, January 1st, 2007.
Bible Alive November 2006. Uncredited article on prisoners' use of Bible Alive magazine.
Bible Alive. Daily reflections November 2006-November 2007 (individual dates given in text references)
Byrne, Peter, C.SsR. *The Power to Heal.* Limerick: Redemptorist Monastery, 2007.
Callanan, Frank. *The Literary and Historical Society 1955- 2005.* Dublin: University College Dublin, 2005.
Conry, Michael J. *Dancing the Culm.* Carlow: Chapelstown Press Ltd, 2001.
Corporate Tanzania, Annual Business Trade and Investment Guide 2006/2007. Switzerland: IMC, 2006.
Deering, Paul. "'Nuclear family' alive and well and living in Sligo." *Sligo Champion* June 20th, 2007.
Delphi Fishery News 2007, Galway, Delphi Fishery, 2007.
Sligo Champion. Editorial "Where we're going." *Sligo Champion* August 8th, 2007.
Fairchild, Phil. "The Singleminded Salmon Fisher." *Trout and Salmon* July 2007, p. 79-82.
Flanagan, Patrick. *Some Notes on Leitrim Industry.* Cavan: Breifne Historical Society, 1970.
Flanagan, P.J., "The Arigna Valley." *Journal of the Irish Railway Record Society* no. 34, vol. 7, 1964.
Flanagan, Fr. Edward Joseph, *Father Flanagan's Sayings.* Nebraska: Girls and Boys Town Hall of History, 2007.
Girls and Boys Town Home, Nebraska. *Management Documents.* Nebraska: 2007.
House of Commons. *Report of the Select Committee of The House of Commons into "Origin, Management and present State of the Arigna Iron and Coal Mining*

Company". London: House of Commons,1827.

IDA Report 1969-70, Dublin: Industrial Development Authority, 1970.

Irish Catholic. Uncredited report on comments made by Bishop Donal Murray, Bishop of Limerick "It's Not Just the Economy, Stupid." May 24th, 2007.

Irish Catholic. Editorial "Senator Mansergh." March 1st, 2007, p. 10.

Irish Times Motor News Section. "The Great Biofuel Fraud." *Irish Times* April 11th, 2007.

Jacobs, Francis. "Climate Change." *Sligo Champion* May 9th, 2007.

Kavanagh, Joe, O.P. "Hints of a Springtime in the Church." *Irish Catholic* February 22nd, 2007.

Keenan, Paul. "Over half of births to under-30s outside marriage." *Irish Catholic* August 9th, 2007.

Keenan, Paul. Report on Pope Benedict's comments ahead of Corpus Christi procession in Rome. *Irish Catholic* June 14th, 2007.

Kelly, Michael. "Tánaiste says PDs must respect religion." *Irish Catholic* February 22nd, 2007, p.4.

Kelly, Michael. "Tip-toe back to Church PDs told." *Irish Catholic* February 22nd, 2007, p.4.

Lynas, Mark. Comments on Global Warming as reported by Brian O'Connell. *Irish Times* March 17th, 2007.

Meehan, Joseph, C.C. "The Connacht Mineral Area 1 – Iron Mines." *New Ireland Review* 1907.

Meehan, Joseph, C.C. "The Arms of the O'Rourkes." *Journal of the Royal Society of Ireland* 1906.

McDonald, Frank. "Dumping it all on Africa." *Irish Times* November 18th, 2006.

McGarry, Patsy. "Priest says Ireland now 'secularised, vulgarised'." *Irish Times* March 13th, 2007.

McGarry, Patsy. "Bishop calls for tax system to encourage stay-at-home parents." *Irish Times* August 6th, 2007.

National Climate Change Strategy 2007-2112. Dublin: Department of the Environment, 2007.

O'Brien, Carl. "Wedded bliss beats seven-year itch." *Irish Times* April 24th, 2007.

O'Reilly, Peter. *Flyfishing in Ireland*. Great Britain: Merlin Unwin Books, 2000.

O'Reilly, Peter. *Trout & Salmon Flies of Ireland*. Great Britain: Merlin Unwin Books, 1995.

Plunkett, Dr. Dudley. *Saving Secular Society*. Stoke-on-Trent: Bible Alive/Alive Publishing, Easter 2007.

Purnell, Gareth, Alan Yates and Chris Dawn. *The Concise Encyclopedia of Fishing*. Bath: Parragon, 2001

Quinn, David. "Huge Majority Supports Archbishop's Podge and Rodge Remarks." *Irish Catholic* January 25th, 2007, p. 3.

Quinn, David. "Taoiseach Attacks Secularism." The *Irish Catholic* March 1st, 2007, p. 2.

Quinn, Dr. R. J. *The History of County Leitrim, Part 2: 1691 to Modern Times.* Dublin: Rialtas na hEireann, 1978. (Original slides by Dr. R. J. Quinn, Notes by M.O' Faolain, O.S.)

Redemptorist Communications. Bulletin for Sunday Mass of May 27th, 2007: Commentary on Christian peoples' respect for human beings. Dublin: Redemptorist Communications, 2007.

Reville, Prof. William. "It's time to reduce our gas emissions." *Irish Times* August 9th, 2007.

Reville, Prof. William. "Persuading ourselves that it is not too late to save the planet." *Irish Times* September 13th, 2007.

Reville, Prof. William. "Prof Dawkins should target PC rather than religion." *Irish Times* January 4th, 2007, p.13.

Robinson, Dr Howard W. *A History of Accountants in Ireland.* Dublin: The Institute of Chartered Accountants in Ireland, 1983.

Roche, Desmond, "John Leydon" (obituary). *Administration* vol. 27 no.3: Autumn 1979, p. 233-254.

Rockwell College Union Diary. Tipperary: Rockwell College Union, 2007.

Sargent, Trevor. Report on Green Party Conference relating to climate change. *Irish Times* February 26th, 2007.

Scally, Derek. "Pope Says Understanding Origins of Life Requires Both Reason and Science." *Irish Times* April 12th, 2007.

Schneider II, Dr A. Patrick. "Cohabitation: Ten Facts." *New Oxford Review* September 2007. (Available from www.lifesite.net/ldn/2007/oct/07100902.html).

Simmons, Charles E., "President Julius Nyerere: A Great Teacher and Devoted African Leader." 1999. (http://www.zmag.org/sustainers/content/1999-10/tributetonyerere.htm).

Sunday Tribune. "Rockwell College Still Living Up to Its Motto." *Sunday Tribune* Tipperary Supplement May 13th, 2007, p.5.

Sutterby, Roderick and Dr. Malcolm Greenhalgh. *Atlantic Salmon: an illustrated natural history.* Great Britain: Merlin Unwin Books, 2005.

Sweeney, Dr. John and Dr. Laura McElain. *Key Meteorological Indications of Climate Change in Ireland.* Cork: Environmental Protection Agency, 2007.

Tullock, Sara. *The Oxford Dictionary and Thesaurus.* Melbourne: Oxford University Press, 1993.

Walsh, Bishop Willie, "Why Saying 'I Do' Still Matters to Couples." *Irish Times* April 24th, 2007.

Weld, Isaac. *The Statistical Survey of the County of Roscommon.* Dublin: Royal Dublin Society, 1832.

Whelan, Richard. "Secularism – The EU is the Odd-Man Out." *Irish Catholic* March 1st, 2007.

Films

Evans, Michael. *Spey Casting and Salmon Fishing with Michael Evans, Volume 1.* Cowden (UK): Rapid River Productions, 1998. (Video)

Gore Al. *An Inconvenient Truth.* USA: Paramount Classics, 2006. (DVD)

Vincent, Jim, Simon Gawesworth and Leif Stavmo. *International Spey Casting.* USA: Scott Nelson Productions, undated. (DVD)

SOFT Skills REVOLUTION

Pfeiffer™
A Wiley Brand

SOFT Skills REVOLUTION

A Guide to Connecting with Compassion for Trainers, Teams, and Leaders

MAXINE KAMIN

WILEY

Copyright © 2013 by John Wiley & Sons, Inc. All Rights Reserved.
Published by Pfeiffer

An Imprint of Wiley

One Montgomery Street, Suite 1200, San Francisco, CA 94104-4594 www.pfeiffer.com

No part of this publication may be reproduced, stored in a retrieval system, or transmitted in any form or by any means, electronic, mechanical, photocopying, recording, scanning, or otherwise, except as permitted under Section 107 or 108 of the 1976 United States Copyright Act, without either the prior written permission of the Publisher, or authorization through payment of the appropriate per-copy fee to the Copyright Clearance Center, Inc., 222 Rosewood Drive, Danvers, MA 01923, 978-750-8400, fax 978-646-8600, or on the web at www.copyright.com. Requests to the Publisher for permission should be addressed to the Permissions Department, John Wiley & Sons, Inc., 111 River Street, Hoboken, NJ 07030, 201-748-6011, fax 201-748-6008, or online at http://www.wiley.com/go/permissions.

Limit of Liability/Disclaimer of Warranty: While the publisher and author have used their best efforts in preparing this book, they make no representations or warranties with respect to the accuracy or completeness of the contents of this book and specifically disclaim any implied warranties of merchantability or fitness for a particular purpose. No warranty may be created or extended by sales representatives or written sales materials. The advice and strategies contained herein may not be suitable for your situation. You should consult with a professional where appropriate. Neither the publisher nor author shall be liable for any loss of profit or any other commercial damages, including but not limited to special, incidental, consequential, or other damages. Readers should be aware that Internet websites offered as citations and/or sources for further information may have changed or disappeared between the time this was written and when it is read.

For additional copies/bulk purchases of this book in the U.S. please contact 800–274–4434.

Pfeiffer books and products are available through most bookstores. To contact Pfeiffer directly call our Customer Care Department within the U.S. at 800-274-4434, outside the U.S. at 317-572-3985, fax 317-572-4002, or visit www.pfeiffer.com.

Pfeiffer publishes in a variety of print and electronic formats and by print-on-demand. Some material included with standard print versions of this book may not be included in e-books or in print-on-demand. If this book refers to media such as a CD or DVD that is not included in the version you purchased, you may download this material at http://booksupport.wiley.com. For more information about Wiley products, visit www.wiley.com.

Library of Congress Cataloging-in-Publication Data

Kamin, Maxine.
    Soft skills revolution : a guide to connecting with compassion for trainers, teams, and leaders / Maxine Kamin.
      pages   cm
    Includes bibliographical references and index.
    ISBN 978-1-118-10037-0 (pbk.); ISBN 978-1-118-22363-5 (ebk.);
    ISBN 978-1-118-23705-2 (ebk.); ISBN 978-1-118-26206-1 (ebk.)
      1. Communication in management.   2. Interpersonal communication.   3. Interpersonal relations.   4. Management—Social aspects.   I. Title.
  HD30.3.K346   2013
    658.4'5—dc23
                                        2012048001

Acquiring Editor: Matthew Davis   Editor: Rebecca Taff
Director of Development: Kathleen Dolan Davies   Manufacturing Supervisor: Becky Morgan
Production Editor: Dawn Kilgore
Printed in the United States of America
PB Printing   10 9 8 7 6 5 4 3 2 1

*This book is dedicated to my Mom, Enid Kamin,
a master of soft skills.*

Contents

Tables, Figures, and Activities	xi
Preface	xv
Acknowledgments	xvii
Introduction	1

1. What Are Soft Skills?   **7**
- A Simple Definition   8
- The Importance of Soft Skills in Business   8
- Soft Skills in Practice   10
- A Progressive Definition of Soft Skills   12
- The Evolution of Soft Skills   13
- Teaching Soft Skills   14
- Soft Skills for the 21st Century   15
- The Leader's Connection   16

2. The Hidden Side of Communication   **19**
- Behind Our Human Interactions   19
- Aligning and Clarifying Your Motives   25
- Unpleasant Organizational Players   29
- What Is Clear Communication?   31
- Removing Communication Barriers   34
- The Leader's Connection   37
- Activities   39

3. The Power of Positive Intentions   **43**
- The Law of Attraction   43
- Kindness, Positivity, and Self-Esteem   46
- The Reciprocity Effect   47
- Why "Yes" Is So Powerful   51
- The Rewards of Altruism   53
- The Leader's Connection   54
- Activities   56

4. Tact and Diplomacy — 61
- What Diplomacy and Tact Accomplish — 62
- Ten Ways to Invalidate Others — 64
- The Language of Acceptance — 68
- Five Steps to Effective Listening — 69
- The Power of Questioning — 75
- The Leader's Connection — 79
- Activities — 81

5. The Challenge of Problem Solving — 87
- A Model for Problem Solving — 88
- The Nine Steps to Effective Problem Solving — 88
- The Role of Intuition in Decisions and Problem Solving — 99
- Other Elements to Consider — 100
- The Leader's Connection — 102
- Activities — 104

6. Soft Skills and Teams — 111
- Types of Teams and Their Uses — 112
- The Two Sides of Teams — 112
- Four Stages of Team Growth — 115
- Interventions That Encourage Results — 122
- Team Member Roles — 123
- The Leader's Connection — 129
- Activities — 131

7. The Personality Factor — 137
- Understanding Personality Styles — 137
- Finding Your Source of Energy — 141
- Discovering How You Gather Information — 144
- Identifying How You Make Decisions — 148
- Describing Your Personality — 150
- The Leader's Connection — 153
- Activities — 155

8. Taking the Sting Out of Feedback — 159
- The Challenges of Feedback — 159
- Types of Feedback — 162
- Giving Helpful Feedback — 162
- Receiving Feedback — 166
- Making Feedback Positive — 172
- The Leader's Connection — 173
- Activities — 176

9. Conflict and Cooperation — 181
- The Stages of Rage — 182
- Dealing with Difficult or Angry People — 185
- Assertive Behavior Techniques — 192
- Take Care of You — 194
- The Leader's Connection — 196
- Activities — 198

10. Conclusion — 205
- How Philosophy Grounds Practice — 205
- Your Purpose — 205
- Content Review — 207
- Parting Thoughts — 212

References — 215
About the Author — 219
Index — 221

Tables, Figures, and Activities

Chapter 1	**What Are Soft Skills?**	**7**
Table 1.1	Basic Knowledge and Applied Skills	9
Chapter 2	**The Hidden Side of Communication**	**19**
Figure 2.1	Circle	20
Activity 2.1	Values Ranking	39
Activity 2.2	Forced Choice	41
Chapter 3	**The Power of Positive Intentions**	**43**
Table 3.1	Reciprocity	50
Activity 3.1	Higher Self	56
Activity 3.2	What Do You Want?	57
Activity 3.3	An Attitude of Gratitude	57
Activity 3.4	Gifts from the Universe	58
Activity 3.5	From Negative to Positive	58
Activity 3.6	Thoughts That Serve	59
Activity 3.7	From Me to You	59
Activity 3.8	Random Acts of Kindness	59
Chapter 4	**Tact and Diplomacy**	**61**
Activity 4.1	Tact and Diplomacy Baseline	81
Activity 4.2	Validation or Invalidation?	84
Activity 4.3	Dialog	84
Chapter 5	**The Challenge of Problem Solving**	**87**
Figure 5.1	Problem-Solving Model	89
Figure 5.2	Root Cause	93

Figure 5.3	Overcoming Indecision	96
Activity 5.1	Practice the Model	105
Activity 5.2	What Is the Problem?	105
Activity 5.3	Tech Confusion	106
Chapter 6	**Soft Skills and Teams**	**111**
Table 6.1	Types of Teams	113
Figure 6.1	Two Sides of Teams	114
Figure 6.2	Sample Ground Rules	115
Activity 6.1	Why Teams?	131
Activity 6.2	Determine Ground Rules	131
Activity 6.3	What Is Not for Teams to Decide?	132
Activity 6.4	Initial Team Assessment	133
Activity 6.5	Your Trust Factor	133
Activity 6.6	Team Functioning Questionnaire	134
Activity 6.7	Brainstorming	136
Activity 6.8	Transportation	136
Chapter 7	**The Personality Factor**	**137**
Activity 7.1	Your Personality Type	155
Activity 7.2	Types and Teamwork	156
Activity 7.3	Relationships	156
Activity 7.4	Your Ideal Work Environment	157
Activity 7.5	Demonstrate Differences	157
Chapter 8	**Taking the Sting Out of Feedback**	**159**
Figure 8.1	The Johari Window	161
Table 8.1	Sample Chart	174
Activity 8.1	Giving Feedback	176
Activity 8.2	Team Feedback	177
Activity 8.3	Feedback Wanted	177
Activity 8.4	Just What I Need to Know	178
Activity 8.5	Appreciation	179

Tables, Figures, and Activities

Activity 8.6	The Appreciation Cape	179
Activity 8.7	"I Appreciate You!"	179
Chapter 9	**Conflict and Cooperation**	**181**
Activity 9.1	Button-Pushers	198
Activity 9.2	Common Reactions	198
Activity 9.3	How I Learned	200
Activity 9.4	What I Will Do	201
Activity 9.5	Skills Test	201
Activity 9.6	Stages of Rage	202
Activity 9.7	Practice Sorting	202
Activity 9.8	Angry Person	202
Activity 9.9	Role Plays	203
Activity 9.10	Appreciating Personalities	203
Activity 9.11	Insights and Endings	204
Activity 9.12	Be Good to Yourself	204

Preface

Welcome to the soft skills revolution, not only the book but, I hope, a cultural shift that raises the practice of soft skills to what I would call its "deserved place." Of course, an author of a book like this would say that! As you will see through the stories, research, and activities in *Soft Skills Revolution*, I do have a genuine belief that we can all be our best with a little help from our friends, co-workers, family, and extended family. Communication is such a gift—real communication. We all want to connect. It's part of what makes us human.

Some months ago, I read a quote on a friend's Facebook page stating that the definition of communication was "texting, except you talk out loud." OK, then! This book is about talking face-to-face. I hope that the ideas and activities offered here will expand your repertoire of communication skills and encourage you to connect in ways that are personally meaningful, however you choose to relate.

Many of the books that have been written about communication in recent decades mention that we live in a tumultuous world, with struggles to balance the effects of technology with the need for the human touch. This truism seems to be more necessary every day. Whether it is technology or other demands of life, we don't always make time for important things like genuinely communicating.

I founded my company, TOUCH Consulting, eighteen years ago with the high-tech/high-touch theme in mind, a concept that I first read about in John Naisbitt's book, *Megatrends*. I had been working in the field of human relations since the inception of my career, but the prediction that soft skills would become even more important intrigued me. Today, studies confirm Naisbitt's insight; soft skills are a major topic in books, magazines, and online, including *Chief Learning Officer*'s recent article "The Shift to Soft" (http://clomedia.com/articles/view/the-shift-toward-soft/).

New research and articles are coming out quicker than I can report them, even though major studies are included in Chapter 1. Technical skills are changing with such speed that the real challenge in today's workforce is the ability to learn and to communicate. Daniel Goleman, a pioneer in the field of emotional intelligence (EQ), believes that EQ is at least as important as IQ. In the *Chief Learning Officer* article mentioned above, Goleman is reported to say that he fears that business leaders might actually be "moving backward" in their EQ development. This would be a shame if it were true because, in the end, it's the lives we have touched along life's path that really matter. When we think about who has been most important to us, we remember those who gave us hope, inspiration, and a touch of kindness. For me, I remember some great bosses, including Dr. Eduardo Padron, president of Miami Dade College and on *Time* magazine's Ten Best University and College Presidents list; Steve Hendryx, retired partner with Accenture, and former director of training at American Express; and Betsy Pelz, teacher and former pre-school director at the University of Massachusetts. They are always "with me." I aspire to live up to their expectations, because they lived up to mine. They are in my heart. Many of my former colleagues are dear friends as well. I hope that work affords you the opportunity to establish meaningful relationships that you cherish in the same way I hold dear so many people with whom I have worked . . . and enjoyed.

In the years that I have been a consultant and an internal director in organizations, I have learned that the first step in the application of soft skills is the desire to practice them. Compassion and kindness are powerful motives. One has to want to be compassionate. I hope that, in the near future, we honor the need for compassion and trust and learn ways to establish relationships that are not only productive at work, but in our personal lives. We need interpersonal connection to avoid the isolation that so many feel these days. We need people who care about us. Learning soft skills can help us show others we care and foster the reciprocity that comes with relationship building, so we are able to both give and receive the joys of personal connection. With connection comes more joy and productivity in the workplace and more depth in our personal lives.

If I could prescribe ways in which communication would work all the time in all circumstances, I would be a sage indeed. Of course, this isn't the case. I can suggest ways that I have learned from many different avenues, including research-based practice, results of thousands of training classes, leadership experience in public, private, educational, and nonprofit sectors, and people. People teach me every day. I learn every day. Fortunately, all my lessons, even the tough ones, have made a positive difference in my life.

May you learn from the people in your life, and may they learn from you. You have the resources within you to be all that you can be and to make this world a kinder place. I wish you kindness in return, and the joys of camaraderie.

With best regards,
Maxine Kamin

Acknowledgments

First, I would like to thank my family for their patience and understanding in supporting me with this venture, and understanding my absence when I was writing. Everyone has been wonderful, from my ninety-one-year-old mom, to three year-old Emma. Jennifer, my niece, and a first-grade teacher, and Brandon, her husband, have both been incredible sources of delight. They are good people, and good friends as well as family. Thanks to Aunt Judy for checking in with me to see how I was doing at various points while I was writing, cheering me on, and to my brother, Stan, and sister-in-law, Linda, for their encouragement.

"You've Got a Friend," written by Carole King, is one of my favorite songs. The words apply to the people in my life who "are there for me." To those people who bolstered me, I would like to extend sincere appreciation.

A special thank you goes to Dr. Brad Stocker for his day-and-night (literally) review of the book, not to mention the countless hours of discussion about its contents and the articles and information he provided. More important, his long-time friendship and inclusion of me in his family are a special source of pleasure for me. Knowing that they are there is a gift.

Thanks to Mimi Clark, a trusted friend who gives me confidence not only by her support with writing, but in so many ways. From high school to the present, Mimi has been a friend I can turn to. She makes me laugh and smile, even through turbulent times and impending deadlines, and she shares the good times as well. There have been many! I also extend gratitude to Audrey Ressler, Steve Miller, and Rick Angelone, for bearing with me and talking about "the book," especially in its beginning stages.

I extend sincere gratitude to Greg Trulson for his model on problem solving and his great contributions to Chapter 6. I have admired Greg for years as a colleague at Miami-Dade College and as a seasoned presenter and consultant. I always remember his presentations and am honored that he contributed to this book.

Kathy Shurte is also a long-time friend and associate in many endeavors, including my working with her in various consulting and training programs and through our participation in the American Society for Training and Development (ASTD). A local, regional, and national leader in ASTD, Kathy took time out from her busy schedule to provide the terrific examples of how people might be motivated in Chapter 2 of this book. She did a great job. I'm looking forward to seeing books from Greg and Kathy in the future!

To the folks at Pfeiffer, I extend my gratitude, including thanks to acquiring editor Matthew Davis; director of development Kathleen Dolan Davies; development editor Mark Morrow; senior production editor Dawn Kilgore; Ryan Noll, editorial assistant; manufacturing supervisor Becky Morgan; and the kind and generous editor of this book, Rebecca Taff.

Thanks is not enough to all of you.

Introduction

In this fast-paced world of electronic communication and busy schedules, there is no doubt that we need quality human connection more than ever to offset the somewhat impersonal effects of quick exchanges through email, texting, video conferencing, and other technologies. Although these electronic pathways are convenient and efficient, sometimes there is just no good substitute for face-to-face, genuine interaction for building trusting relationships at work and at home.

Soft Skills Revolution is about how important it is for people to relate and connect, in person. The book is designed to help staff members, trainers, supervisors, managers, executives, and even families practice sound communication skills for better workforce and personal interactions. Using the principles in the book can also help build relationships in leisure time, not that many of us have much of it these days. With the information provided, you will think of ways to open up conversations in all walks of life.

The content of this book goes beyond "techniques." The emphasis is on the core philosophy that. to be a genuinely effective communicator, the wish to connect and communicate has to come from a desire to be authentic yourself, and also to see the world from someone else's point of view. These are two big concepts. You will have an opportunity to delve into them in a variety of ways, including by your own reflections, by reviewing short case studies, through examples of dialog, and by scenarios taken from actual situations and research.

Questions and Tips

Questions at the end of each chapter allow you to take what you have read and make it personal in a way that is meaningful for you. In and of themselves, the questions are learning tools. Taking the time to respond provides an open door for valuable insights into how chapter content may relate specifically to you. The increased perception that you gain from your answers may reinforce your self-knowledge, as well as point you in a direction of further learning and application. Tips follow the questions and are simple suggestions of ways to hone and practice skills.

Activities

Activities at the conclusion of each chapter start the ball rolling for you to focus more intently on applying what you learn. Most activities in the first part of the Activity sections may be done individually. It's your own workbook.

Following the activities are "Instructor Notes" for trainers and leaders to use in different combinations, including duos, trios, teams, and classes. Activities prompt thought, allow skill development and practice, and provide ways to transfer learning to the workplace and other venues. Trainers and leaders can use the activities one at a time or create full days of training.

The questions at the end of each chapter may also be used for instruction, for example:

- After a discussion about soft skills and their definition;
- In communication classes as icebreakers;
- In team meetings to define the topic of the chapter and to conduct a dialog or a discussion; and
- In individual conferences to highlight strengths;
- As ways to identify skills needed for personal development or team development.

The tips that follow the questions provide additional ways to apply concepts.

The Leader's Role

To reinforce the importance of leadership support and practice, there are questions and tips at the end of each chapter just for leaders in the section titled The Leader's Connection.

Organizations that value soft skills need buy-in from leaders to "practice what they preach." A positive workplace culture begins at the top. Leaders set the tone to encourage soft skills to be practiced throughout the organization and to recognize the value of meaningful discussion, dialog, feedback, and teamwork.

About the Chapters

Each chapter has a theme, and chapters build on each other. Below is a short description of each chapter.

Chapter 1: What Are Soft Skills? Chapter 1 offers a brief history of soft skills training and a progressive definition based on present-day use and global understanding of the term. A review of research demonstrates how important business leaders consider soft skills in their quest for finding competent staff. Soft skills are described in detail, as are employer demands for soft skills *over* traditional "hard" skills. Importantly, top leaders describe how essential they believe soft skills to be for the nation's ability to continue a leadership role in the world economy.

Chapter 2: The Hidden Side of Communication. Human communication is complicated, which is why it is important to recognize motives that are beneath the surface, whether or not they are acknowledged. This chapter speaks not only to verbal language, but also to the significance of nonverbal language. I discuss universal motives for communication and possible hidden agendas.

Chapter 3: The Power of Positive Intentions. Negativity can be a real energy drain. After examining possible motives, it is important to determine a positive reason for communicating. This may take some revision of an initial thought. If we had positive thoughts all the time, soft skills training would be easier. As human beings, we have all kinds of feelings, and we should. How we communicate those feelings is important. Focusing on positive intention helps. This chapter explores ways to turn negative thoughts into positive ones and explains "reciprocity," how we live in a social world with expectations and the give and take of everyday interactions.

Chapter 4: Tact and Diplomacy. You may think that tact and diplomacy are relative concepts, and you would be right. Some commonalities exist in all cultures, however. This chapter identifies those common qualities and describes what most people look for in healthy, validating relationships with others. A five-step process for effective interactions is presented, and ways to put your point across without hurting feelings is addressed. Solution-focused questions are covered as a method to promote understanding.

Chapter 5: The Challenge of Problem Solving. Research for the 21st Century, noted in Chapter 1, firmly states that high school and college graduates lack critical thinking skills. Chapter 5 offers a nine-step process for building the practical and intuitive skills necessary in today's work environment. By following this basic method, creative ways to solve problems emerge naturally. You can use this structured method independently or with others. For trainers and leaders, the model affords a way to approach problem solving for any team in an organization.

Chapter 6: Soft Skills and Teams. Everyone works in at least one team. Most of us work in more than one. With quality of problem solving at stake, it is important that work team members know the impediments that poor communication and other soft skill deficits pose to accomplishing goals. It is also critical to know how teams develop, much like infants develop into adults—from curiosity to productivity. Chapter 6 includes ways that people help or block team performance. The chapter provides interventions for each stage of team development; principles for knowledgeable facilitation and brainstorming; guidelines for when to use dialog and discussion; ways to handle disruptive behaviors; and appropriate techniques to move the team to greater understanding of root causes and solutions for effective problem solving.

Chapter 7: The Personality Factor. Literary works on personality and personality traits span centuries. Today, personality surveys, inventories, and training tools are used daily in the workforce to enhance job matches, supervisor and staff compatibility, and team makeup. In a positive way, personalities count a great deal in healthy companies. We all have strengths and challenges, which account for our different personalities and how we see the world. Recognizing and supporting team members' strengths is paramount to teamwork, as is helping teammates with challenges. Individuals must understand the dynamics of personality and have the tools and techniques to work effectively together. This chapter explores a number of these factors, including personality type.

Chapter 8: Taking the Sting Out of Feedback. Who really wants feedback? Why is the answer usually: "Not me!" Perhaps it is because nobody wants to be wrong. Self-esteem is often mistakenly tied up in being right. Knowledge of ways to give and receive feedback mitigates the sting that is often associated with the "feedback" word. Productive techniques encourage growth: the purpose of feedback. Chapter 8 includes principles of giving and receiving feedback and offers practical suggestions on how to begin a feedback discussion, how to gain buy-in, what to focus on, and how to conclude a session concretely.

Chapter 9: Conflict and Cooperation. Stuff happens. Even if you have tried your best to manage a situation, conflict may be hard to avoid. It's not much fun. This chapter discusses the causes of workplace conflict and how to turn it into useful communication. Conflict is not bad, but it does have to be handled expertly, and everyone can become an expert. With the practice of soft skills, tough interchanges have the potential of increasing understanding. Chapter 9 provides ways to uncover the source of a particular conflict and come to common ground.

Examples of communication techniques will help you learn ways to reach consensus and other forms of agreement and use suggestions to help others resolve issues and concerns.

Chapter 10: Conclusion. The title of this book, *Soft Skills Revolution,* implies actions that catch on to foster a change in the way we interact with one another. In order for this important transformation to occur, we have to be believers. That's what a "revolution" involves. Chapter 10 highlights the importance of putting your personal philosophy into action. A summary of the chapters is included for you to review what you have read and how the concepts and learning that you achieved through activities fits together with your personal mission.

Chapter 1

What Are Soft Skills?

WHAT'S IN THIS CHAPTER?

- A Simple Definition
- The Importance of Soft Skills in Business
- Soft Skills in Practice
- A Progressive Definition of Soft Skills
- The Evolution of Soft Skills
- Teaching Soft Skills
- Soft Skills for the 21st Century
- The Leader's Connection

There are a lot of interpretations for the term "soft skills." Some are even humorous. The truth is that the term is bolstered by years of research in the fields of psychology, sociology, and education, with a long history of practitioners past and present who promote and base their businesses on soft skills, but use a variety of other names. The reason for the expansive list of descriptors is that soft skills encompass a lot of areas, and experts are not always masterful in all of them. Just the definition is challenging, spanning the many components of communication, all of which would be impossible to name. For a beginning, we will trace the roots of soft skills briefly, and use a simple definition as a foundation.

A Simple Definition

"Soft skills" was a common term in the 1960s and 1970s. Students and teachers considered the term akin to human relations, interpersonal communication, and team building, all of which encompass skills that form the foundation for building relationships. A definition of soft skills from that time would encompass *listening, empathy, interpersonal communication, team building, group dynamics, sensitivity to others, compassion, integrity, and honesty.*

In recent years, forward-thinking companies have brought soft skills back into the foreground as critical to business success and have determined that they are a major factor in the country's continued prominence in the global economy. How companies define these skills now exceeds previous definitions, and that is testimony to the importance that soft skills have garnered. The following synopsis takes a look at research by major corporations that recognize just how important soft skills are to the advancement of business, government, and communities.

> For further history of how soft skills evolved, see the box entitled "The Evolution of Soft Skills" at the end of this chapter.

The Importance of Soft Skills in Business

A 2006 report entitled "Are They Really Ready to Work? Employers' Perspectives on the Basic Knowledge and Applied Skills of New Entrants to the 21st Century U.S. Workforce" revealed that employers view "soft skills" as even more important than the three R's (reading, writing, and arithmetic). The study, conducted by The Conference Board, Corporate Voices for Working Families, the Partnership for 21st Century Skills, and the Society for Human Resource Management, reported survey results from more than four hundred employers who rated skills on a scale of relative importance. Employers that participated included companies such as Microsoft, the Annie E. Casey Foundation, Dell, Inc., Phillip Morris, State Farm, Ford, and Pearson Education.

Table 1.1 Basic Knowledge and Applied Skills

Basic Knowledge/Skills	Applied Skills
English Language (spoken)	Critical Thinking/Problem Solving
Reading Comprehension	Oral Communications
Writing in English (grammar, spelling)	Written Communication
Mathematics	Teamwork/Collaboration
Science	Diversity
Government/Economics	Information Technology/Application
Humanities/Art	Leadership
Foreign Languages	Creativity/Innovation
History/Geography	Lifelong Learning/Self-Direction
	Professionalism/Work Ethic
	Ethics/Social Responsibility

Source: "Are They Really Ready to Work? Employers' Perspectives on the Basic Knowledge and Applied Skills of New Entrants to the 21st Century U.S. Workforce." (2006). New York: The Conference Board., p. 9.

The "Ready to Work" study reviewed a variety of skills, including what was defined as "applied skills" (termed "soft skills" in the introductory presidents' message) and "basic knowledge skills." See Table 1.1 for the breakdown.

As you can see, the types of skills that companies are looking at now reflect the changing nature of society and business, and include broad categories. Once related mostly to "personal growth," the new soft skills have emerged as essential to business and community organizations, even more so than reading and writing, as mentioned earlier.

Why the New Emphasis on Soft Skills?

The intent of the Conference Board study was not only to identify important skills, but to evaluate workforce entrants as to their capabilities in the areas determined to be most critical. This is particularly important because it raises the bar for soft skills as requirements for employment. If applicants are going to be judged on expertise in communication, teamwork, creativity, ethics, social responsibility, and other areas in Table 1.1, they will be evaluated in those areas at work as well.

In the overview letter from the group of presidents involved in the study, the consensus was that "far too many young people are inadequately prepared to be successful in the workplace." Their conclusions were based on survey results that showed that over one-half of new entrants are deficient in the most important skills—oral and written communication, professionalism/work ethic, and critical thinking. Applied skills trumped basic knowledge skills as being the most important.

Other research mirrors the 2006 study, including the 1991 report "What Work Requires of Schools: A SCANS Report for America 2000." In this study, conducted by the Secretary's Commission on Achieving Necessary Skills, listening and speaking were pronounced "basic skills." Their category of "interpersonal" skills includes:

- Participates as a member of a team,
- Teaches others,
- Serves clients/customers,
- Exercises leadership,
- Negotiates, and
- Works with cultural diversity.

Soft Skills in Practice

Although communication training programs are taught in many companies and organizations, the actual practice and acceptance of expanded definitions of soft skills is not elevated to optimum potential in all industries and organizations. Customer service, a field based on soft skills, is considered by many to be the worst it has been in decades. There is definitely an opportunity for training and development.

As far as executive leadership, Zenger, Folkman, and Edinger (2009) say, "Possibly because it has been so hard to define, social scientists have shied away from soft skills on the grounds that if the topic of interpersonal skills was a soft subject, this was simply over the top (p. 11)." For many trainers, Zenger is the king of soft skills curricula and programs for frontline staff and leaders. If Zenger admits that it is hard for executives to practice soft skills, you can bet that he has explored the difficulty of using soft skills at an executive level, where communication and workplace culture start. Similarly, in the article "Creative Leadership, Tough Times: Soft Skills Make the Difference," John Fleenor (2003) of the Center for Creative Leadership writes that today's leaders are struggling to use leadership styles that will help their organizations through the transitions required of the current business environment and that "soft" leadership skills, such as trust, empathy, and communication, are confusing for executives to balance with bottom-line approaches. A Center survey mentioned in the article found that the more stress that an organization is facing, the more important a leader's soft skills become, and that the likelihood of managerial flaws that cause leader derailment included problems with interpersonal relationships, difficulty building and leading a team, and difficulty changing and adapting.

A Change in Perception

Perhaps the word "soft" needs a boost of credibility. We know the "reputation" of the word:

> He's just a softie.
>
> He's soft on her.
>
> She's soft—thin skinned.

Should we always be "hard"?

> He took a hard line.
>
> She gave the hard facts.
>
> He's hardcore.
>
> She came down hard.
>
> She's hard as nails.

Because of the many perceptions of the term, "soft," soft skills remain an enigma. This is troublesome because soft skills are evident immediately, and are almost as obvious as hair color.

When you meet someone for the first time, you form an immediate impression. The impression has nothing to do with titles, whether the man or woman is a director or counselor. The impression you have is how the person chooses to communicate with you.

A Progressive Definition of Soft Skills

> Soft skills are the skills that really count. They are the skills that employers look for, that promotions are made of, and by which families thrive.

As we have seen, soft skills are hard to define, and the meaning has changed over the years with the inclusion of new competencies, such as cultural diversity. Because this book goes beyond traditional approaches, it calls for a more expansive, progressive definition and discussion of soft skills, an approach that is more appropriate for today's socially networked workforce. To change the perception of soft being "less," and to demystify the term, we will use the following definition from here on to more amply describe soft skills in terms of competencies and the categories that progressive companies recognize.

> Soft skills are interpersonal skills that demonstrate a person's ability to communicate effectively and build relationships with others in one-on-one interactions as well as in groups and teams. Skills include listening and responding in a receptive way to others' points of view; cooperation, and the ability to be flexible and take positive action in situations that require understanding of the circumstance, environment, and the culture of the person, organization, team, or family in which specific interactions occur. The practice of soft skills aids in communication and promotes problem solving, negotiation, conflict resolution, and team building.

As the touchstone for the discussions that follow, this progressive definition forms the foundation for subsequent chapters as well as suggested examples, activities, and tools that you may use to incorporate learning into your professional development plan and perhaps your personal life.

Questions

- What soft skills do you practice and consider strengths?
- What would you like to improve?
- Who is someone that you admire for his or her ability to excel in soft skills?

- If you have received soft skills or communication training, what was most helpful?
- What soft skills would you like to see your colleagues practice?

Tips

- Listen more than you speak.
- Keep an open mind.
- Reinforce others.
- Embrace diversity.
- Be positively proactive.

The Evolution of Soft Skills

The humanistic education movement was predicated on human potential and a value system that included self-knowledge as paramount to human growth and development. Soft skills in the 1960s and 1970s were taught in progressive universities, colleges, and community colleges and were the subject of workshops all over the country. At the University of Massachusetts School of Education, one of the most progressive learning entities at the time, courses in sensitivity training, group dynamics, and "Education of the Self (Ed Self)" were part of the curriculum. Classes were suspended at regular intervals in favor of modular credit workshop weeks offering an array of communication seminars. The "School of Ed," home to such faculty greats as Ken Blanchard, Sidney Simon, and Gerald Weinstein, was a haven for enlightenment about Rogerian (Carl Rogers) listening techniques and Gestalt therapy (Fritz Perls). Jack Canfield, co-author of the *Chicken Soup for the Soul* books, gave workshops close to the campus.

The movement encouraged people to examine their own motives, behaviors, patterns, values, beliefs, and attitudes. Topics that were traditionally ignored in academia rose to an elevated status, such as racism, religion, culture, sexism, and whatever emerged from students' personal histories. Feelings were not only accepted, but they were considered crucial for understanding every type of human interaction and for responding with empathy. The humanistic education movement challenged the status quo of sweeping feelings under the rug and embraced the learning that ensued from personal discovery.

Who *Got* It?

Those who were in classes and workshops had varied responses to learning and practicing self-disclosure and interpersonal skills. Faculty, staff, and community were divided as well. Students who "got it" were those who had positive self-esteem and could reflect on their own actions without self-incrimination or judgment—more as observers, intent on improving knowledge of their own intentions and responses. This also required "out of the box" thinking and suspension of judgment for the purpose of hearing the thoughts and concerns of others and practicing positive regard. People who were threatened or unaware of the educational principles involved in humanistic education referred to such teaching as "touchie-feelie." In that way, valuable realizations and practices could be dismissed without the naysayers having to show any type of expertise in the practice of soft skills.

Teaching Soft Skills

Experiences in the form of structured activities were the mainstay of personal growth sessions, rather than lectures. Leadership courses were a natural expansion of the practice of human relations skills and allowed participants to look at how their behavior affected other people and how their values influenced their decisions. Types of experiential activities that allowed people to work at developing relationship skills are included in the final section of this chapter.

After knowing oneself, the next set of humanistic education skills involved learning about and facilitating teams. Traditional group dynamics included sensitivity groups ("T" groups). The Esalen Institute was the most well-known organization that taught alternative education and sensitivity training. Founded in 1962, Esalen explored "human potentialities," a term coined by Aldous Huxley (Anderson, 2004). Many Esalen staff members and guest lecturers came up with their own theories and became (or already were) famous on their own accord; these included Deepak Chopra, R.D. Laing, Abraham Maslow, Rollo May, Dean Ornish, Ida Rolf, Paul Tillich, and Arnold Toynbee, to name a few. Folk singers and musicians who lectured and performed at Esalen included such favorites as Joan Baez, Judy Collins, Joni Mitchell, Jim Messina, John Sebastian, Ravi Shankar, Crosby, Stills, and Nash, and individual members of The Beatles.

In the outside world, peace and love were embraced by at least part of the boomer generation (underlying messages of which were depicted in the long-running musical, and now period play, *Hair!*), and *s*oft skills were considered essential for a worthy life. At the same time, students were protesting about war and the military-industrial complex, as well as the relevance of college courses to life in general. Richard Nixon, then President, was disturbed that the universities would become a sanctuary for radicals, and professors were blamed for not being able to figure out what relevance meant.

Gerald Weinstein, the initiator of the Education of the Self course at the University of Massachusetts, was a mentor to humanistic education faculty nationwide. "Ed Self" addressed various areas of personal growth within a framework of discovery and choice. Sid Simon, author of many books on values clarification, contributed to and taught the course as well. Dr. Simon also taught a host of other courses across the country that spread humanistic education to anyone interested in developing his or her communication skills.

Soft Skills for the 21st Century

Fast forward to the first quarter of the 21st Century, and the field of training and development abounds with the very same soft skills to learn, improve, and practice. You can find an infinite number of activities in books for trainers and consultants. Most companies that create training programs for supervisors have something like "The Supervisor as Self" as the first part of a series or have similar modules emphasizing the importance of knowing yourself before you supervise others. These include personality type, learning style, values, and leadership style. After one examines oneself, the next level of learning is team dynamics.

Team Training Approaches

Since the 1960s, we have seen all kinds of training for team building transpire: ropes courses where people do physical tasks with team member support; constructing toy cars, real bikes, and creating structures from newspaper, cardboard, pipe cleaners, Popsicle sticks, and whatever exists in the surrounding area. We have seen teams protect eggs with straws and drop the eggs off roofs to see whether the eggs have been properly nurtured by the team. In all these types of activities, "processing," that is, talking about what happened, how it happened, and how the people on the team felt is the most important learning that takes place. Many other types of team activities analyze the make-up of the team and use the expertise of facilitators and consultants to "unstick" the team and move on to more productive work. Quality teams have evolved from quality circles to Six Sigma to non-linear creative problem-solving teams. Since teams are such a large part of our work lives, their failure or success is crucial to business.

The Leader's Connection

Staff members look at a leader's soft skills first, whereas leaders sometimes think that how much they accomplish determines their success. This is true, of course, but how a leader treats people is really the road to accomplishment. Although much of motivation comes from within, it also comes from being valued by others. The most well-respected people in an organization are those who listen, respond with encouragement, allow free thought and meaningful discussion, and bring people together. In order to do that, soft skills are essential.

Kouzes and Posner, in *The Leadership Challenge* (2007), say that it's a job of a leader to create an environment of passion and pride. Performance will be the natural result. To build a cohesive and collaborative team, developing trust is a must, and trust comes from the simple acts of treating people with respect and fostering positive relationships. From the trust that the leader builds, a healthy team learns to trust and value all of its members. From that comes excitement in collaborative work and enthusiasm in continuing to work together toward common goals.

Leaders sometimes are unaware of the profound effect that they have on the people within an organization. A small slight may be blown out of proportion. An outright attack at a team meeting can hinder the whole team. (If it happens to one, it can happen to another.) People learn to be silent. They do not do their best. Their motivation diminishes. They may still produce what is necessary, but not what they could contribute if allowed, respected, and encouraged.

Soft skills are often difficult for leaders because they think they are unnecessary. They may think: "People get paid to do their jobs. Why should I thank them?" This is the hard line. It has no soft skill about it—no appreciation. On the other hand, leaders who use soft skills, and recognize the talent within their organizations, enlist people to use their strengths, and appreciate them for it. These sage leaders succeed in engaging their workforces and experience optimum results.

If employers are looking for new people in the workforce to be adept at soft skills, employers need to have the skills themselves, model the skills, support training of those skills, and consider soft skills just as important as "hard" skills. Onward to a new era in understanding.

Questions

- What are some of the soft skills you reinforce in your team members?
- How do you appreciate contributions to team goals?

- In what ways do you demonstrate that you trust your team members?
- What are the types of soft skills you use?
- What types of soft-skill training do you offer?

Tips

- Take the time to listen to people who seek you out. Consider it an investment.
- Encourage opinions other than your own.
- Probe for understanding before you respond.
- Appreciate your staff regularly.
- Provide courses and coaching in soft skills.

ABOUT THE NEXT CHAPTER

The next chapter examines motives that promote or inhibit people from practicing soft skills. Behind every action is a thought, feeling, or both. The practice of soft skills includes a close examination of motivation.

Chapter 2

The Hidden Side of Communication*

WHAT'S IN THIS CHAPTER?

- Behind Our Human Interactions
- Aligning and Clarifying Your Motives
- Unpleasant Organizational Players
- What Is Clear Communication?
- Removing Communication Barriers
- The Leader's Connection
- Activities

Behind Our Human Interactions

What lies in the resources of someone else's mind? Most of us don't have a clue unless we are told. Sometimes, we get the whole story truthfully and accurately. But at other times, we are met with interference. In this chapter, we will explore how

---

*Special thanks to Kathy Shurte for contributions to this chapter.

Figure 2.1 Circle

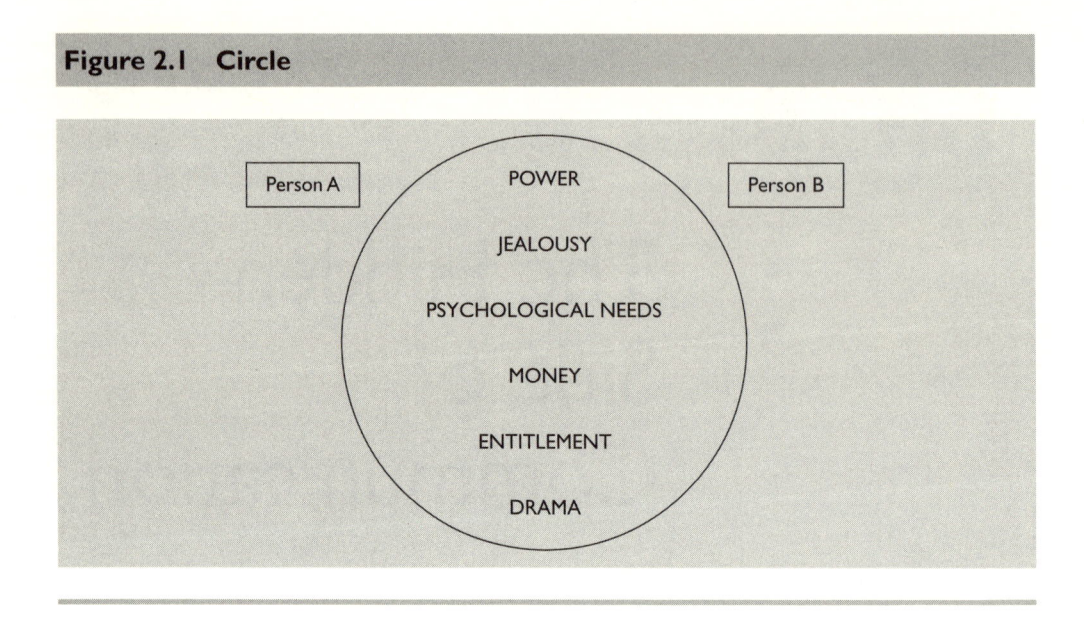

```
        ┌─────────────┐         POWER         ┌─────────────┐
        │  Person A   │                       │  Person B   │
        └─────────────┘       JEALOUSY        └─────────────┘
                       PSYCHOLOGICAL NEEDS
                              MONEY
                            ENTITLEMENT
                              DRAMA
```

others' motives (the reasons for taking a particular action or saying something) influence what is ultimately communicated.

Motives are influenced by beliefs, attitudes, opinions, stereotypes, psychological issues, environment, money, influence, power, fame, and core values. These filters appear in all sorts of ways. If we suspect that someone has a reason other than communicating clearly about a topic, that suspicion will hinder an honest interchange. Consider this schematic in Figure 2.1.

In order to have clear communication between people, the circle that separates Person A from Person B has to be addressed. The problem is how to uncover ulterior motives, since the very nature of the term "ulterior" suggests a lack of truth and sincerity. First, let us look at clear intention, and then we will look at how "perceived injustice" may lead us to recognize confused or muddled intention caused by motives like those depicted within the circle in Figure 2.1.

Intention

Intention is powerful. To understand intention, first consider some reasons we often intend to communicate:

- To get a point across,
- To be understood,
- To exchange thoughts,

- To provide support,
- To clarify,
- To present an alternative point of view,
- To summarize,
- To mediate,
- To promote, or
- To understand.

Presented with clear, transparent intentions, these communication goals help solve problems, increase self-esteem, widen perspective, encourage others to contribute, and increase individual and workplace motivation.

Perceived Injustice

It looks like the ten reasons listed above are clear, but sometimes one may sense that something else is going on. This may be just a hunch or an observation about tone, rate of speech, or word emphasis. If we think something is "off," we may feel violated by what we perceive as dishonesty. For instance, if we suspect that a colleague has a selfish motive for suggesting a plan, a need for power and control, or an ego requiring constant feeding, our suspicion may cause us to shut down or react to something other than what was actually said. In some cases, the actual underlying motive is the message. Here's a workplace example of a clear ulterior motive:

> Art, a manager in a large construction company, wanted to be the operations director of the company. He thought that gaining informal political power by negating ideas put forward by the current director would eventually land him the job he wanted. Art's staff members didn't outwardly challenge his actions, although it was clear what was going on. Many liked the current director's programs, which allowed the workers to be more self-sufficient, empowered, and included in front-line decisions. Even the union appreciated the current director's policies, and the members followed them as prescribed. Union grievances dropped to near zero because everyone felt heard and empowered to ask for change. Art was against the concept of inclusion, and he met any success with pessimism.
>
> When Art eventually realized his goal of becoming the director, he ended the programs, which resulted in a much less productive and

complaint-free work environment. The business suffered. Art didn't last long in his dream job.

In cases like Art's, personal motives are often known to an organization and staff, but politics and loyalties get in the way of productive communication. Those who may like new ideas are afraid of supporting them for fear of ramifications. Leaders who support the status quo and resist positive change may win for themselves temporarily, but in the meantime, people in the organization may not reach their potential, teams may suffer, and the company may not experience its potential. On the other hand, courageous leaders can embrace change, communicate their visions, and move organizations forward:

> Brian wanted to improve customer service in the airport restaurants and snack bars he managed. To do this, Brian embarked on a comprehensive plan to train managers and front-line staff and committed himself to leading a culture change. He involved the corporate office in the planning and gained the support of his superiors, including the president of the corporation,. He read books on the topic and eagerly participated in discussions about the content of training and what he wanted to achieve. His managers gained interest and were willing to try new ways of serving the public and of encouraging staff to provide "uncommon courtesy." "Uncommon Courtesy" banners were hung across airport eateries. Staff came to understand that customers deserved to enjoy the dining experience while waiting for a flight. The change resulted in the employees enjoying their work more. Sales at the restaurants rose, and customer satisfaction rates increased, as measured by delighted customers filling out comment cards. Customer comments went from 67 percent negative to 88 percent positive as the comment cards poured in (up from an average of twenty-seven per month to 277). Everyone felt good for being part of the heightened excitement of serving customers with care and kindness.

Results of Clear Motives

Clear motives are more likely to produce clear action, while ulterior motives may produce a whole host of unintended drama and unproductive behavior; senseless arguing, backstabbing, and ridiculing or blaming others instead of solving problems. This is the definition of a win-lose philosophy. A win-win mindset is more productive. It encourages all parties to win.

The C Shield Theory

I remember an old commercial on television about eliminating cavities. It showed an image of a tooth on one side of a huge clear shield that was supposed to indicate the power of the brand of toothpaste to prevent cavities; germs resided on the other side. It made an intimidating impression on me because whatever knocked up against the shield fell to the ground, no longer moving. The shield was impenetrable, and the cartoon germs were no longer with this world. Ominous for a kid.

Years later, I was explaining to a friend of mine who was having difficulty with his girlfriend, that I had a theory—the C Shield Theory—involving the way people might think that their emotions, desires, and opinions cannot get through an "invisible shield." My friend was questioning why he still had a connection to his ex-girlfriend, and she to him. I proposed that there was no shield separating them, like the toothpaste commercial, and that his body language and tone of voice told the true story of his continued affection for his ex, and that she knew it and felt it every time they ran into each other. When he smiled, frowned, shrugged, stared, or looked sad, she caught his emotion and intent. His emotions did not hit up against a shield that protected his feelings from getting through to the other side, and his feelings, unlike the germs, did not crash and die on the spot.

No "C Shield" exists in real life. Just about everything gets though the barriers we put up. In fact, according to a landmark study on communicating emotions and attitude, Albert Mehrabian (1981), a professor at the University of California, Los Angeles, found that 93 percent of what we communicate is through tone of voice and body language:

- Seven percent in the meaning of the words that are spoken,
- Thirty-eight percent "paralinguistic" (the way the words are said), and
- Fifty-five percent of meaning is in facial expression.

Here is an example of how these statistics play out in the real world:

> The chief executive officer (CEO) of "Do Good Things" tasked his vice presidents and directors to increase the number of good deeds they do so they could satisfy their funding source and meet specific goals to prove that, indeed, they were doing good things. The twelve-member group convened. All departments were represented. The stage was set. The leader of the group told the company representatives that they needed to do more good deeds or their contract with

the funding source would be discontinued. His tone was threatening and accusatory.

At first, everyone was silent as they thought through the implications for their work and future with the company. Everyone knew they could improve, but all decided to stay silent and hope the idea would blow over.

However, within five minutes their reactions were broadcast loud and clear. Several people rolled their eyes as they looked at each other. One person folded her arms and another looked down at the table. Another person sat up straight and did not move, while others doodled on pieces of scrap paper.

An hour later, few people had spoken, and those who did sounded defensive. The leader continued on, finally concluding the meeting by asking people to create a chart of what they would do to increase proof they were doing good things, since nothing had been accomplished at the meeting.

The leader had hoped the meeting would result in the creation of an improvement plan that everyone would buy into. Clearly, it didn't happen. So what did happen? Were group members willing to improve? Yes. Did they want to figure out ways to do that? Yes, but not at the expense of being humiliated. From the perspective of the team members, they were hindered from progressing with positive recommendations by the leader's tone and responded with their own self-protective body language. After the meeting, a great deal of discussion went on about tone and body language and how other participants reacted, all as a cathartic response to release anxiety. Little was said about the actual purpose of the meeting.

Erving Goffman, a social psychologist, writes about "sign vehicles" that convey information about interactions. "The expressiveness of the individual (and therefore his capacity to give impressions) appears to involve two radically different kinds of sign activity: the expression that he gives, and the expression that he gives off" (Goffman, 1959, p. 2).

Goffman used the terms "actors," "performers and performances," "observers," "co-participants," and "audiences" to explain how people communicate, recognizing that most adjust their behavior depending on the circumstance. For example, in the meeting scenario above, the backstage water cooler discussion one-on-one with a trusted colleague might be very different if the CEO of the funding source appeared after the meeting and asked how it went. Instead of describing names and gestures of specific individuals, such as, "And you know that [this person] always does this," the conversation might have a different spin. You might hear meeting participants say something like "we came up with many solutions to improve outcomes," and smiles would be the order of the day. This would be much more politically correct, which can be a good thing, depending on the circumstances.

Authentic communication is truthful communication. If your thoughts are congruent with the outward manifestation of what you are thinking or feeling, you are communicating authentically. Read on to discover techniques that will help you communicate using soft skills to accomplish your goals and help you to be clear in your motives.

Aligning and Clarifying Your Motives

There is a reason we say "A picture is worth a thousand words." It is because a graphic representation clearly shows how the parts fit together, who was seated where, or what shade of blue was woven into the tablecloth. When we communicate, we are in essence painting a picture in the other person's mind; we are trying to show him or her graphically what we are seeing in our mind's eye. If the speaker and the listener have different motives, communication will not happen. Here's an example:

> Pete and Ken work together. Pete has very strong feelings about some recent changes that have been made in the organization, especially about how they affect him. Pete wants to share his feelings with Ken. Ken, meanwhile, considers workplace conversations to be "verbal volleyball," where you simply hear what the other person is saying and then lob back your own version of how something similar happened to you. Pete's motive is to share his perspective and find someone who is sympathetic to that point of view, so together they can convince management to go back to the old way of doing things. Ken's motive, just as when he plays beach volleyball, is to win. As far as Ken is concerned, as long as he provides a comeback to each of Pete's statements, Ken feels that he is listening and winning—or controlling—the conversation.

Communication is an active, two-way process. Ken may think he is communicating with his co-worker, but because he is not actively listening to Pete's message, Ken is only hearing verbal cues that it is his turn to say something. Pete is talking into a void, and Ken is causing more confusion than clarity. Pete and

Ken's motives are not aligned, so their communication is compromised. Here are some other ways that communication is compromised. Do you ever find yourself talking to any of these caricatures?

The Light Bulb
Light Bulbs think they are the most intelligent people in the room and therefore must speak on every topic. After all, if you don't hear their wisdom, the conversation will not be able to move forward. Light Bulbs often have good ideas, but because they consider themselves to be above everyone else, after a while, they are ignored, or worse, made fun of behind their backs. What do you think the Light Bulb's motives might be in a conversation or a problem-solving session? You will not often hear this personality type support others, unless someone else in the group serves his or her purpose, most likely someone higher in the organization structure.

Light Bulbs' motives are to ensure their intelligence shines through. Here's an example of recognizing a Light Bulb's need and inviting his collaboration. Just imagine you are meeting with a Light Bulb to plan an office event and this is a transcript of your conversation:

> Lee, thank you for taking the time to meet with me. As I mentioned, it's my office's turn to plan the charity golf tournament this year. I know your group has done it several times in the past, and you always seem to have the best successes. Although I've planned conferences and other large events before, fun and fund-raising are not my forté. I would love to run some ideas by you and hear how you handled the different committees.

The Cynic
The *Cynic* often thinks everything everyone else is doing is worthless, boring, and a waste of time. Whereas the Light Bulb discounts others' ideas as inferior to his own, the Cynic's wisdom comes from simply knowing "we've tried that before, it didn't work then, and it won't work now." This may actually be the case, but the Cynic is more likely to vocalize that point of view. What are the Cynic's motives? Everyone knows he or she can go to Cynics when they don't agree with something progressive, because Cynics do not like much of anything new.

Although you might think the Cynic's motive is to make you look bad by pointing out how your old ideas are useless, Cynics perceive they are adding value to the discussion. They believe that, by showing you the error of your ways, you will appreciate their insights and consider them important members of your team. By acknowledging the perspective of Cynics, you may receive the benefit of their contributions, rather than be annoyed by their presentations. Here's an imagined transcript of a successful interaction with a Cynic:

> Claudia, I'm sure you've heard by now that headquarters (HQ) wants to bring back the annual charity golf tournament. I have to admit, when I heard our office was tapped to plan the event, I wasn't sure how successful we could be. After all, the economy is still suffering, and even in good times, it seems like Lee's group was the only one that could make this the premier event HQ wanted. I was thinking we could take a different approach and make it a fun event for the whole family, rather than an elite day for the VPs. Before I start pitching this, can you help me look at this from both sides?

By asking Claudia to help you look at both sides of your approach to the event, you will hear everything Claudia thought was wrong with previous events, and she will predict everything that can go wrong with your new approach—allowing you to develop a broad contingency plan and pull off a successful event.

The Heart

Hearts often have the emotional pulse of the organization. They have the trust of others because they are clearly as concerned about how people feel as they are about the productivity goals of the organization. Hearts recognize that dignity and respect go a long way. Sometimes, a Heart is the lone "voice of the people" who is disregarded in favor of charts, graphs, checkboxes, and measures. What are the Heart's motives for listening to a business discussion?

A Heart's heart is in the right place. We know how important relationships are in the workplace and how easy it is to get caught up in our work and overlook the human side of those doing the work. A Heart's motive is to be sure everyone feels O.K. and that no one is left out. It is important to genuinely acknowledge the Heart's ability to understand people so well and to capture the collective feeling of contributors. Here is a transcript of a successful Heart interaction:

> Helen, I'm so glad you're on our team! As you know, there are high expectations for this golf tournament. We are being held to a high standard. Lee's office has raised the bar every year—and our budget is conservative, to say the least. I was thinking that we should make it a fun event for the whole family, rather than an elite

day for the VPs. If we stay focused on being inclusive and cost-sensitive, the participants will respond to the fact that all donations will stay in our community this year—you know, neighbors helping neighbors.

In this interaction, you give Helen lots of reasons to stay focused on the business of your plan. And since you have already committed to family, being inclusive, and helping the community, you have addressed Helen's motives, and she is free to focus on the business at hand.

The Spirit

Spirits have the capacity for courage and determination. These individuals try to work through issues and pinpoint how to move forward with the goals in mind, including productivity and people. You want people with the capacity for courage and determination on your team. Use your communication skills to encourage the Spirit to achieve a positive outcome, as in this example:

> Steve, you've always impressed me as a guy who is not afraid of a challenge. Our office has been tasked with planning the charity golf tournament this year. In spite of the twists and turns in the economy, I believe we can pull off a very successful event. It will mean doing things differently than they've been done in the past, which is a little risky, but I believe it will end up being very rewarding for everyone. I'm putting the team together now and could really use someone with your tenacity and focus.

By acknowledging Steve's strengths and letting him know up-front that this will be a team effort, you have given him a good challenge. Your project has all the elements that he likes, and he has the skills to assist the team in moving forward.

The Leader

Leaders are not always the actual people in charge. Leaders can emerge from the group as competent professionals who can manage the interactions of diverse individuals and move the group forward. Good Leaders move the people from being a group to being a team so that everyone is working together to achieve a goal or to improve the organization. Leaders' primary motive for listening is to understand. They want to know your level of support, and why. They want to hear your ideas and concerns and create an environment in which you will feel safe and supported. A Leader listens with intent. In the scenario below, Michelle is a Leader at the time she is speaking to Charlie:

> Just think, me, an accounting clerk, on a high-profile team like this! I am very excited about this opportunity, but it sounds like you may have some reservations about this project. What is it that concerns you? [Charlie replies that he's been single for a lot of years and does not like family events.] There will be plenty of events behind the scenes, or you can drive the beverage cart and be the most popular guy there! Plus, we really need your expertise from the shipping department to keep everyone moving in the right direction and to get them to the food and entertainment on time. That is no different than getting parts in and the finished product out of our warehouses. Can we count on you, Charlie, if we promise to keep you away from the kids.

Although it is easy to stereotype how some people behave, recognize that we all have the capacity to play these roles. Few behaviors are absolute. The Light Bulb can also be a Cynic or a Leader; the Heart can be a Leader or a Light Bulb. The Spirit may also be the Leader. Based on our personality types (a comprehensive description is in Chapter 7) we see what we see, we make decisions on our own information and preferences. Although the characters above may sound extreme, each has value. The Light Bulb often does shine light on facts and perspectives we have not considered; the Cynic may suggest ways to be more productive and effective; the Heart may indeed be heard and improve motivation and pride at work; and the Spirit may permeate through chaos at a time that is right for the group to gain consensus.

Unpleasant Organizational Players

It would be remiss to ignore those in an organization who demonstrate psychological dysfunction. Unfortunately, some people thrive on ulterior motives, including bullies, sociopaths, and narcissists. These dysfunctional personality types are difficult to interact with, so be aware of typical types of behaviors and how to handle the challenges these people bring to an organization.

Bullies, Sociopaths, and Narcissists

Bullies try to make themselves right and their targets wrong, often in a way that is hurtful. Their tactics are to control, manipulate, blame, criticize, nitpick, whine, complain, find fault, undermine, degrade, and scheme. The principle motive for their behavior is to make themselves look good. Psychologists generally agree that bullying behavior is tied to lack of self-esteem; however, it is hard for targets of a bully to see their hurtful and often mean-spirited behavior as due to a lack of confidence. Some bullies are outright brilliant; so it is difficult to imagine such a dark personality turn.

The "targets" often are appalled by not only the bully's behavior, but by those who are silent and allow the bully to dominate. As Namie and Namie point out in *The Bully at Work* (2000), targets who speak up and confront the bully may tap into the guilt others feel for letting the bullying behavior continue. Targets are often strong and capable people the bully considers "nice" and cooperative. Because competition for attention and recognition drives the bully, nice people may be targets until they stand up for themselves and their beliefs. This often is too much for a bully to handle, and he or she will move on to an easier target.

Sociopaths and *narcissists* may be worse than bullies, as they often seem to lack a conscience and have little or no empathy for others, regardless of the consequences. Like bullies, they want to be in control and, according to experts, have protective patterns that are deep-seated based on their biological makeup and childhood experiences (Behary, 2008), as described in Chapter 9. These people have extreme personalities, yet they are present in the workforce and can wreak havoc in many ways. Sociopaths and narcissists can also be very charming. Thus, their outbursts and disrespectful behavior often take co-workers off guard.

How to Deal with Bullies, Sociopaths, and Narcissists

In dealing with bullying and personality disorders, the first priority is to be sure that you are not intentionally or unintentionally exhibiting any of the negative behaviors yourself. Second, you can choose to confront people's behaviors directly when they are directed at you and refuse to buy into or support the behavior when it is directed at others. Some bullying behaviors can be mitigated if everyone in the organization refuses to tolerate them. Other psychologically based personality disorders are hard or even impossible to change; but you will find some solid techniques in the next section and throughout this book to help you cope.

Still, you won't find a magic wand that will erase personality dysfunctions in others. Although some techniques can help, the most important thing to remember in dealing with dysfunctional behavior is that it's not you who has the problem. Make sure you maintain your dignity and self-worth, and perhaps reserve a bit of human empathy for the one with the disorder.

What Is Clear Communication?

You have to *want* to communicate clearly if genuine interchange is to occur, including embracing sound motives, distinctly expressing thoughts and ideas, hearing what the other person has to say, and accepting the response. This does not mean that you have to agree with the person who is speaking; however, it does mean not being quick to pass judgment and to give an opinion before really understanding what another person says or means. Reviewing the basic communication tenets that explain the communication process helps define the process, beginning with the source of the message.

Source/Speaker

If you are the speaker and have something you want to share, then your goal is to put that exact thought into someone else's head so he or she can see it through the filters and lenses of your life. That's exactly why communication is so difficult. No matter how complex or how simple that thought is, it is uniquely yours, shaped and colored by your entire life's experiences.

As the sender of the message, you have to first encode it—putting your message in a format that will allow someone else to not only recognize, but to be able to understand the message with every nuance and shade you intended it to have.

Here is a very basic example of encoding. Consider that you were born in the United States and you speak English as your primary language. You might think, "What's there to encode? I simply have to use the appropriate words and my listener will know what I mean; perhaps not. Let take a phrase from the earlier conversation examples about a company golf tournament—"This year, our golf tournament is going to be a family affair." Watch how the message changes through the communication cycle that follows.

Channel

The *channel* is the vehicle or vessel that will carry your message to the listener. Your options are many: face-to-face conversation, email, memo, poster, telephone conversation, text message, live or recorded video message, and you can think of more. The channel gives context to your message.

As the sender of the message, the onus is on you to select the best and most appropriate vessel for your message. If your message is important enough to send, you should carefully consider how you package it. Would you send your five-year-old off to kindergarten by packaging him in a cardboard box and floating him down a canal to the school? NO! Most parents today don't even trust the public school buses. Your child is so precious, you have to personally drop him off and pick him up in your personal vehicle equipped with safety belts and five-way air bags. If your message is worth sending, it deserves the same kind of attention. Continuing with our example, you have now called a meeting to discuss the golf tournament face-to-face with employees.

Decoding

The listeners must *decode* your message. That is not as simple as it sounds. Your listeners may not have been born in the United States. Your listeners may speak more than one language. Your listeners may never have played golf. The word "family" can be a highly emotionally charged minefield to some people; ditto for the word "affair."

Receiver

The *receiver* is the person who will "catch" the message. You try to be clear and keep your message simple and uncomplicated, but it doesn't always work. Returning to the golf tournament example, it would seem simple enough to assume that everyone in the room should understand your intention: to make the golf tournament a family affair. Despite the fact that the team is diverse, they all heard the same words, delivered the same way, at the same time. How do you think members of the team received your message? Here's an imagined transcript of what the members might be thinking:

Phil: Family golf? Oh! It will be a miniature golf tournament!

Wendy: Golf tournament? Why is it always about the "good old boy" network?

Charlie: Family? Well that should be a totally dysfunctional day. I'll volunteer to work the beer tent.

Michelle: Now this sounds interesting. My kids will love it. I wonder if we'll have a bounce house?

Claudia: I'm not sure about a golf tournament in this economy, but it sounds like the boss is willing to try something a little different. I think I'll take a wait-and-see approach for now.

Helen: This will be great! We can do age-appropriate activities while the golf game is on, then bring everyone together for a concert at the end!

Steve: No one is doing golf tournaments because of the economy, but if we position this as a family event and focus on our goal, we can eliminate most of the risk. I'm in!

You thought your message was clear and would not be affected by the filters and lenses of the listeners' lives, but nevertheless there was more than one version of your original thought. One would think that your clear message, packaged so neatly, had been opened and contaminated before it reached your audience!

In many organizations, communication is a one-way process. The boss, or someone up the chain of command, sends out a message and assumes it is received as intended and will be acted upon appropriately. No thought is given to shaping, coloring, or filtering—the message is just "communicated" out to the masses. And then chaos follows. Fortunately, you recognize that communication is a two-way process, and so do your listeners.

Response

Hearing is the physical act of allowing your ears to do what they were designed to accomplish. *Listening,* on the other hand, is a skill that must be learned and continually practiced to keep it sharp. *Responding* is to listening what a whetstone is to a knife—the tool that keeps it sharp. Responses come in two varieties: verbal and nonverbal, as we discussed earlier.

It is a beautiful present when your listener gives you a response. You will know whether the listener received your message as intended or you need to go back to the drawing board. Some very overt forms of nonverbal responses will also tell you when your message was not received as intended. Quite often, the response is somewhere in the middle, and it takes a volley of skilled listening and feedback to ensure communication has happened as intended.

What can you conclude from the following responses?

Phil (with a huge smile on his face): Great idea! I haven't played in years, but it's always fun… although it can be very frustrating, especially at the windmill.

Wendy (snarls): I'd rather do something a little less elitist, like a bake sale.

Charlie (simply puts his head down on the table):

Michelle: This sounds very interesting. My kids will love it, especially if we have a bounce house.

Claudia(nods her head): We've never done this before.

Helen (smiling): I'm excited! I have some great ideas for a theme. Oh! And the invitations… and the posters. This is going to be a huge success!

Steve (nodding): With the right people on the right committees, I can see this being the surprise success of the year. It's different, and we're the team that can pull it off!

Your characters, the Cynic, Heart, and Spirit, are on board. Michelle seems to "get it," Phil is up for something, but maybe not what you have in mind, Wendy and Charlie are sending very clear negative messages, and Steve sees the potential for the team to succeed.

Removing Communication Barriers

Analyzing how to deliver your message effectively is essential, as is breaking down potential barriers at each stage of the communication process. Thoughtfully considering each stage helps your message to be received well. Some of the suggestions below can help you remove the barriers.

Message

If your message is too lengthy, too short, disorganized, or contains errors, it may be misunderstood and misinterpreted. Poor verbal skills and inappropriate body language can also confuse the message. If you choose to encode your message in writing, proofread it aloud before sending it. For particularly important or sensitive messages, have someone else proofread them for you. Always consider your audience. What is their knowledge level relative to the topic? How are their language skills in general? Even if everyone around your conference table has earned a college degree, communication experts suggest that you communicate at about an eighth-grade level to ensure comprehension.

Barriers in context tend to stem from senders offering too much information too fast. There are two theories around this issue. Some say, when in doubt, less is often more. It is best to be mindful of the demands on other people's time, especially in today's ultra-busy society. On the other hand, and in the case of our example, you offered too little information too fast. Your message was lost in translation to some of your listeners.

Instead of starting your meeting by saying, "This year, our golf tournament is going to be a family affair," it might have been helpful to provide more context for the listener:

> Some of you may have heard the announcement that we are going to reinstate our annual charity fundraisers. Although the economy has

not totally solidified, our organization has been very fortunate. Sales are beginning to increase, and last week we offered two part-time employees full-time positions. We believe it is time to take a leadership role in our community and once again help those less fortunate than ourselves.

Our office has been tasked with planning the first event. Although we've always done a golf tournament in the past—and quite frankly, I believe HQ thinks we'll do it again—I've been given free reign to plan the event as I see fit.

We've all become closer over the last couple years as we collectively tightened our belts and made sacrifices together. Now I'd like to celebrate that. My idea is to do a golf tournament, and to add the element of family to it. I'd like to have something for everyone. Lee has promised to share his project plan with us, so we can learn from his best practices, and I'm sure you all have ideas as to how we can make this a great event and a successful fundraiser.

Sure, it is a little more information. However, the result is closer to your intended message. Phil no longer suspects he'll be playing miniature golf, Wendy understands why it's golf and not a bake sale, and even Charlie gets in the spirit as he asks, "Do we have to bring our real families, or can we bring a friend we like better?"

Once you understand context, you will become more aware of how you deliver your message so it is received as intended. You will become more considerate of the filters and lenses of your co-workers and, by the way, your family and friends. Good communication is not limited to the workplace!

It is the responsibility of all parties to ensure that communication transpires correctly. Senders must send clear messages, and receivers must send clear responses to indicate messages were received as intended. The following passages present examples of what that might look like. Let's go back to your original message, the one without the additional context.

Phil's response might have been: "Family golf? Where the entire family plays together? So are we playing miniature golf, or are we forming foursomes with our spouses and children?"

You know immediately that his vision is not the same as yours.

Even if Wendy's response was sent sarcastically: "And what will we do with the women and less privileged among us?" you will know that something is amiss! "Wow, Wendy! I'm not sure I know what that means. Let me explain a different way."

Charlie's response was clearly negative, but it was not enough to let you know what was behind it. You spoke, he gave his response, and now it is your turn to make the communication more clear. "Charlie, that's not the reception I was hoping for. Please tell me exactly what it is you object to … the golf, the family, your anticipation of the work it will take to execute this event? Please help me understand your objection." If Charlie does not respond, communication has not occurred. You definitely want to follow up with him offline after the meeting.

These are just a few examples of how people interpret interactions. Most consider a simple discussion or conversation—simple. For the most part, it can be effortless. The more people know about you and your general motives—kind, compassionate, or otherwise—the more communication can be easy. When people do not know you, they have a tendency to attribute qualities to you based on what they have heard or what they see. Organizational transparency means an open slate for the public to see your operations, budget, strategic plans, and the like. Personal transparency means you demonstrate that you are honest and congruent with your values; you are compassionate and kind; and you honor your organization's mission. If you show that on a regular basis, your transparency will aid in smooth communication because your motives will not be suspect.

Questions

- What do I practice to ensure my communication is authentic?
- How can I make sure I have heard others correctly?
- What ulterior motives have I noticed in the past?
- How have I chosen to respond?
- How do people know when I am looking for "the greater good"?

Tips

- Think about your motives when you communicate.
- If your motives are not authentic, wait to speak until your communication is reliable.
- Practice with another when you have an important message to impart.
- Respond to your colleagues.
- Verify that others have received your message as you intended.

The Leader's Connection

People trust leaders whose motives are not self-centered and line up with the organization's mission. Employees know when leaders have the best interests of their employees at heart. Even mistakes or differences of opinion can be worked through when staff members know a leader cares about them and shows it.

It is the leader's responsibility to recognize the importance of the communication cycle to provide clear messages and give meaningful responses. Leaders need to spend time thinking about and preparing messages, especially when the messages carry sensitive content. This extra care can save time and avoid rumors that result when people fill in what they consider "the blanks." The more questions you can answer with your message, the less you will have to answer later.

Leaders receive responses from their messages. Taking the responses seriously and responding with care and concern for staff goes a long way. Ignoring responses, positive or negative, only serves to send an "I don't care about you" communication, regardless of the topic initially addressed. Give everyone the chance to exchange ideas. Give them your full attention and your clear mind. It will pay off.

Questions
- How do I express authenticity to staff?
- In what ways do I manage business priorities and staff concerns?
- How can I do better?
- What steps can I take to ensure that my messages are clear?
- What have I learned from past communications?

Tips
- Review your messages before you send them out.
- Think before you speak.
- Use your influence for the common good.
- Avoid distractions when you are with others.
- Respond with respect.

ABOUT THE NEXT CHAPTER

In Chapter 3, we will carry on the journey to healthy communication. "The Law of Attraction" is explained and the positive outcomes of using the concept are examined. "What goes around comes around." The chapter will assist you in thinking and acting in a positive manner and being responded to "in kind."

Activities

Notes to Reader: The activities in this book are designed to be done individually or in a training environment. Whether you are in a group with others or working on your own, you may go back to the activities in the chapters at any time and learn from them on an individual basis.

Notes to Instructor: Suggestions for how to use the activities in a learning environment are included at the end of each activity.

Purpose: To recognize how motives and values align and to explore values that we act upon.

Background: Steven Reiss, Emeritus Professor of Psychology and Psychiatry at the Ohio State University, suggests that values and motives are related (*Psychology Today*, www.psychologytoday.com/blog/who-we-are/2201204/universalmotives-and-intrinsic-core-values, July 10, 2012). His supposition is that an intrinsic motive can be broken down into what people want and how much they want it. He also suggests that some values are universal; such as social contact, understanding, and order. He sees motives as an expression of values.

Criteria for Identifying a Value: Raths, Harmin, and Simon (1966), consider the *processes of valuing* as a means to assist people identify their values. They see values based on three processes, *choosing, prizing,* and *acting*, and offer the following criteria for defining a value:

> Choosing freely from alternatives after thoughtful
> consideration of the consequences of each alternative

Whether values are universal or merely personal, they play an important part in what people will stand up for at work, and sometimes what conflict ensues because individuals feel strongly about their values.

The following values clarification activities include learning techniques such as forced choice, rank ordering, prioritizing, choosing, and other ways to sort out areas of confusion and conflict.

Activity 2.1. Values Ranking

Instructions: Rank order the following values by choosing ten values from the list and ranking them from most important, "1," to least important, "10." There are spaces to add your own values if they are not listed. Answer the questions that follow the ranking chart.

Value	Rank
Achievement	
Compassion	
Competition	
Control	
Cooperation	
Expertise	
Family	
Fitting In	
Flexibility	
Helping Others	
Honesty	
Inclusion	
Learning	
Persistence	
Producing	
Recognition	
Respect	
Responsibility	
Social Interactions	
Standing Out	
Winning	

Top Value:

How I chose it:

How I demonstrate it at work:

How I feel and react if I do not practice my values:

Activity 2.2. Forced Choice
Forced-choice questions bring awareness of values differences and preferences. Look at the words below and choose the word on the left or the word on the right for each set of words.

Choose between:
1. Structure   Freedom
2. Gourmet dinner   Fast food
3. Camping   Staying in a hotel
4. Writing a letter   Texting

Write the reason you chose each word. Reflect on how that choice influences your everyday actions.

1.

2.

3.

4.

Note to Instructor: For Activity 2.1, form groups of five and have each person share only his top value, how he chose it, how he demonstrates it at work, and how he feels and reacts if he does not practice those values. This may be used as a work team activity as well.

For Activity 2.2, post the words on construction paper or flip charts, one pair at a time. Instruct people to move to one side of the room or another, based on choices. Once they reach the side of their choice, have them pair up, still standing, and discuss their choices. Feel free to add other choices to the list. If you have a small group, ask people to circle the answers they prefer and then pair up. Process with the whole group without evaluation.

Chapter 3

The Power of Positive Intentions

> **WHAT'S IN THIS CHAPTER?**
> - The Law of Attraction
> - Kindness, Positivity, and Self-Esteem
> - The Reciprocity Effect
> - Why "Yes" Is So Powerful
> - The Rewards of Altruism
> - The Leader's Connection
> - Activities

The Law of Attraction

You've probably heard the expression, "what goes around comes around." Well-known proverbs such as the Golden Rule (Do unto others as you would have them do unto you) or Platinum Rule (Do unto others as they want done unto them) describe a reciprocal process in communication and in action that we have heard through religious teachings or from parents and teachers. Theories in psychology, philosophy, religion, sociology, and social psychology provide explanations for "you get what you give" and "what you put out there in the universe you get back." One is the Law of Attraction.

You Get What You Give

Put simply, the Law of Attraction says that when you think positive thoughts and take positive action, others pick up your optimism and are likely to respond in the same way. When you think negative thoughts and act unkindly, others absorb your thoughts as well and may respond with similar intent and action. The Law of Attraction has existed in history for centuries, but it recently hit pop culture with the book, *The Secret* (Byrne, 2006), and the law of attraction books after this one took off like wildfire. That so many law of attraction books have been sold points to a growing awareness that behavior is catching—and not only behavior that is expressed verbally or by action. In addition to what is said, what we *mean* and what we *wish for* may be absorbed as well, the essence of another proverb: "Be careful what you wish for."

Thinking positive thoughts and acting in a receptive manner open up your natural ability to draw people to you. Energy travels. Endorphins, body chemicals, are released when people are treated in a pleasant and courteous manner. When someone is attacked physically or emotionally, other chemicals such as adrenalin are released, and the fight-or-flight response kicks in.

Key Principles

Key principles of the Law of Attraction include:

- Like attracts like. As you think a thought, you are attracting the same kind of energy.
- The more you think a thought, the more similar thoughts will come into your consciousness.
- The Law of Attraction does not recognize "don't," "not," "no," or any other negative words.

If you like a person, that person usually knows it. If you don't like a person, unless you are a good actor, that person has an idea that he or she is not on your favorites list. Turning to literature, *Lady Chatterley's Lover* (Lawrence, 1960) is an example of one person sending out positive intent to a person of a different class in early 20th-Century Britain. Lady Chatterley takes a liking to the gamekeeper,

Mellors. Although they are worlds apart in society, their initial connection turns into a love affair. As you think a thought, you are attracting the same kind of thought.

When interacting, you are sending energy. If you really believe in what you are saying, you attract enthusiasm. In positive environments, people listen. They become inspired. Colleagues expand your ideas, contribute, and enlist others. Here's an example:

> Roy is new to a company as its talent management director. One of the first observations he makes is that people deserve more recognition than they receive. Along with his team, he initiates a Token of Appreciation (TOA) campaign, whereby appreciation cards may be given by staff for any reason as a means of thanking colleagues for their work, support, or ideas. He is really excited about the program and goes "door to door" handing out cards to everyone in the organization, personally explaining the program. One of his staff members wants to lead the project. She sends out emails encouraging people to participate. Each month, prizes are awarded from recipients' cards that are placed in the TOA box. People are excited. The first month, 520 are dropped in the box. The second month, 655 are collected. By the eighth month, 695 potential winner cards are in the TOA box. Of course, everyone who receives a TOA is a winner. Some post the cards in their offices because they don't want to part with them, even though the cards are returned after the selection ceremony. The positive intent takes flight. Year to date, 4,357 people have been recognized, some several times.

Everyone wants to be recognized for his or her worth and value. Given the opportunity and the encouragement, people will recognize each other. The best-selling book *1001 Ways to Reward Employees* (Nelson, 1994) and its sequels confirm what motivation theorists have written about throughout history: recognition is the most powerful form of motivation.

Recognition is one way to be kind. Pierro Ferrucci in *The Power of Kindness* (2006) calls kindness a central power in our lives, with the power to transform us, possibly more so than any other attitude or technique. It feels good to be kind and to be the recipient of kindness. Kindness spreads, just as the TOA campaign caught on and multiplied in numbers and good will. The Random Acts of Kindness movement, now a foundation, is proof that a few people can create and spread kindness throughout the world. The foundation is the U.S. delegate to the World Kindness Movement. (See www.randomactsofkindness.org.)

Kindness, Positivity, and Self-Esteem

The same Law of Attraction applies to your thoughts about yourself. Affirmations or self-appreciations are often some of what coaches and counselors recommend in promoting healthy self-esteem. Positive affirmations help identify those qualities that you like in yourself. And if you like those qualities in you, others will, too. Here are some examples of affirmations:

- I am good at my job.
- I have great problem-solving skills.
- I am attractive.

Self-esteem starts with you. Everyone is good at something, and more often than not, at many things. This is not to say that we don't have areas in which we can grow. In a healthy environment, people are encouraged to share their talents and are mentored in the areas in which they can improve. Author Marcus Buckingham (Buckingham & Clifton, 2001) is a mastermind at teaching people how to "go for their strengths." His books emphasize the importance of knowing who you are and being proud of it. Leaders are encouraged to know their team members. Instead of using a one-size-fits-all list of expectations, Buckingham recommends sharing the wealth among team members and allowing a person's natural talents to be recognized and reinforced by others. This saves a lot of time and increases productivity. Instead of boxing people in, the strengths approach allows for creativity and initiative, skills that everyone can access if they are allowed to in a way that suits their strengths. Let's take a look at a scenario that demonstrates the concept:

> Joan is a creative leader who enjoys thinking of ways to improve her organization. Although she is good at detail, she would rather work with the big picture, figure out how to accomplish things, and do them, which is part of the definition of her job as a director. Some of the detail work that she is required to complete, she doesn't particularly like. It takes a lot of time because she is in a position of leadership, and going back and forth between meetings and projects that move the organization forward and working with necessary data input is a chore. At times, she wishes she could do one or the other, but not both. She has very talented professional staff members. She doesn't want to burden her staff members with clerical tasks; however, she experiments with using her team's talents to do some of the work.
>
> One of Joan's staff members, Eric, is a stickler for detail. He enjoys teaching one-on-one and showing counselors how to input data that is

critical for them to maintain their credentials in the field. One day Joan asks Eric whether he would like to take on the task of preparing everyone for an extensive training program. Rather than piecemeal the project, she genuinely inquires as to whether he would like to do the whole process. He says he would. She is grateful for the help, and thinks, "I hope I'm not giving him too much to do on top of all the other assignments he does with such expertise." Within a few days, Eric has the project organized and is whipping out administrative tasks and appointments with staff at record speed. Joan is copied on all the emails from grateful employees who appreciate his assistance. They range from "I can't thank you enough" to "I love you, Eric!" Eric is pleased. Joan is freed up to do what she does best, and the organization continues as a leader in the state for training and documentation.

Self-esteem comes from within; however, it is built through experiences. New experiences can enhance self-esteem greatly, especially if the basic fabric of skill is evident. Eric is now considered a guru in the project he successfully coordinates, and he has taken on even more responsibility with another area of the company in need of similar talent. His increased visibility puts him in a good position for future assignments that bring value to the company. The Law of Attraction is at work: he puts out good intentions, followed by action. Others respond with appreciation and good will.

The Reciprocity Effect

What if Joan took all the credit for Eric's project? Eric might not be as enthused and motivated. He might not work to his capacity. There would be an inequality in the interactions between Eric and Joan, and Eric might feel slighted and unappreciated. What if Joan demanded that, in addition to his project, he teach a new class? He might be resentful. Instead, Joan teaches classes to free him up to excel. She loves it. They both gain in the reciprocal interactions.

In 1964, sociologist Peter Blau published the first edition of *Exchange and Power in Social Life*, which looked at the concept of "reciprocity." Reciprocity involves people responding "in kind," exchanging good deeds for good deeds and negative behaviors for negative behaviors. It includes how much people perceive they are giving, and how much they believe they are getting back. *Perception* is the key word. It's all in the eye of the beholder.

If someone says hello to you, he or she expects a hello back. If you extend your hand, you expect someone to shake it. If you let someone stay at your house, you may not expect the favor returned immediately; but, if a hurricane sweeps through, you probably have the number of the person who stayed with you, and you might ask him to provide a safe haven.

At work, we expect cooperation. If we don't get it, we may refrain from giving it. There is a difference between going out of your way for a colleague (exceeding expectations), meeting expectations, or not meeting them.

> Carole is not very techy. Periodically, she has trouble with her computer. Bob is part of the technology team that troubleshoots technology problems. Whenever Carole calls him, he comes over to her station with a smile on his face and a kind word. She knows Bob likes ice cream. Every now and again, she buys his favorite brand of chocolate and puts it in the company freezer for him to enjoy. Although this is not expected, Carole appreciates the extra understanding he shows her, and the way he teaches her to troubleshoot on her own. Both are exceeding expectations.

PRINCIPLES OF RECIPROCITY

People expect that you will respond in kind and that positive actions will be returned, and of equal value to theirs.

If you "give of yourself," you are investing emotional energy in another person. The investor (not monetary) expects a return that is perceived to have as much emotional value as the emotional "gift" he or she gave initially.

Men Are from Mars

John Gray, author of *Men Are from Mars, Women Are from Venus* (1992), had the bestselling book since the Bible at one point in time. He was the nation's most renowned "relationship expert" for years. Gray also coordinated a series of national workshops for couples to attend. During the mini-retreats, instructors explained how men and women keep score. The class objective was to learn how to keep romance going forever.

According to the workshop principles, keeping score involved points based on values that the genders put on emotional support. Although the *points game* was considered playful and not highly scientific, it served the purpose of illustrating that men and women may have different ways of appreciating each other. For example, suppose a husband (Martian) gives a big gift (car) to his wife (Venutian).

He gives it out of love. However, he isn't the type who thinks about the little things that his wife likes; such as greeting her with a hug when he comes home, validating her feelings when she is upset, offering to help her when she's tired, or really listening, including looking away from the television or computer.

If a woman counts 1 point for each gesture of love, the car gets as many points as picking up groceries on a man's way home. The theory goes that the car is worth lots of points to the man, and if little things are forgotten, they aren't as important as the grand gesture of buying a car. But a woman still expects the little kindnesses that she desires.

Transfer this to the workplace. These are common expectations of staff members:

- Courtesy
- Greeting
- Cooperation
- Expediency
- Listening
- Supporting
- Remembering
- Following through
- Understanding
- Honesty
- Accurate work
- Initiative
- Problem solving
- Technical expertise
- Documentation
- Reporting

If we were to assign points to each one of these behaviors, it might look like a values clarification exercise, where those who value courtesy more than documentation assign a higher value to courtesy. If a CEO were assigning values, problem solving might rate higher than a greeting. In any situation, these values may vary, depending on the circumstance and other values that come into play. If the chairman of the board of directors did not say hello to the CEO, this may be more of a slight than if an engineer at her desk did not look up and offer a greeting when the CEO passed her office. The value of power has now entered into the mix.

We often keep score, even if it is not at a conscious level. Soft skills can mitigate the potential reciprocity imbalances that occur on a regular basis, whether or not they are intended. Positive language opens up communication and tells the receiver that the sender is willing to work in a cooperative manner. Consider these positive and negative statements and reciprocity principles that correspond to the positive column in Table 3.1.

Table 3.1 Reciprocity

Positive	Reciprocity Principle	Negative
I'd be glad to help with that.	Colleagues often seek help from their peers. This avoids asking the boss for direction and exposing a weakness. The helper receives respect.	That's not my job. Figure it out yourself. Nobody ever helped me when I came here.
How was your weekend?	Social interactions form the basis for positive relationship building.	It's none of your business.
Thanks so much for getting that report to me so quickly.	What causes pleasure to some may cause displeasure to another. Although affection is well received by many, some people do not like to be touched at work. It violates their personal space.	Let me give you a big hug! (Conditional – positive or negative)
Your project was excellent. It was so well thought out and you included credible back-up data.	If one-on-one, this can be well received. If in a group, outstanding work and recognition can be received with jealousy and resentment when someone is not recognized for his work.	Why do you always get credit for what you do? What about everyone else?
It was so much fun talking with you, my friend!	There is gratification in associating with friends and colleagues—just because it is rewarding in and of itself.	Nobody can be trusted here.
We all agree! That means the project will fly! Let's give ourselves a round of applause!	The sociability in a functioning work group involves experiences that are intrinsically gratifying.	Some people are so mushy.

Positive	Reciprocity Principle	Negative
I can put that display up for you.	Most people like helping others and doing favors for them.	I'm not going to do manual labor.
You really got me out of a bind with the display. If you ever need me to help you with anything, I'm there in a heartbeat.	One good deed deserves another. If people help each other out, they strengthen their relationship.	Look at those fools who helped put up that display. They are really kissing up.
I'm glad you asked me to help. You were so kind in helping me out last week.	If favors are not reciprocated, a person can be perceived as lacking gratitude.	Just because you helped me—that's your job. I don't have time to help you.
I liked the way you presented that. It helped all of us understand the challenges better.	Social approval is critical in building teams and relationships. Disrespect and disregard cause ill feeling, ill will, and have productivity consequences.	Your team is the one responsible. You'd better get on the stick.

Source: Reciprocity concepts from Peter Blau, *Exchange and Power in Social Life*, 2008.

Why "Yes" Is So Powerful

Earlier in the chapter, it was said that the Law of Attraction does not recognize "No." This is a point to remember. Whether or not you believe that thoughts are transmitted and "answered," "No" is a formidable way to receive minus points.

"Do you know how many hours this whole course takes?"

"No."

"Do you know where I can find a phone to use?"

"No."

In the Law of Positive Attraction, and in customer service research, "No" is distasteful and causes an immediate reaction.

Even children do not like to be told "No!" Early childhood educators try to use positive terms to show children what to do, instead of telling them what they cannot do. "Tell Johnny in words that you want to play with the blocks." "Let's see, would you like to play with the truck or the house until you can play with the blocks?"

Imagine approaching a building and seeing these signs in *red letters*:

STOP! DO NOT PARK IN SPACES THAT HAVE GREEN LETTERS. YOU WILL BE TOWED.

Better:

Please Park in yellow spaces that are designated for this building. We appreciate your cooperation.

If the Law of the Universe does not recognize No (or not), then you *can* park in spaces that have green letters.

Think of ways to say "Yes" instead of "No." "Yes, I'd be glad to find a phone for you." "Let me quickly count up all the hours in the courses that you would like to take." Soft skills are all about ways to put ideas and thoughts into positive terms.

Think of ways to say "Yes" instead of "No."

Positive

- I can.
- I will.
- Let me show you.
- Thank you.
- I appreciate your help.
- I like your spirit.
- I'm available for you.

Negative

- That's not my job.
- Not my area… I'll transfer you.
- I don't have time.
- You should know better.
- What about "closed" don't you understand?
- Look it up on our website.

Body Language

As described in Chapter 2, your body language gives you away. You can project a positive outlook or a negative one.

"What's wrong?"

"Nothing."

How many people have been asked "What's wrong?" If you were asked that question, something in your demeanor was giving cues to a companion that you were not pleased. Imagine the body language of the people asked these questions:

"Are you listening?"

"Don't you like the food?"

"You think that's a chick flick?"

"You don't agree?"

If you are in a store and the salespeople do not acknowledge you, how do you respond? How many points did they lose? Will you buy from them? What if you are at the grocery store and the checkout person says, "Did you find everything you wanted?" while she has already started scanning your order and has not looked up once? What if she looks at you before she starts, smiles, and says the same thing? You may know that she has been directed to say that to every customer, but you just may smile back.

People are always watching. If you are feeling tired and suffering from contact overload, try taking a walk if you can. Look at the scenery. Empty the thoughts that are exhausting you or the physical aches that come from sitting too long. When you are walking, breathe deeply. Listening to music is also a way to improve your mood. It can even improve your performance.

The Rewards of Altruism

Altruism is positive regard for others in an unselfish way. There are no points in the practice of altruism, and it comes from the heart. Mother Teresa was considered to be altruistic. Her image is one of giving to improve the welfare of others, with no expectation of anyone giving back. Princess Diana looked as if she had transcended this earth when she was involved in charity work. Her tenderness was apparent working with children. It gleamed in her eyes.

Buddhists believe in the accumulation of merit. Merit comes not only from good deeds, but from thoughts, images, and feelings, said to be a mind stream. Marc Ian

Barasch, author and former editor of *Psychology Today*, describes the belief: "Whatever we drop into [the mind stream] tends to keep circulating, whether a rusting beer can or a lotus petal. The idea is to place more positive intentions and loving thoughts into the stream while refraining from tossing in any more junk, thus purifying the waters and restoring what Buddhists consider the mind's natural ecology of benevolence" (Barasch, 2005, p. 143).

We have much to learn in the practice of giving—if we want to learn it. The Law of Attraction would say that the more you give, the more the universe will give back to you. The first step is unconditional positive regard for the people we meet and work with on a daily basis. From there, the rest will unfold.

Questions
- What do you expect from colleagues?
- What do you give?
- In your opinion, do you give more than you receive?
- What more would you like?
- What more can you give?

Tips
- Just give.
- Recognize what others do for you.
- Thank people each time they do something for you.
- Appreciate your colleagues verbally as well as nonverbally (smiling, nodding).
- Recognize that the universe does give back to you. Look for it.

The Leader's Connection

You can be the catalyst in the Law of Attraction. By your thinking and responding in a positive way, those whom you touch will naturally want to give back. Their gifts may be in kindness returned to you or in working harder for your organization.

Leaders sometimes think they have to be perceived as tough. If that's the case, tough mirrors tough, and staff will respond in kind with behaviors that may be considered defensive. Once a defensive stance is assumed, it's hard to eliminate

The Power of Positive Intentions

it. If you are a leader, you can turn your mindset from suspicion to appreciation. Appreciation will catch on.

Questions
- What "vibes" do you give out?
- What are you receiving from your staff?
- How much positive and how much negative are you hearing?
- Do you take responsibility for what you are sending out?
- When was the last time you reinforced someone for doing a good job?

Tips
- Be aware of the people in your surroundings and acknowledge them.
- Recognize your staff.
- Recognize your colleagues.
- Give credit where credit is due.
- Thank people for little things.
- Practice random acts of kindness.
- As a leader, you have people who support you. Support them.

ABOUT THE NEXT CHAPTER

The next chapter is about the art and skill of listening. We can immediately shut someone down by not listening, with consequences that transcend that one conversation. We can also gain respect and make another person feel validated.

Activities

Notes to Reader: The activities in this chapter are designed to be done individually or in a training environment. Whether you are in a group with others or working on your own, you may go back to these activities at any time and learn from them on an individual basis.

Notes to Instructor: Suggestions for instructors to use activities in a learning environment are included after the activities.

Purpose: To practice the Law of Attraction

Background: The science of quantum physics has demonstrated that everything in the universe is simple energy and that energy can make matter. Scientists have proven that thoughts can actually change matter. Our thoughts, beliefs, and feelings, waves of vibrational energy, drive our behavior. The Law of Attraction, as explained in Chapter 3, takes this concept to practical levels. One of the precepts is that what you give out, you receive back.

Some people call the energy that resonates on a positive level "source energy," "higher power," or "higher self." Generally, when we are in alignment with our "best self," feelings follow, such as happiness. Good feelings are usually followed by positive, productive action.

Activity 3.1. Higher Self

Instructions: Imagine a situation at work in which you did not feel 100 percent positive. Ask the "all knowing" part of you (you do have it), "How would I like things to be?"

- Be clear about why you want things to be different.
- How do you want to feel about it?

Ask yourself:

- How would my higher self view this situation?

- What can I think or do in this situation to feel better?

- How can I imagine myself positively influencing this situation?

Activity 3.2. What Do You Want?
Rather than pushing against what you do not want, find what you do want.
What do you want in the following categories?

- Time

- Tasks

- Skills

- Personal relationships

Some say that if you put what you want out in the universe, the universe will carry what you want back to you. You have to believe that it will happen. This doesn't happen immediately. It can work, however, if you are clear enough about what you want. For instance, if you want to increase your technology skills, once you identify your desire, you may find that a course in just that is offered at work or in your vicinity.

Activity 3.3. An Attitude of Gratitude
In order to manifest what you desire, live with an attitude of gratitude. This sends out positive energy that attracts more of what you want.
What positive emotions do you already have about:

- Job

- Family

- Friends

- Co-workers

Activity 3.4. Gifts from the Universe
Keep a journal about what you want and how the universe gives it to you.

Activity 3.5. From Negative to Positive
Change the negative statements below to positive ones, using the following as an example:

Negative: Nobody listens to me. (If you think this way, you are not likely to have people listen to you.)

Positive: I am worth listening to. (If you think this, you will exude the confidence that comes with the thought.)

Negative Statements

Because I had an upset with a co-worker, I cannot trust her anymore.

I am going to wreck my computer for its incompetence.

My boss doesn't like me.

Activity 3.6. Thoughts That Serve

Consider the questions below and whether a change might influence your thoughts and the energy you give out.

- At work, where do you give most of your attention?

- Are your thoughts about this serving you or not serving you?

Activity 3.7. From Me to You

Make a list of five people at work you would like to thank for something.

Create handwritten cards that describe why you want to thank each person and put it on his or her desk.

1.
2.
3.
4.
5.

Activity 3.8. Random Acts of Kindness

Make a conscious effort to do something kind during the day: open a door for someone, say hello to a stranger, drop by a co-worker's office to say hello and express appreciation for something she has done or to say how he helps others and you.

Notes to Instructor: Most of the activities in this chapter can be shared in duos, trios, or teams. Some are intended to be done individually, as described. Variations on the activities include different ways to share with others. You might:

- Have people share just one part of an activity;
- Suggest that they share the "An Attitude of Gratitude" with their families;

- Post appreciations;
- Suggest they make up their own negative statements and turn them to positive;
- Have participants make up negative statements and give them to team members to turn into positive statements; or
- Role play the negative to positive statements.

Chapter 4

Tact and Diplomacy

WHAT'S IN THIS CHAPTER?
- What Diplomacy and Tact Accomplish
- Ten Ways to Invalidate Others
- The Language of Acceptance
- Five Steps to Effective Listening
- The Power of Questioning
- The Leader's Connection
- Activities

Diplomacy encompasses having your needs met in a way that does not demoralize or hurt another person. *Tact* includes taking the feelings of another into consideration and responding in a way that demonstrates understanding and sensitivity. Consider the interactions below in light of tactful and diplomatic responses and the consequences of repeated insensitivity.

A patient says, "I've been to so many doctors. For a year, I've been feeling horrible. I've been given one pill after another. They just keep shoving pills in my face. They don't listen. They hear one sentence, write a prescription, and that's it. To make it worse, one doctor called me a hypochondriac because I have been to him for the same condition repeatedly. I'm still sick. Nobody cares."

A new counselor says, "My supervisor doesn't want to listen to my concerns about clients. She says that she learned the hard way and I should, too. I feel so bad. I want to do well. I'm new at this. I'm afraid I'm going to make a mistake. People get fired for making mistakes, so I try to pretend that I know the rules. But I'm scared. I need help. If I don't do everything I'm supposed to, a client could relapse, or worse…."

A letter carrier tries to explain to his supervisor that routes can be handled in a more efficient way so he doesn't have to go back and forth to areas that are in the same vicinity as the schedule demands. He can save the post office time and the taxpayer's money. The supervisor won't have it. She says, "Who are you to recommend changes? When you have my job, you can do what you want."

In the quotes above, it is clear that the doctor, supervisor, and administrator did not understand the seriousness of listening nor the consequences of ignoring important dialog. More than simple disagreements, the lack of focused attention caused personal and organizational harm, some of which could be grave. Suppose the patient stopped going to doctors altogether? This has actually been the result for many patients. Years after unproductive encounters with doctors, illnesses have been discovered that are life-threatening. Proper diagnoses could have saved lives. In the case of the supervisor, intelligent help and instruction could have increased the staff member's confidence and improved service to clients. For taxpayers, more efficient postal routes could have saved money, time, and delivery services to the mail carriers in the whole district.

What Diplomacy and Tact Accomplish

Why do some people listen and others do not? Is it because we do not want to be *bothered* with listening? Is it because listening is not recognized as just as important as telling? Is it because the competition to be right overrides paying attention?

At times, the reasons for ignoring the thoughts and feelings of others may just be oversight. But in a larger sense, we are used to prime time disrespect; it actually is approved and accepted in the media, a powerful cultural influence. For years, people have cheered television hosts and judges for insults, jeers, and insensitivity. Children have watched our "idols" and discovered that being nasty is amusing and lucrative. They have seen television and movies in which doctors, business leaders, and politicians have atrocious people skills. These are our role models, our heroes.

In Jay Carter's book, *Nasty People: How to Stop Being Hurt by Them Without Becoming One of Them* (1989), Carter suggests that invalidation, the way people hurt each other by discounting them, is contagious. He believes that invalidation is learned and passed down from one generation to another and from person to person. Feeling inadequate and compelled to control, the person who invalidates frustrates others enough for them to become just like the invalidator, and the cycle continues. Carter states that 1 percent "intentionally spread this misery to manipulate and control others" and that "20 percent do it semiconsciously as a defense mechanism" (p. 9). He notes that all of us do it at times, most not intentionally.

Invalidation has been called one of the most lethal forms of emotional abuse, killing confidence, creativity, and individuality. In this chapter, it is especially important to address this most blatant form of abuse, because it is the antithesis of tact. Invalidation is an action that denies another's right to be heard and understood. What does invalidation look like? It looks like judgment in many ways, including saying:

- "I don't care about your feelings."
- "Grow up."
- "Lighten up."
- "Be happy."
- "I was only kidding."
- "You are the only one who feels that way."
- "You are too sensitive."

"Maybe she was just trying to help you," is another form of invalidation. Years ago, a good friend gave me some prudent advice: *"Don't take the other person's side when I am trying to tell you how I feel."* This remains some of the best advice I have ever received. "Siding" with the adversary comes across to the speaker as betrayal. *Often, the listener is actually trying to help and appear understanding.* Invalidation is not always intentional, which is why it is so necessary to bring to the foreground as a communication technique that can be easily changed. In the exchange below, consider whether Janie intended to help or discount Benny.

Benny: "I had a tough day at work today."

Janie: "What happened?"

Benny: "My boss jerked me around like nobody's business. He made me do a job over that was done perfectly the first time."

Janie: "Well, maybe he was really trying to help you… teach you a new technique."

Benny: "He wouldn't know a new technique if it hit him in the face."

Janie: "There must have been a reason he made you do the work over."

Benny: "Hey, you weren't there. This guy wouldn't have a job without me. Who are you to be taking his side? I thought you were married to *me*! "

Without thinking of how her comments would affect Benny, Jamie had an almost automatic response to take the "other side." Did she mean to start an argument? If the answer is, "No," she missed the mark by discounting Benny's feelings.

Ten Ways to Invalidate Others

To categorize invalidations, consider these ten ways that may deflate people. Examples depict actions that are not helpful. We will discuss ways to be supportive later.

Ordering

- "I don't care what your boss told you to do. I'm telling you that I want you to do it my way."
- "Get those pictures to me immediately!"
- "Stop your whining. Do your job."

Threatening

- "I'll see to it that Mr. Santos knows that you are the only one who didn't submit your information in time."
- "If you don't come up to speed, you won't have your job for long."

Preaching
- "You shouldn't act like a spoiled brat. Maybe that worked when you were a little girl, but it doesn't work now."
- "You ought to be respectful."

Giving Solutions
- "This is how you should solve the problem."
- "You should just do what's obvious…."
- "Just tell the woman that you're tired of her playing loud music."
- "Just ignore him when he insults you."

Lecturing
- "In this economy, you should be happy you have a job."
- "If you do your work every day and manage your time well, you will not be stressed out."
- "When I had your position, I saw all of my clients on a regular basis. You should be able to do the same thing."

Criticizing
- "You're a jerk."
- "You are wrong."
- "Your opinions are irrelevant to this discussion."
- "You are inept."

Blaming
- "If it weren't for the sales department, we wouldn't be in this fix."
- "John was the one who insisted we do it this way."
- "Maryanne caused all the distractions. It's her fault we failed."

Minimizing
- "Oh, it's not that bad."
- "You're making too much of this."
- "She probably forgot all about your disagreement."

Changing the Subject

- "Forget about your concerns. How was your weekend?"
- "So, I heard that you're working on a new project."
- "Let's talk about happy things."

Denial

- "You don't really feel that way."
- "You will see it differently tomorrow."
- "Don't worry. It will all work out."

As you can see, the way we invalidate is almost a cliché in many instances. We do it almost by rote. Rather than using tact and diplomacy and listening, we practice behaviors that belittle and chastise, hardly realizing the effect.

It's Me and Not You

If a person is taking the time to talk with you, it's about that person… not you. As the "My Fair Lady," song goes: "It's me and not you….Don't rain on my parade." Raining on my parade in this context means . . . "Just don't tell me what to do or what you think. It's my life. It's my thought. It's my time to speak. It's all about me right now."

Being a good listener is the key to being diplomatic. In order to practice the skill, try putting yourself in someone else's shoes. Like any other skill, listening takes intent to succeed and practice. In general, think about the value that others have to you, and you to them.

- Put your ego aside.
- Clear your head of anything but the speaker.
- Listen to the whole thought without evaluating.
- Give the speaker a chance. Make sure you have allowed time for him or her to complete his or her thoughts.
- Put aside judgments about clothes, appearance, mannerisms, and distractions.
- Listen with receptivity to what is being said. Avoid focusing on your own opinions and what you want to say in response.
- Pause before responding in case the speaker wants to continue.

- Listen "holistically." Hear the whole presentation; facts, suggestions, assertions, tone of voice, body language, intent.
- Pay attention with the energy it takes to understand.

These are hefty skills. Practiced, they are worth the reward in so many ways. The patience that you show is compounded over time. Trust builds. Relationships form; you know each other's thoughts and accept each other's feelings. Deeper communication occurs. When you have to ask for something in a hurry, the "I need this now" is understood as your need, not an invalidation, because you have formed a relationship in which you understand beyond words.

As worthwhile as listening is, few can argue that it can be daunting. In the beginning stages of a relationship, and with those who need more of your time than others, their immediate needs may be distressful. You may not be able to give your full attention. "Noise" may be interfering. Noise is distraction in the form of personal thoughts about the many things that you have to do, haven't done, wish to do, wish you hadn't done, etc.: cell phones going off, hands flying across the keyboard while you're speaking, interruptions, email, emergencies (everything), and anything that does not involve the speaker. This is all just normal in our environment. Some deal with their emotional needs for connection in different ways, waiting patiently for their turns. Take a little time to look around and notice these folks. Here is a story about one of them:

> Sue once worked in an office where she was surrounded by commotion and the activity of co-workers. She kept to herself, but really wanted to establish relationships with her co-workers. It was difficult amid the conversations others were having and the din of the office environment. Because she found it hard to "break in," she was quite certain some of her co-workers did not believe she was a good listener. She quietly did her job and was good at it. She was happy and successful in her work. Her co-workers seemed to be unhappy in theirs. Sue's perceived aloofness was a minor source of irritation in the office, but it never really created any hardships.
>
> A funny thing happened in December. Sue brought in gifts for all of her co-workers. They weren't just gifts; they were the best gifts ever. One by one, as her co-workers unwrapped their presents, they were stunned by how meaningful each gift was to the person who received it. "How did you know that I paint with watercolors?" "This is my favorite artist!" "I had one just like this when I was growing up, and

I lost it when we moved!" The best gift of the day, perhaps, was learning that Sue did listen when her co-workers spoke, and she thought about them with good will. As it turned out, she paid a lot of attention to the personal conversations in the office because she wanted to build relationships with her co-workers that were meaningful. She wasn't sure how to do it. But she listened. They benefited, and so did she. At the spring picnic, they all asked her to sit with them and chat.

There are many people out there who would benefit from a kind word and being recognized as valuable. Being observant and taking time to listen can be comforting enough for people to gain renewed spirit and energy. Take the situations below:

A graduate school student says to her colleague, "Wow, thanks for listening to me about my course and the paper I have due. You really took an interest in what I was saying. It's great talking with you. I think I have a better understanding now of what was blocking me. Tonight, I'll be able to finish my paper, for sure!"

The patient who was bumped around from doctor to doctor says, "Now that you've found the problem, I can get off all these pills and on with my life."

The nervous presenter says, "Thanks so much for listening to my fears. Now I can do this."

The Language of Acceptance

The most practical book I have ever read on listening is *Parent Effectiveness Training* (P.E.T.) by Thomas Gordon, first published in 1970. P.E.T. has been the basis for many workshops for teachers, parents, and clients. Whether you are interacting with a child or discussing products with a customer, the acceptance with which you need to speak is the same, as are the listening principles.

Acceptance, feeling that you are understood and recognized for being you with your own unique thoughts and feelings, is paramount to any interaction. The person to whom you give credence can develop, change, solve problems, be creative and productive. Gordon uses an analogy of soil that enables a seed to become a flower, purporting that if you listen, you provide the nourishment for growth.

We live in a critical society. Parents often think it is their responsibility not to be accepting. They think that teaching their children to become worthy adults involves criticizing what they do wrong. Then children go to school and are criticized by teachers, especially if they don't do exactly what is expected. In the workforce, criticism is commonplace. In the best case, criticism is considered for the person's "own good." In the worst case, it is just demeaning and ignorant. Unfortunately, criticism is remembered with more potency than praise.

Acceptance is an overall condition that insulates a person's soul. *If I know that you will accept me, I will disclose my fears, concerns, real feelings, and insights.* Acceptance is like unconditional love. You don't have to love your colleague in the romantic sense of the word, but it behooves you to listen with acceptance in the moment, unconditionally. You might at this point be asking: What if I disagree?

There will be time for you to disagree. You will have your say. But hearing a person out first is more important than giving a premature response. Again, listening is about the other person. It is an art and a skill. It requires concentration on what the other person is saying, not on what you think. It is about understanding first.

Five Steps to Effective Listening

Listening takes all of you. It is a state of mind. The whole is more than the sum of the parts. However, there are specific skills that one can learn, especially if listening does not come naturally to you. The goal for listening is to focus on the other person entirely, using your body language, which was discussed in Chapter 2 and again in Chapter 3. Eye contact is essential when listening to a person face-to-face and for being tactful.

Step 1: Focusing

Eye contact is important, whatever your business communication encompasses. It is a way to focus your attention. We all know that but, like listening in general, eye contact is not always practiced. You can tell when people have been trained to have eye contact and they feel *compelled* to do so. Eye contact can be half-hearted and awkward if it is forced, rather than natural.

Note: Some cultures are taught that eye contact is disrespectful. If you know that this is the case when interacting with someone, focus on his or her face, not the eyes. Most people in the U.S. workforce do understand that eye contact is an expectation.

International companies teach eye contact and nonverbal communication not only because it is important to demonstrate respect, but because they have speakers of many languages among their guests, and nonverbal communication is the only way that certain staff members can communicate with customers.

> Recently, I had the good fortune of taking a cruise, my first real vacation in a long time. Not everyone on the ship spoke English. By the end of the cruise, I wished I had everyone's name and address so I could keep in touch. That's how much "at home" they made me feel. There was not a staff member on the ship who didn't connect by eye contact and say "hello" when he or she passed us in the hall, took our names for dinner, or played music. When I say connect, I mean connect. You feel it when someone "catches your eye." It's different from staring. They caught my eye, and not in a flirtatious sense, which is how we usually think of "catch your eye." They were so genuine in their greetings. I still remember them. There is an old American Indian saying that goes: "Certain things catch your eye, but pursue only those that capture your heart." In the case of the staff on the cruise, it was both at one time.

If you really look at someone, you, too, can be endearing immediately. But, just like authentic verbal communication, you must be authentic in your eye contact. In couples counseling and human relations workshops, sitting face-to-face and maintaining eye contact is a powerful exercise. It causes emotions to surface. The exercise is used to bring people closer together quickly and to completely focus on the other person without words.

When you focus on people, they are the center of attention. They are in the spotlight. It is their show. With the rapt attention that you would give an actress on stage, you transfer that type of receptiveness to the speaker. Although you might not be as enraptured as you would be at a performance, the receptivity needs to be noticeable. You need to be quietly engaged, not just there, in present time; in the moment.

Step 2: Encouraging

In addition to eye contact and other nonverbal indicators of being "present," we encourage one another when we validate by sounds and phrases such as, "Uh, huh," "Mmm," "Right," "Got it," "Ug," or "Understood." These comments are usually accompanied by gestures like head bobbing (up and down), eyes widening, eyebrow raising, frowning, head shaking (no!), laughing, mouth opening, and cues that let the other person know that you caught the message. People can speak for hours, literally, with only this kind of encouragement. Most people need more than that, but given an opportunity, some can talk "until the cows come home."

> **Just an aside:** Cows are known to take their time and make their way home at their own unhurried pace. The phrase "until the cows come home" was coined before 1929, according to the writers at www.phrases.org.uk/meanings/382900.html, accessed March 3, 2012. The first known reference was in Scotland's *The Times* referring to how the Duke of Wellington should conduct business: if he proposed a certain bill, it was said that he could be minister "until the cows come home." Groucho Marx used the phrase in *Duck Soup*: "I could dance with you till the cows come home. Better still, I'll dance with the cows and you come home."

These little acknowledgements go a long way. Even over the phone, one receives encouragement by sounds that people make on the other end of the line. If you talk on the phone a lot and people continually ask you, "Are you there?" it would be a good thing to remember to use "uh huh" validations more.

Step 3: Paraphrasing

If you can paraphrase, you will most probably be known as a good listener and be on your way to being tactful and diplomatic. You may also be able to make a lot of money. Take Oprah Winfrey. She will always be known for "opening up" her guests so they revealed their innermost thoughts and feelings. Oprah paraphrased often, eliciting deeper responses as a result of her understanding of what her guests said, and sometimes what they didn't say, but was obvious.

Jerry Springer (talk to the hand) is also a big star. What images do you have of Oprah Winfrey compared to Jerry Springer? Consider these terms: warmth, acceptance, curiosity, caring, clarifying, supporting. Which of the two celebrities embodies those terms? Which would you rather be interviewed by?

Let's take a look at the paramount skill of paraphrasing as a way to increase understanding. Paraphrasing is repeating or rephrasing something someone has said. It has the effect of putting a person at ease, if it is done well, and of reinforcing the speaker's intent:

> *Ellie:* "I think we should ask the waitstaff what customers say about the vegan dish we just put on the menu. It seems to be selling, but I'd like to know more about why. Is it the taste, or do we have a lot of vegan customers?"

Jimmy: "So you are curious as to whether the taste of the new dish is making it popular or rather that we have so many vegan customers?" (The question mark at the end of the sentence is there to indicate that the voice can raise a bit as if to say, "Did I get this right?")

Ellie: "Yes. That's it."

When you hear the "yes," you have paraphrased well. You want to feel as though you have made a basket in a basketball game or caught a fly ball. The degree that the speaker answers, "Yes," in terms of emphasis and body language is the grade you receive on paraphrasing. The better you are, the more the speaker will let you know that you have it right, not only what was said, but what was understood, as in the following example:

> The other day, I got an A. I was talking to my niece's two-year-old daughter, Emma. She was telling me that she had a phone in her hand and that it had numbers on it. She wanted me to "call her number and talk." I had to listen to her really carefully… because she's two. So I said, "Oh, you have a phone in your hand with numbers! You want me to call you!" She looked at me for a second, surprised that I understood exactly what she said, and replied with a resounding, "Yes." It was such a "you got it in the pocket" response that it startled me. Just then, I was reminded that even a two-year-old knows when you are really listening. And she was so delighted that I understood her! And I was delighted that she was delighted!

If you want to build a relationship, paraphrase. If you want to please a customer, paraphrase. If you want to understand a client, paraphrase. If your response is, "People say I'm parroting and not to do that," then you may not be getting the speaker's intent. When you pause after the speaker finishes a thought, and you have listened intently, think about the speaker's real message. Then paraphrase your understanding of the communication. Avoid starting with, "What I hear you saying." For some, it is a hackneyed phrase and annoying, like hearing screechy chalk on a blackboard. But you can say that in your head if you need a reminder that, indeed, what you need to listen to is what a person is saying, and to be as close to the intent as you can when you paraphrase.

It is not as easy for people to paraphrase. When asked the question, "Do you know the definition of paraphrasing?" most answer, "Yes." They can also define it.

Tact and Diplomacy   73

In role plays, most can't do it. Why? People want to solve the problem they "hear." The real problem is that they don't give people enough time to really describe what happened and convince the speaker that what she said was understood. *Initially, the understanding is more important than solving what the listener thinks is the problem. This is part of being diplomatic.*

To demonstrate understanding the speaker, let's observe a situation by reading about Marlene's plight in trying to resolve an issue of concern to her. There are two scenarios. See which one you like better:

Marlene: "There is a tear in this blouse…."

Glenna: "So, do you want to return it. We have a thirty-day policy. If you bought it more than thirty days ago, you can only get a credit. That's the store policy."

Marlene: "I didn't say I wanted to return it."

Glenna: "Yes, you did. When did you buy it?"

Marlene: "I bought it yesterday."

Glenna: "Well, didn't you see the tear when you bought it?"

Marlene (getting annoyed): "Of course not!"

Glenna: "Do you have a receipt?"

Marlene: "Yes."

Glenna: "May I see it?"

Marlene: "Yes. Here it is."

Glenna: "This says you bought it day before yesterday."

Marlene: "That could be true. Time is really flying these days."

Glenna: "It's only a small tear. Your dressmaker can fix it."

Marlene: "I don't have a dressmaker."

Glenna: "We have one in the store."

Marlene: "I don't want a dressmaker!"

Glenna: "Well, what DO you want?"

Marlene: "I want to exchange it for another blouse, the same size, the same color, without a tear."

Glenna: "Oh. Too bad you didn't come in yesterday. This blouse was on sale."

Compare the scenario above to:

Marlene: "There is a tear in this blouse...."

Glenna: "The blouse has a tear?"

Marlene: "Yes, I was so disappointed to see it when I got it home."

Glenna: "I bet you *were* disappointed!"

Marlene: "It's such a pretty blouse and I spent so much time getting just the right one."

Glenna: "It *is* a pretty blouse. And I know how hard it is to take the time to shop and finally find the right purchase. What would you like to do?"

Marlene: "Do you have another in stock?"

Glenna: "We sure do. Let me get it for you. It was on sale yesterday, but if you have the receipt and it is within thirty days of purchase, I'm going to refund the original, and give it to you for the sale price today. I'm awfully sorry for the inconvenience."

Step 4: Reflecting Feelings

When Glenna said, "I bet you *were* disappointed!" she was reflecting back to Marlene a feeling she intuited from Marlene's exchange. She paraphrased and reflected a feeling. She demonstrated a deeper understanding of Marlene's situation. Marlene really liked the blouse and was disappointed that it had a tear. Although the example was a simple conversation, it was meaningful. It was kind. It demonstrated caring. It was diplomatic.

Feeling words are not as commonly used as organizational and business words. Identifying what people feel takes more skill than paraphrasing only, but it builds the relationship, temporary or long-lasting. Letting someone know you care is a major factor in customer loyalty. It is a factor in building trust in the workplace and at home.

It is not difficult to identify feelings if you are willing to do it. We all have feelings. We experience them on a daily basis. Reflecting feelings helps a person release what we think of as "negative" emotions: sad, angry, and misunderstood. (All emotions are just emotions. It is hard to avoid labeling them.) Understanding "positive" feelings helps the speaker relive them, as described in the wedding save:

- "Wow, I bet you were glad that this came in before the wedding!"
- "I sure am! Thanks so much for putting a rush order on this. You made my day… and the wedding!"

Empathizing further validates a person when it is appropriate. "I understand how you feel," "That must have hurt," "I can imagine your pain," "I feel the love!"

Step 5: Summarizing and Supporting

Summarizing is a skill we learned in school. Everyone can do it. It is also a skill we don't always use. Consider this example:

> *Glenna:* "So, I'm going to put this on a hanger for you, as you wanted, and I'll get you cashed out right away. I hope you enjoy the blouse, and I'm glad that we could make your experience a good one this time. Please come back and see me whenever you'd like to shop. We appreciate your patience and I would like to help you the next time you're here."

Glenna summarized what she was doing to close the loop on the transaction, and she supported Marlene as well, as a person and as a customer. Summarizing is that last step that ensures closure. In the workplace, it also makes clear what assignments are given, when the assignments are due, or what action is to be taken. If a lot of discussion has transpired, summarizing serves to clarify important parts of the conversation as they relate to action:

> "So you will follow up with Donna to see whether there is enough money in the budget for a motivational speaker, and I will contact Tiffani to see whether we can use her training room for the presentation."

The Power of Questioning

Once you are sure that you have allowed time for the five steps of listening, closer examination of issues, concerns, suggestions, and options can be illuminated by questioning. The two most well-known types of questions are open- and closed-ended. Open-ended questions allow the speaker to reveal new points, voice deeper concerns, and provide additional information without being interrupted. It is up to the listener to ask good questions, based on what he or she has heard, intuition, and need to know. These types of probing inquiries may begin with "tell me about," "what were the circumstances surrounding," and the most beloved question of psychotherapists and counselors, "How did that make you feel?" Open-ended questions help the speaker reveal more.

Closed-ended questions allow the listener to obtain specific information and the speaker to provide particular facts and observations. Along with open-ended questions, they are often used in investigations. "What time did the robbery occur?"

"Who was there?" Amusing closed-ended questions include "Who's on first?" and (again) "Do you have a receipt?" Ellen DeGeneres's J.C. Penny commercials were prime time in 2012 with scenes from the past and present depicting Ellen trying to return a toga (it only has one shoulder) with the salesperson's response, "When did you buy it?" and Ellen's musing that it was right after the time of the locusts. Still, "Do you have a receipt? is the retort, with Ellen's response, "This is ridiculous." Closed-ended questions sometimes annoy people. In legal proceedings, you often hear, "Just answer the question with a 'Yes' or 'No.'"

Leading Questions

"You do not get along with her, do you?" is an example of a leading question. It puts the person who is answering in a bind and may cause misinformation that the questioner wants confirmed for his or her purpose. It is not clear communication. "Why did you jimmy the figures for the quarterly report?" (This implies that the figures *were* jimmied.) Avoid leading questions. Use open-ended questions instead to elicit truthful responses. "How did you get the figures for the quarterly report?"

Socratic Questions

Did you think of Socrates when you read the "Socratic Questions" heading? What did you think? The Greek philosopher and teacher is often depicted with students at his feet while he is asking question after question, without giving answers. Socrates was known for his devotion to creative thinking, and for the exploration of deeper meanings and the pursuit of alternative thought patterns. "What could we suppose instead?" would be an example of a Socratic question designed to analyze "the opposite" to uncover assumptions that might be erroneous with the original presupposition. For those of you who tackle complex problems every day, you might have said at one time or another, "How can we look at this differently?" "What are the implications of the decision that we are about to make?" These are Socratic questions.

If you are involved with research, you know the meaning of the term "null hypothesis." You might want to prove that there are differences between two groups of people, those who have blue eyes and those who have brown eyes. You think that blue-eyed people receive more attention in classes. Your null hypothesis might be that there are no differences between the attention that blue-eyed people receive and the attention brown-eyed people receive.

Here's an example of a father and daughter conversation as it relates to the Socratic method. The father looks at a situation in a different way than his daughter does and poses a question that is an alternative to her viewpoint.

> Sarah is a beautiful young woman who is a college senior. She hasn't had a lot of time to date, so she takes the plunge into online dating. After a few emails with an interesting man, she accepts his invitation to meet. They have a nice time. There doesn't seem to be much chemistry though. After the date, Garth, her father, asks her how the date went. She says that it was very pleasant, but that there was no particular chemistry. She doesn't think they will go out again. Her father says, "Does there have to be chemistry on the first date?" Her father is testing her assumption. She can choose to keep her assumption that there should be immediate chemistry or can explore different trains of thought.

Solution-Focused Questions

Solution-focused questions are a type of open-ended question with a visionary, historical, or exacting purpose. These types of questions are often used in counseling, but they can have a profound effect in the business world as well. Such questions might look like those that follow:

Miracle Questions—Imagining a successful future; creating hope in counseling

- If you woke up tomorrow and a miracle had happened while you were sleeping, and your life could be any way you wanted it, what would it look like?
- If the miracle occurred, what would you do first?
- What would people notice about you that has changed?
- What would be the best-case scenario regarding your family?

Past Success—Remembering what was successful, how it felt, and creating hope that it can happen again

- What has worked for you in the past?
- How did you find the strength to overcome all the obstacles?
- Who was a person you trusted?
- What would it take for you to regain the confidence you had before this happened?

Exception-Finding Questions—When similar circumstances occurred but were overcome

- When you did not lose control, what was different?
- What would have to happen for you to gain back the control you had?
- When you reached out before, what were the circumstances?
- What would you need to reach out again?

Scaling Questions—Making complex problems more concrete

- On a scale of 1 to 10, with 10 meaning great confidence, and 1 meaning no confidence at all, how confident are you that you can do this?
- If you moved up the scale just one step, what would it look like?
- On a scale of 1 to 10, how would you rate your self-esteem right now?
- What would it look like if you moved up the scale?
- On a scale of 1 to 10, how would you rate your progress?

In a business situation, combining questions might look like these:

- What do you hope to gain from this meeting, class, or project?
- How will you know whether this project has been successful?
- As a result of the 360-degree feedback instrument, what will you do differently?
- The last time you tried this solution, how did it work?
- What would you repeat?
- What would you not repeat?
- What have you learned?
- What worked well today?
- What would you like to see next time we meet?
- On a scale of 1 to 10, where 10 equals you at your very best, where are you now?
- What would you like to do to move up the scale?
- What will you take away from this interaction?
- What will look different when you facilitate tomorrow?

Tact and Diplomacy

The five steps of listening and intuition in questioning are paramount to tact and diplomacy. Asking the wrong question can be insulting and discouraging. "Why on earth did you do that?" is different from "Tell me how you came to that conclusion." Using positive language, as described in Chapter 3, is also important to establishing rapport, one of the reasons we use tact and diplomacy. Another reason to use tact and diplomacy is to achieve the results you want.

Questions

- On a scale of 1 to 10, how would I rate my listening skills?
- What distracts me when I am listening?
- If I do not paraphrase, what is getting in the way?
- How comfortable am I in reflecting feelings?
- Do I summarize transactions?

Tips

- Pause before you respond.
- Consider how your words will affect another.
- Apologize if you have not used tact and diplomacy (it happens).
- If you question whether you can be diplomatic in a situation, suggest that you take some time to think and get back to the person.
- Think of a time in the past when you have been diplomatic and how it worked out for you and the other person.

The Leader's Connection

Listening has rules of engagement associated with it. The five steps apply to leaders as much as they apply to associates. There is no better way to be well received than to listen. Public speaking is important, of course, and that is a lot of what leaders do, as well as planning, organizing, staffing, directing, coordinating, and budgeting, age-old responsibilities that students of management and leadership know. Are leaders remembered for staffing? Budgeting? They may be remembered for pulling a company out of financial crisis, but to do so takes a lot of listening to customers, staff, and advisors.

More recent thoughts and research on leadership emphasize inspiration, motivation, developing people, and the ability to foster commitment (Zenger, Folkman,

& Edinger, 2009). An example of the power of listening in these endeavors is described by Eikenberry (2007). He talks about his intent to attend events and listen rather than speak, letting others do the talking. His comments about how he was received when he practiced this, and he did have to practice, were that he was complimented on being "very interesting" and a "great conversationalist." Without much talking, he was perceived as a great communicator. People who are admired for their communication aplomb are inspirational. Be inspiring.

Questions

- Has anyone ever told you that you are a good listener?
- What are your strengths as a listener?
- What do you need to improve?
- How often do you listen without giving your opinion?
- What do you consider inspirational?

Tips

- Hold "fireside chats" with your staff members. Listen. Ask them what they are working on and what their goals are for the coming week or month.
- Ask staff what inspires them.
- Honor emotion.
- Practice the five steps of listening.
- Hear people out.

ABOUT THE NEXT CHAPTER

The next chapter is about problem solving. Once you have listened with positive intent, if there are problems to be addressed, the problem-solving model depicted in the next chapter will help you move through tried-and-true steps to come to solutions.

Tact and Diplomacy

Activities

Notes to Reader: The activities in this chapter are designed to be done individually or in a training environment. Whether you are in a group with others or working on your own, you may go back to these activities at any time and learn from them on an individual basis.

Notes to Instructor: Suggestions for instructors to use activities in a learning environment are included at the end of the chapter.

Purpose: To apply concepts of tact and diplomacy by exploring predispositions, perceived skills, and practicing guidelines for dialog.

Background: For productive communication to transpire, tact and diplomacy play a large role in paving the way for trust and understanding. Practicing ways to put tact and diplomacy into action affords skill development. Activities in this section are for insight and practice.

Activity 4.1. Tact and Diplomacy Baseline

The more honest you are on the following Tact and Diplomacy Baseline survey, the more you can identify the skills you want to improve. This is for your growth and development.

Answer **D** for Disagree, **SD** for Somewhat Disagree, **SA** for Somewhat Agree, and **A** for Agree.

Statement	D	SD	SA	A
1. I consider tact and diplomacy equally important to practice with every work associate.				
2. I consider how my interactions affect others.				
3. If I have hurt someone's feelings, I apologize.				
4. I shy away from feelings at work.				
5. I think about tact and diplomacy as being more necessary with top leadership.				
6. When someone wants to talk, I am able to clear my mind and give that person my full attention.				

Statement	D	SD	SA	A
7. If I am not able to give my full attention, I suggest a specific time to contact me when I will be able to talk.				
8. When I have an urgent task for which I need input from another person, I express the urgency and expect an immediate response.				
9. I can do two things at once; I read email while someone is speaking.				
10. I paraphrase often.				
11.				
12.				
13.				
14.				
15.				
16.				

Answers

1. If you did not answer A (agree) for this question, describe your reasons for not agreeing.

2. If you answered D or SD for this question, think of a time when what you said had an undesirable effect on your listener. What did you say? How and why did the person misunderstand your intent or take offense? If you answered SA, in what situations would you be less likely to consider others' emotions?

Tact and Diplomacy

3. If you did not answer A, what were you considering when you answered? How difficult is it for you to apologize? In what situations would you not apologize?

4. If you answered A or SA, describe your discomfort with discussing feelings at work. Think about some underlying assumptions; such as "feelings have no place at work." Think about your own feelings and how you expect others to respond to you.

5. If you answered A, what were your thoughts? How do you define tact and diplomacy? How do you think others view what is evident as you practice this belief?

6. If you answered D or SD, what gets in your way? How can you mitigate distractions?

7. If you answered S, SD, or SA, what alternatives do you offer when you cannot meet a colleague's need to talk with you?

8. If you answered A, do you consider what the other person is doing? Do you ask for assistance and whether the other person can meet your time frame, or do you demand that your task be done immediately?

9. If you answered anything but D, recognize that reading email while you speak with someone is a form of invalidation.

10. If you answered D or SD, consider practicing paraphrasing more. You might choose conversations that you know will be ensuing to not only converse, but paraphrase.

Activity 4.2. Validation or Invalidation?

Instructions: Put a **V** for validation or an **I** for invalidation next to each statement.

_____ 1. I appreciate that you came so quickly to fix my computer.

_____ 2. Get to the point.

_____ 3. What a great idea!

_____ 4. I thought you said you would be here in five minutes.

_____ 5. Your desk is a mess.

_____ 6. Your input clarified the problem.

_____ 7. You know he meant it for your own good.

_____ 8. Do you have to state the obvious?

_____ 9. Read my lips.

_____ 10. Calm down.

Activity 4.3. Dialog

Note to Instructor: Ask participants to brainstorm topics of interest to them—topics that are not controversial, but would be valuable to share. Ask them to pose the topic of interest in the form of a question. The question does not need to be about work, but might be, depending on interests. (What are the qualities of a good leader? What does it mean to be content?) Have participants pick one topic from the list to discuss by whatever decision-making technique you choose, making sure there is consensus. Explain that the purpose is to express thoughts and that everyone will have an opportunity to speak about the subject that was chosen. The difference between dialog and discussion is that, in discussion, decisions are reached or expected. In dialog, thoughts are expressed; no decisions are made.

Once participants come up with a question that describes their interest, explain the ground rules (see Chapter 6 for a definition of ground rules):

- One person speaks at a time.
- Everyone listens.
- One person follows up on the thoughts of another.
- Judgment is suspended.
- Debate is not accepted.
- Everyone is treated respectfully.

Conduct this activity by having people sit in a circle. If you have more than ten people, you might want to split the group in two, with another facilitator for the second group.

As facilitator, describe the topic the group chose. Allow a few minutes for reflection and for participants to write down their thoughts. Open the dialog, and facilitate to be sure that the ground rules are followed. That will be your primary role. After 30 to 35 minutes, thank the people in the session and close the dialog activity. Pose questions for review and processing:

- How did it go?
- Did everyone feel heard?

If you have done this activity in a work team, you may want to repeat it with additional thought questions that most likely came up in the dialog. For more information on creativity and dialog, go to www.minervas.org.

Notes to Instructor: If you use Activity 4.1 with a group, ask the participants to take the survey at their seats. After they have responded and answered the questions in the "Answers" section, ask them to think about one area in which they would like to improve. You may have them discuss that in pairs, trios, or in the group, depending on the comfort level of participants.

Activity 4.2 can be done in pairs, trios, or a team. You may also ask group members to come up with other invalidations that they find hurtful and add those to the survey.

Chapter 5

The Challenge of Problem Solving*

WHAT'S IN THIS CHAPTER?
- A Model for Problem Solving
- The Nine Steps to Effective Problem Solving
- The Role of Intuition in Decisions and Problem Solving
- Other Elements to Consider
- The Leader's Connection
- Activities

Every time you make a choice or take an action, you are making a decision. We make hundreds of choices every day, from deciding what to wear to preparing for a big presentation. That is why developing problem-solving skills is so important for both new and existing employees, especially considering the research we covered in Chapter 1, which showed that problem-solving expertise is lacking in those currently entering the workforce.

---

*Thanks to Greg Trulson for his contributions to this chapter.

Compared to one hundred years ago, our daily lives force us to make many more critical decisions than our forbearers had to make. How many phones, computer software programs, television programming devices, and other communication instruments have you had to learn to operate in the last year just to find answers to even simple questions, never mind gathering information for important decisions? For solving problems in a sometimes chaotic world, what techniques can we use to determine what success would look like? This chapter serves as a review of ways to do that and presents a method for defining problems and solutions.

Problem solving requires creativity, adaptability, and the willingness to confront the uncertainty and ambiguity of complex scenarios. With any decision, consequences factor into the equation. Depending on the circumstances, the decision-maker can experience paralysis because of how the decision may affect others, the decision-maker, and the organization. To prevent stagnation, learning and assessment techniques are instrumental for moving forward with decisions. Tools and models offer step-by-step approaches for gathering information for optimum results.

A Model for Problem Solving

Models are ways to organize information within a familiar mental image. They provide structure for looking at a situation. Having a model, a planned way to analyze the situation and take action, can assist a problem-solver who is overwhelmed and cannot decide where to start. It may also mitigate his or her fear.

There are many problem-solving models, none perfect for every situation. We will describe Greg Trulson's model in this chapter. Trulson's model offers a flexible framework to assist in the decision-making process.

Trulson wraps decision making and problem solving together, even though each has its own unique elements. That is, problem solving is primarily concerned with the definition of the problem, whereas decision making addresses the development of choices to solve the problem.

As we cover the model, keep in mind that the process is flexible and open to modifications depending on the circumstances. The bi-directional arrows shown between several steps in Figure 5.1 indicate that you may have to return to a previous step for further discovery. You may want to skip to the section on The Role of Intuition (shown in the center of the figure) and come back to the steps of the model later.

The Nine Steps to Effective Problem Solving

The nine steps in the problem-solving model are described in the following paragraphs.

Figure 5.1 Problem-Solving Model

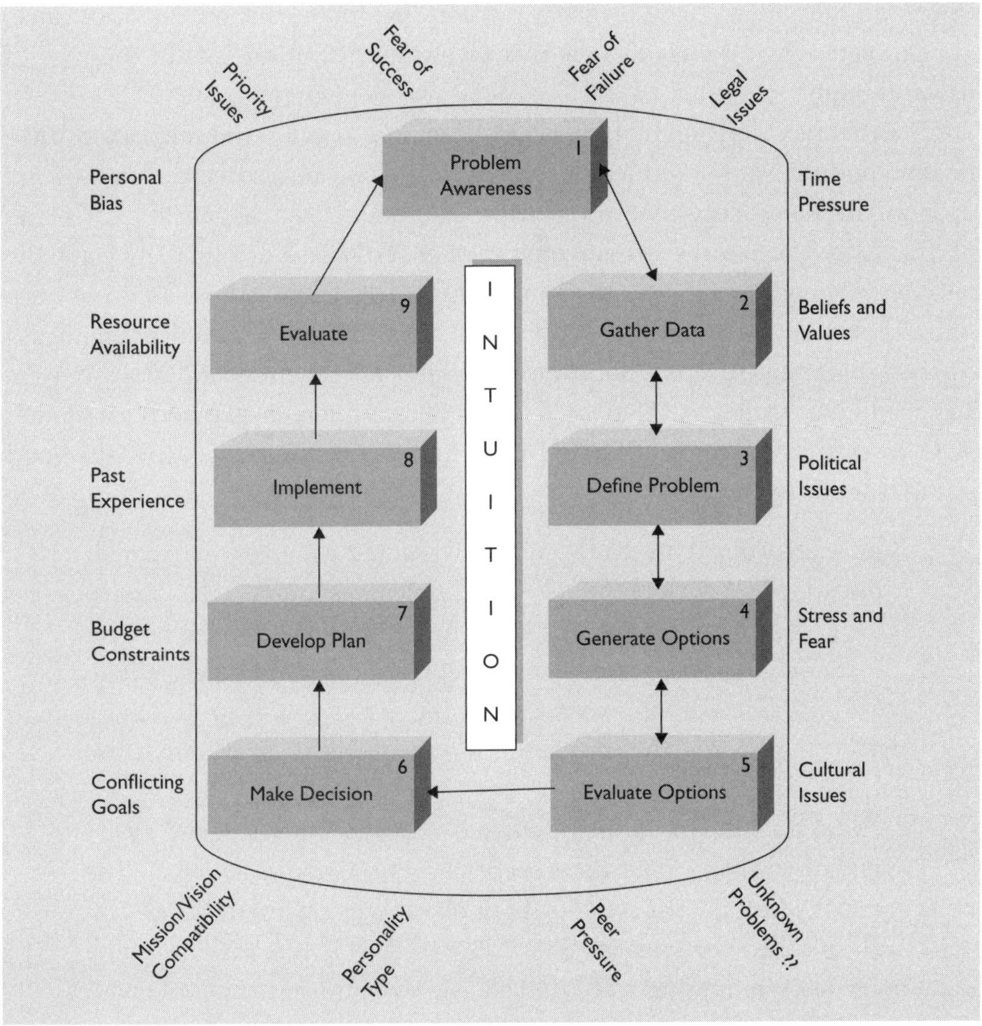
Priority Issues
Fear of Success
Fear of Failure
Legal Issues
Personal Bias
Problem Awareness
1
Time Pressure
Resource Availability
Evaluate
9
I N T U I T I O N
Gather Data
2
Beliefs and Values
Past Experience
Implement
8
Define Problem
3
Political Issues
Budget Constraints
Develop Plan
7
Generate Options
4
Stress and Fear
Conflicting Goals
Make Decision
6
Evaluate Options
5
Cultural Issues
Mission/Vision Compatibility
Personality Type
Peer Pressure
Unknown Problems ??

Step 1: Problem Awareness

Something isn't right. You've turned on your intuitive radar and scanned the environment to discover suspicious symptoms. The military would call this step raw intelligence gathering. Family counselors would call it family assessment. The goal in this step is to connect the dots and make sense of patterns that emerge from the data.

Step 1 is easy when the symptoms of a problem are obvious. The difficulty comes in challenging the status quo and exploring new approaches. This is the "head in the sand" stage. Sometimes, people are afraid to try alternative possibilities and ignore the obvious. New alternatives require work. Sometimes, teams and individuals would rather put out fires than confront the root cause of a problem. Or if the root cause is a mystery, frustration gets in the way of logical thought.

Crisis-to-crisis decision making is also common. "Do it now" instead of "Take the time to do it right" produces a self-reinforcing cycle of solving a problem by repeating the same steps that didn't work last time. Those responsible for errors may have doubts. In order to overcome anxiety and meet a deadline, they assume that the only answer is to do the same things over again. Albert Einstein once said, "The definition of insanity is doing the same thing over and over again and expecting different results." Substantive organizational transformations require changes in the system. As Newton's first law of motion says, a body in motion tends to stay in motion until acted upon by an outside force. Here's a good example of this tendency:

> Brad's department has had significantly higher turnover than similar groups in his division. He uses the human resources (HR) department to recruit candidates. The department has voiced concerns over the continuing costs of providing replacement candidates, not to mention the relocation expenses and the disruption of productivity that comes from the revolving door of hired and departing employees.
>
> Brad is a little inconsistent when candidates interview and rarely spends the appropriate time preparing questions in advance. The sessions often are just conversations about outside interests like golf and favorite sports teams. Brad believes the key selection criteria boils down to finding well-dressed, highly enthusiastic people with good chemistry and a great handshake.
>
> The HR department is taking heat for not providing a continuous stream of qualified candidates to fill the vacated positions. HR has scheduled Brad for a class on management coaching to help him develop the skills to counsel his underperforming team members. Is the HR plan on track?

In this example, HR does not dig deeper to expose of the real problem. The next step they should take is to gather information about root causes.

Step 2: Gather Data

This step provides a foundation for defining the problem. The symptoms in Step 1, combined with the data gathered in this step, can result in a hypothesis about the underlying problem.

A classic example of gathering data occurs after an airliner crash. Investigators are anxious to recover the "black boxes" that contain a record of the aircraft's technical performance and cabin recordings. This data is combined with other input to help determine the cause of a crash and reduce the chance of a similar calamity in the future. In the same way, you have to gather your organizational black box information.

Often, there is a tendency to not spend enough time asking relevant discovery questions. It is also possible for people to spend too much time on this step to avoid moving on. This may be an indication of procrastination and low tolerance for risk taking. At some point, the accumulation of more and more data can threaten the decision-making process.

Another issue to be aware of is the tendency for most people to look for information that supports their own conclusions. People are not always aware of their own biases and may believe they are neutral.

Like a detective trying to solve a crime, one must ask lots of questions and consider all the evidence. An interesting source to help format questions comes from Rudyard Kipling:

"The Elephant's Child"

"I kept six honest servants,

(They taught me all I knew)

Their names were What and Why and When

And How and Where and Who."

To apply Kipling's wisdom, try forming discovery or solution-focused questions:
- What symptoms do we have? What symptoms don't we have?
- What or who has failed? Who has not failed?
- Where do we have the symptom? Where don't we have the symptom?
- When did it start? When was everything O.K.?
- Why did this fail and not that?
- What has changed? How has it changed?
- When was it changed?

- Why is it doing this and not that?
- Why did it start then and not before?
- Why did it show up here and not there?
- What's strange or peculiar?
- What are your feelings about the situation?
- Who does it impact? Who doesn't it impact?

The answers to these and many more questions provide insight to define the problem in Step 3.

Step 3: Define Problem

Clearly defining the problem is the most critical step in the process. Problem definition is often much more difficult than solving the problem once it has been defined. The quality of the decision will be a direct reflection of the energy committed to understanding the situation. Making the right decision but seeing the wrong problem ends up being a waste of time; even a less than perfect decision on the right problem would be more beneficial. Take the appropriate time here to ensure you are working on the "real" problem and not just a symptom.

> In problem solving, clearly defining the problem is critical.

Data gathered in Step 2 is analyzed to prove the hypothesis that a problem exists. Analysis paves the way to determine problem cause(s). In Step 3, careful thinking is required to isolate and separate symptoms to find the "seed"—the problem. This requires postulating the suspected causes of the problem.

The definition of the problem comes from finding the root cause. Again, according to Newton's first law, things generally stay on the same course unless something changes. Figure 5.2 depicts a situation and the riddle that needs to be solved to find root cause.

Now it is time to put your Sherlock Holmes hat on and determine the causal influences that brought about the problem. Some of the potential sources might be:

- New or different policies
- New or different procedures
- New or different suppliers

Figure 5.2 Root Cause

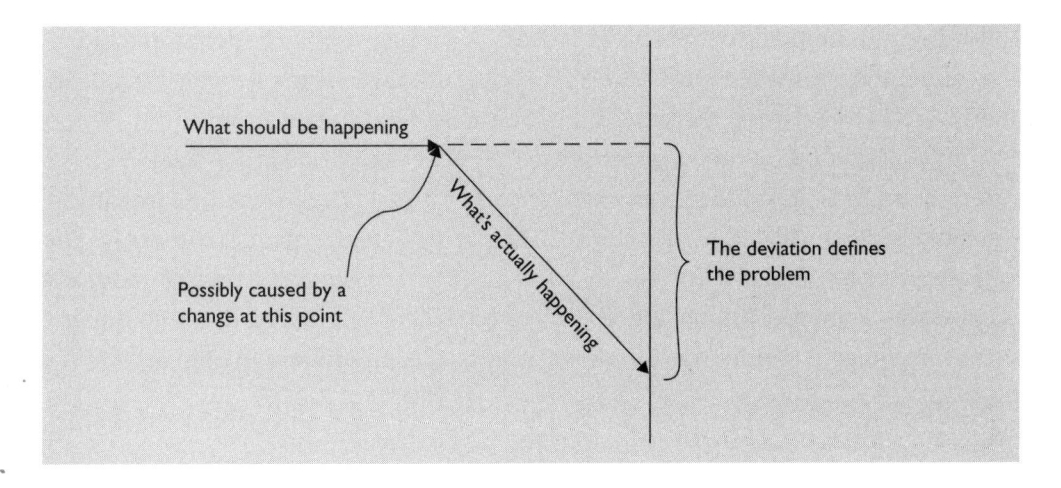

What should be happening

Possibly caused by a change at this point

What's actually happening

The deviation defines the problem

- New or different parts
- New or different materials
- New or different personnel
- New or different equipment
- New or different facilities
- New or different reward systems
- New or different control systems
- New or different working conditions
- New or different feedback systems
- New or different leadership
- New or different competitors
- New or different regulations
- Anything new or different from the past
- Misinformation

Once the cause is determined, a problem statement must be written that is concise and allows everyone to focus clearly on alternative ways to solve the problem. At this stage, part of the iceberg below the waterline becomes apparent. The problem statement lays the groundwork to generate options in Step 4.

Step 4: Generate Options

After the problem is defined in explicit terms, creating the most effective range of options requires creativity. The basic process of problem solving/decision making is essentially the same for individuals or teams, although trying to solve a problem in a group is not always the way to go. Some decisions need group input; some may be made based on the knowledge and perspective of one individual.

For team decision making, the techniques of "Teaching Ways to Gain Group Agreement" are included after Activity 5.4. Specific benefits of and more strategies for team decision making are discussed in Chapter 6. Using a variety of methods helps teams manage options. Once choices have been narrowed down to a manageable number, it's time to evaluate the merits of each of them in Step 5.

Step 5: Evaluate Options

There is always a degree of risk and uncertainty when selecting the option to implement. It requires full consideration of the options and a close look at the pros and cons of each. Good analysis reduces the risk of implementing a decision that has been evaluated insufficiently, lowering the risk of surprises that may surface later.

Step 5 is achieved best by the team that helped develop the alternatives, although guests can be invited. Consensus is easier with those who have gone through the process earlier. Evaluation may require another meeting, depending on the time allotted for solving the problem. It is important to move on and not rehash alternatives. The risk at this stage is continuing to belabor the decision and avoiding action.

"Outsiders" can be invited to give feedback on the options being considered. Often they say something like: "Have you thought about…?" and suggest unexplored solutions, which is possible because they're not so close to the problem.

STRATEGY

To be sure all options are being given full scrutiny, you might want to assign the role of "devil's advocate" (a Socratic approach) to a team member during the discussion. This person opposes all options and suggests the disadvantages and questions the value of each alternative. Being assigned the role includes the instruction and understanding of "no ridicule," since the devil's advocate is providing a service to the team. If everyone evaluating an alternative can see nothing wrong with the option, be careful! It is a rare alternative that has full unconditional support and someone may be withholding his or her critical view because it's politically dangerous.

Always consider the option of doing nothing. It could very well be the alternative that makes the most sense. Hurricane forecasters use the term "cone of uncertainty" to describe the probabilities for the track of a storm. What you are doing at this point is forecasting the "cone of probabilities" for a successful implementation of a solution. To help you understand the implications of each option, the group must discuss the following questions:

- Does the solution line up with our core values as an organization?
- Is there time available to implement the decision?
- Is the solution practical and something that could be implemented?
- Do we have the budget?
- Is there a high probability of acceptance by those impacted by the decision?
- Are the team resources available to implement the decision?
- Is there a reasonable risk/reward potential?
- Will the decision impact customers positively or negatively?
- Will new precedents be set in the organization?
- What other groups or departments will be affected by the decision?
- What are the major obstacles to be overcome?
- What are the pros/cons of the solution?
- What will the effect be on our competitors?
- Will the solution create bigger problems than we are solving?
- What are the potential unexpected consequences of implementing the decision?
- Is the solution legal and ethical?
- Will the implementation help the organization achieve its goals?

Perhaps the answers to most of the questions are not necessary to explore, but if the answers cause alarm bells to ring, take the opportunity to revisit options until you're fully confident about the choices you've made. Assuming a few alternatives have been selected, move to Step 6, making the decision.

Step 6: Make Decision

When all alternatives have been reviewed and analyzed, it is time to decide among the options. Ultimately, you or the team has to ask one final but serious question: Is the implementation of the decision going to solve the originally defined problem with manageable downside risk?

Figure 5.3 Overcoming Indecision

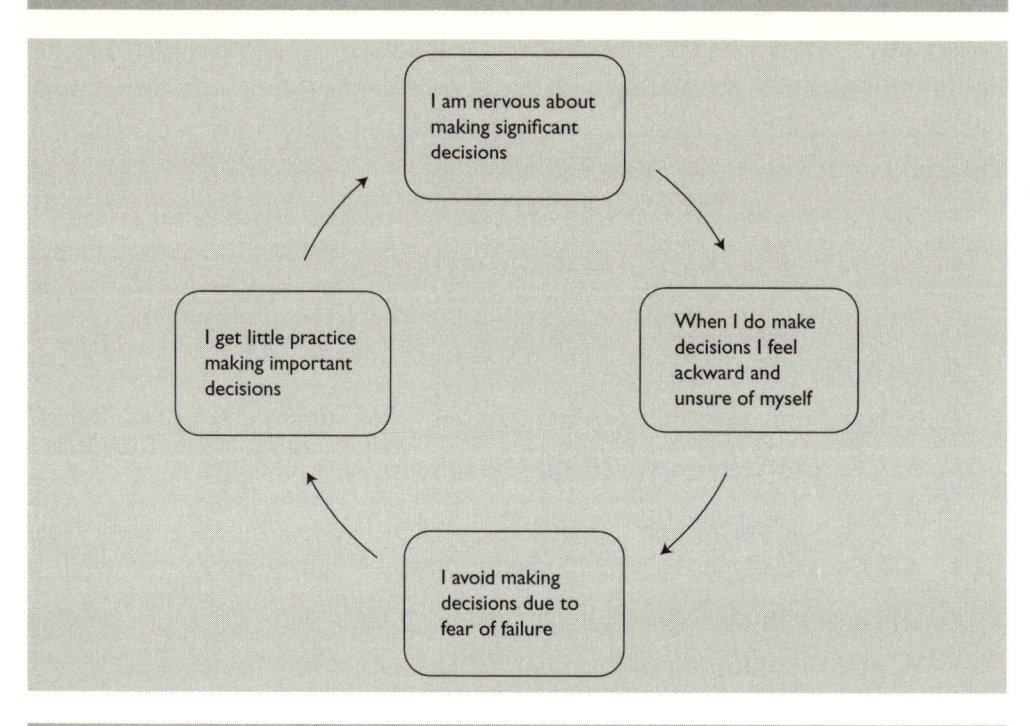

- I am nervous about making significant decisions
- When I do make decisions I feel ackward and unsure of myself
- I avoid making decisions due to fear of failure
- I get little practice making important decisions

Indecision or slow decision making is often the kiss of death. Delays born out of the need for perfection or fear of failure can destroy all work done to this point. Figure 5.3 depicts the vicious cycle of indecision that must be overcome.

The best way to break the cycle is to start making decisions based on the information gathered in Step 5. A forced-choice technique might help if options have been narrowed down to a few good choices and you or the team are feeling perplexed about the decision.

QUICK DECISION TOOL

1. What is the optimum benefit that could result from this choice?
2. What is the worst possible result with this choice?
3. Is the benefit of Number 1 worth the downside of Number 2?
4. Could you ultimately accept the results of Number 2?

Two other techniques are to:

1. Ask what decision you would make if you were forced to make up your mind in three minutes.
2. Flip a coin and see whether the winning decision resonates with all you know about the decision. If it doesn't, that choice is not the better option.

When all the information is in and options, intuition, and consequences have been thoroughly assessed, it's time to select the best option. Absolute certainty may still be elusive, but with the time, effort, and work put in, it's necessary to make the call. Congratulations are in order for progress to date on Steps 1 through 6.

Step 7: Develop Plan

Once you've made a decision, notify all those who will be affected by it and will be involved in the implementation. To make sure each part of the plan has an owner, assign responsibilities and detail the steps required. You will also need to develop the measures that will be used to assess the results. What will things look like when you are successful? How will you know you have achieved your goals?

No matter how skilled you are at making decisions, it requires both formal and informal conversations with others to gain the needed "buy-in." This step might also be called "sell the plan," since much of your time will be spent gaining support. Often the solution to the problem spills across organization boundaries and involves departments that were not involved in the decision-making process. Be ready to educate others about the decision and champion your case throughout the organization.

For large-scale decisions, a champion, serving as a single point of contact, needs to work with those responsible for doing what was agreed to. From now on, reasonable speed is required in the implementation. Long delays will dampen enthusiasm and become yet another problem to solve. Step 8 gives you some guidance moving the project along.

Step 8: Implement

You have the budget and resources allocated. You've published the plan and assigned responsibilities. It's time to launch your decision.

The best decision ever developed is of no value if it isn't put into action. There's little risk until you reach this step. Thousands of great decisions die at this point because of procrastination and fear the decision might be wrong. President John F. Kennedy captured the essence of this moment during the Cuban missile crisis (Sorensen, 2005):

> "The essence of the ultimate decision remains impenetrable to the observer often, indeed, to the decider himself . . . there will always be the dark and tangled stretches in the decision-making process . . . mysterious even to those who may be most intimately involved."

Your intuition is telling you to go ahead and you have to trust that all of your life's experiences have prepared you for implementation. A simple formula explains the critical need for successful implementation of the decision.

$$Ed = (Qd \times Id)$$

The overall effectiveness (Ed) of a decision equals the quality of the decision (Qd) times the implementation of the decision (Id). Be ready for second thoughts after you activate the plan. You are likely to second-guess your decision. Look past this and press on to the final step, where you evaluate and celebrate your success.

Step 9: Evaluate

All decisions must be tested in reality. The ultimate measure of all your effort comes when you assess whether the problem you set out to address has been solved. The best solutions on paper often have to be modified for the real world.

Put the decision under the evaluation microscope to determine whether the symptoms you originally identified have been resolved. Or have some unintended consequences surfaced? Keep management informed about your progress and make sure status reports provide feedback for all those who are contributing to the implementation.

Decision errors will happen and, when they do, admit the mistake without too much fanfare and move on. If the problem persists, try another option you considered in Steps 3 through 5.

After you have achieved success, pat yourself on the back, and be sure to recognize all those who contributed to the success of the effort. You might host a special event for everybody to celebrate, with special prizes awarded to those who went above and beyond. If you succeeded in an individual decision that you made, celebrate the accomplishment by treating yourself to something special.

The Role of Intuition in Decisions and Problem Solving

The problem-solving model we've just covered relies on a very rational, logical, sequential process. Bear in mind, though, that intuition also plays a large part in the problem-solving and decision-making process. If a purely rational step-by-step approach would always suffice, we could simply use computers to solve all our problems.

Intuition is not a magical sixth sense but a subconscious process that assists us in the decision-making process. Reasoning occurs beneath the surface of conscious thought as your mind finds links between past events and elements of the problem you are facing.

We've all had that blinding flash of brilliance while we are in the shower or on a beach. Somewhere along the way, our minds started processing information about a problem and, in that moment, a solution emerged.

It is possible to increase your intuitive capability with a little work on your part. Some of the things you can do are listed here:

- Really listen to people and reflect on their viewpoints.
- Pay close attention to the big picture of personal and professional events.
- Read diverse materials.
- Listen to internal thoughts that surface while you are at rest or walking.
- Attend events you've never experienced before.
- Read case studies for vicarious learning experiences.
- Seek training on creativity and intuition.
- Keep a private journal with no concern for spelling or grammar.
- Find some new friends.
- Join new associations and attend meetings.
- Take time out to be by yourself and listen to your heart.

All of these ideas provide your mind with new experiences it can use to serve as a launch pad for intuitive ideas.

Other Elements to Consider
More Than Just Following Steps
The vast majority of the decisions you make would rarely need all the steps in the Nine Steps model. For the most part, your intuition helps you navigate through life. However, when the importance of the decision is high and the risks are significant, use the model to guide you through the process.

The valid concerns in the outer ring of Figure 5.1 can either derail or add value to the decision-making process. Some have been touched on already; such as time pressure, political issues, fear of failure, personal bias, past experience, budget constraints, mission/vision compatibility, stress and fear, peer pressure, and unknown problems. All of the concepts are topics of books in and of themselves. However, a few that are shown deserve to be highlighted.

Legal Issues
Legal issues can put a halt to what may appear to be a creative solution. For example, consider this scenario:

> A team recently interviewed a candidate with adequate credentials, degrees, and experience. The candidate had some learning disabilities that members thought could be managed by special accommodations. The talent management recruiter walked the candidate to his car. While the manager was out of the room, the team continued discussing how adjustments could be made for the candidate to succeed. Everyone was aware of the Americans with Disabilities Act, which requires accommodations for disabilities when people can do the job with reasonable assistance. The team was about to finalize the decision, but when the talent management recruiter returned she told the team that the candidate had a DUI conviction within the last year. Since the job required transporting children, DUIs within five years of application were against state law and local policy.

Suggestion: Include HR, your legal department, and contract managers if a decision might have any legal implications.

Cultural Issues
Knowledge and awareness of cultural diversity has recently been included in performance evaluations in progressive companies. With the increase in international commence, worldwide information exchange, and diverse populations in the

workplace, cultural sensitivity is important. In *Diversity Training* (Wildermuth & Gray, 2005), the U.S. Census Bureau reports that, between 1995 and 2050, the American population will increase as follows:

- White, non-Hispanic people, 7.4 percent
- People of Hispanic origin, 258.3 percent
- Black, non-Hispanic people, 69.5 percent
- Native Americans, 83.0 percent
- Asian and Pacific Islanders, 269.1 percent

Suffice to say that listening, inclusion, collaboration, accepting differences, and understanding are necessary skills and abilities to allow decisions to be made that take into account the richness that cultural dimensions provide.

Beliefs and Values

As we discussed in Chapter 2, thoughts are defined by beliefs; actions are taken based on values. For example, consider this scenario: If someone believes that new trainees should be treated just the way she was—thrown into the fire—then this same person may also value independence and treat new staff members with a hands-off approach. If this colleague or co-worker is a supervisor, and your project involves a mentoring program with new staff being mentored by supervisors, you'll have a hard time convincing this person that mentoring and coaching help people to become independent and that support helps confidence in the long run.

Personality

Personality is discussed more fully in Chapter 7. However, when it comes to decision making, personality conflicts often arise when some people are big-picture folks and others are intent on getting the details. Also, by nature, some are more concerned with organizational results and some with the harmony of the team. Some act quickly. Some prefer thoughtful consideration and time to think. All perspectives are good. Somewhere along the way, they all must mesh together for the good of the organization.

Who Should Make the Decision?

One of the tenets of decision making is to have the right person solve the problem, and that might just be the person with the problem. "How can that be?" you might ask. After all, if this person knew how to solve the problem, wouldn't he or she just solve it? That may be true; however, by asking the right questions, the person who has the problem may be able to solve it with the team's help or individually with the help of the decision-making model in this chapter. One strategy would be to have the owner of the problem lead discussions as a facilitator. If several own the problem, people can take turns. The best-case scenario is to allow problem owners to be problem-solvers.

Questions

- What process do I presently follow to solve problems?
- How can I improve?
- What step of the model is the most difficult for me?
- When have I questioned a decision I have made?
- When has a decision turned out well?

Tips

Like a child, be

- Boundlessly creative and curious
- Totally honest
- Courageous to the extreme
- Spontaneous; living in the moment
- Trusting
- Fun-loving and playful

The Leader's Connection

Possibly, the sagest advice that can be offered to leaders is to avoid thinking that you have to solve the problem alone or thinking that you can always solve problems from your perspective only. Leaders are often intuitors, leaving the details to others. Sometimes you need the details, as well as the workforce harmony, the organizational perspective, and the insight of others. Look at the ways to gain thoughts and insight listed in "Ways to Gain Perspective and Insight" in the Activities section of this chapter.

One strategy for leaders to encourage more collaboration is to ask team members to go through Steps 1 through 6 of the model prior to a problem-solving discussion. The team members can present their analysis independently or in assigned subgroups. The conversation then becomes a coaching opportunity for the leader

The Challenge of Problem Solving

and a great way for the team members to gain confidence and self-esteem. Any individual can practice this approach as well.

Questions

- How often do I make decisions independently?
- What is the method I use to involve others in decision making?
- Once I accept a decision, do I implement it?
- How often do I have the sense that the root problem is still elusive?
- What was one of the best decisions that was made cooperatively? How did we do it?

Tips

- Follow the tips in the previous Tips listing.
- Use the problem-solving tools in this chapter.
- Embrace the diversity of your team.
- Ask your direct reports to use the model.
- Encourage creative thought and intuition.

ABOUT THE NEXT CHAPTER

The next chapter is about teams. When you communicate one-on-one with a person, it is sometimes easy, and sometimes difficult. Skills and practice help ease the way for effective discussions and problem solving. When you are in a team, the communication challenges are multiplied and the solutions to engaging effectively are increased as well. Chapter 6 looks at team challenges and communication solutions.

Activities

Notes to Reader: The activities in this chapter are designed to be done individually or in a training environment. Whether you are in a group with others or working on your own, you may go back to these activities at any time and learn from them on an individual basis.

Notes to Instructor: Suggestions for using these activities in a learning environment are included at the end of the chapter.

Purpose: To practice problem solving with actual issues or concerns.

Background: The problem-solving model in this chapter walks you through how to solve a problem, taking into consideration the process to follow, not just making a quick decision. Of the activities in this section, one is for real problems, one uses a learning tool to think about the process, and one gives a scenario for practice. If you conduct the activities, they will require time to complete. You may not be able to finish in one sitting. It is important that participants choose a problem that can be solved without approval from anyone else in the organization. If a problem is systemic, figure out what part of the problem the person can help with and how he or she can make things happen. This will allow everyone to complete the entire process. After people become familiar with the nine steps, they can use the model for problems that require more assistance and cooperation from others.

Overview of the Problem-Solving Model

Use the explanations for each step of the model that were provided in Chapter 5. There is a brief description below of each step.

1. *Problem awareness:* What do you think the problem is, and what is the root cause?

2. *Gather data:* What data do you need to be sure that you are correct in identifying the problem? (For instance, say that you think the problem is turnover. What are the turnover statistics? How do they differ from previous years? What is the norm for turnover in your business?)

3. *Define the problem:* After discussion, define the problem. This may be difficult to do. (Perhaps you discovered what you believe to be the root cause of turnover. It may be hiring practices. Then you might want to revise your original view of the problem and define it differently.)

4. *Generate options:* What can your department do about the problem? What are some ideas to resolve the issues? (Using "hiring" as the problem, and assuming you are not HR, one option may be for all members of your team to be

The Challenge of Problem Solving

on the lookout for potential recruitment areas and to submit names of candidates you think qualify for the job. This is a big problem [turnover] narrowed down to a sub-problem in which you can execute resolutions. Another small problem might be "We cannot get in touch with team members when we need to reach each other." One option might be to create an electronic shared calendar. Another might be to have a whiteboard showing where people will be for the day. Another option is to have a five-minute team meeting in the morning to touch base with each other regarding the day's activities.)

5. *Evaluate options:* Which options are the best? What can you do immediately? What might take more time? How can you prioritize what might be done? (Expanding the shared calendar option, this is a task that can be completed by a person in the department. Action steps would include ensuring that accurate information is provided to that person by a certain time.)

6. *Make decisions:* Decide on the best solutions. (If this is your first time using the model, you might choose only one solution that can be implemented. You will obtain more timely resolution with only one solution, and you can determine how the model worked and ways you could improve next time.)

7. *Develop a plan:* Create an action plan with people assigned to tasks and due dates. Set up meeting dates for progress reviews in person or with online conferences to determine when actions are met.

8. *Implement:* Like the Nike commercial, "Just do it!" This, of course, would be according to your well-thought-out plan.

9. *Evaluate:* How did it go? Were you able to solve your portion of the problem? If not, why not? If so, celebrate your accomplishments.

Activity 5.1. Practice the Model

Instructions: Make a list of problems that you would like to solve. Choose one. You will not be solving the problem. You will be using the problem to determine what you might do at each step of the problem-solving model. This is for learning purposes and to discuss an issue by using the model to try it out.

Activity 5.2. What Is the Problem?

Instructions: Read the scenario about Brad and turnover in his department in Chapter 5. Complete the nine steps of the problem-solving model using the scenario. You can make things up to fill in the story. After you have completed the activity, see Greg Trulson's Scenario Notes at the end of the chapter. He created more background, just as you can do. Don't look until you have completed your process!

Activity 5.3. Tech Confusion

Instructions: In the case below, identify the steps that were taken by the salesperson to solve the problem. What steps are missing?

Tech Confusion

Susan was about to head off to college with a dinosaur-aged laptop computer. She needed to acquire a new computer and was overwhelmed with all the choices of equipment. Her Internet searches and visits to the electronic retailers only deepened her confusion and immobilized her. One of her friends had the decision made for her by overeager parents and Susan wasn't sure she liked the brand her friend received.

Susan decided to visit one last retailer before throwing in the towel and heading off to campus with her old computer. When she entered the computer department she was shocked to see the number of laptop options they had available. While standing there, she was approached by one of the sales personnel who looked like a character from central casting. What she expected was a tirade of features for each machine, which would only have created more confusion.

To her amazement, the salesperson seemed like he had been to the Rudyard Kipling school of sales. Instead of pointing out a specific laptop, he started asking questions and actually listened to her answers. "How will you use it? How often?, Where will you use it? Do you store lots of music and pictures? What types of classes will you attend? What is your budget?" and many more pertinent questions. After listening to her answers and crafting additional probing questions to determine her needs, he offered a limited pallet of options for her to consider. "Based on your needs, I suggest you consider two models that will fit your requirements. Let me tell you why…."

Susan made her selection with confidence and headed off to pursue her dreams.

Notes to Instructor: If you are working with a large group, you can conduct the activities with teams. Ask people to form groups of five. To identify problems to tackle in Activity 5.1, ask each team to brainstorm problems that they would like to solve in the organization. Ask them to choose problems that are in their control and do not require many levels of approval for follow-up. One problem can be addressed per team; the team members should agree on the problem. Have the nine-step model posted or hand it out. Give teams enough time to work the problem through Step 7. See the techniques described on the next page for the discussion phase.

Teaching Ways to Gain Group Agreement

The methods described below can aid in group decision making.

Brainstorming

The word brainstorming was coined by Alex F. Osborn, the co-founder of a large advertising agency. The focus of the process is to develop creative ways to solve a problem, as opposed to critical or evaluative thinking.

The facilitator of a session explains the reasons for the event and reviews the rules to be followed. The number of participants is best kept from six to twelve. The idea of deferred judgment of ideas is critical for the approach to be effective. Full participation of the group members must be accomplished without letting anyone dominate, while encouraging the quiet participants to contribute. If time allows, the facilitator should use an icebreaker with the group to encourage creativity before the ideas are generated. The success of a brainstorming session depends on the group following these rules:

1. Generate as many ideas as possible/quantity without concern for quality.
2. Combine ideas and piggyback parts of ideas.
3. Visibly record all ideas for everyone to see as they are developed.
4. Refrain from criticism or evaluation of ideas until the idea generation is complete.
5. Encourage very creative, even far out, ideas without ridicule.
6. Set a time limit and leave some time for the group to reflect on the ideas.

The evaluation of the ideas does not take place until the end, and preferably at a later time. The delay will often help participants develop additional ideas before they start the evaluation phase. Ideas are critiqued and reduced to the final accepted solutions for analysis in Step 5 of the model.

Nominal Group Technique

The nominal group technique was developed by Andre Delbecq and Andrew Van de Ven while at the University of Wisconsin. This technique is designed to achieve equal participation by all participants and lessen the chance for individual domination or dysfunctional conflict within the group. The technique follows a prescribed series of steps:

1. Each member generates ideas silently, often on 3 x 5 cards. A time for this phase will usually be limited to 10 to 15 minutes.
2. The facilitator gathers all the ideas from each group member one at a time in a round-robin fashion and records them visually or posts the 3 x 5 cards on a board.

3. Each idea is discussed for clarification and understanding. New ideas may come to mind as this step proceeds, and they are posted as well.
4. A letter is assigned to each idea that is posted and the group members use a numerical weighting system to rank order the ideas. The most common approach of forced ranking asks the group to silently vote by ballot using a scale from 1 to 10 points, with 1 being the best.
5. The preliminary vote is tabulated and the rankings are discussed. If clear winners surface, skip to Step 7 of the problem-solving model. The options may be narrowed down for the next round of voting.
6. Repeat Steps 4 and 5 of the process to reduce the options down to the target number of ideas for further evaluation.
7. The final vote is disclosed and the top option is put through Step 5 of the problem-solving model.

Delphi Technique

The Delphi technique was originally developed by the Rand Corporation. The technique was named after the Oracle at Delphi in Greece in the 6th Century BCE, who received written questions from afar. This technique also has been called "absentee brainstorming," since it parallels the same idea-generation process but through electronic or snail mail means. The approach allows people to think without others jeopardizing the integrity of their ideas. There are generally five steps in the process:

1. Questionnaires are distributed to each participant explaining the goals of the process and asking them to anonymously generate suggested solutions to the designated problem.
2. The questionnaires are returned to the facilitator and the ideas are combined and tabulated.
3. If necessary, the facilitator talks to the contributors to gain clarification of their ideas prior to the next round of emails or mailings.
4. A second and possibly third and fourth round might be used to narrow down the solutions. Much like the nominal group technique, a forced ranking might be applied to determine the top suggestions.
5. A final report is distributed to all participants presenting the results and thanking them for their participation.

The Challenge of Problem Solving

Scenario Notes

Here are some suggestions regarding the scenario about Brad and turnover in his department.

Step 2

- The HR department:
    - Reviews exit interview data derived from departing employees
    - Reviews performance appraisals for ex-employees
    - Compares turnover statistics prior to Brad with current trend
    - Reviews Brad's personal appraisals done by his manager
    - Interviews Brad concerning the turnover
    - Discovers Brad cancelled attending two company-sponsored seminars on interview skills
    - Discovers the turnover increase corresponds with Brad's arrival
    - Discovers that Brad did not use the structured interview process that is company policy

Step 3

- The problem is redefined from a turnover problem to improving the interview and selection process Brad uses, plus the enhancement of his coaching skills.

Step 4

- Direct coaching of Brad by his manager
- Brad attend a seminar(s) concerning interviewing and coaching skills
- Brad could shadow a successful counterpart manager during an equivalent hiring process
- Brad could use self-study courses followed by intensive coaching by his manager

Step 5

- Coaching and attending a seminar or several seminars were the options chosen.

Step 6

- Brad will be directly coached and observed by his manager following the attendance at the company-sponsored structured interviewing seminar.

Step 7

- Brad will register for a seminar within two weeks.
- Brad's manager will conduct a coaching session before the seminar.
- Meetings will take place every two weeks for continued coaching and for follow-up.

Step 8

- Brad attends a seminar and debriefs with his manager upon return.
- He starts using his newfound skills in upcoming interviews.

Step 9

- After an appropriate time, HR will assess the turnover in Brad's department to be sure the training and coaching helped him overcome his lack of interviewing expertise.

Chapter 6

Soft Skills and Teams

WHAT'S IN THIS CHAPTER?
- Types of Teams and Their Uses
- The Two Sides of Teams
- Four Stages of Team Growth
- Interventions That Encourage Results
- Team Member Roles
- The Leader's Connection
- Activities

When you work with others, freedom of thought and validation of others is a priority. With a high-functioning team, not only can these goals be attained, but you can experience great rewards in terms of better problem solving and productive interaction. Great team connections spark enthusiasm and creativity. The question then becomes how to get to the place where you look forward to team meetings and the advantages that working with colleagues affords you and your organization. Exploring the elements of group dynamics may give you some answers.

The difference between a *group* and a *team* is that a team has a common goal. It could be to improve sales of a product, increase staff motivation, plan a company event, improve a process, develop procedures, or solve a specific problem. Organizations form teams to gain different perspectives and to use the expertise of the individuals on the team. A team is more than the sum of its parts. In discussing issues and problems, new ideas are expressed and the team elicits valuable insights and resolutions. Minds expand when one person says something that might work, and then another person piggybacks on that thought and adds another piece to the puzzle. In addition to producing an outcome, a healthy team will leave members feeling productive, inspired, and confident. Trust will build. People will want to work together more and will gain respect for each other. Healthy teams don't just happen, however. It takes work and structure to allow free thought. Although that might sound like a contradiction—structure and freedom—think about how children grow: with structure that allows their safety and promotes their exploration without harm.

Types of Teams and Their Uses

Most people are on more than one kind of team. From the team descriptions in Table 6.1, determine the types of teams you are participating in now.

You may be on several of the types of teams described in Table 6.1. It is useful to know the parameters of the teams in which you participate. If you are unclear, ask the person to whom you report to give the team some definition and boundaries. If you are to be together for a month, this is good to know. If you are on a standing committee, you may want to know whether members rotate in and out. If you are on an ad hoc team, you may want to know if you are just planning, or planning and executing an event or project.

The Two Sides of Teams

Teams have two major "sides" or functions: task and maintenance or the intellectual (thinking) and the people (feeling) sides. Both sides are equally important. The task side of teams requires planning, goal setting, analysis, review, decision making. and evaluation. The maintenance side requires attention to how the process is unfolding and how to involve participants. A smooth process will allow the tasks at hand to be done efficiently.

Table 6.1 Types of Teams

Type of Team	Description	Examples
Traditional Work Unit	Primary work group, unit, section Department Division Focuses on daily tasks and outcome measures Where you have your office or work space	Client Services Accounts Payable Warehouse Management Information Services Customer Service Budget Public Relations
Problem-Solving Team Task Force	Comprised of members from different functions, divisions, departments, or teams Focuses on specific problems Responsible for solving the problem Usually has a time frame for resolution	Pros and cons of a new software system Improve an operating procedure Reorganize space for optimum storage Select office furniture
Quality, Process Improvement, Six Sigma, or Action-Planning Teams	Cross-functional teams Looks at processes Develops standards, procedures, efficiencies, and action plans for various parts of the organization Makes recommendations to leadership	Determine plant standards Work-flow improvements, such as quicker service from intake of auto to delivery to customer Improve recruitment and retention Action planning for strategic plan
Standing Committee	Studies specific issues or needs and plans certain actions or events Is ongoing; usually is long-term	Safety committee Management Councils Steering Committees
Task Committee	Formed for a certain cause	Planning a training event

Figure 6.1 Two Sides of Teams

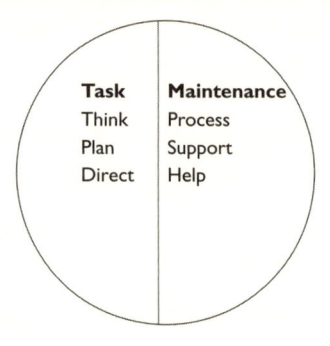

Task
Think
Plan
Direct

Maintenance
Process
Support
Help

Determine Ground Rules and Process

Ground rules have been mentioned in other chapters. They are so important that the purpose is being reiterated. To ensure that both the thinking and feelings sides of the team are paramount in team members' minds, ground rules or norms need to be established. Ground rules are behaviors that we expect of one another to encourage tact and diplomacy. Without rules, chaos can impede progress. Imagine a dance troupe that had no rules, or an orchestra that has no sheet music. If there were no traffic lights, what would occur? In these instances, the rules of the game are clearly communicated.

Members must agree on rules and also on consequences for violating the rules (such as paying a quarter for every broken rule). Without clear expectations of how people will treat each other, the team members can easily run amuck, talking over each other, disagreeing before a concept has been explored adequately, attacking people personally, and other behaviors described later in this chapter. By firmly sticking to ground rules, a safe and trusting environment can be established.

Ground rules may look like those behaviors described in Figure 6.2.

To help you in setting ground rules for your own teams, the following questions might be useful to ask:

- What do we expect of each other?
- What behaviors do we want to support?
- What behaviors do we want to discourage?
- What behaviors are not tolerable?

Although some of the questions elicit what is not acceptable, these answers can be expressed as positive statements. For example, "We will not demean each

Soft Skills and Teams

Figure 6.2 Sample Ground Rules

We will:

- Begin the meetings on time and end on time
- Complete any pre-work assigned
- Be prepared to discuss assignments and actively contribute
- Honor confidentiality
- Seek clarification
- Turn off phones and electronic devices
- Listen to each other
- Respect everyone's point of view
- Address issues directly
- Validate thoughts and feelings
- Ensure understanding
- Treat everyone with dignity

other" can be turned to "We will treat each other with dignity and respect." Responsibility for maintaining the ground rules is the leader's. However, when someone violates a ground rule, anyone on the team can call that member on his or her behavior and ask him or her to honor the rules.

Four Stages of Team Growth

Just as stages of development have been identified for children—what to expect at what age—teams go through stages, too. It's helpful to know the process so you can help keep the team on track. To use the analogy of children growing up, when babies are born, they are naturally curious, dependent on Mom for nourishment, support, and structure, and not sure how to relate to the world. As they grow older, they learn what is expected: how to eat, when to sleep, not to touch electrical outlets or draw on the walls. Around the time they discover that using the potty is a real accomplishment, they develop a sense of independence, affectionately known as the "terrible two's." They say "no" a lot. They refuse to take direction. They give you orders. From a cuddly cherub, they turn into baby Godzilla.

In a few years, children start to be more self-sufficient. They can play with others. They go to school, know the rules, have friends, and function within a civilized society. They progress in their culture. They continue to learn and abide by societal norms.

As children reach adulthood, they become more proficient, find jobs, continue their studies, and become valued members of society. They create, innovate, problem solve, and produce. They work with others to achieve goals. They function on many different teams.

Teams are similar. Although the stages are not totally congruent, we could use childhood, adolescence, and adulthood to mirror team stages. The concept of observable behaviors at certain points in a team's life comes from Bruce Tuckman (1965), who described these developmental stages: forming, storming, norming, and performing. Later he added adjourning. We will focus on the first four stages.

1. Forming

When a team forms, there is a combination of excitement, pride in being considered a member of the team, and concern about the job that needs to be accomplished. There is also some suspicion. Members do not want to reveal too much about themselves until they have a better grip on what the team will be like. Team members are hesitant as they start to explore boundaries of what is considered acceptable in the way that they act, express themselves, and reveal their identities.

> **STAGE ONE—FORMING**
>
> Behaviors might include:
> - Attempts to clarify the purpose and the outcomes expected
> - Discussion on ways to produce results
> - Philosophical and theoretical discussions about the point and significance of tasks
> - Impatience to get on with the first steps
> - Expression of perceived organizational barriers
> - Concern about what members think more important than the task at hand
> - Attempts to figure out why the team was convened

- Complaints about how the team was formed or political discussions about how the company is functioning as a whole
- Internal concern about how people fit in and how the individual will feel a sense of belonging

Behavior in the Forming stage is mostly polite. People are searching for their fit. The facilitator is the focus for the group, and cues are taken from him or her as to what is expected. There are a lot of internal and external unknowns at the beginning of the process, and thus the team is not highly productive in accomplishing tasks, nor is it expected to be.

2. Storming

The Storming stage is pretty much how it sounds. People begin allowing their discomfort to be known. They form alliances, cliques, and factions, and may pit one against another, with blame and criticism. Comments such as, "There is a hierarchy here: those who are considered important are heard and those who aren't take a back seat." Arguments break out, and interpersonal conflict may take center stage. Although participants may agree on the issues, they may not have consensus on how to address them.

STAGE TWO—STORMING

Behaviors and feelings might include:

- Surprise that there is more involved than expected
- Insecurity with new methods such as the problem-solving and decision-making concepts
- Uneasiness regarding giving and receiving feedback
- Distress about accountability
- Competition
- Vying for recognition
- Defensiveness

- Suggesting going beyond the purpose and scope of the group
- Anxiety and tension
- Jealousy

In the Storming stage, there is a lot of disagreement about how the team should move forward, what steps should be taken, how to organize tasks, who should do what, and in what order. Anxiety about lack of decision making increases and members experience a sense of unrest. People want to demonstrate their expertise and worthiness; individuals look at the process only from their individual points of view and background experiences. Control issues emerge, and collaboration is difficult. With the amount of dissention, it is difficult to remain on task and progress. However, in the fight for recognition, people do learn about each other's talents and proficiencies. Although this is a tough stage, members begin the process of disclosure and start to gain a sense of where others are coming from and why.

3. Norming

Although the Storming stage seems ominous and dysfunctional, it does not last forever. As thinking individuals, people realize that there is a time frame for completion and that their own agendas may not be the only ones that merit discussion and thought. People start to suggest ways to come together. Ground rules are followed.

STAGE THREE—NORMING

Behaviors may include:
- More inclusion by and for members
- Increased engagement
- Better use of feedback
- Consensus building
- Open discussion
- Increased harmony and cooperation

- Statement of norms and adherence to team standards
- Recognition and respect
- More productive conflict resolution

The Norming stage happens as people learn more about what others expect, not just about the expectations of the facilitator. Working through the conflicts of the previous stage brings the team closer. Humor is more apt to emerge and good faith is extended so the team can carry on with the goals that they have set in ways that are acceptable to the other team members.

4. Performing

In the Performing stage, the team takes off. Tasks are accomplished. People feel more comfortable emotionally and produce without anxiety and mistrust. They take each other's strengths into account and allow creativity and innovation to emerge. They listen to each other and encourage reciprocity. They agree on overall expectations.

STAGE FOUR—PERFORMING

Behaviors may include:
- Resolution of problems at a quick pace
- Receptivity to others' ideas
- Recognition of special talents and contributions
- Creating action plans for goals
- Cooperatively assigning tasks
- Volunteering to take on jobs

In the Performing stage, there is a high affinity for the team and for belonging to it. When the team reaches this stage, it is ready to achieve high performance. An example follows:

> Ellen was working for a Fortune 100 company. Although the company was extremely progressive at the time, it still had vestiges of hierarchical foundations. Out of the blue, Ellen's chief executive

officer asked her to take on the assignment of coordinating a week-long training program for eighty worldwide CEOs. The heads of the company in Germany, Great Britain, France, and other countries were the participants. The responsibility for conducting this big event rotated among CEOs each year. Ellen's CEO handed her the curriculum. She could hardly carry it. He told her that he had forgotten all about the event and that it was very high profile. His credibility as a CEO was on the line. She had two weeks to figure out how she was going to train the trainers, vice presidents from North American sites. And the CEO wasn't going to be able to make the training session the first day, so Ellen would have to handle it herself.

The training program was very complicated, requiring vice presidents to learn operations areas other than their own in detail and then conduct several three-hour workshops for the CEOs; give speeches on their topics to start out each morning; and be able to answer all the questions that the "trainees" had to answer as part of their in-class assignments. It was a bear. To train the VPs, Ellen had to learn the most intricate parts of each department at the CEO level, including finance, customer service, application processing, data processing, and more.

After Ellen arrived in the convention hotel and arranged all the materials, the group members convened. They were not especially enthusiastic. Ellen welcomed everybody and explained how delighted she was to be working with them for such a well-respected event. They just looked at her. She tried to make light conversation to break the ice. Silence. Some side-talking. This forming stage lasted for quite a while until Ellen put the schedule for the rest of the day on a flip chart. One of the VPs said, "You know what you can do with your schedule." The team had moved into the storming stage. There was laughing, and some VPs threw spitballs at each other.

Ellen was aghast. These VPs were going to be "on stage" for the next week; they hadn't even read the curriculum. They were one-upping each other with everything they said, expressing less than VP-like behavior in a critical situation where their own derrieres were on the line.

When it was time for a break, Ellen consulted with the person who had coordinated the event the previous year. He said, "They aren't happy." She said, "I can tell that." He continued, "You're a woman manager. They don't want to take direction from you." "Oh, I get it," she responded, and said, "Well, tell them that it's their show, their careers. I will set expectations again when we reconvene."

Fifteen minutes later, the group walked in, one by one, with very sheepish expressions on their faces. Ellen waited until they all sat down. She let them sit in silence for a few seconds, looked at all of them, and said, "Gentlemen, are we ready to work?"

The rest of the week, they took every direction Ellen had to offer and listened to their peers, all highly intelligent individuals. To make up for the time lost, they stayed up until 3:00 a.m. every day, going over workshops and their speeches. They had a lot of fun. About 2:00 a.m. one day, one of the team members was laughing so hard he was rolling on the floor in front of the stage. Their rehearsal of speeches started with some trepidation and ultimately ended with confidence. The humor was thrown in as the topping on the cake—or perhaps everyone was just giddy from no sleep.

Each member of the team performed with the charm, expertise, and professionalism that CEOs would expect. On a scale of 1 to 5 on evaluations, the team received all 5s. Ellen's CEO was ecstatic. The team lifted her up at the end of the workshop, and her CEO exclaimed, "Let's do it again next year!" Ellen about fainted.

The team did it again the following year with equally impressive results.

Sometimes, when the team goes through normal stages, it is hard to be the leader and awkward, possibly, to be a participant. As a leader, the only saving grace is that you know that every team will go through these stages. It does not matter what level you are facilitating. Like little ones growing up, all teams grow up with similar developmental stages. There are ways to encourage growth and discourage dysfunction, both with children and with teams. The next section gives you an idea of ways to move a team forward.

Interventions That Encourage Results

Teams can progress through the forming to performing process more quickly if some interventions are made that are appropriate to the team's stage of development. The interventions are ways to eliminate confusion, model positive behaviors, and suggest methods to encourage healthy discourse.

Forming

- Clarify expectations.
- Explain how and why the team was formed.
- Explain or create the mission.
- Determine how the mission fits into the larger mission of the organization.
- Welcome contributions.
- Determine whether training is needed in group process or in areas that the project requires.
- Explain who needs to approve the final result and whether the team can implement recommendations.
- Have a timeline for completion.

Storming

- Ask for one person's opinion at a time.
- See what the team members can agree on.
- Explore disagreements to see whether there are ways to incorporate some ideas into what the team already agrees on.
- Ask different team members to summarize others' points of view.
- Allow experts in their field to give their perspectives and/or explain history.
- Use the "yes… and" concept: "Yes, we can paint the lobby ourselves *and* we can ask art students to give us design tips—both ideas can be combined to save money."
- Introduce simple team-building activities or icebreakers.

Norming

- Follow ground rules.
- Allow for creativity.
- Set up action plans for goal completion.
- Have people volunteer for or agree to tasks.
- Be prepared for changes in direction and regroup.
- Understand that going back to storming or forming may happen, but only for temporary periods.

Performing

- Encourage efficiency.
- Take up suggestions for moving the project to goal completion.
- Guide the team if members are biting off more than they can chew.
- Support team members.
- Use resources.
- Watch that all are contributing and support those who need encouragement.
- Confirm direction on how plans will be implemented.

There are other stages that theorists have added over the years, including "adjourning." When the team is finished with its task, members need to say goodbye. It is common for people to want to keep in touch and for there to be some sadness in saying goodbye to what has become a performing team. As all good things must come to an end, celebrations of the work accomplished is a good way to ease the disappointment of adjourning and to recognize the hard work members of the team accomplished.

Team Member Roles

People play roles in teams, although they are not always prescriptive. Behavior can change. However, it's important to note that some people do behave in ways that can move a team toward its goal, or stop the team in its tracks. Just being aware of the roles can help team members react in ways that are honest and at the same time kind. Sometimes, it's hard to bring out the "kind" when people are blocking the path. Let's take a look at some common roles.

Benne and Sheats (1948) proposed the following roles played by team members:

Task Functions

- *Initiator:* contributes, suggests new ideas and perspectives, initiates tasks, makes recommendations
- *Information Seeker:* asks for clarification of the facts relating to suggestions or ideas.
- *Opinion Seeker:* asks for clarification of the values involved in a suggestion.
- *Opinion Giver:* gives his or her beliefs or ideas on what should be the group's evaluation.
- *Elaborator:* spells out, explains further, looks at possible outcomes of proposed actions.
- *Coordinator:* attempts to show relationships between ideas, to bring them together.
- *Orienter:* Defines the position of the group or outlines the direction the discussion is taking.
- *Evaluator:* critic: examines the group's production in relation to standards of performance.
- *Energizer:* attempts to stimulate or arouse the group to greater or higher quality activity.
- *Procedural Technician:* performs mechanical and routine tasks to expedite work.

Maintenance Functions

- *Encourager:* Praises, agrees with, indicates warmth and solidarity.
- *Harmonizer:* Mediates differences, reconciles disagreements, relieves tensions, searches for common elements in conflicts.
- *Compromiser:* Yields status, admits errors, comes halfway, persuades others to find common ground.
- *Expediter:* Keeps communication channels open, encourages or facilitates participation of others.

- *Standard Setter:* Stresses quality standards to attempt to achieve.
- *Follower:* Goes along with group movement, serving as audience.
- *Climate Tester:* Asks members how they feel about the way in which the group is working and about communication; shares own perceptions.
- *Active Listener:* Listens and serves as an interested audience for other members; is receptive to others' ideas, goes along with the team when not in disagreement.
- *Trust Builder:* Accepts and supports openness of other group members, reinforcing risk taking and encouraging individuality.
- *Interpersonal Coach:* Promotes open discussion of conflicts and processing.

Negative Roles

- *Aggressor:* Attacks the group or its problems, deflating the status of others, joking aggressively, expressing disapproval of values, acts, or feelings of others.
- *Blocker:* Resistant, stubborn, negativistic, disagreeing, or opposing beyond reason.
- *Recognition Seeker:* Works to call attention to himself or herself by boasting and trying to maintain a superior position.
- *Self-Confessor:* Uses group as audience for expressions of personal and emotional feelings; not group oriented.
- *Help Seeker:* Attempts to gain sympathy, expresses insecurity, personal confusion, and personal depreciation.
- *Social Interest Pleader:* Claims to speak for some special group and covers his or her own bias in this way.

As you can see, roles are sometimes positive and sometimes negative. The important point to remember is that people do sometimes play these roles, and you can predict behavior. Once you know what a person is predisposed to do, you can figure out ways to respond. For instance, for the "Self-Confessor" and "Help Seeker," you can volunteer to talk about personal concerns after the team meeting. For the "Social Interest Pleader" you can ask, "Is that your opinion?" For the "Recognition Seeker," you can praise the seeker's contributions and ask, "What do others think?" For the "Blocker," you can make an observation about his or her behavior: "You don't seem to like any of the ideas that we have presented. Is there a reason that you are not receptive? You know that we would like to hear your ideas, too. Do you have ideas that you haven't shared with the team yet?" And for the "Aggressor," "We would like to hear your opinions about the topic." The degree to which you confront an aggressor in a team meeting is tricky. Ideally, the facilitator would have an off-line discussion with the person and request compliance with the ground rules. If the facilitator does not do that, referencing the ground rules is appropriate for anyone on the team. "Respect" is usually included in ground rules and is a way to take the aggression from the individual back to group norms. Here are some additional phrases you can use to help with negative behaviors.

SUGGESTIONS FOR DEALING WITH NEGATIVE BEHAVIOR

Aggressor: Paraphrase the concern and ask for the opinion of others. Or paraphrase the concern and express an alternate opinion: "Let's consider another solution." (Socratic method)

Blocker: Describe the behavior: "It seems as if you don't like any of the suggestions on the table. What would be your way of handling the issue?" "It's hard for us to reach consensus when you don't agree. What would you agree on?"

Recognition Seeker: "You have great ideas and have contributed a lot. It may be time to hear from Jane. She has some valuable opinions too."

Self-Confessor: "Maybe we can talk about that after the meeting. It sounds like you might need to express some feelings that are holding you back from contributing."

Social Interest Pleader: "Let us hear from *you*. We would like to hear your own opinions. It's easier to address your concerns rather than try to imagine what the whole employee population believes."

Aggressive people need you to respond with strength. Although they may seem intimidating, they respect assertion and clarity. Always backing down will allow them to run over other people—and you. Sit straight, make sure your

Soft Skills and Teams

body language is confident and that your tone of voice is strong, though not aggressive.

Attacking back is never a good tactic, although it's hard sometimes not to want to do it. Just when someone pushes your buttons and you want to say, "Take a hike" (or worse), breathe deeply and remember that self-esteem may be at stake for the person who attacks, for you, and for the team. More suggestions for avoiding button-pushers are covered in Chapter 9.

It is up to everyone on the team to carry his or her weight. Being on a team is an important assignment. It means that you have been chosen as someone who can give suggestions for improvement and someone who is respected by your peers and supervisors. As such, you are expected to conduct yourself with the team's goal as first priority. If your only team assignment is to engage with your work team, the same expectations apply. Once hired, you are part of whatever team you serve on. Common roles of a team member are to:

- Attend all meetings, including staff meetings.
- Be on time.
- Submit items for the agenda.
- Identify opportunities for improvement.
- Participate in selection of items to work on.
- Gather, prioritize, and analyze data.
- Implement team decisions.
- Track effectiveness of solutions.
- Share experience and knowledge.
- Assist the designated leader with positive productivity and process roles.
- Provide feedback to leader and team members.
- Assist with presentations.
- Maintain a positive attitude.

The positive roles are the ones you want to practice. To be a valuable contributor to the team, it is not necessary to only initiate. It is also important to listen, clarify, reinforce, and bring the ideas of others together. Questions and paraphrasing are good ways to accomplish the task of moving forward. Here are some samples of ways to keep the team moving forward.

- "What do you think?"
- "I liked John's idea."
- "Maybe we can combine those two recommendations."
- "We could do that! That sounds like a good plan."
- "Can you explain a little more about what you said?"
- "I liked the way you were open about your experience."
- "If we did that, we might expect some pushback. How can we overcome objections?"
- "How do you think the team is functioning at this point?"
- "Do we have unresolved issues?"
- "Is everyone comfortable with the direction we are taking?"
- "Maybe someone else can think of a way to roll this out in our time frame and still practice good change management."

The Facilitator

A facilitator helps teams come to consensus, identify areas of concern in group process, and assists the team in reaching its goals. The facilitator:

- Listens well
- Pays attention
- Helps the team focus on organizational objectives
- Does not evaluate or contribute ideas initially
- Gives clear directions
- Focuses the energy of the team on a common task
- Elicits alternative methods and procedures from the team
- Protects individuals and their ideas from attack
- Encourages members to participate
- Helps the team find win/win solutions

Specific behaviors include:

- Defines the role of a facilitator
- Helps to educate the team by drawing out resources within the team

- Paraphrases to clarify feelings
- Summarizes when necessary
- Boomerangs questions back to team members
- Is positive
- Gets agreement
- Has a sense of humor
- Does not talk too much

Questions

- What roles do you play in teams?
- How can you use your strengths to move teams forward?
- How will you apply what you have learned about the stages of team development?
- How would you describe the stage of development that your work team is in presently?
- What is one way that you can move a team you are on to further growth?

Tips

- When a new member joins the team, the team may go back into the forming stage, since there is a new influence.
- When the direction changes, the team may experience some storming.
- Make sure all people express their opinions.
- Look for agreement; find ways for people to agree by accepting parts of different solutions or by combining solutions.

The Leader's Connection

It's an honor to lead a team. Your team members depend on you for support and encouragement. The most important interventions may come from you or come from team members who learn from you. Group dynamics is often taught in university programs. That means that studying on your own may be the way to learn how to be an expert. Of course, your position demands that you are the head of many teams: work teams, process improvement teams, and a variety of task teams. As a leader, you do this naturally. Learning more can increase your effectiveness and your company's productivity. Lead by example.

Questions

- Are the teams you lead and facilitate clear on their mission?
- How do you know that the mission is clear?
- Is there a trained facilitator on the team for which you are responsible?
- Do you listen more than you speak?
- What method do you use to gain consensus?

Tips

- Lead the team meetings according to an agenda.
- Teach and refresh on group process.
- Share experience and knowledge.
- Document the progress of the team.
- Balance task and maintenance functions.
- Communicate program updates.
- Track and measure progress.
- Lead by example.
- Communicate with others regarding progress.
- Provide feedback.

ABOUT THE NEXT CHAPTER

The next chapter looks at the many personality types that contribute to our work life. Based on the Myers-Briggs Type Indicator™ and the theories that relate to it, there are sixteen personality types. Although no two people are alike, the characteristics of "type" that have been studied help us understand each other and embrace our similarities and differences.

Soft Skills and Teams

Activities

Notes to Reader: The activities in this chapter are designed to be done individually or in a training environment. Whether you are in a group with others or working on your own, you may go back to these activities at any time and learn from them on an individual basis.

Notes to Instructor: Suggestions for using these activities in a learning environment are included at the end of the chapter.

Purpose: To explore how using soft skills can build relationships with team members.

Background: Teams go through stages of development. Commitment to a team requires adherence to ground rules and the team's progress through the stages. Activities in this section help people to think about what a team is for and how they can contribute in a professional way.

Activity 6.1. Why Teams?

Instructions: Answer the questions below to explore the reasons for teams.

- Why do we have teams?

- What are the advantages of working in a team environment?

- What are the disadvantages?

Activity 6.2. Determine Ground Rules

Ground rules are the norms that people determine will be followed within their teams. All team members must agree on the ground rules.

Create ground rules that you would like your teams to follow based on the questions below:

- What do we expect of each other?

- What behaviors do we want to support?

- What behaviors do we want to discourage?

- What behaviors are not tolerable?

Activity 6.3. What Is Not for Teams to Decide?

There are times when decisions have to be made only by the organization's leaders or by one individual. Not all decisions are appropriate for teams to make. Factors include the time available to make a decision, adequate information, necessity for confidentiality, and so forth. What are some other issues that you think would not be appropriate for teams to address?

Activity 6.4. Initial Team Assessment

Think about your work unit, the primary team in which you are involved on a daily basis. Answer the questions below to identify areas of strength and weakness:

1. What do you think are the keys for success in a team's approach to work and problem solving?

2. How effective and satisfying is your team?

3. What are the team's greatest strengths?

4. What would you like your teammates and/or resource people serving your team to learn or relearn?

5. What forces, obstacles, barriers, and sources of resistance will need to be overcome in order for your team to become great?

6. What forces exist that may push for greater success with your team?

7. What would you expect from your supervisor in working with you and your organization to facilitate team excellence?

8. What should your supervisor be able to expect from you when working with your team?

Activity 6.5. Your Trust Factor

Answer True or False to each of the following statements:

_____ 1. I meet performance standards.

_____ 2. I put the team's mission, goals, and needs ahead of personal agendas.

_____ 3. I follow ground rules.

_____ 4. I share information.

_____ 5. I meet deadlines.

_____ 6. I recognize the contributions of others.

_____ 7. I do not talk behind anyone's back.

_____ 8. I bring up issues I think are important.

_____ 9. I tell the team when I think things are not going well and can be improved.

_____ 10. I volunteer for the hard jobs as well as the easy ones.

_____ 11. I follow through on what I say I will do.

_____ 12. I address issues directly with the people concerned rather than avoid the issue or go to the team leader.

_____ 13. I don't exaggerate problems.

_____ 14. I ask questions to clarify and to increase my understanding.

_____ 15. I admit when I am confused about my role and responsibilities.

Activity 6.6. Team Functioning Questionnaire

Instructions: For each of the statements below, use the following scale to indicate your level of agreement with the statement; then write the number in the blank to the left of the statement.

1 = Strongly Disagree   2 = Disagree
3 = Agree   4 = Strongly Agree

_____ 1. The team's goals are clear, including how they relate to the organization.

_____ 2. Job descriptions reflect responsibilities for department goals.

_____ 3. The team members know who is responsible for tasks that are essential to the unit. There is limited overlap.

_____ 4. Ground rules are created and followed.

_____ 5. Decisions that can be made within the team are put into action.

_____ 6. All members of the team have input into decisions for which they are involved.

Soft Skills and Teams

_____7. Team members are honest and forthcoming with each other and the team's supervisor and work through conflict.

_____8. There is a high degree of camaraderie on the team.

_____9. The team members know the influence they have on the organization and on other units.

_____10. Team members know how they affect each other.

_____11. Team members share information freely.

_____12. Team members can identify and solve team problems.

_____13. Team members understand team process and are adept at making recommendations for improvement as well as appreciating team members for success in personal and team development.

_____14. Team members support team goals and contribute regardless of personal inconvenience.

Team Assessment

Based on your answers to the Team Functioning Questionnaire, please answer the following questions:

What would you like to see continue within your team?

What suggestions do you have to improve the team's ability to function? (What might be changed?)

What specific suggestions do you have to optimize the strengths of the supervisor? (What do you like and want to continue?)

What specific suggestions do you have to assist the supervisor to lead this team? (What might be changed?)

Activity 6.7. Brainstorming

Conduct a brainstorming activity with the group. Pick a topic or have the group choose one. Follow the steps in "Teaching Ways to Gain Group Agreement—Brainstorming" in Chapter 5.

Activity 6.8. Transportation

Ask participants to draw a type of transportation that represents their team. Split the group into teams of five or six and give each team a flip-chart and felt-tipped markers. Give them ten minutes. Have leaders of the teams present their drawings and explain them to other participants.

Notes to Instructor: The activities in this section can be used for teaching team functioning or used with intact teams when you want to facilitate discussion about team functioning.

Activities 6.1 through 6.6 can be used at different times during one session or several sessions. Each is a questionnaire to hand out to team members. You can distribute the questionnaires, compile the results, and distribute them to the team members. Or you can have participants fill out the questionnaires and respond in the group using their answers. To facilitate a discussion of this nature, assist team members to keep comments positive and productive, including ways to improve.

The last two activities are suggestions for ways in which you can lead a team meeting.

Chapter 7

The Personality Factor

> **WHAT'S IN THIS CHAPTER?**
> - Understanding Personality Styles
> - Finding Your Source of Energy
> - Discovering How You Gather Information
> - Identifying How You Make Decisions
> - Describing Your Personality
> - The Leader's Connection
> - Activities

Understanding Personality Styles

Did you ever have the feeling that you could finish a person's sentences without even knowing him or her very well? On the other hand, have you run into those you can listen to, look straight in the eye, ask questions of, and still not totally understand not only what they said, but how they got there?

One might think that, when it comes to communication, there is some kind of systematic way to approach the process. After all, we learn how to talk when we are just a few years old; we understand at least some of what is said even earlier. People communicate in the language they are taught, and verbalizations are common ways of moving thoughts to speech. So the rules of the game must have some logic behind them, as we have discussed throughout this book. Why, then, is it sometimes just impossible to "get through"?

What we take in and how we analyze words depends on characteristics we were born with, our experiences, and our background. The inborn part of the communication process comes from personality type. To get a small taste of your personality type, follow the directions below.

In each of the four sets of statements below, choose which list (A or B) is closest to your preference. There are no right or wrong answers.

A1	B1
I express my thoughts easily.	I prefer to ponder before I speak.
I like gatherings and engage easily with friends and strangers.	I need some alone time to regroup in a quiet setting.
I enjoy working with groups rather than by myself.	I may not say much during a meeting, but I will be listening and thinking about the discussion.
I am easy to get to know.	People sometimes think I'm reserved.
I prefer to act rather than reflect a lot.	I am reflective.
A2	**B2**
I am good with details.	I have keen intuition.
I like facts rather than hunches.	I have hunches that cannot always be "proven" with data.
I am good at carrying out policies and procedures.	I am imaginative and creative.
I follow directions in sequential order and complete one step before I go to the next.	I may skip steps in a project and come back to them later.
"Big picture" people drive me nuts.	I leave the details to last, and preferably to others.

The Personality Factor

A3	B3
I am logical and objective.	I have strong values and work from them.
The same principles should apply to all in the same way.	I give people chances and sometimes modify expectations.
I have been told I can be critical and condescending.	I am warm-hearted and enjoy appreciating people.
I value precision.	I value the work that people put in.
I am analytical.	I believe that harmony is essential in the workplace.

A4	B4
I am organized and decisive.	I go with the flow and prefer spontaneity.
I am uncomfortable when closure is not reached.	I like to keep an open mind and like change and flexibility.
I plan ahead and meet deadlines.	My planning is conditional and I don't mind interruptions.
On vacation, I need to know where I'm staying, how long it will take to get there, and what the schedule entails.	On vacation, I would prefer to see what happens, experience the moment, and avoid schedules.
My desk is either clean or acceptably neat.	My desk is a mess and so is my closet.

You may have had a hard time choosing columns. This is natural. We are never just one way or the other. However, everyone has certain areas of comfort, even though they may be able to operate outside their comfort zones. For example, while you may enjoy "going with the flow," learning to be decisive in certain situations is, of course, a part of life and necessary for survival.

Instruments such as the Myers-Briggs Type Indicator™ (MBTI®), based on Carl Jung's theory of psychological type, provide a comprehensive picture of the areas in which you are most comfortable, termed "preferences." When you answer the questions on the MBTI and score it, your "type" is confirmed by your own knowledge of what you prefer. Depending on the strength of inborn preferences, you lean somewhat or strongly toward ways of getting your energy, gathering information, making decisions, and practicing a certain lifestyle or relating to the outside world. Learning about the Myers-Briggs can be eye-opening, validating, reassuring, and informative.

Myers-Briggs preferences are designated by letters:

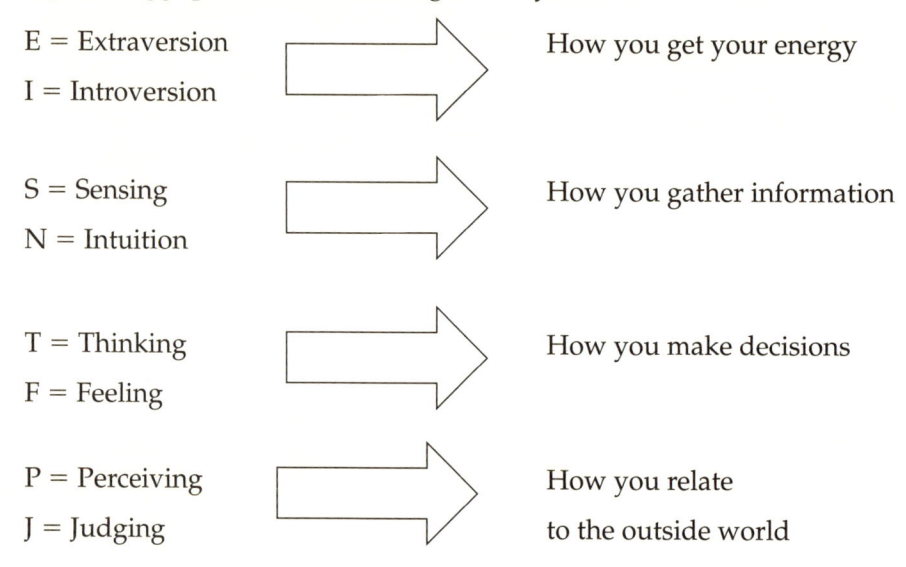

E = Extraversion → How you get your energy
I = Introversion

S = Sensing → How you gather information
N = Intuition

T = Thinking → How you make decisions
F = Feeling

P = Perceiving → How you relate
J = Judging   to the outside world

The dichotomies of the two columns, taken together, form sixteen different personality types. Each dimension has its own common characteristics; however, for an accurate description of type, all four of your preferences interact in ways that have validated attributes and are more descriptive than any one dimension. In the discussion below, each preference will be reviewed; but the descriptions used, such as "extraverts," are only one part of a person's makeup. Knowing your integrated Myers-Briggs type and the types of others provides a wealth of information. Organizations such as the Center for Applications of Psychological Type (CAPT) and Consulting Psychologists Press (CPP) provide resources for you to learn more about your preferences and your type. You can also access www.kiersy.com to take David Kiersey's Temperament Sorter, another way to look at personality. Kiersey is the author of the *Please Understand Me* series, available in bookstores and on the site.

With knowledge and practice, you can increase your soft skills and communicate in ways others can understand based on what you know about your own and others' preferences. Personality type requires much more than a chapter; however, some key principles can help you think about why people do what they do, how they do it, and how you can be a catalyst for better communication.

Finding Your Source of Energy

The activities you just completed gave you an idea of your personality preferences. Each selection you chose was an area you are prone to favor. The first columns (A1 and B1) represented extraversion and introversion. In the discussion of these preferences, as with others, consider how you can use your strengths at work and in your personal life.

The Extravert Experience

Columns A1 and B1 relate to how you get your energy. Extraverts usually have characteristics of Column A1. They get their energy by interaction with others. They like to put their thoughts out for people to hear. It is somewhat torturous for extraverts to be alone all day long or to sit in a meeting where they cannot express themselves. They get their energy from talking, socializing, bantering, telling stories, and letting others know them. "Getting energy" is much like charging a battery. Energy keeps us going, and *people* keep extraverts' batteries charged and running. Put an extravert in a cubicle with no people or phone contact, and at some time during the day, he or she will get up, talk to someone, visit, or engage in some kind of human contact. You don't see many extraverted bookkeepers or data entry staff members.

Extraverts give life to parties and company events. Energized after one celebration, they can go to another and have just as much fun. They are easy to get to know and are generally perceived as friendly and approachable. They are eager to articulate and quick to give opinions and verbalize thoughts. In their desire to "share," they can dominate a conversation, repeat what others have said and think it's their own, and become annoyed if someone says something they were thinking and they didn't say it first.

The Introvert Experience

Introverts (Column B1) get their energy from being pensive and thoughtful. A tough day for an introvert is to attend three meetings and a company event, be a part of a focus group, and end the day with a team discussion. Whew! This is a bit too much outward direction. Batteries drained from no time for reflection, it is likely the introvert will not even want to turn on the radio on the way home. Quiet is the goal.

Introverts are often good listeners because they take in what is said and think about it. They are less likely than extraverts to interrupt or to pull the focus back to themselves. In a meeting they may be the ones who, at the end of the discussion, reflect back what people have said and come up with a solution that no one else considered. Without needing the stage, they are good synthesizers of opinions and create new solutions.

Although introverts may end up in large venues, they prefer small groups or one-on-one discussions. Intimate settings allow them to comfortably participate. They are not competing with extraverts to put their points across. Because introverts prefer to be with few people they know well and who know them, their best environment is with friends or colleagues who have established a trusting relationship. They do not linger much after gatherings and may be the first to leave a big party, especially if they have not connected with one or two others.

There are no right or wrong preferences. Those with different preferences help each other, as long as there is understanding of the wealth and depth of thought that can be experienced with different people's gifts. And every person has gifts to offer. To be annoyed or exasperated by someone who is not like you is like missing parts of the equation, and possibly overlooking the best answers, results, or outcomes. Corporate think tanks have been known to make sure that all personality types are represented for the purpose of coming up with the best solution seen from different angles. NASA and Southwest Airlines are two of the many companies that use the Myers-Briggs to study high performers and to revise curriculum and training opportunities to include soft skills for different personality types in learning sessions.

A Personality Type Demonstration

Inborn preferences are part of every person. Under usual circumstances, preferences do not change. Here is an activity that Myers-Briggs trainers use to demonstrate the principle of preferences.

Instructor: Sign your name on any piece of paper you have handy.

Instructor: How did that feel?

Participants often stare at the instructor before they answer, some thinking "What do you mean 'How did it feel?'" Then someone will say something like, "Natural, effortless, easy, didn't have to think about it, just did it, felt fine; it was easy."

Instructor: Now change hands and write your name.

Some groan, laugh, chuckle, grimace, and look at how others are doing it.

Instructor: How did that feel?

There is almost always someone who says, "I'm ambidextrous." But most say something like "awkward, hard, can't read it, looks like my three-year-old's attempts; had trouble doing it," and there is a lot of laughter in the room.

That's a simple way to demonstrate how preferences work. On a more complicated level, neuroscientists have studied this exercise and others for evidence about how the brain works. Try the exercise yourself.

Soft Skills for Extraverts and Introverts

Since extraverts like to express their thoughts aloud, allow them to do it. If you are extraverted, too, take the time to listen and then express your point of view. Here are some ways to get a word in edgewise:

- "Thanks for giving me your thoughts. I'd like to tell you mine. Then we can see if there's a conclusion here" (or middle ground or compromise).
- "I agree with what John is saying, but I'd like to add something for the group to consider."

Keep your tone of voice and body language in an accepting mode, but assertive. This is important because, otherwise, you might communicate frustration and intolerance. Bear in mind that you're an extravert, too, and others may struggle to get their own points of view across. You may have to use questioning techniques to obtain the opinions of introverts.

- "What do you think, Irene?"
- "Let's hear from some of the people who haven't spoken."

One cautionary note is that introverts may not want to speak on the spot. Teachers who give extra credit for "participation" favor extraverts. It is a shame that those teachers are not educated in personality type and learning style. Expecting all students to speak up over the extraverts who pontificate naturally (sometimes at length and on and off of the topic) is ignoring the nature of introverts, who prefer to think about the topic deeply or aren't as quick on the gun and do not like to present off-the-cuff answers.

Encourage introverts to reveal what they are thinking by using writing and reflection. Suggest they email their thoughts, allowing time for reflection and organization of responses. You could also say, "Let me come back in a few minutes and continue the discussion." Introverts will often give you the hint anyway and say, "Let me think about that." I was in a discussion the other day and my colleague said, "Let me marinate on that."

If you are an introvert talking to another introvert, questions and paraphrasing work well. Also, acting on the person's suggestion is motivating. "Oh, that's a good idea. Let's go with that for action step one." Supporting is a positive behavior to practice with fellow introverts, providing, of course, that you agree. Encouragement leads to further contributions.

Discovering How You Gather Information

Once you have gained some knowledge about how you get your energy, the next preference is between sensing and intuition, two distinct ways to observe the world around you, what is there for sensors, and what may not be there, but somehow intuited for intuitive types.

Put simply, a person is either a big picture type (Intuitive—N) or a detail type (Sensor—S). People who prefer sensing are usually very good with details. They are the staff members you want on your team to make the schedules, order the food, collect data, construct the charts, and follow procedures. They take numbers at face value and are good at administrative work that requires standardization. Remember the old TV series "Dragnet"? Sergeant Joe Friday was famous for saying, "Just the facts, Ma'am. Just the facts." In other words, I believe what I see, hear, touch, taste, smell, and observe.

Here's a conversation that might occur between a sensor and an intuitive:

S: "How much did we spend on the employee event?"

N: "Not that much."

S: "How much?"

N: "It was well received."

S: "How much did we spend?"

N: "Around $500."

S: "How much *exactly*?" (getting frustrated)

Sensors need exact information, and sometimes they cannot fully move on until they get it. Here's another example of a phone conversation between a leader (L) and some participants (P):

L: "Training in the state will be changing. Instead of being centralized it will be up to individual organizations. We will hold a meeting sometime in August to discuss how we will roll out the program. This is a big change, and we'll have to all put our thoughts together. We'll be discussing standards that all can follow and competencies to give us a baseline."

P1: "So, we'll use the competencies to create our programs?"

L: "Yes, and we will be able to individualize the curriculum based on local needs."

P2: "This is a big change, and there are a lot of ramifications. Let's think about a few."

P3: "What time is the meeting?" (Silence from all others.)

P4: "What?"

P3: "What time is the meeting?"

L: "We haven't decided that yet."

P3: "Where is it?"

L: "We haven't decided that yet."

P5: "Can we get back to the discussion?"

Here we have a sensor who needs to have exact information in order to proceed. Although the time and location of the meeting are important, the leader said it would be "sometime in August." P3 may have a tight schedule. Changing schedules is hard for sensors, and until that one question is answered, she is going to be uncomfortable and could miss important parts of the discussion.

More on the Sensing Experience

Sensors are practical. They are good at conserving energy and materials, often figuring out the best price or the closest location. They go step-by-step in following directions and like a structured approach to discussions, such as reviewing action plans. They like things that are definite and measurable.

Sensors are often literal. They ask specific questions and want specific answers. If you don't give them what they want, they may discount your explanation or ask the same questions again. Consider this child's question:

Boy: "Mommy, where do I come from?"

Mom: "Well, I thought you would want to know one day."

Boy: "Where?"

Mom: "Well, your Daddy and I had so much love that we wanted a little boy like you, and we got together, and Daddy planted a seed in Mommy, and it grew to be you!"

Boy: "But where did I come from?"

Mom: "Well, I carried you in my womb. When you were inside me, it made my tummy look big. And then you were born."

Boy: "But where do I come from?"

Mom: Silence. Mom doesn't really know what else to say at this point. She figures that sex is not part of the conversation; he is too young to get it.

Boy: "Bobby comes from New York. Where do I come from?"

Mom: "Oh. . . !You come from Massachusetts, honey. We moved here to New York when you were only one year old."

Never underestimate the tenacity of a sensor who wants an answer.

The Intuitive Experience

Intuitives (N) are interested more in meaning than specifics. (The N is capitalized so as not to confuse the dimension with introverts,) They want to know what's behind the numbers, how they were collected, and whether there is any meaning to a chart, graph, or directive. Or they can entertain themselves in their own worlds and not even notice that the graph is posted on the wall. Their minds are usually active, thinking about solutions, creations, innovations, theories, and dreams. They often overlook what's in front of them and, deep in thought, miss exits on the highway, trip over something they didn't see, or forget where their cars are at the mall. They are perfectly capable of creating an excellent presentation, working hard on the overall theory as well as details (not their favorite) and then forgetting to copy the presentation on a zip drive for presentation in another location the next day. Introverted intuitives live in their heads a lot; extraverted intuitives are more likely to express their plans, ways of doing things better, and their creative innovations.

Intuitives enjoy variety. While sensors like to make lists and cross things off in pleasure, intuitives would rather do different, intriguing projects and aren't that interested in accounting for the details and crossing off specific tasks. With vivid imaginations, intuitives appreciate possibilities and delight in envisioning what could be rather than what is. Top-level leaders are often Ns, moving the world's companies and organizations to better and longer sustainability based on changes in the environment and economy. They are often backed up by sensors, who keep them grounded with facts they might not consider.

Soft Skills for Sensors and Intuitives

Sensors need facts based on reality. If your boss is a sensor and you are an intuitive, you will probably hear, "Give me some concrete facts to back up what you are suggesting" more than once. He or she needs data to show others to support your intuition, even though you may have used facts to come to your conclusion. Soft skills for you include your presentation style (to include charts, graphs, raw data, and predictions based on past history and current demonstrated trends); listening to reactions and accepting that more facts might be needed to put your intuition into action, and validating your boss for pointing out areas that you might have missed. These principles don't apply only to your boss. You can get support from your sensor teammates in the same way, and you can also engage other areas in the organization to help make your points by collecting data that you might not have readily available.

Soft skills for sensors working with intuitives (and in personal situations) require faith and trust. Since this concept may not be the norm for sensors, it does take some learning. Trust is built on acceptance and belief in the person with whom you are engaging. Instead of punching holes by firing questions and tearing apart assumptions, listen first. Intuition may be off the deep end, it may be right on, or be a little of both. Practice listening. Think about the times when colleagues offered their gift of intuition and they were right. Sometimes, it is too late to take advantage of insight after the fact. It may take years for what is obvious to intuitives to be validated with enough facts for sensors, and by then the project or the company may be so far gone that the suggestions may be moot or the company may be out of business.

Identifying How You Make Decisions
Thinkers
People who prefer the thinking function make decisions based on logic. Talking about a situation and analyzing the benefits, obstacles, consequences, and outcomes, a thinker applies rationality in coming up with final answers. Once a decision is made, since it has been analyzed with the information available, the thinker wants to apply it to all in the same way, because, as thinkers think, this is fair. Fairness, considered "the same for all," is important.

Thinkers may be perceived as harsh and critical. Picture Clint Eastwood in *Dirty Harry*, and Meryl Streep in *The Devil Wears Prada*. More likely to find the mistakes and criticize, thinkers are often considered cold and condescending. Donald Trump is also a good example of a thinker, both in real life and on "Celebrity Apprentice."

At work, thinkers can motivate by providing logic and helping people analyze plans, projects, and processes. They are good at correcting errors and finding holes in others' logic. They can also demotivate by assuming they are always right. This would be because, as they see it, they have analyzed everything with great thought—their thoughts. Their behavior could come across as arrogant, abrasive, or rude. They can put a red pen to the most earnest of reports and consider it a gift of feedback.

Feelers
Those who prefer to make decisions by their feeling preference consider their own values, which most often include harmony in the workplace, personal relationships, and supporting those on a team or at home with understanding and compassion. They are keenly aware of the feelings of others and take those feelings into account when making personal and organizational decisions. Feelers often have the pulse of the workforce, especially of intuitive feelers, and they can capture what may not even be verified by surveys. Sometimes, people do not reveal the truth on surveys. This is not to say that feelers are right. It is just to say that they may have some information that can be very useful.

If the people with whom feelers work are going to be negatively affected by a decision, they go to their defense. Feelers often support those who are negatively impacted by social norms where dignity and respect are denied to groups or vulnerable individuals. Consider Martin Luther King, Jr., Mother Teresa, Nelson Mandela, and Carl Rogers.

The Personality Factor

Feelers can be very persuasive when they are passionate about a topic. Take budget cuts, a common organizational necessity in tough times. Here's a familiar discussion between a CFO thinker (T) and feelers (F).

T: As your CFO, I must tell you that there will be serious budget cuts this year.

F: How will they determined?

T: We will look at the whole organization and see where we can save money in every area.

F: What about people's jobs? There are rumors out there that people may be cut.

T: We are considering all aspects.

F: There are plenty of ways we can save money without people losing their jobs. Without the front line, we compromise services to the people who count on us, and to our internal employees. Morale is already low.

T: The workforce comprises the highest costs in the organization.

F: People will not stick around if they think they are not supported by the administration. Why don't we eliminate the new technology that will cost millions?

T: We will take your feelings into consideration, but reducing expenses is an organizational priority that may involve staff layoffs. Technology is important to keep the company on the cutting edge.

Although people are generally affected by the possibility of losing their jobs, feelers are most likely to be concerned about others as well as themselves. Loyal to the people in the business (and the organization, too), they may feel wounded by the pain that will be caused if fellow staff members are laid off with no means of supporting their families. They understand people's needs and are empathetic. They are usually willing to take responsibility for their own actions and are more likely to apologize, appreciate, and express caring. Those who have a Thinking preference may not see the rationale of those who prefer to make decisions from the Feeling perspective and may think of them as emotional and "soft."

Soft Skills for Thinkers and Feelers

Thinkers need to listen to feelers and, by learning soft skills (sometimes ascribed to feelers, as noted above), reflect back the feelings that are being shared. If you are a thinker, you might wince at the term "shared." If you are a feeler, sharing is a gift. Feelers know who wants their gifts and who doesn't; but they will take risks anyway if they think their feelings substantiate values that they cherish. It is important to hear feelers out. Just listening and demonstrating that you care can go a long way in establishing trust and motivating a feeler to do his or her best work. Thinkers may respond that listening to feelings is unnecessary and that "People have jobs; they need to just do them." Feelers might react with a song title like: "Take This Job and Shove It." They will respond silently though, because they wouldn't want to be so unkind out loud.

One intuitive feeler whose boss made the "people have a job" comment responded with, "They may have jobs, but in the same way people who are victims in domestic violence situations have a home." Fortunately, the boss understood the analogy. Neither comment got them any further with action, but the feeler made her point and the boss understood that people at work were really feeling stressed from an environment that could be improved. Let it be said that there was some trust between these two individuals; and let it also be said that neither comment is an example of soft skills, lest anyone misunderstand.

Describing Your Personality

Judging

The "judging" preference does not refer to evaluation or to being judgmental; it is defined differently in Myers-Briggs language. It refers to how people use this dimension in the outside world and how it is reflected in their lives.

One's lifestyle at work and at home may be different. However, for the judging (J) preference, planning, organizing, scheduling, and deciding are critical, even if they look a bit different in the workplace and in personal life.

Those who have the judging preference are not comfortable with leaving things up in the air or with last-minute changes. Their inclination is to be methodical enough to avoid last-minute stress. Interrupt a judger's schedule and he or she will not be thrilled. You may hear something like: "I have to finish this report; and then I have to work on the talent management project; and then I have lunch; and then I have a training class; and then I have to order our supplies." Their minds take one step at a time. For a motivated judger, his or her schedule might look like this:

8:00–8:15	Make or double-check the list for the day. Read emails that came in since 5:00 yesterday.
8:15–10:30	Complete the field report; Section 1 by 8:45; Section 2 by 9:15; Section 3 by 10:30.

10:30–10:45	Take a break.
10:45–11:45	See client offsite. (Directions already MapQuested.) Checklist of questions in folder. Put folder and directions in briefcase.
11:45–12:00	Complete documentation on client.
12:00–1:00	Lunch, preplanned meal.
1:00–4:00	Scheduled meeting with Team 1 in Conference Room B.
4:00–4:15	Check emails that came in during meeting and respond. (All other emails have been addressed on the BlackBerry.)
4:15–4:30	Return telephone calls that came in during meeting.
4:30–4:45	Make a "to do" list for tomorrow. Cross off "done's."
4:45–5:00	File and clean desk. No stray papers. Put chair back in place before leaving.

Order for judgers is a necessity. Getting things done is motivating and reinforcing. In their personal lives, judgers want to know what is happening and when. They plan ahead and anticipate what needs to take place for systemized functioning. They can get a lot done by keeping to the schedule. They can be stressed by interruptions and unexpected events.

Perceiving

Those who prefer the perceiving process enjoy going with the flow. Too much scheduling can be draining for them. They like to be flexible, take pleasure in surprises, and are receptive to what comes their way in terms of life experiences. They like to remain open. They can wait for decisions; delays do not drive them nuts. Too much structure will. Today they might want to do one thing; tomorrow they may want to do another. Someone may suggest something totally different and they might be just fine with that, too. This is not to say that people who are perceivers do not make decisions. They are just more open to change, and that also depends on the rest of their type dimensions. For instance, a judger who is also a feeler may not change his or her mind on certain values that he or she considers indisputable such as: "We will not discriminate." But he may easily change his mind if his colleague wants to go to a restaurant for lunch that is different than planned.

Vacations are a "trip" (excuse the pun) for those who differ on the J/P scale. Myers-Briggs trainers have a lot of fun asking participants divided by Js and Ps to prepare on a flip chart how they would plan for a trip. Do the plans need to be made far in advance, or spur of the moment? Should there be a schedule, or would a schedule defeat the purpose of a vacation? For a perfect vacation, Js and Ps might differ a lot! The difference might be seen in the comments below.

Judging Preference
The plans must be made far in advance. Each day has to be scheduled so we can decide beforehand where to stay, what time we will get there, and when we will leave the next day, so we can book appropriate places to stay and be there on time. We also need to decide what clothes to bring well before leaving because we have to make sure that they fit in the suitcases and the suitcases fit in the car or plane in such a way as to carry or not be charged for unnecessary luggage. We also need to schedule where we want to go every day and what events we want to see, and we need to make sure that they meet the overall time plan for arrival and departure. We can't stop for too many bathroom breaks.

Perceiving Preference
Vacation! Go with the flow—whatever happens. We do whatever we want, when we want, and where we want. We don't schedule anything. We just take off and see where we end up. We eat at places that look interesting, and we stop for the night wherever there's a vacancy in a decent motel where we have landed. We get up when we want to get up in the morning. We eat at the motel or, if we've slept too late, we find an interesting breakfast nook or run into the 7-Eleven for coffee and whatever we can find that isn't too gross. We'll make up for it at lunch. Or we'll have a great breakfast and skip lunch. Pack? We'll throw things into the suitcase at the last minute. If we forget something, we'll stop at a Wal-Mart or mall. Or we'll buy it in the motel's store.

If you would like to do this fun and insightful activity with a colleague or team, or apply other personality concepts, see the "Activities" section at the end of the chapter.

Questions

- Based on the information you have, what would you predict your personality to be?
- What strengths do you bring to your team?

- When have you been able to present your perspective and be heard?
- When have you been challenged to put your ideas across?
- What do you think accounted for the difference between your answers to the last two questions?
- What personality characteristics make you proud?

Tips

- Take pride in your personality.
- Learn the personality types of your team and your supervisor.
- Be tactful and diplomatic when you work with personalities other than your own.
- Notice those with whom you have conflicts.
- Determine whether their personality types may be different from yours. Listen to their thoughts and try to appreciate their points of view.

The Leader's Connection

Your personality type is recognized by your staff members. They may not be able to tell what "letters" you are (T, F, etc.), but they know something about how you think and your decision-making style. At times, leaders discount people who do not think in the same way that they do. After all, being a successful leader, you must know something! This is true. The question becomes: Do you want to know more? Do you believe that you can be even more successful if you consider the perspectives of others in your organization, especially those who have diverse preferences and see the organization in a different light? Would you be willing to reach out to those with personalities that are different from yours? Extending your vision in this way serves the purpose of recognizing everyone, not just those who are like you or those you like (sometimes the same).

If some of the top companies in the United States are working with curricula related to the Myers-Briggs Type Indicator, it may benefit your organization as well to "type" yourself and your team, especially if you have the mindset that you can learn from everyone on your team. Your "opposite" will give you great perspective. Instead of discarding different views, consider embracing them, for understanding and to obtain a broader view. You may make the same decisions that you would have without additional input. Or you may do one or more things differently that will make the difference between buy-in and dissent. It is worth considering for you—and for your team.

Questions

- Does your team know your personality type?
- Do you know the "types" on your team?
- Are you willing to receive training on the MBTI?
- What do you think will be the advantages?
- Are there any disadvantages as you see it?

Tips

- Hire a certified instructor in administering and interpreting the MBTI.
- Have the consultant "type" your team and discuss the results.
- Determine how you can adjust how you motivate each individual.
- Work toward greater consensus through validating all types and listening and taking into account different points of view.
- Do not expect everyone to be like you.

ABOUT THE NEXT CHAPTER

The next chapter, "Taking the Sting Out of Feedback," shows you how you can express observations, feelings, and perceptions without sounding critical. Feedback is a positive way to gauge how you are coming across to others. It is like setting a train back on track when it is about to derail. Your true intentions are in your heart and mind. Feedback can help you realize whether your actions are being received in a way that mirrors your intent.

Activities

Notes to Reader: The activities in this chapter are designed to be done individually or in a training environment. Whether you are in a group with others or working on your own, you may go back to these activities at any time and learn from them on an individual basis.

Notes to Instructor: Suggestions for using these activities in a learning environment are included at the end of the chapter.

Purpose: To identify the importance of personality in relationships and in work behavior and productivity.

Background: Past and present, the concept of personality has been researched and discussed as a way to understand ourselves and each other. The Myers-Briggs Type Inventory, developed by Isabel Myers and Katherine Briggs, identifies preferences and "type," a concept that allows us to look at how people we work and live with get their energy, take in information, make decisions, and conduct themselves in their work and personal lives.

Activity 7.1. Your Personality Type

Instructions: Review the list early in Chapter 7 and decide which of each pair you are most like. Read the descriptions of preferences in the rest of the chapter. Then answer the questions below:

1. Based on your Extravert or Introvert (E or I) preference, what would you consider to be the strengths that you have at work. At home? What communication difficulties do you have that may be related to your preference?

2. Answer the question above as it relates to your Sensing and Intuition preference (I, N).

3. Answer the question above as it relates to your Thinking and Feeling preference (T, F).

4. Answer the question above as it relates to your Judging and Perceiving Preference (J, P).

Activity 7.2. Types and Teamwork

Instructions: Read the following scenario and answer the questions in the space below.

> You are participating in a project in which you have been asked to design a new communication process for your organization, including a statement and a logo. What personality preferences would you like to see demonstrated on your team?

Activity 7.3. Relationships

Instructions: Think about those you get along with best. Based on what you determine to be your preference similarities, with whom are you most compatible? How do you communicate? How do your similarities help you in understanding the other person, and vice versa?

Es with Es, Is with Is

Ss with Ss, Ns with Ns

Ts with Ts, Fs with Fs

Ps with Ps, Js with Js

What communication struggles do you encounter with those who have opposite preferences?

Is with Es

Ss with Ns

Ts with Fs

Js with Ps

Activity 7.4. Your Ideal Work Environment

Notes to Instructor: Split participants into four teams: ST, SF, NF, and NT. Give each team a piece of flip-chart paper and some markers. Ask team members to draw their ideal work environment. Have them present it to the large group. Process the activity after the presentations and note the differences in what each team chose as its primary criteria for an ideal workplace.

Activity 7.5. Demonstrate Differences

Notes to Instructor: For the I and E preference, split the group into introverts and extraverts. Give them a topic to work on that involves discussion. Assign an observer to watch the groups. You and the observer can watch for how quickly the teams begin, how much conversation transpires, and how animated each team is in expression.

For the S and N preference, use a half-filled water bottle to display how people see things differently. In front of the group, ask those with the S preference to raise their hands. Roll the water bottle from side to side and up and down, swirling the water in the bottle. Ask the Ss to describe what they see. You will hear comments such as "A water bottle with water in it." Then ask the Ns to describe what they see. You may hear comments such as, "A river flowing through an empty field." Process quickly, identifying the differences, including creativity, imagination (N qualities), and specificity (S qualities). Ask how that might relate to the workforce, and how each preference complements the other.

For the F and T preference, post flip charts on either side of the room. Ask the Fs to go to one side and the Ts to the other. Give each group markers and ask them to write this question at the top of the flip-chart sheet: "What is love?" and to answer the question.

Give participants fifteen minutes, or until you see the flip-chart paper has been written on. Some may need more than one piece of flip-chart paper, but probably for only a few sentences or phrases. Process the activities, being careful not to evaluate the responses, but to see how others view such an "emotional" word (usually Fs).

For the P and J preference, split the participants into the two groups, as above, with a flip chart and markers. Give them this instruction: "You are going on a vacation. Determine what you need to do to get ready." Give the participants fifteen minutes to list on the flip-chart paper what they will do. Process the results.

Notes to Instructor: The activities in this chapter can be used with individuals, pairs, or teams. For pairs, give participants enough time to talk with another person and then process everyone's insights as a group. For teams, have each person write his or her responses individually and ask each participant to share his or her responses in the team, one person at a time.

For Activity 7.2, teams of up to six people can complete the task described and present their slogans and logos. If done in a large group, all teams can present one at a time. Additional activities could include teams that have been formed by "type" writing a song or poem and then comparing differences.

Chapter 8

Taking the Sting Out of Feedback

> **WHAT'S IN THIS CHAPTER?**
> - The Challenges of Feedback
> - Types of Feedback
> - Giving Helpful Feedback
> - Receiving Feedback
> - Making Feedback Positive
> - The Leader's Connection
> - Activities

The Challenges of Feedback

We all worry about being judged or criticized by others. Whether we are questioning our attractiveness to our spouses or partners or wondering whether our supervisor thinks we are doing a good job, we question our worth to others. It is natural to want to be the best at what we do at work, and for the benefit of those we care about outside the job. In literature, sports, and entertainment, heroes are idolized for being the best; who received the trophy or award for best actor, player, or CEO is often front-page news. Sometimes, heroism goes to one's head, and any less than "you are perfect" feedback is blown out of proportion. Take a fairy tale, for example:

"Mirror, mirror on the wall, who's the fairest of them all?"

In the story, *Snow White*, Snow White's evil queen stepmother asks her magic mirror, "Mirror, mirror on the wall, who's the fairest of them all?" Time after time, the mirror answers, "You are, my Queen!" This reinforces the queen's vanity. One day, the queen asks her question: "Mirror, mirror on the wall, who's the fairest of them all?" To her horror, the mirror answers, "Snow White." The queen is furious. She becomes hysterical. Her jealousy explodes into such a rage that she demands Snow White's death.

Snow White and the vain evil queen, still obsessed with her power and image, live on in present-day television and movie tales, now not only for children, but for adults intrigued with the storylines. Myths, including Snow White and Cinderella, portray evil step-relatives who have very distorted "mirrors." For those of you who are more into music than fairy tales, in a song Snoop Dogg (Snoop Lion) asks, "Mirror, mirror on the wall, who is the top Dogg of them all?" After five minutes of contemplation, the mirror answers, "You are a conceited bastard."

Believe it or not, those are Snoop Dogg's lyrics, and he goes on to describe his morning primping to look as great as he can with the help of Oil of Olay, Johnson's baby powder, and new underwear to impress the girls. Times have changed, but the tales of vanity and jealousy have not.

Those of us who are not fairytale characters or songwriters have mirrors, too. We peer into them in the morning, in the restroom, in hotel lobbies, and the like. How do we look? Who is behind the image? How are we being judged?

Do my colleagues respect my opinion?

Am I being too critical?

Should I care?

Most people care about what they project, whether they admit it or not. Those who say, "I don't care what people think" are suspicious to others in their self-awareness. Even those who might be considered self-actualized want to be known as such. Think of the present Dalai Lama. He does not want the image of being god-like, demonstrating that he cares about the perceptions of others. He wants to be considered a spiritual human being with sincere motivation as a Buddhist monk (his ideal perception), separate from politics or godliness.

Figure 8.1 The Johari Window

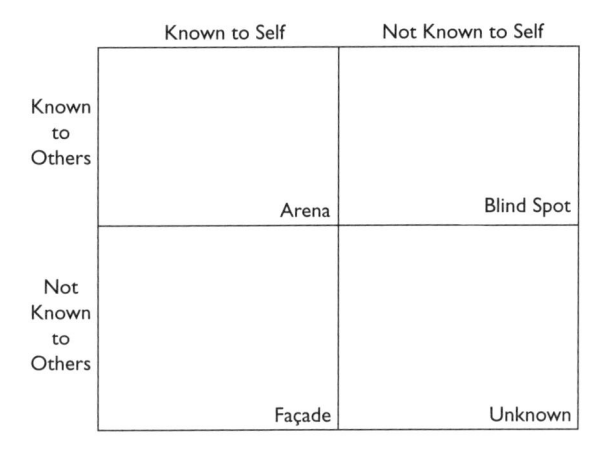

	Known to Self	Not Known to Self
Known to Others	Arena	Blind Spot
Not Known to Others	Façade	Unknown

Those in the helping professions assist people to manage their own perceptions and the perceptions of others. Trainers use techniques to create environments for self-awareness. The Johari Window, shown in Figure 8.1, one tool for self-discovery, was named for its creators, psychologists Joseph Luft and Harry Ingham. Used to uncover "blind spots," the tool reflects back the information seeker's perception of self and what colleagues can see that he or she cannot. The Johari Window tool paves the way for people to open up to others for better communication and teamwork. Some of the activities at the end of this chapter will help you put the Johari Window concepts into practice.

Using the Johari Window theory, one starts with equal squares. The Arena is the "open" space that is shared information. The Blind Spot is unknown to the participant, but known to others. The Façade is the part of a person that he knows about himself, but others do not. The Unknown Area reflects what neither the participant nor others know. One use of the tool is to give participants words that describe emotions, knowledge, and attitudes to place into the quadrants. Sample words include able, accepting, energetic, proud, patient, nervous, and witty. As trust grows, some squares grow larger. The best case is for the Arena to expand. Other squares, such as the Blind Area, shrink. As the model can be used in teams, the team members disclose more, trust more, and move from the forming stage to other more productive stages, as described in Chapter 6. The results depend on the amount of self-disclosure that the participant chooses and the learning that comes from feedback.

Types of Feedback

People receive feedback constantly from peers, supervisors, family, athletic instructors (golf, yoga, tennis), neighbors, and strangers. Ever see a fight break out over who was first in line at the grocery store? "Can I take someone over here?" when a new line opens up could provide some serious feedback. "I was first! You are inconsiderate!" "Thank you for letting me go first. I always remember a kindness."

Feedback at Work

"Please come into my office. I'd like to give you some feedback."

The curse of death! That's how most would take the statement above. Our first response is to think, "Oh, no. What does she think I did wrong now?"

If you eliminate the "Right" and "Wrong" labels, it is possible that you can learn something from the feedback of others. If you are giving feedback, it is also possible to impart your impressions so the other person can hear them and change behavior. After all, that's what you want.

In recent times, feedback and disclosure have become very important in the workplace, with all kinds of feedback instruments. 360-degree feedback has become commonplace, with co-workers, staff, and others giving feedback on the behavior of their bosses or peers. Self-scoring is also important to the concept. What does the mirror say? What do others think it says?

With the many feedback tools that exist on the market, data can be plotted with charts and graphs to depict areas of strength and weakness. However, in order for feedback to change behavior, a trainer's expertise in using soft skills is critical to encouraging the person to accept it. If the person has asked for feedback, he or she may be less defensive than if it is thrust upon him or her by organizational edict. If the person has not asked for nor seen the value of feedback, it takes great skill to present the data to be of benefit to the organization and to the person.

Giving Helpful Feedback

There are ways to give feedback that do not have to hurt people's feelings. It is best to think about what you are going to say before you say it. Otherwise, even the most kind of us can pop a cork and appear *mean*, intentionally or unintentionally, by attacking character or values. In this section, feedback is about everyday work situations. It is not about performance appraisals or discipline. Here are some suggestions for giving feedback to a partner with whom you want to maintain and improve a working relationship.

Give Feedback in Person

Because of the sensitive nature of feedback, give it in person. We have all seen enough email feedback that is either a copout from sitting down with the person who deserves attention and support or is used as a quick way to put a point across. (See an example of what can happen with email feedback in the section that follows.) There are several steps for giving feedback. Some of those cannot be accomplished unless you are with a person or you are using Skype. Even Skype is not the best mechanism. Although feedback should not be "personal," it is not a report. It is human. People have feelings: positive, encouraged, fearful, concerned, and often anxious.

The most important concept is that feedback should be for a positive purpose. If you cannot think of a positive reason for giving feedback, do not give it. This is a huge requirement. How many times have people given feedback to each other only to make their own points? Maybe they have been sitting on feedback for months, years, or more. Couples end up in marriage counseling if they can't give each other feedback at the time the feedback is relevant. If five years into a marriage, Jerry tells Anna that it really bothers him when she goes out with her girlfriends and does not call when she is going to be late, that is five years of being annoyed that may turn into a whole array of other irritations concluding with "and you don't put the cap back on the toothpaste" or, much worse, "I want a divorce." Five years ago, the first time Anna did not call, if Jerry had brought it up, Anna may have said, "Oh, thanks for telling me. I didn't want to wake you up. If you don't mind being disturbed, I will be sure to call."

Use "I" Statements

When you give someone feedback, you are giving *your* views, *your* interpretation, your screens, and your opinion. How you see an event or situation may be very different from how someone else sees it. Own your perceptions.

- "I wanted to talk to you about something you said at the meeting," instead of "You made everyone angry at the meeting."
- "I felt uncomfortable when you told Gaston that his ideas were too lofty," instead of "You never listen to anyone else. We are all tired of it."
- "I want to discuss the fundraiser we collaborated on," instead of "You always let other people do your work for you."

Using "I" statements has several advantages:

1. It is hard to argue with what you are saying about how *you* responded.

2. If you add others to the feedback ("People think you are arrogant"), the first thing someone is going to want to know is "Who thinks that?" Then the discussion can easily turn into a "he said; she said," argument or an attack on the other person ("She's one to talk!").

3. "I statements" set the tone of wanting to take responsibility. ("This is how *I* responded.")

Make an Observation

Making an observation is another way to start giving feedback.

- "I noticed that you have the report that is due tomorrow and it is under other projects on your desk."
- "We talked about sending out that training announcement about team building."
- "Based on our studies, the scanning project seems to be taking more time in preparing files than we thought."
- "The new receptionist is forwarding calls to where they need to go."
- "That fix in the computer department was successful. Now, people are able to get into the portal and work from home."
- "Relating the benefits of home health care compared to a nursing home seemed to please the Ruiz family. They thanked you several times."

Describe the Value

There should be value in the feedback you provide. Saying something without the value it has to you, the team, or the organization is not as meaningful as it could be.

- "Your files were selected to review for the scanning project. Once your files were submitted, it took more time preparing the files than we projected. Documents were out of order, requiring sorting to determine in which section of the electronic file the documents belonged. This is time-consuming and could lead to inaccuracies and misunderstandings."
- "Julie, thank you for getting calls where they need to go and for taking the initiative to answer questions yourself. This has really helped me serve our clients better because I can solve customer problems more easily without

working through their frustration of being bumped around from one department to the other. It saves time with our customers and builds trust."

Let the Other Person Respond

There is a tendency to spend too long and go on and on when giving feedback. Feedback should be about *one* incident or topic. It should be quick and to the point and only take a minute or so to give. That's why you have to think about what you are going to say. "What do you think?" is a way to let the feedback receiver give you his or reaction. It is amazing what you sometimes learn. Take the scanning feedback. Here's a plausible response:

- "The procedures state to put the legal documents in the legal section. They also state that some of the legal documents should go in the court review section. I wasn't sure where to put court orders. I also wasn't sure where to put notes of legal proceedings. If I did not know where to place a document, I put it in the side pocket of the binder. I didn't want to make a mistake."

Allowing discussion maintains the dignity of the other person. You only have your own observations or data to work with. There may be much more than you see or the numbers show. A feedback session can be rich with new information. If you keep your mind open and try to avoid judging, you can be instrumental in solving problems and uncovering systematic or personal issues that prevent people from doing their best work. Use the listening and paraphrasing skills you reviewed in Chapter 4. Let the other person know that you have heard what he or she said. Otherwise, you will discount an explanation that could provide you with what you want—changed behavior.

Lend a Hand

The feedback session is not over until you offer to help. Helpful feedback is just that, and after you have heard from the receiver, it is time to come to some positive action. Provide your thoughts. Listen to the other person's thoughts. The best scenario—mentioned several times in this book—is that the other person comes to similar conclusions him- or herself.

- "Oh, I see now. I think it will be easier for me to organize the documents."
- Or "I will submit the suggestion for procedure clarification and a training aid. That will help others, too."

Offer Confidence

At the end of your feedback session, let the receiver know that you have confidence in him or her.

- "I'm so glad we talked. I know that you will follow through with what we discussed. If you have any more questions about the process, I'm here to assist."

This ends the session on a positive note and demonstrates your willingness to resolve the issue. **Note:** this is different from "sandwiching" feedback, which is a popular method. Although educators have diverse views on it, "sandwiching"—giving positive, then observational, then positive feedback—is suspicious to the receiver. Just like a sandwich with two pieces of bread and meat in the middle, the receiver immediately thinks, "Where's the beef?" He or she knows it's there. It's just a matter of time until the giver gets it out.

One more caveat is worth mentioning. If you use the conjunction "but" in a sentence, people often discount anything that precedes the "but."

- "Denise, I notice all you do for the department. You are always here and I can count on you to work well with my customers when I need you to fill in for me when necessary. *But* I have been receiving your activity reports two or three days late, and it is making me late in rolling up the final report to the district office."

Do you think that Denise is going to remember what was said before the "but"? It would be better to say, "Denise, I have been receiving your reports two or three days late. It's causing me to be late with reports to the district office. Is there any way you can get your part to me earlier?" Let Denise respond. She may tell you that she has had other priorities from the district office herself, always at the last minute. Or she may say that she is just buried. Listen. You have offered feedback and made the request. "Is there anything I can do to help?" would be a good way to see whether you can help with the problem. Then express confidence.

Receiving Feedback

Turn the tables and now you are the recipient of information. Going back to the Johari Window, how open are you to suggestions? How self-aware are you? If you think you cannot be wrong or do not have anything to learn, feedback can cause conflict. Conflict that is resolved can bring people closer and add to

Taking the Sting Out of Feedback

the trust building that is necessary for authentic communication. But it can be hard to hear that your actions might be improved. Perhaps you think that your results are just fine. You may think that if your colleague or boss really knew what you did, he or she would not be so hung up on minor details. Maybe the person doesn't know how to give feedback. Maybe he or she has held some information from you and, at some time convenient for him or her, dumps all of his or her irritation on you, making it difficult to hear perceptions. Here's an example:

> Janie and Reisa work together. They are both competent and bright staff members. Janie has an important presentation to give in the morning. It includes members of staff at all levels, including executives and community presenters significant to the company. At 4:00 p.m., Janie receives a phone call from her son Bobby's school saying that he is sick. She tells Reisa. Janie decides she will stay home with Bobby the next day. Reisa, who also has a child, supports her decision. They spend time discussing that Shelly, their supervisor, will be very upset. Shelly is very conscientious and has her own supervisor, who expects excellence in all work activity, especially presentations. Canceling the presentation is not an option. After forty-five minutes of conversation, Janie and Reisa decide that it's time to tell Shelly the bad news. It is almost 5:00 p.m.
>
> Shelly is caught off-guard. Janie has been out several times because of her son being sick. He has allergies. Although it has never interfered with Janie's work, Shelly has been concerned that at some point, this type of situation could happen. She reacts. She is upset. She blows up. She says, "How can you be so irresponsible? I've asked you before to have some back-up in case Bobby gets sick. How many times have I asked you to find a babysitter who could take care of Bobby if you had to be here? I have spent hours giving you ideas for this presentation, and it is all set. I cannot cancel it. You have to present."
>
> Janie does not receive this feedback well. She takes offense at the term "irresponsible" since, in her mirror, she is a highly responsible person, both to her work and to her family. She retorts, "You are a single woman and have no idea what it's like to have a family. You

are all about work. My family is the most important part of my life. This is just a job." The discussion escalates.

Shelly, despite her fears of being left in the lurch, thinks the world of Jamie. This does not come across in this particular conversation because values are clashing and tempers are flaring. Both individuals take extreme positions.

If you were Shelly, how would you rewind and play this over? If you were Janie, how would you receive the feedback in a way that would promote problem resolution?

We cannot control the behavior of other people. We can influence it. It takes a secure person to gracefully accept feedback. Here are some tips:

1. Recognize Your Strengths

Be proud of your strengths. Be proud of your desire to do the right thing. If you have trouble thinking of your strengths, go back to the last chapter on personalities. Think about what you are good at doing. Think about what you feel natural doing and remember that all tasks are not equally easy.

2. Be Open to Improvements

What may have been your best intention could have a result that could be even better than what you accomplished. You are not the sum of just one bit of feedback. You have many talents. Try not to feel attacked and don't explain until you have listened sufficiently. Look at what happened when a gifted individual misunderstood an exchange:

> Corinne is a talented, intelligent, wise, and experienced presenter. She is highly respected in her organization. Among the many professional tasks she accomplishes, she conducts training on financial subjects that are not inherently interesting, but staff members in her company have to know the details of the process she is training. Without proper knowledge, the result can be thousands of dollars lost to children who receive money to live.
>
> Corrine's vice president asked her to prepare a PowerPoint presentation. It was to be Corinne's first experience with PowerPoint. Corinne worked tirelessly on the presentation. Although she had debilitating arthritis in her hands, she did the whole presentation herself.

The presentation was sent to the training director, who was not aware of the project. The PowerPoint presentation was written impeccably and had fifty-five slides filled with exact information, all of which was needed. But it was in PowerPoint and should have no more than six bullets to a slide. The director emailed Corrine and said that she would be glad to help revise it. Unbeknownst to the director, the vice president and Corrine had a meeting in which they discussed the email. Corinne was not a happy camper. Her interpretation of the email was that the director thought that she was not a good writer. Indeed, she was an excellent writer, and the director was very impressed with her talent.

The director was called into the vice president's office. She was pleased to see Corinne. Corinne was not so pleased to see her and greeted her with, "Are you saying that I'm not a good writer?" The director was stunned. She had been trying to figure out how to take all the great information Corinne had written and pare it down for slides, a hard task because Corinne was a "tight" writer—no unnecessary fluff.

The director explained about the "rules" for PowerPoint. Corinne asked, "But what about all the information I wrote?" The director responded that it would be great if she could copy the information **as is** for a handout. She lauded Corinne for being such a good writer and thanked her for doing an excellent job on the research and the content for the proposed handout. Suddenly, Corinne laughed and the vice president had a huge grin on her face. In a matter of minutes, Corinne went from "Who are YOU to correct me" to saying, "Next time, talk to me in person, and not in emails."

As a fitting end to the story, the director attended the presentation because she really wanted to know more about the topic. With the ease and humor that only a pro presenter has, Corinne mesmerized the audience with stories and information that resonated with the participants. She used PowerPoint like a presenter should, as a visual for visual learners. In this presentation, although the information was extensive, not too many people looked at the PowerPoint. Just as an aside, a good presenter trumps a PowerPoint slide.

3. Listen

Listen until the person who is giving you feedback either gives you the option to respond or there is a pause in which you can say what you would like to convey. Acknowledge the feedback as meaningful if it indeed presents a different perspective. Here's an example about listening:

> Laura is an instructor. She is bright, articulate, energetic, motivated, dedicated, and can produce in a half-hour's time work that would ordinarily take two hours. She is always still raring to go. She once received an award for the "person most likely to go back to work after the company picnic." She will do anything anyone asks with competence and a great attitude.
>
> One day, Laura's director asked her to help out with an employee who was out of compliance with a policy. Laura had trained the individual on many occasions in class and in one-on-ones. Laura pointed out that since the employee had been on the job for several years, it was more appropriate for his line supervisor to address the issue in terms of complying with policies. She was right. The director made arrangements for both her and Laura to talk with the supervisor and coach the supervisor if needed.

In the case of Laura and her director, there is a factor that is important to consider: trust. When you receive feedback from someone, the more you trust the person to be a reliable source, the more you might take the feedback as valid. People who give you good feedback help you with your blind spots and help you learn. If you perceive feedback that way, you might receive more of it, and you might learn a lot, even if you think you already know your strengths and weaknesses.

4. Acknowledge the Feedback

Here's where paraphrasing is a great tool. It is important to acknowledge the feedback. Paraphrase what the other person is saying. It is his or her perception. Acknowledging is not agreeing. Paraphrasing will let the giver of the feedback know that you have heard it. If the person had enough courage to give you feedback, he or she deserves to know that you have heard it.

- "So you think the process I'm following needs to be simplified."
- "You would like to see more output."
- "You saw me be abrupt with a customer."

- "A client complained that she was waiting for me a long time in the lobby."

You have to acknowledge what the other person has said, even if your emotions are kicked into gear and you know more about the situation than the other person does. This is a hard thing to do. It is normal to "fight back" or explain. Responding to feedback is a skill, just like any other skill. It takes thought and practice.

5. Clarify

If you know something that may help in a feedback discussion, facts may help to clarify a situation. Try to use facts though, instead of a defensive discourse. If you do not think the feedback is accurate or think that the other person is unaware of the details, expand on his or her thought, as in the examples:

- "So you think the process I'm following needs to be simplified. Let's see if we can take it step-by-step to determine how it can be easier."
- "You would like to see more output. Do you have any ways that you think we could produce more?"
- "You saw me be abrupt with a customer. That must have been when I talked with Mr. King. He was rude to me. At the time, I thought a very direct response was actually appropriate. In retrospect, I should have suggested that we go somewhere private and discuss the contract he did not want to sign. That would have given us both an opportunity to catch our breath and diffuse some of the dissention."
- "The client who complained that she was left in the lobby for a long time might have been Mrs. Thompson. I was waiting for her to call me so I could go get her. If she called, I didn't hear the phone. I will contact her and find out what happened. I will apologize for her being inconvenienced and waiting so long."

Notice that none of these responses was negative. Negative responses would be like:

- "It wasn't my fault."
- "She should have called back if she was waiting so long."
- "He was rude enough to be thrown out of the building."
- "Why do you always believe what you hear?"

Make a Plan

Sometimes, a plan for correction is easy. "I'll correct that next time." Other times, it might take more thought. Work with the other person to see whether the problem should be corrected immediately, whether it needs to be researched, or if it is a pattern that can be rectified. Your receptivity speaks louder than the problem.

- "I'll keep my cell with me or be around a phone when I am expecting a call."
- "The process that we revised sounds good. I'll try it with two others first and we'll see whether it works."

When feedback involves a pattern, such as being abrupt with more than one customer, training or coaching might be helpful. Or both might be the most effective. The best scenario is for you and the person giving the feedback to come up with a solution and to agree that the solution is worth trying.

Say Thanks

You are both professionals in the feedback process. Thanking someone for giving you feedback enhances your working relationship. As resolving conflict brings you closer, so does giving and receiving feedback if it is done in the right way. Express appreciation for the interchange.

> Review these tips before you give feedback and, if you can, before you receive it. Keep the tips in mind. They will help you if you use them.

Making Feedback Positive

Positive feedback is powerful. A kind word or gesture can make someone's day, make a person smile, and let a colleague know that you appreciate his or her contributions. As much as we have to think about giving and receiving constructive feedback, we need to think about praise and recognition. The best type of recognition depends on the person. Those with a "thinking" preference like to be recognized for their work contributions. Those with a "feeling" preference enjoy being recognized for their values. The best way to find out how a person likes to be recognized is to ask or observe responses. That being said, everyone likes a "thank you," an "I appreciate your help," or even a "hello." From the *Jerry Maguire* movie, take heed with one of the famous lines: "You had me at 'hello.'"

Questions

- What is the best feedback you ever received?
- What change in behavior did you experience as a result?
- What do you not want people to know?
- What about your image would you like to change in the "mirror"?
- How do you feel about receiving feedback?

Tips

- Evaluate your own performance on a project, listing strengths and weaknesses.
- Ask someone to give you feedback on the same project.
- See how closely your perceptions match.
- Appreciate a co-worker.
- Give some positive feedback to your supervisor.

The Leader's Connection

As a leader, you are the primary person from whom your staff members want feedback. Use your words well, and think about the responsibility you have chosen to take as a leader. Recognize each person on your team at least once a week for accomplishments and contributions. If you need a reminder, make a simple chart like the one in Table 8.1 with staff members on the left side and weeks up top. If you would like to save the particular comments, make a section for comments.

You can think of something for everyone.

The way in which you give feedback is as important as the feedback you give. "Can we talk for a few minutes?" is a better way of starting out than "What were you thinking when you . . . ?" Your responsibility to your team and to the company requires that you give members of your team feedback. You provide the map, the way to success. If you fail to provide the map, you limit possibilities and leave people to their own perceptions of not only what they should do, but what you want them to do. Negative feedback is always remembered

Table 8.1 Sample Chart		
Name	**Week 1**	**Comments**
J. Maguire		Your sales really paid off this week. Thanks for your perseverance.
M. Streep		Your body language is so expressive. Thanks for the support.
C. Eastwood		I appreciated your honesty. I like it when you are direct.
T. Swift		I really appreciated the heart and passion you demonstrated in your speech. People responded.
S. Tyler		You tried something so different. I appreciate your courage.

more than positive feedback. Praise often. It tells people that they are on track. If they derail, bring them back quickly. Recognize each step of their progress. You do not have to wait until they have done exactly what you want to say, "Thank you." You also do not have to thank people on your team only. There are many people at work who help you achieve your goals. Thank them.

Questions

- When have you been pleased with the feedback you gave and the response?
- When have you received good feedback?
- How do you feel about feedback from staff?
- What is one feedback step that you would like to improve?
- What is your philosophy about appreciating direct reports? Other staff?

Tips

- Find small actions to praise.
- Appreciate frequently.

- Encourage feedback at all levels.
- Provide training on giving and receiving feedback.
- See whether what you praise is done more often.

ABOUT THE NEXT CHAPTER

Using soft skills, including giving and receiving feedback, is more challenging when others are upset. There is no doubt that tempers can cause emotions to escalate. In the next chapter, we will be looking at ways to mitigate damage from temper flares and discourteous behavior, moving from conflict to cooperation.

Activities

Notes to Reader: The activities in this chapter are designed to be done individually or in a training environment. Whether you are in a group with others or working on your own, you may go back to these activities at any time and learn from them on an individual basis.

Notes to Instructor: Suggestions for using these activities in a learning environment are included at the end of the chapter.

Purpose: To provide ways to take and give feedback that maintain self-esteem.

Background: Feedback does not have to be bad news. When feedback is recognized as a way to enhance a person's effectiveness on the job, it can be invaluable if the intent is positive and the feedback is received with professionalism.

Activity 8.1. Giving Feedback

Instructions: Review the feedback guidelines in Chapter 8. Think of a person to whom you would like to give feedback. Write out your beginning statement and the value of the feedback. Imagine how that person would respond. Imagine how you would come to resolution. Think of what you would say to thank the person for listening and receiving your viewpoint. Role play the scenario with a trusted colleague, one who does not know the person with whom you would like to talk.

Activity 8.2. Team Feedback

Discuss the giving and receiving feedback guidelines in Chapter 8 with your team. Ask someone to give you feedback. Match your responses with the tips on receiving feedback and see how you fare. Ask your colleagues to provide feedback on how you responded.

Activity 8.3. Feedback Wanted

Instructions: Read the scenario below and address the question at the end.

> Darby tries to keep work and life balance by keeping in touch with friends. She enjoys conversations with people she has known a long time, as well as new friends. Her "oldie goldies," though, are a treasure to her. In spite of her very busy and hectic schedule, she calls and writes personal letters frequently. Lately, she has been hurt by the lack of response and communication from friends. It seems to Darby that Facebook posts (to all) and mass texts are all that she receives. Her personal communications are not returned. Darby feels that "real communication and friendship" are expressed by caring enough to connect on a personal basis. She thinks that if her friends cared about her, as she cares about them, they would write, call, or visit.

Darby has decided that she would like to give some feedback to Anne, her long-time friend, as a start in expressing her feelings.

How would you coach Darby?

Activity 8.4. Just What I Need to Know

Instructions: Read the scenario below and answer the question at the end.

> Wanda is an executive director in a mid-sized company. She has a busy job and receives innumerable emails on a daily basis. She prefers to communicate via electronic communication. She finds it more efficient, and she can also refer back to emails to refresh her memory regarding decisions and background. She has priorities, and sometimes overlooks emails that are in her inbox. She especially overlooks long emails. Sometimes, the long emails regard decisions that only she can make.

> Arthur is the director of HR. New rules come out from the government periodically that the company must follow. Arthur needs the support of the executive director to inform the company of new procedures. He offers long explanations as to how the procedures will affect the company. Arthur cannot seem to get Wanda to respond to what Arthur sees as urgent, both legally and procedurally. Arthur suspects that Wanda does not read his emails.

If you were Arthur's supervisor, what feedback would you offer for Arthur to get better results?

Activity 8.5. Appreciation
Ask your team members how they like to be recognized. Then recognize them based on their answers. You can practice this in a team setting first and then remember to do it often.

Activity 8.6. The Appreciation Cape
Instructor Notes: Use masking tape to tape half of a flip-chart sheet to the back of each person in the group. Give each person a bright-colored marker, such as red, blue, purple, or green. Have participants walk around the room and post an appreciation statement on each person's "cape." Be careful about ink bleeding through to people's clothing.

Activity 8.7. "I Appreciate You!"
Instructor Notes: Start with one person. Have that person turn to the right and appreciate the person sitting next to him or her. Continue with the second person doing the same for someone on his or right, until every person in the room has said to a colleague:

"I appreciate you for . . ." or I appreciate you because . . . ."

Notes to Instructor: The activities in this chapter can be used in a workshop as well as individually. Activity 8.2 can be used as homework or pre-work. The scenarios can be discussed in teams or pairs and then processed in a large group discussion. Activity 8.7 is a group activity that is fun and demonstrates another way to give appreciation.

Chapter 9

Conflict and Cooperation

WHAT'S IN THIS CHAPTER?
- The Stages of Rage
- Dealing with Difficult or Angry People
- Assertive Behavior Techniques
- Take Care of You
- The Leader's Connection Activities

Everyone "goes off the deep end" occasionally. Tact, diplomacy, and constructive feedback fly out the window as we fully embrace anger or outrage. No matter how expert we are in using soft skills, strong emotions are hard to handle—both our own and those of others. Sometimes, it seems impossible to resolve a dispute agreeably. With people planted firmly on opposite sides, Rudyard Kipling's phrase about East and West, "never the twain shall meet," can describe the gulf that is created. Add anger, and the divide grows larger.

Although disagreements may seem irresolvable, there are strategies to try, ways that you may mitigate full-blown outbursts rather than escalating them. In the rest of this chapter, we will explore methods to manage conflict. But first, it is important to understand how control gets away from us in the first place and how rage takes on a life of its own.

The Stages of Rage

We are all subject to psychological stressors that impede our rationality. When anger erupts, behavior changes emerge in stages. Stages build on one another. The first stage, feeling powerless, is uncomfortable and disturbing. Emotional agitation brews. If no resolution to the underlying feelings of not being heard, being ignored, rejected, or otherwise feeling emotionally harmed is not resolved, the body and the brain proceed to frustration. The third stage, enraged, is when a person feels *completely powerless and frustrated* to affect any change.

> **STAGES OF RAGE**
> 1. People feel powerless. Nothing they have tried has worked.
> 2. They feel frustrated. Continued efforts produce more of the same roadblocks, resulting in a feeling of disappointment, dissatisfaction, and worthlessness at not being able to effectuate results.
> 3. They become enraged. The combination of events and feelings causes a type of stress overload that overcomes the ability to be rational.

Physiological Factors of Stages of Rage

There are no time elements that we can attribute to the stages of rage, but they do follow a pattern and take a toll emotionally and physically. When the brain senses that a threat is present—unmet needs or bodily harm—it activates areas of the brain, including the amygdala, which creates a feeling of distress and a "ready for action" response, releasing hormones such as adrenaline. This occurs rapidly; so once the process starts, it is hard to stop. Consumed by physiological responses, and gripped by what may seem like uncontrollable forces, the person goes into a fight, flight, or freeze mode. When confronting a truly dangerous or life-threatening situation, this response can be invaluable. Unfortunately, the brain doesn't distinguish between exasperating and life-threatening. Daniel Siegel (2001) calls this a low road of functioning which can essentially shut off higher brain activity. Although all people do not respond to threats in the same way,

Conflict and Cooperation

people do go through the same stages of rage, and they experience similar reactions. The following story of Tom and his plight with the driver's license office is an example of how stages of rage build on one another:

Powerless

Tom needs to renew his driver's license in person at the driver's license office (DLO). He took time to ensure that all the documentation needed was in order. He cannot take off work more than two hours, so he looks up DLO hours online. He heard that you can get an appointment online to save time. He goes through the process of keying in five pages of information. Finally, he gets to the appointment screen. The next appointment available is June 5. His license expires May 15. He is not pleased. He calls the DLO to request the best time to come in, a time when lines may not be wrapped around the street. He is on hold with ghastly music for fifteen minutes, and finally hangs up.

On his way home, Tom goes to the DLO. The office closest to work is half an hour away, but near his home. It is past 5:00 p.m., but he sees that people are still waiting in line. He goes toward the door to get information about days that are better than others to come in. The door is locked. The guard at the door shouts, "We're closed!"

When Tom gets home, he and his wife fix a quick dinner, and at the table, he asks his daughter if she has homework. The daughter says, "I'm not doing it. It's dumb." Tom yells at her. The rest of the night doesn't go much better.

The next day, Tom asks his boss if he can take several hours off to have his license renewed. The boss says, "Sure." Although Tom still has at least a week before the deadline, he wants the task out of the way. Swamped with work, he rushes out before lunch to go to the DLO and, in his haste to get there, does not realize that he is speeding in a school district. He receives a $400 ticket. He is feeling powerless.

Frustrated

When Tom gets to the DLO, the line is a quarter of a mile long. He asks someone leaving the office how long it took to complete the whole renewal process. The customer says, "Three hours." Now Tom is frustrated. He did his best to manage his two-hour time slot, and still it did not work out. He has to go back to work.

Tom is usually accurate in his job. Upset from the incidents of the day, he quickly completes a spreadsheet that the boss wants immediately. Five minutes later, his boss calls and reams him out for a mistake that he made. He is angry that his work is being affected by a silly driver's license.

Enraged

The next day, Tom asks his boss if he can leave at 3:30 to make it to the DLO before the doors lock at 4:00 p.m. Someone at work was kind enough to tell him the closing hour. His boss says, "I thought you did that." Tom, somewhat embarrassed, explains briefly.

Tom's work buddy is right about the time to arrive at the DLO. Tom is the last customer who makes it through the door before it locks. He waits an hour. At 5 p.m., he hears a loudspeaker voice say, "One of our clerks has to leave the office. If you have not been taken yet, please come back another time."

Tom is furious. He has reached a stage of rage. He walks over to the first person who is wearing a DLO shirt and says, "You idiots could care less about whether or not citizens who want to do the right thing even get their licenses. You treat people like cattle and just put them out to pasture when you feel like it. Someone had to leave the office? Well, I had to leave my office, too! Who is taking care of my work? Do you ever think about the inconvenience and trouble you cause people? No! You just want to get your paycheck. Well, I'll tell you something. I pay your salary! I'm a taxpayer."

Like Tom, most of us have "been there" in one way or another, although we all respond to inconvenience in our own ways. Tom really tried to do the right thing at every juncture until he blew up. But what about who he blew up *at*? Someone wearing a DLO shirt got his wrath, someone who had no idea of Tom's struggles, disappointments, and fears. As described earlier, when a person reaches the rage stage, that person is not necessarily rational. We do not even know the name of the gentleman in the DLO shirt. We do not know his function. Neither did Tom. *"It just happened."*

Reasons for Anger

There are many reasons why people become angry, some based on the perception that their values have been violated, reciprocity infringements, and perceived unfairness. Psychological "schemas," mental structures that reside within our psyche, may also come into play. As a result of our biological make-up and past experiences, we sometimes are angered by a behavior or interaction that reminds us of needs that were not met at another time, perhaps in childhood. Wendy Behary (2008) describes eighteen early maladaptive schemas that may influence how someone perceives a situation. Whether a maladaptive schema or a buildup of life's everyday experiences, all of us have personal "button-pushers."

What Pushes Your Buttons?

What annoys you? Chances are that there are certain situations that make your blood boil. Maybe it is when someone is lying to you, or when someone suggests that *you* are not being truthful. Maybe it is rude, arrogant behavior. Perhaps you are infuriated when people are late, or when you are inconvenienced by policies or processes that seem totally illogical. Screaming, cursing, threatening, and denigrating are other personal button-pushers that often cause an immediate knee-jerk reaction.

Even in role-play situations, participants reveal what pushes their buttons. It is easy to spot. Muscles tense. Facial expressions reveal displeasure. Voices rise. Some people say that their hands sweat and their breath is short. If even hypothetical situations cause flare-ups, what happens in real life?

If you know what triggers your own anger, you can work on ways to deal with it. Awareness is the first step. It takes work and commitment to understand your button-pushers and to practice taking a deep breath instead of reacting. Button-pushers evolve into behavior patterns that are hard to break. *So practice not letting others get to you.* Use the activities at the end of this chapter to examine your button-pushers and to learn more about coping with unpleasant circumstances. The next section describes some behavioral characteristics that research shows are the most perplexing.

Dealing with Difficult or Angry People

Many books are on the market these days about dealing with difficult people. Some of the titles are very descriptive; such as *Nasty People: How to Stop Being Hurt by Them Without Becoming One of Them* (Carter, 1989); *Why Is It Always About*

YOU? (Hotchkiss, 2002); *Disarming the Narcissist: Surviving and Thriving with the Self-Absorbed* (Behary, 2008); *The No Asshole Rule* (Sutton, 2007); *Since Strangling Isn't an Option* (Crowe, 1999) and more, especially if you include books about bullying. Seminars and workshops with "difficult people" in the title also abound. There are numerous theories about why so many books on the topic are adorning our bookshelves. Suffice it to say, interpersonal times are tough.

Difficult Behaviors

Robert Bramson, one of the pioneers on the topic of difficult or angry people, developed a commonly observed set of difficult behaviors. *Coping with Difficult People*, originally published in 1981, has been the staple for a host of print articles, web posts, and discussions on the topic. Amazon.com readers rate the book five stars. One person said that you need this book wherever you are, even on a desert island. Think about that one! Let's take a look at what has stood the test of time in the difficult and angry people field.

Bramson's categories of behaviors, illustrated with identifiable "characters," are

- Hostile aggressives (Sherman tanks)
- Hostile aggressives (snipers)
- Hostile aggressives (exploders)
- Complainers
- Negativists
- Expert know-it-alls
- Unresponsive clams

In the discussion that follows, we will explore the behaviors and ways to address them. We are not making judgments about any of these types of people. Rather, we hope that examining the categories will help you to work in productive ways with people who exhibit these behaviors.

Hostile Aggressives (Sherman Tanks)

Sherman tanks are the most difficult of all types. They can be aggressive and hostile and behave just as the term sounds, running over obstacles in their path like a tank. Their actions have often worked for them. They are used to getting their way. Sherman tanks often invalidate others in ways that are discussed in Chapter 4. Tanks' invalidating statements and behaviors might look like:

- Excessive use of the word "I" in a self-centered way. ("I think that the way I have analyzed the situation is right. I have looked at all possibilities.")
- Blunt responses that are insensitive to others' feelings. ("You are flat out wrong.")
- An all-knowing attitude, indicating that his or her own opinions expressed are *facts*. ("The election will undoubtedly go to the incumbent senator.")
- Sweeping generalizations. ("Everybody knows that. Why do you always do things backwards here?")
- Assumptions. ("This is the way she wants things done, so do it!")
- Sarcastic remarks. ("Oh yeah, somebody like you would think that. Get a grip.")
- Criticizing. ("You shouldn't have done it that way. Don't you know any better? This is awful.")
- Patronizing. ("Be a good girl and do this for me, will you?")
- Swearing. ("Has anyone ever told you that you are a b——?").
- Blaming others. ("This is the way you people do things. I, of course, would do it differently.")
- Hostile tone of voice. ("I told you that before. Did you forget to take the earphones out of your ears?")
- Piercing eye contact. (Body language includes leaning over too far; violating someone's personal space.)
- Threatening body language such as finger pointing, sweeping gestures, fist thumping, turning away, throwing hands up in the air, stomping, putting hand on hips, or rolling eyes.

How to Deal with Sherman Tanks

Fighting with a Sherman tank is usually a career-limiting move, especially if this person is your boss. If someone started to hit a bully in a school yard, what do you suppose the bully would do? Think of the Sherman tank as the bully in the school yard, wound up for the fight. In terms of what to do with this behavior in real life, instead of buying into the altercation, be assertive, not aggressive. Stand tall, literally. Listen. The tank wants your reverence; you need to understand the problem (the initial divide). When you can get a word in, clearly state the problem and how you will work on it. Be firm, straightforward, and audible, ensuring that your voice and body language say, "I am perfectly capable of handling this." You may even have to interrupt. Any sign of reticence or fear will put fuel in the tank.

You may also suggest that you work together for a cooperative solution and reinforce that resolving the issue is really important to you, while you keep eye contact and maintain control. Try practicing this kind of assertiveness with a colleague friend to hone your skills, and use the activities at the end of this chapter to develop skills and strength to transfer learning to life's challenging moments. More on assertiveness is covered later in chapter.

Hostile Aggressives (Snipers)

Imagine someone with a bb gun shooting play bullets. This is what a sniper does, although with words. Snipers gossip behind others' backs and make unkind remarks. They also demean people to their face and in groups. The barbs are hurtful. Friends have to defend or not defend the person being attacked behind his or her back, or the person him- or herself must decide how to respond when comments are directed face-to-face. Snipers are not direct. Their sarcastic remarks come from the same place that the Sherman Tank's do ("I am right"); but comments are couched with a menacing, mocking intent. The tactic that works best with snipers is to smoke them out. Uncover their disguise. Their tactics are dangerous and unprofessional.

How to Deal with a Sniper

Here are some suggestions on how to shut down sniper attacks:
- Confront snipers with the truth: "Actually, I followed the action plan as we agreed. Can you tell me why you think I missed part of it?"
- Ask them what they meant: "Did you mean that training was dull?"
- Refuse to accept responses like, "I was just joking."
- If the attack is not on you, suggest that the person talk to the other person involved if there is an issue.

- Be assertive in your interactions and refuse to play along or "dis" a colleague.
- Do not accept ridicule.

Sniper personalities are bad for an organization's external customers, but these individuals are particularly harmful to other co-workers and colleagues. Their shots can sting. They attack underhandedly. Unless you smoke them out and confront them for their behavior, they will continue to be insulting to anyone who will listen. If you do not listen to their gossip about others and do not let them undermine you, they will go on to someone else. If nobody listens, they are all smoked out.

Hostile Aggressives (Exploders)

Hostile aggressives explode when they feel under attack, whether real or perceived. The slightest hint of disagreement may set them off.

- "Mr. Hinge, thanks for meeting with us. We need to go over a few of the facts you presented. We need clarification."
- "What do you mean you need clarification? I followed your directions precisely! It took a long time to fill out your forms. You would think I'm being interviewed for the FBI! Where is your boss?"

How to Deal with Exploders

If at all possible, find a way to let the exploder "win."

- First, let the exploder blow off steam.
- See whether you can take the exploder to a private place to talk.
- Offer help and have a plan of action.
- Make a positive statement.
- Find a way to take a break and let the person calm down: "Let's go over this again. Can you wait a few minutes and we can regroup?"

Complainers

Complainers talk a lot. They can find something wrong with just about every co-worker they meet. They think there should be a cafeteria at work. They think there should be a gym. They can tell you why the lack of all these conveniences shows that management doesn't care about them. Complainers feel blameless and innocent. They are not known to take responsibility for their own actions or to be predisposed to finding solutions.

How to Deal with Complainers

When responding to complainers, help them look at solutions to problems, but engage them in questioning so as not to invalidate their concerns. Avoid agreeing with them, which is usually the easiest thing to do (in hopes that they will just go away or because you have *some* of the same feelings yourself). Listen actively and show that you understand. Use closed-ended questions to stop diatribes. "Was that the intent?" Try to encourage them to come to at least one alternative viewpoint. You might use Socratic questions.

Negativists

Picture a child blowing bubbles and a parent bursting them all. Negativists like to burst everyone's bubbles. Pop. Pop. If you do not like to have your bubbles burst, try some of the techniques below. Bear in mind that negativists think people cannot be trusted, especially those in power. By the way, they choose to see the world as they do; they are often just unhappy, and they want you to be, too.

How to Deal with Negativists

If you want to maintain a relationship, you do need to listen a bit. After getting the essence of the negativist's most recent dissatisfaction, you might try infusing your own optimism in a way that is not condescending. As with the complainer, your encouragement of an alternative point of view (and a dose of optimism) may be helpful. Do not be surprised if your efforts are not appreciated. He or she may just walk away, but the negativist may at least think about what you have said.

Expert Know-It-Alls

Expert know-it-alls have all the "right" answers. They feel powerful in their "knowing." They are often smart people. Since knowing it all is part of the expert's self-esteem, what he or she presents may indeed be of value and well-thought-out.

Dealing with Expert Know-It-Alls

In order to convince an expert know-it-all that you might have a good point, too, have your facts ready, along with back-up explanations, examples, or research.

Knowledge is power. Try not to discount the expert's contributions because of the affect that comes with it.

Unresponsive Clams
Unresponsive clams may use silence as a form of aggression, as a way to mask fear or embarrassment, or just because they do not know how to express what they are thinking. By not contributing, they say a lot; as a natural response, others try to fill in the blanks by guessing what is on the clam's mind. To unlock the thoughts and feelings of someone who is silent, demonstrate that you do want to know what he or she thinks. The person's behavior may be a result of feeling that he or she has not been heard. Offer an "in" to the conversation, but do it gently.

How to Deal with an Unresponsive Clam
Ask open-ended questions. Use open body language that shows interest. Look at the person and, after asking a question, be silent. Avoid the need to fill the silence. It is possible that the person is naturally submissive. If this is the case, you will notice that the person is hardly audible when he or she does speak and might fidget, slump, not look directly at you, not focus, play with hair, or tap his or her fingers. It may be hard to tell whether these behaviors are from anger or from uneasiness. If you hear something like, "I'm just going along with the crowd" or a self-deprecating comment like "I'm just a new person here. I don't really know what you all are saying" or something like "I'm not that bright, but I am persistent," you will get a clue as to the reason behind the silence.

Super-Agreeables
Super-agreeables have a strong need to be liked. They have a tendency to commit to things they cannot do. They want approval.

How to Deal with Super-Agreeables
Give super-agreeables a win-win scenario. Help them take on tasks that they can do, and walk them through steps that they can accomplish. That way, they are more likely to be able to complete the tasks they take on and to obtain your approval. The fact that they want to please is a motivator. Help them keep motivated by recommending reasonable activities that are doable. Then thank them for their accomplishments.

Indecisive Stallers

Indecisive stallers like to delay and want to think about things. This is not necessarily bad; however, sometimes decisions must be made and their input and commitment are needed in short order. They do not like conflict or confrontation.

How to Deal with Indecisive Stallers

When you need an answer, help stallers be honest about their concerns, if they have any. Propose solutions. You might offer different solutions to the same problem and see which they prefer. Giving direction can help them sort out what their concerns are and what they can support or propose on their own.

Assertive Behavior Techniques

Assertive behavior starts with listening. With all the difficult behaviors described above, use the steps for listening presented in Chapter 4. You will need to pick what step to use, in what order, and for how long, as explained for the negativist above. (For example, you would not want to use open-ended questions and you would paraphrase and empathize only so much with a negativist.) When dealing with difficult behaviors, it is important to take responsibility for communicating clearly, directly, and with understanding. There are times when this type of understanding can take the form of not responding at all. This is an intuitive communication process. Although it is important to respond when behaviors such as sniping are directed at you, at times you might not want to respond other than to listen.

Sorting

Sorting is skipping over a hostile remark or something that was said that could take the conversation someplace other than solving the problem at hand. When you use the sorting technique, you address only the important issues and ignore insults, hostile remarks, and unproductive dialog. If you choose to go back to a time in the conversation when the person was not so upset, then you have to use your judgment about how to do that.

Example: Carol is a customer service representative at the phone company. Mrs. Garnor is an upset customer. In the dialog below, Carol uses her skills to move from conflict to cooperation:

Carol: "Hello, may I help you?"

Mrs. Garnor: "This place never helps. It is a haven for aggravation."

Conflict and Cooperation

Carol: "I'm disappointed that we haven't been able to help you. Maybe I can do better today." (*Sorts insult, empathizes, and extends a hand.*)

Mrs. Garnor: "I doubt you can do any better than the last time I called when the service was cut off to my area. I'm at a friend's now. If you don't turn my phone back on, I'm going to sue you." (*Attack.*)

Carol: "When was your phone turned off, Mrs. Garnor?" (*Asks a close-ended question and sorts the attack.*)

Mrs. Garnor: "Today. Do you think I'd let it stay off a week and then call?"

Carol: "No, I don't think you would. Let me see what I can do." (*Sorts sarcasm, offers assistance, and begins to find a solution, assertively.*)

Mrs. Garnor: "Just get the phone back on before I call my lawyer."

Carol: "Do you have your account handy?" (*Sorts demand and obtains more information to help solve problem.*)

Mrs. Garnor: "This place drives me up a wall. Didn't I just key in my account? Didn't I tell you my mother's maiden name? Didn't your recording say, 'Please wait while we access that account?' I am waiting for what, exactly?"

Carol: "Yes, you did key in your account, and I'm sorry that I need the same information again. I know your time is important. Let me see if I can get this done quickly." (*Uses "I/me statement," sorts sarcasm.*)

Mrs. Garnor: "I was out of town and just came back today. I have never been late on a bill. So this time I was late. One time. Big deal. National crime. For this I have wasted twenty minutes already. I need another vacation."

Carol: "I can understand that! Do you have a credit card to pay over the phone?" (*Sorts comments. Asks closed-ended question.*)

Mrs. Garnor: "Yes. Here's the number."

Carol: "Thanks for taking the time to go to your friend's house to call first thing in the morning. Your prompt call means we can have your phone on today. It certainly must be an inconvenience to not have phone service as soon as you get back from a trip. I'm really sorry that the phone was disconnected. You're a very good customer." (*Empathizes, provides solution, apologizes for the inconvenience, expresses support.*)

Mrs. Garnor: "Glad you noticed."

Carol: "We're all set. Your phone will be connected shortly. Thanks again for calling so quickly so we could resolve this. I want us to provide you with the best service we can." (*Summarizes, verifies solution was found, and offers support.*)

Mrs. Garnor: "O.K. Thank you. You were better than the last rep I called when your lines were out. She practically hung up on me."

Carol: "Well, if there is anything else we can do for you, let us know." (*Sorts comment.*) "I'm glad your phone will be on soon." (*Offers help and shows caring.*)

Mrs. Garnor: "Thanks. I'm glad we resolved this. I'll be going home now. Thanks for your help."

Mrs. Garnor may not have been ecstatic during this transaction, but she did cooperate. Tone of voice, which you can almost "hear" in this scenario, was a key factor in Carol's success. Her tone was understanding and supportive. Even though she was on the phone, her body language was receptive, and she demonstrated that she was listening to every word Mrs. Garnor said. Escalation was avoided, and Carol's professionalism deterred a full-blown episode of rage. When resolution is reached, an angry customer can come around more quickly than you might imagine and could end actually become friendly.

Take Care of You

Dealing with difficult or angry people can take the wind out of your sails. No matter how adept you are at dealing with it, anger is disturbing. Here are some ways that you can ease your discomfort. Some examples pertain to direct sales, but can be applied to any business environment.

Journals

Use journals to:

- Document what happened and what resolutions you worked out. This will help if there is a dispute of any kind on a customer's part. You will have a record.

- Release emotions. Start with, "What I'd like to say to . . ." and/or "What I'd like to say to me." Take the journal home with you to keep it safe.

Be Firm and Tactful
If a situation occurs during which you think it is best to use a direct intervention, take a deep breath and be firm:

- "I want to hear what you're saying, but I've got to ask you to slow down a bit."
- "Please respect me. I will respect you."
- "Let's talk about this. Can we agree to listen to each other?"
- "Perhaps we need some time to reassess the problem. Would you like to call me back?" (If the person says, "No," and you think that his or her rude or insulting jabs are too inappropriate to continue the conversation, you can say, "I want to give you my attention. But you are screaming at me, and I am going to have to call you back. When is a good time?"

Take a Break
Taking a walk can clear your mind and give you additional oxygen. Your distress might not seem as bad afterward. Your day can improve. No doubt, there will be other customers who let you know that you are appreciated and valued. Remember to value yourself. Give yourself a break and smile at a passerby when you are walking. The person may smile back at you (you!), the one who has just overcome obstacles and managed conflict in an admirable way.

Is It Personal?
Most of the time, it is not personal. It is not about you. Anger can be displaced, and considering the many ways that people's buttons can be pushed, angry customers may be simply venting powerlessness and frustration about the situation or about previous situations. Or the anger may be about an unrelated event. The person might have had an altercation that had nothing to do with you or your company. You just happened to be there at the wrong time, in the wrong place. There is a lot of stress in everyday living and impersonal interactions dehumanize us in many ways. Of course, it is not your job to be a therapist (unless you are a therapist). You can be kind, which goes a long way to remind people that someone cares.

Questions
- When was the last time a customer became angry with you?
- What were the circumstances?

- What did you do?
- What could you have done differently?
- What will you think about the next time you are confronted by a difficult customer?

Tips

- Smile at customers when they approach or when you first hear them on the phone.
- Practice working through conflicts with friends and family.
- Read more about how to handle difficult situations.
- Think of flight (ignoring or walking away) or fight (fighting back) as unacceptable reactions.
- Be good to yourself. You are important.

The Leader's Connection

Challenges for leaders involve being the person who has to take the responsibility. "The buck stops here." The angriest person might end up in your office. Leaders are often very good at soothing angry customers. They know that, just because of their formal positions, they may have a calming effect: "I talked to the president!" "The vice president saw me and promised to look into my concern."

As the leader, it is important to recognize that sometimes you become angry too. When leaders let their own anger show, the effect is amplified, largely because of their role (Conger & Kanungo, 1998). The leader's emotions are "super contagious" (Brief & Weiss, 2002). The comment, "It comes from the top" is tossed around many organizations. Emotions trickle down. If you are disgusted, it shows. If you are pleased, it shows. There is no sure way to hide your emotions. This is true of all of us. The leader is prominent, in a visible spotlight. It comes with the job. As a leader, it is nearly impossible to avoid being angry at times. Think about using some of the techniques in the "Take Care of You" section above, especially taking a walk or writing your thoughts down before you express them. The truism, "It's lonely at the top," must be remembered when confiding your thoughts to others. When you are angry, try calling a trusted friend or colleague outside work rather than share your thoughts within the organization.

Questions

- How often do you think about the emotional consequences of your own behavior?
- What is your take on letting your emotions show at work?
- What did you learn from the last book you read on leadership?
- Who is your emotional role model?
- What positive emotions have you spread lately?

Tips

- Think about what you say before you communicate.
- Get in touch with your emotions and name them.
- Notice when people are "tiptoeing" around you.
- When you are having a bad day, limit your communication.
- Let people get to know you, especially when you are feeling good.

ABOUT THE NEXT CHAPTER

After reading the chapters in this book, you can see that the revolution in soft skills is underway. The term "revolution" often implies an upheaval. In the book's context, revolution implies change, a soft change in values to consciously include actions that are kind, inclusive, and trusting. You have read some scenarios in which people wanted to be right, without thinking about how to be assertive and to use soft skills without being aggressive. You have also read examples in which people expressed warmth and understanding, wanted to be kind. I hope you have completed some activities that have given you insight into soft skills you want to practice for yourself and, if you are a trainer, for your participants. Read on in the next chapter to further explore pathways to kindness.

Activities

Notes to Reader: The activities in this chapter are designed to be done individually or in a training environment. Whether you are in a group with others or working on your own, you may go back to these activities at any time and learn from them on an individual basis.

Notes to Instructor: Some objectives for using these activities in a learning environment are listed at the end of the chapter. These activities can also be used as a one-day program for trainers.

Purpose: To recognize how emotions influence interactions and learn ways to work with common forms of conflict.

Background: Conflict comes from clashes of all sorts, including difference in values, motives, and personalities, as we have seen. When conflicts arise, they are almost automatic. When someone else's behavior causes an immediate reaction in you, the behavior may trigger a "knee-jerk" response in you. Activities in this section will help you uncover some of the ways you react and provide some ways to move from conflict to cooperation.

Activity 9.1. Button-Pushers

As discussed in Chapter 9, certain behaviors push our buttons. Think about what makes you angry. Is it when you think someone is disrespectful? Is it when someone confronts you and yells? Imagine a game show in which a button must be pushed to give the right answer. That's how quickly someone can annoy you or you can irritate someone else and push his or her buttons, even if it is unintentional. Make some notes on what pushes your buttons. Be honest. Refer back to Activity 2.1 if you need a jump start.

Find a partner, friend, colleague, or supervisor. Give each other three minutes to explain your button-pushers. Use active listening techniques. You do not have to come to any resolution. This is for awareness only.

Activity 9.2. Common Reactions

Take one of your button-pushers to explore in more detail, such as someone screaming at you. Write your answers to the following questions:

What is your usual reaction to the behavior?

Here are some common reactions you may have listed:

- Freeze—stop, look, and listen
- Flight—leave the scene
- Fight—engage in conflict to establish dominance over another
- Fright—become passive in light of a traumatic event or the experience of panic, such as in post-traumatic stress disorder

Describe an incident in which you exhibited your reactions to the button-pusher you selected.

Is the reaction you had common for you?

Describe a time when you experienced this reaction.

Activity 9.3. How I Learned

Instructions: Consider a task you had to learn that required your full attention. What did it take for you to learn the task? How many times did you have to practice the task before it became "second nature"? What emotions are associated with the task?

Now think back to the button-pusher you selected in Activity 9.1. Describe the ways in which you learned to cope with the behavior. Just reflect: it took you a long time and many circumstances to learn your coping mechanism. Changing behavior requires awareness of what is bothering you before you can find productive ways to cope.

Activity 9.4. What I Will Do

Instructions: Review all of your button-pushers. Decide what you can do to avoid being run by them. Practice with friends. Use the listening and assertiveness techniques that have been provided throughout the chapters of this book. Decide what else you would like to address, such as affirmations ("I am capable and competent and can handle anger"). Set up a schedule to check in with yourself at least weekly to reinforce how you have used new behaviors.

Activity 9.5. Skills Test

Notes to Instructor

1. Tell participants that you are going to test their skills to create a baseline for the group's ability to use communication skills.

2. Say that you will give the directions only once. Ask for a timekeeper and explain that the activity will be timed, since in real life, interactions and problem solving must be completed quickly.

3. Give this instruction: "Please line up in order of your birth date, month, and day. Our timekeeper will start timing when I give the 5, 4, 3, 2, 1, start. Count down. . . 5, 4, 3, 2, 1, Go!"

4. The participants have to determine where January is and how to ensure that each person is in the right place. When you see that they have finished their line, ask: "Are you finished?"

5. Ask the timekeeper for the time taken. With twenty-five people, it should not take much longer than two minutes. Some groups finish in less than two minutes.

6. Tell the participants that you will do a "quality check." Start with January and have each person say the month and date of his or her birth. (Quality is usually 100 percent.)

7. While they are still standing, ask the participants what it took to complete the activity. Frequent response are "teamwork, cooperation, body language, and leadership." Ask questions, such as: "Who were the leaders?" "How did you know where to go?" "Did you see any conflict?" "How was conflict resolved?"

8. After the debriefing, let the participants know that they have now practiced the skills necessary for dealing with difficult people and for cooperating. Give them a round of applause and let them take their seats.

Activity 9.6. Stages of Rage

Notes to Instructor: Explain the stages of rage. Ask participants whether they have ever experienced an instance when they were in a full stage of rage or a customer or colleague went through the stages. You may also tell a story of your own or show a video or YouTube examples.

Activity 9.7. Practice Sorting

Notes to Instructor: Create a scenario or use the one in this chapter to demonstrate sorting. Ask participants to pair and play the people in the scenario, switching roles after the first round. Ask for reactions.

Activity 9.8. Angry Person

Notes to Instructor

1. Split the group into teams of five and give each group a flip chart and markers.

2. Tell them that they will be drawing pictures of a difficult person and listing the behaviors on one-fourth of a flip-chart sheet. Draw a stick figure as an example and give some examples of words, such as aggressive, curt, and arrogant. Each team draws only one person.

3. Allow fifteen to thirty minutes for the teams to draw their figures.

4. As you see that teams are finishing, ask them to choose a leader to present the team's creations. Post one team's drawing at a time. After the spokesperson describes the drawing, have each member of the team introduce him- or herself, giving name and place of work.
5. After each group presents, circle categories of behavior that are common to all pictures, such as rude, mean, or disrespectful.
6. Break after the processing, or at a time that seems right for the group.
7. Review the categories of behaviors that have been presented and how they may be collective button-pushers. Review the behaviors described in this chapter, those that were categorized by Robert Bramson. Do this one behavior at a time and brainstorm ways to deal with each behavior, adding your own suggestions to theirs.

Activity 9.9. Role Plays

Notes to Instructor: Explain that participants will create a role-play scenario for *each type* of difficult type they identified in Activity 9.8. Assign each group a type. Give fifteen minutes for them to create role-play situations. Ask each team to present its role play, using the techniques you have discussed. Provide suggestions if the role plays go astray. The rest of the group can provide suggestions as well, and "instant replays" can be enacted by the players. You may also expand this activity to how *not* to address each category discussed by role playing what *not* to do and then role playing what to do. Another alternative is to use a film to demonstrate behaviors.

Activity 9.10. Appreciating Personalities

Notes to Instructor: Use the Myers-Briggs Type Indicator (MBTI) to identify personality types. If you are not a certified instructor, use the quick chart in Chapter 8 of this book.

Discuss personality types and how they may affect perception of difficult behaviors. Have people give examples of conflicts that they have had that might have been based on lack of understanding of a particular personality type.

Break groups into Introverts on one side of the room and Extraverts on the other side. Have each group describe their characteristics and what they need from the other group. Do this for the four preference pairs.

Activity 9.11. Insights and Endings

Notes to Instructor: Ask the participants to share an insight that they gained from the workshop, either about themselves or about the topics presented. Allow enough time for people to respond. Use a ball if you would like to throw to the first responder, and ask that person to throw to another for a response. Continue the process until everyone has had a chance to respond.

Activity 9.12. Be Good to Yourself

Notes to Instructor: This activity can be used as an alternative ending to a workshop on the topic of dealing with difficult people.

Describe ways in which people can help themselves to stay calm, as noted in Chapter 9. Ask the group to provide other ways to maintain "sanity" and health, both physical and mental. Ask them how they can be good to themselves while at work and in their personal time.

Notes to Instructor: Following are some brief objectives for a one-day program in dealing with difficult people. Or you can use the activities in other programs as you choose.

Objectives: These are the objectives for a one-day program:
- To indentify personal button-pushers
- To find common behaviors that are difficult to address
- To determine ways to deal with difficult behaviors
- To discover how personality type contributes to behavioral responses
- To affirm one's capability to deal with difficult people

Chapter 10

Conclusion

> **WHAT'S IN THIS CHAPTER?**
> - How Philosophy Grounds Practice
> - Your Purpose
> - Content Review
> - Parting Thoughts

How Philosophy Grounds Practice

We have journeyed together on a path of discovery, contemplating reasons for action, reflecting on answers to questions, and learning ways to enhance cooperation. The content in this book spans decades of thought, both on a philosophical plane and in activities that promote authentic communication and understanding of others. Philosophy and action are often intertwined, knitting the fabric of life, what we practice, and why.

Your Purpose

If you were asked, "What is your purpose in life?" it might be a foreign concept; it could be in your mind from religious teachings; or it might be a metaphysical question for you. Depending on your background, you have thought about the question deeply, it has crossed your mind on occasion, or anything in between.

It is rare for a person in this enlightened age not to at least consider reasons for being. If you close your eyes for just sixty seconds and ask, "What is my purpose?" what are your initial thoughts?

"Making money," "obtaining power," "winning the sports title," or "demonstrating the most shocking persona" were probably not among your choices. Why not? It is probably because, just by nature and socialization, we all have a need to contribute to something beyond ourselves. Your answer may have contained words such as "to be helpful," "to enlighten," or "to be joyous and caring." Steve Pavlina (2012) has this life's purpose:

> Caring deeply, connecting playfully, loving intensely, and sharing generously; joyfully exploring; learning, growing, and prospering; brilliantly, and honorably serving the highest good of all. www.stevepavlina.com/about-steve-pavlina.htm.

Pavlina gave up his lucrative computer games business to write about and facilitate personal growth workshops, and in 2008 Hay House published his book, *Personal Development for Smart People.* Pavlina's book and his blog have received wide attention. His popularity, as well as other authors' success in the personal growth field, are testimony to the interest in this topic now, much like in the 1960s, when it was common as part of the humanistic education movement to search for something more, something to believe in, and something to connect with spiritually and collectively.

Suffice it to say that the theme of connection runs through this book. People want to connect, improve, embrace the greater good, and be a part of a community. Whether we as individuals are immersed in doing this already or longing to be more communally involved, the majority of human beings do wish for a better world, and a gentler society where human "beingness" is as important as production.

Researchers have debated the question of motivation, and rather than choose research that only supports "the greater good," as described above, some other research is worth noting. Douglas McGregor, author of *The Human Side of Enterprise* (1960), described two trains of thought about human personalities that are still studied in research circles: Theory X and Theory Y. Theory X says that people are basically lazy and must be motivated by outside influences, threats, and demands. Theory Y purports that people are self-motivated and, given the right circumstances, will reach for goals and perform based on their inner sense of achievement, honesty, work ethic, and desire for completion. The philosophical construct regarding Theory Y is one of unity and commitment to work, including the overall whole, not just one part, one area, or one silo.

As we ponder Theory X and Theory Y, we move into the realm where philosophy meets research and practicality and look at our own beliefs about the nature of humankind. This is where our study of communication begins, especially at work. Do we think that there is hope and personal satisfaction in communicating with people, or do we think that the effort is not worthwhile unless we are demanding and make threats? These are the two extremes. Few think completely one way or the other. Let's explore some philosophical and theoretical concepts as we review the chapters in this book and see what those concepts have spawned in terms of human communication.

Content Review

Through the book we have looked at situations in which soft skills would enhance communication. Scenarios demonstrated how skills would play out in a typical circumstance, and activities have been offered for practice and personal transfer of learning. A brief review of major concepts presented may help put it all together to see how philosophy and theory play an important role in understanding why skills are so important for better communication and, ultimately, a productive workforce that can compete in the global economy.

Soft Skills

To be proficient in soft skills, one has to believe that the skills are worth the effort it takes to learn them and to use them as often as possible. Even when you think Theory X thoughts, and especially at those times, you can mitigate arguments and achieve better results with imagining that, under the right circumstances (in this case, expert communication), the person with whom you are speaking can come around to your way of thinking.

As we have seen, soft skills are difficult. They are hard to practice and a tough sell in some environments. Thaler and Koval (2006) address the image problem of being "nice," which for the purposes of this conversation we can partially attribute to using soft skills. The authors recognize that some people think that to be nice is to be Pollyanna, passive, wimpy, and Milquetoast, akin to the perceptions of "soft" mentioned in Chapter 1. And to those who think soft is weak, Thaler and Oval say, "'Nice' is the toughest four-letter word you'll ever hear: It means moving forward with clear-eyed confidence that comes from knowing that being very nice and placing other people's needs on the same level as your own will get you everything you want" (p. 3).

Soft skills are powerful. Knowing how to use them not only gives you power, but it empowers others. Giving others power speaks to your self-confidence, your desire to achieve, your compassion, and your trust in another's ability to succeed. Caring about sharing recognition, collaborating, and supporting co-workers' growth takes self-assurance and faith in people. These actions speak to a higher order than just the self. They speak to community, and they are essential to the community at work.

Motives

Personal motives drive behavior. The lessons in Chapter 2 include working from your value system. If you believe that most people are "good" (Theory Y), you may act from a value of respect, communicating in respectful ways. Remembering "the C shield theory," respectful actions would include body language, which tells nearly all and includes how you respond nonverbally, as well as your tone of voice. Values are what we practice. Taking time to illuminate them helps to keep your motives in line with who you are and for what you want to be known.

The greater good is the more expansive motive. Work is a place to explore, create, collaborate, and experience personal and professional growth. It is a place for people to support one another in these endeavors. Working gives us the opportunity to build self-esteem, both our own and that of others. It affords us a place to belong and contribute. Those whose motives are clearly in support of organizational goals are respected for their clarity of purpose. Support makes a difference in so many ways. Motives show like the clothes on our backs. Wear a wonderful wardrobe to work!

The Law of Attraction

Reciprocity works. Thaler and Koval in *The Power of Nice* have some amazing examples, including how being kind makes money. This is not a new concept; customer service research abounds with statistics and stories about how great service translates into higher profits, but an example from Thaler and Koval's book is particularly fun to recount. It is about a security guard:

Frank was a sweet and gregarious security guard in the New York building where the Kaplan Thaler group worked. He had a cheerful hello for everyone in the morning, and it started the day on a positive note for staff who encountered his enthusiasm. One morning, a major potential client was to visit the office. The client was not from New York and had preconceived notions about the big city being cold and unfriendly. When his team arrived, they were skeptical. But when they walked into the building, Frank gave his warm and welcoming greeting to each member of the team, and the client was astounded by the kind reception. The Kaplan Thaler group reported that it was Frank's smile, his warmth and consideration, that helped seal the deal on the multi-million-dollar account. The lead client actually mentioned how impressed he was with such a sincere greeting and that he was automatically favorably impressed, lending credibility to the firm.

Like attracts like. Energy travels. The theme of Chapter 3 was to recognize the messages you are sending out and to keep them positive. That goes for thoughts about yourself as well. Be kind to yourself. Think well of yourself. Recognize your strong points and admire yourself for them. Others will, too.

Tact and Diplomacy

Validate, validate, validate. Tact and diplomacy are based on good will, and good will is built on appreciating interactions, listening, and responding in ways that let others know you have heard them, you care, and you understand. If your co-worker wants to talk with you, listen with attention. Incredible creativity can be released by being a good listener. Sometimes emotions block creativity and clear thought. You can be the catalyst for emotions to be communicated and worked through in a way that keeps your partner on track at work or at home. Acceptance is the key element in building the trust that is needed for disclosure to occur—acceptance in a holistic sense. It is caring unconditionally about the person when you offer support.

In Chapter 4, the important skill of listening was broken into steps: focusing, encouraging, paraphrasing, reflecting feelings, summarizing, and supporting. Questioning was explored as well, and solution-focused questions were highlighted as jewels promoting the process of discovery. It is hard to ask the right questions. Using solution-focused questions can help you avoid the other person shutting down. Try opening a person up and experiencing the wealth of the connection.

Problem Solving

Problem solving has been considered a soft skill because it involves creativity and insight. Both are often practiced with others, but we all solve problems on our own as well. In Chapter 5, Greg Trulson gave us a model to use so we can clarify a problem and take the steps to solve it. Expertise in problem solving helps us and our co-workers. Working through problems in a systematic way demonstrates that we care about really thinking through the steps of problem solving, which saves the time and emotional distress that can come from problem-solving paralysis or lack of attention to important problem elements.

For group problem solving, sensitivity to cultural backgrounds is important. Different perspectives can shed light on the darkness. The light comes from varying experiences and ways of looking at an issue. Different perspectives give life to a problem-solving session. Openness is also a critical element, and evaluation should not come until the very end, when all ideas have been expressed and reviewed. Once more, the receptivity you bring to the table, and your willingness to listen, means a more productive session.

Soft Skills and Teams

A team is more than the sum of its parts, the participants. With each new insight and expression of a creative thought, information multiplies and new possibilities are discovered. Knowing the team's stage of development and the roles people play helps in ensuring that members are heard and that conflicts are resolved. With knowledge of team process, the facilitator and team members can move through the forming, storming, and norming stages to performing, while maintaining the dignity of all members.

One-on-one communication can be challenging. Teamwork can be more challenging, which is why ground rules must be set so everyone has respect. The task is only half of the equation; maintenance is the other. Sometimes the two concepts are thought of as the head (thinking) and heart (feeling) part of teams. Since both are equally important, it takes expertise in facilitation to consider both at once.

Interventions are helpful in working through the stages. Much like helping an infant grow to adulthood, support, understanding, and guidance are necessary for a team to experience maturity. Team members need to feel comfortable sharing their experience and knowledge with others without being evaluated. All members must work toward a common goal and remain focused on maintaining a positive outlook. A healthy group cooperates, produces, celebrates, and experiences the satisfaction of working together in harmony, much like a musical group.

Personalities

Personalities spice up work life. Introverts and extraverts, sensors and intuitors, thinkers and feelers, and judgers and perceivers all balance each other. Soft skills are extremely helpful and important to take advantage of the gifts that all personalities have to offer. Because some types are opposites from our own, using soft skills can be especially demanding. Preferences such as sensing and intuiting and thinking and feeling require a true desire from those with opposite preferences to communicate and make decisions.

Thinkers and feelers may see being right and being kind the most differently, based on their natural tendencies. Thinkers' attention to analysis, in their minds, leads them to a "right" conclusion. After all, every aspect of the problem has been thought out with precision. Feelers are more intent on harmony, accepting others' emotions, being kind, and wanting everyone to get along. The struggle for thinkers and feelers is to consider different points of view. With understanding great relationships have been developed that have proven invaluable to problem solving. Colleagues' divergent views can both be right, and with positive intent and use of soft skills, colleagues can also be kind.

Feedback

If you cannot think of a good reason to give feedback, the rule of thumb is not to give it. Positive intent is necessary for feedback to be useful. Before you give feedback, think about the good that will be accomplished if the feedback receiver takes your message well and is better equipped as a result.

Equally important is to be a good receiver of feedback. Your strengths are still your strengths, so be proud of them. Allow room for growth and improvement. Listen and acknowledge the feedback, which may be hard for the other person to give. Good faith and trust must be a part of any feedback session. Trust that feedback is given to help you to hone your strengths and grow in the areas that challenge you.

Conflict and Cooperation

Being kind when someone is in a stage of rage is an accomplishment. Recognizing different categories of difficult behaviors can help you deal effectively with people who push your buttons, whether they are screaming at you or being antagonistic in other ways. Understanding that anger has a physiological effect and that, at times, listening is the best defense against escalation can help you contain the situation.

Handled well, cooperation can result from what was initially a conflict. We are all human, and unpleasant situations come up now and then. With the many skills you have learned in this book, your confidence should be greatly improved, your vision of "the greater good" reinforced, and your expertise in resolving even the most difficult people problems solidly enhanced.

Parting Thoughts

Is it better to be right or kind? As we have seen in the book, and as we know through instinct and experience, there are times when being right is critical. There are also times when being kind is important. And there are times when we can be both right and kind.

Kindness is comforting. Endorphins, brain chemicals, are released when people feel safe and have a sense of well-being—and kindness does that. You can feel it even from a simple courtesy, as with Frank the security guard's warm hello.

Kindness, being nice, and practicing compassion are not the only components of soft skills, since soft skills encompass so many competencies. In this book, kindness and being nice have been mentioned often. Soft skills allow kindness by taking into account another's feelings, thoughts, values, personality, strengths, and opportunities for growth. Practicing soft skills takes commitment and belief that it is the right thing to do. Either by self-instruction or by participating in training, we become more sensitive to those around us and to their needs. This expands our consciousness and ability to give. It follows that we must value giving if we are to be successful in practicing skills that require it.

Being right is often important in this world of massive decision making. That is why listening, a soft skill, is essential. Better decisions come from examining different perspectives about a problem. This is not to ignore the fact that decision-makers often make decisions on their own without needing other opinions or

Conclusion

because there is no time to explore alternatives. If being right is always a necessity for the decision-maker, however, that motive should be examined.

To leave this journey for now, here are four wishes:

- A wish for you to live the life you want
- A hope that compassion will precede your footsteps
- A hope that contentment envelopes you
- A wish that you are comforted by kindness

References

Anderson, W. T. (2004). *The upstart spring: Esalen and the American awakening.* Reading, MA: Addison-Wesley.

Barasch, M. I. (2005). *Field notes on the compassionate life: A search for the soul of kindness.* Reading, PA: Rodale, Inc.

Behary, W. (2008). *Disarming the narcissist: Surviving and thriving with the self-absorbed.* Oakland, CA: New Harbinger Publications.

Benne, K. D., & Sheats, P. (1948). Functional roles of group members. *Journal of Social Issues, 4,* 41–49.

Blau, P. (2008). *Exchange and power in social life.* New Brunswick, NJ: Transaction Publishers.

Bramson, R. (1981). *Coping with difficult people.* New York: Dell.

Brief, A. P., & Weiss, H. M. (2002). Organizational behavior: Affect in the workplace. *Annual Review of Psychology, 53,* 279–307.

Briggs, K., & Briggs-Myers, I. (1985). Myers-Briggs Type Indicator. Mountain View, CA: CPP.

Buckingham, M., & Clifton, D. O. (2001). *Now, discover your strengths.* New York: The Free Press.

Byrne, R. (2006). *The secret.* Hillsboro, OR: Beyond Words Publishing.

Carter, J. (1989). *Nasty people: How to stop being hurt by them without becoming one of them.* New York: Fall River Press.

Conger, J. A., & Kanungo, R. N. (1998). *Charismatic leadership in organizations.* Thousand Oaks, CA: Sage.

Crowe, S. (1999). *Since strangling isn't an option.* New York: Berkley Publishing Group.

DFW APT. (2011, January). Neuroscience of personality: Insights and applications of leading and coaching. http://dfwapt.org/past_events/01202011_mbti_neuroscience.

Eikenberry, K. (2007). *Remarkable leadership: Unleashing your leadership potential, one skill at a time.* San Francisco: Jossey-Bass.

Einstein, A. (2011, December). BrainyQuote.com. www.brainyquote.com/quotes/quotes/a/alberteins133991.html.

Ferucci, P. (2006). *The power of kindness: The unexpected benefits of leading a compassionate life.* New York: Jeremy P. Tarcher/Penguin.

Fleenor, J. (2003, April). Creative leadership, tough times: Soft skills make the difference. *President and CEO* magazine, pp. 36, 37. Geneva, IL: Nexxus.

Goffman, E. (1959). *The presentation of self in everyday life.* New York: Anchor Books.

Gordon, T. (1970). *Parent effectiveness training.* New York: Plume.

Gray, J. (1992*). Men are from Mars, women are from Venus.* New York: HarperCollins.

Hotchkiss, S. (2002). *Why is it always about YOU: The seven deadly sins of narcissism.* New York: The Free Press.

Just a human being, says the Dalai Lama in Bodh Gaya. (2012, January). NDTV.com. www.ndtv.com/article/india/full-transcript-just-a-human-being-says-the-dalai-lama-165646&cp

Kiersey, D. *Please understand me II.* (1998). Del Mar, CA: Prometheus Nemesis.

Kouzes, J. M., & Posner, B. Z. (2007). *The leadership challenge.* San Francisco: Jossey-Bass.

Lawrence, D. H. (1960). *Lady Chatterley's lover.* London: Penguin Books.

Mehrabian, A. (1981). *Silent messages: Implicit communication of emotions and attitudes.* Belmont, CA: Wadsworth.

McGregor, M. (1960). *The human side of enterprise.* New York: McGraw-Hill.

Myers, I. B. (1998). *Introduction to type* (6th ed.). Palo Alto, CA: Consulting Psychologists Press.

Namie, G., & Namie, R. (2000): *The bully at work.* Naperville, IL: Sourcebooks, Inc.

NASA Systems Engineering Behavior Study. (2008, October). www.nasa.gov/pdf/291039main_NASA_SE_Behavior_Study_Final_11122008.pdf.

Nelson, B. (1994). *1001 ways to reward employees.* New York: Workman Publishing.

Pavilna, S. (2008). *Personal development for smart people.* Carlsbad, CA: Hay House.

Pavlina, S. (2012, August).www.stevepavlina.com/about-steve-pavlina.htm.

Raths, L., Harmon, M., & Simon, S. (1966). *Values and teaching: Working with values in the classroom.* Columbus, OH: Charles E. Merrill.

Reiss, S. (2012, July). Universal motives and intrinsic core values. *Psychology Today.* www.psychologytoday.com/blog/who-we-are/2201204/universalmotives-and-intrinsic-core-values

Sorensen, T. (1963, 2005). *Decision making in the White House.* New York: Columbia University Press.

Siegel, D. (2001). *The developing mind: How relationships and the brain interact to shape who we are.* New York: Guilford Press.

Sutton, R. (2007). *The no asshole rule: Building a civilized workplace and surviving one that isn't.* New York: Warner Business.

Thaler, L. K., & Koval, R. (2006). *The power of nice: How to conquer the business world with kindness.* New York: Doubleday.

The Conference Board. (2006, October). Are they really ready to work? Employers' perspectives on the basic knowledge and applied skills of new entrants to the 21st century U.S. workforce.

The Secretary's Commission on Achieving Necessary Skills (SCANS). (1991, June). What work. http://wdr.doletta.gov/SCANS/whatwork.whatwork/pdf.

Tuckman, B. (1965). Developmental sequence in small groups. *Psychological Bulletin, 63,* 384–399.

Wildermuth, C. (2005). *Diversity training.* Alexandria, VA: American Society for Training & Development.

Zenger, J. H., Folkman, J. R., & Edinger, S. (2009). *The inspirational leader.* New York: McGraw-Hill.

About the Author

Maxine Kamin, M.Ed., was a pioneer in the human relations movement and continues to add to her repertoire in the field of soft skills, evolving with the movement as it changes and expands in definition. As a faculty member at the University of Massachusetts (UMass), she created and taught values clarification and humanistic education courses alongside leaders who have long been pillars in training, development, and consulting. She also taught in a clinical supervision program for early childhood education.

After fourteen years in academia as a UMass faculty member and dean, and director of staff and program development at Miami-Dade College, she entered the corporate world as manager of instruction and evaluation at American Express, and eventually founded TOUCH Consulting, Inc. (Training for Organizational Development, Unparalleled Customer Service, Communications, and Human Resources), headquartered in Plantation, Florida (www.touchconsulting.com). As president, she consulted with companies all over the United States and became known for creatively delivering leadership, human relations, and customer service training, as well as assisting companies to enhance service delivery through improvement of systems and processes.

Recognized as an expert in her field by the American Society for Training and Development (ASTD), she authored the first book in ASTD's well-received training series, *Customer Service Training*. She was asked to participate in the next ASTD project, the Ten Steps books, and is the author of *Ten Steps to Successful Customer Service*. In her quest to expand into new soft-skills areas, she partnered with Cristina de Mello-e-Souza Wildermuth and Ron Collins to co-author "Diversity Programs That Work," an ASTD *Info-line* publication. Some of her other training programs include Uncommon Courtesy, which is used in thirty-six states, Special Guests for the Florida Panthers and Huizinga Holdings, and Eleven Home Runs for Leadership.

Ms. Kamin's clients have included Fortune 500 companies, colleges, universities, city, county, and state governments, entertainment organizations, and small businesses.

Ms. Kamin completed all coursework for a Ph.D. in educational administration at the University of Florida and has been an instructor in leadership and organization development at Florida Atlantic University and the University of Phoenix.

Wanting to give back to the community and combine her humanistic education, clinical supervision, and early childhood background for the benefit of children and families, the author worked for eight years as the director of professional development for ChildNet, Broward County's child welfare organization. She participates in statewide curriculum projects for the Department of Children and Families and was a contributing author for "Supervising for Excellence," a nineteen-module State of Florida program that helps new supervisors learn supervision and leadership. She serves on the advisory board of the Florida Certification Board and Keiser University and continues to present at community, state, and national conferences. She also teaches soft skills in government and corporate settings.

Ms. Kamin operates with the premise that the personal touch in business—respecting and appreciating associates and customers—is the key to success. Her programs are designed to give practical application to these principles.

Index

Page reference followed by *fig* indicate an illustrated figure; followed by *t* indicate a table.

A

"Absentee brainstorming," 108
Acceptance: description of, 68; positive impact on interactions by, 68–69
Action-planning teams, 113*t*
Active Listener role, 125
Activities: for applying concepts of tact and diplomacy, 81–85; for feedback, 176–179; for identifying importance of personality style, 155–158; for identifying motives and values, 39–41; for Law of Attraction practice, 56–60; for managing anger and conflict, 198–204; for problem solving and, 105–106; for using soft skills to build team relationships, 131–136
Aggressor behavior, 126–127
Aggressor role, 125
Altruism: definition of, 53; the merit of, 53–54
Americans with Disabilities Act, 100
Anderson, W. T., 14
Anger: that is personal versus displaced, 195; reasons for, 185; stages of rage in, 182–184; understanding your triggers for, 185. *See also* Conflict
Angry people: assertive behavior techniques for listening to, 192–194; dealing with categories of difficult behaviors of, 185–192
Angry Person activity, 202–203
Annie E. Casey Foundation, 8
Applied skills: list of, 9*t*; as more important than basic knowledge skills, 10
Appreciating Personalities activity, 203
Appreciation activity, 179
The Appreciation Cape activity, 179
"Are They Really Ready to Work? Employers' Perspectives on the Basic Knowledge and Applied Skills of New Entrants to the 21st Century U.S. Workforce" report (2006), 8, 9
Assertive behavior techniques: listening as center of, 192–194; sorting, 192–194
An Attitude of Gratitude Activity, 57–58
Authentic communication, 25

B

Baez, J., 14
Barasch, M. I., 54
Basic knowledge/skills: applied skills as more important than, 10; list of, 9*t*; listening and speaking as, 10
Be Good to Yourself activity, 204
The Beatles, 14

Behary, W., 185, 186
Behavior: altruistic, 53–54; common workplace expectations of, 49; difficult, 186–192, 212; Golden Rule on, 43; how circumstances may determine, 24–25; how personal motives drive, 208; Law of Attraction outcomes for, 44–47; "nice," 207–208; Platinum Rule on, 43; reciprocity effect on, 47–51; suggestions for dealing with negative, 126–128
Being "nice," 207–208
Beliefs: Buddhism merit, 53–54; as problem solving issue, 101
Benne, K. D., 124
Blaming, 65
Blanchard, K., 13
Blau, P., 47, 51
Blind spot identification, 161
Blocker behavior, 126
Blocker role, 125
Body language: cultural differences in acceptable, 69–70; encouraging gestures sounds, 70–71; eye contact, 69–70, 187; holistic listening through your, 67; of hostile aggressives (Sherman Tanks), 187; how communication is dominated by, 23–24; projecting positive versus negative, 53. *See also* Communication
Brad's department turnover scenario: definition of the problem, 90, 105; problem-solving steps for the, 109–110
Brainstorming: Delphi technique as "absentee,"108; group decision making through, 107; team building activity using, 136
Bramson, R., 186
Brief, A. P., 196
Buckingham, M., 46
Buddhism merit concept, 53–54
Bullies: description and motives of, 29–30; how to deal with, 30
The Bully at Work (Namie and Namie), 30
Button-Pushers activity, 198
Byrne, R., 44

C

C Shield theory: description of, 23, 208; examples of how communication is impacted by, 23–25
Canfield, J., 13
Carter, J., 63, 185
Center for Applications of Psychological Type (CAPT), 140
Center for Creative Leadership, 11
Changing the subject invalidation, 66
Channels: definition and options for, 31; how communication and messages are impacted by, 31–32
Chicken Soup for the Soul book series, 13
Chopra, D., 14
Clear communication: hearing, listening, and responding components of, 33–34; how leaders' can impact, 37; how listeners decode the message impacts, 32; how the channel can create, 31–32; how the receiver "catches" the message impacts, 32–33; what the source/speaker contributes to, 31
Clifton, D. O., 46

Index

Climate Tester role, 125
Closed-ended questions, 75–76
Collins, J., 14
Common Reactions activity, 198–199
Communication: as active and two-way process, 25–26; bullies, sociopaths, and narcissists,' 29–30; honesty of authentic, 25; how behavior changes depending on circumstances of, 24–25; how leaders' can impact, 37; how perceived injustice can block, 21–22; how soft skills can improve, 12; illustration of emotions driving, 20*fig*; intentions for, 20–21; one-way, 33; questions and tips on, 36, 37; removing barriers to, 34–36; using Skype for, 163; tone of voice and body language dominating, 23–24. *See also* Body language; Feedback; Messages; Motives
Communication motives: of the Cynic, 26–27; of the Heart, 27–28; of the Leader, 28–29; of the Light Bulb, 26; of the Spirit, 28
Compromiser role, 124
"Cone of probabilities," 95
Conference Board, 8, 9
Confidence, 166
Conflict: dealing with difficult or angry people during, 185–192; as inevitable, 181; philosophical review of handling, 212; understanding the stages of rage in, 182–185. *See also* Anger
Conflict resolution: assertive behavior techniques for, 192–194; the leader's connection to, 196–197; taking care of yourself component of, 194–196
Conflict resolution activities: Angry Person, 202–203; Appreciating Personalities, 203; Be Good to Yourself, 204; Button-Pushers, 198; Common Reactions, 198–199; How I Learned, 200; Insights and Endings, 204; Practice Sorting, 202; Role Plays, 203; Skills Test, 201–202; Stages of Rage, 202; What I Will Do, 201
Conger, J. A., 196
Consulting Psychologists Press (CPP), 140
Cooperation, 212
Coordinator role, 124
Coping with Difficult People (Bramson), 186
Corporate Voices for Working Families, 8
"Creative Leadership, Tough Times: Soft Skills Make the Difference" (Fleenor), 11
Criticizing: comparing acceptance with effects of, 69; invalidating by, 65
Crosby, Stills, and Nash, 14
Crowe, S., 186
Cuban missile crisis, 98
Cultural differences: eye contact and, 69–70; as problem solving issue, 100–101
Cynic personality type, 26–27

D

Dalai Lama, 160
Decision implementation: developing a plan for solution, 97–98, 105; Ed = (Qd X Id) formula for, 98

Decision making: crisis-to-crisis, 90; finding the right person for, 101–102; Kennedy's Cuban missile crisis, 98; leader's connection to process of, 102–103; other issues to consider for, 100–102; overcoming indecision during process of, 96*fig*; process and techniques for, 95–97, 105; questions and tips for, 102, 103; Quick Decision Tool for, 96; role of intuition in, 99; "Teaching Ways to Gain Group Agreement" techniques for, 94, 107–108. *See also* Problem solving

Decisions: evaluating the, 98–99, 105; implementation of, 97–98, 105; process for reaching a, 95–97

Decoding messages, 32

DeGeneres, Ellen, 76

Delbecq, A., 107

Dell, Inc., 8

Delphi technique, 108

Demonstrate Differences activity, 157–158

Denial as invalidation, 66

Determine Ground Rules activity, 131–132

The Devil Wears Prada (film), 148

Dialog Activity, 84–85

Diana, Princess, 53

Difficult behaviors: complainers, 189–190; expert know-it-alls, 190–191; hostile aggressives (exploders), 189; hostile aggressives (Sherman tanks), 186–188; hostile aggressives (snipers), 188–189; indecisive stallers, 192; listed, 186; negativists, 190; review of how to handle, 212; super-agreeables, 191; unresponsive clams, 191

Diplomacy: being a good listener as key to, 66–68; description of, 61; examining consequences of insensitivity and lack, 61–62; five steps to effective listening as paramount to, 69–75; philosophical review of, 209–210; the positive impact of, 62–64; the power of questioning as part of, 75–79; rapport established through, 79. *See also* Tact

Diplomacy activities: Dialog, 84–85; Tact and Diplomacy Baseline, 81–84; Validation or Invalidation?, 84

Dirty Harry (film), 148

Disarming the Narcissist: Surviving and Thriving with the Self-Absorbed (Behary), 186

Displaced anger, 195

Diverse U.S. population (1995–2050), 101

Diversity Training (Wildermuth and Gray), 101

Duck Soup (film), 71

Duke of Wellington, 71

E

Eastwood, Clint, 148

Ed = (Qd X Id) formula, 98

Ed Self, 13, 15

Edinger, S., 10, 80

"Education of the Self (Ed Self)" course (University of Massachusetts), 13, 15

Eikenberry, K., 80

Einstein, Albert, 90

Elaborator role, 124

"The Elephant's Child" (Kipling), 91

Index

Emotional abuse: invalidation as form of, 63–64; ten ways to invalidate others and causing, 64–66

Emotions: anger, 182–195; C Shield theory on myth of "invisible shield" of, 23–25, 208; how words reflect feelings and, 74–75; Law of Attraction creating positive, 44–55, 56; related to perceived injustice, 21–22; "super contagious" nature of leader's, 196. *See also* Feelings

Employers: applied skills more valued than basic knowledge skills by, 10; soft skills in demand by, 12

Encoding messages, 31

Encourager role, 124

Encouraging gestures/sounds, 70–71

Endorphins, 212

Energizer role, 124

Enraged state, 184

Esalen Institute, 14

Exception-finding questions, 78

Exchange and Power in Social Life (Blau), 47, 51

Expediter role, 124

Expert know-it-alls, 190–191

Exploders (hostile aggressives), 189

Extravert personality type: energy of the, 141; review of how to work with, 211; soft skills for the, 143–144; testing for, 138–139

Eye contact, 69–70, 187

F

Facial expression, 23–24

Feedback: challenges of giving, 159–161; different types of, 162; Feedback Chart as reminder to give, 173, 174*t*; how to give helpful, 162–166; Johari Window theory on giving, 161*fig*; leader's connection to constructive, 173–175; philosophical review of giving, 211; positive, 172–173; questions and tips on, 174–175; receiving, 166–172; 360-degree, 162; workplace, 162. *See also* Communication

Feedback activities: Appreciation, 179; The Appreciation Cape, 179; Feedback Wanted, 177; Giving Feedback, 176; "I Appreciate You!," 179; Just What I Need to Know, 178; Team Feedback, 177

Feedback Chart, 173, 174*t*

Feedback strategies: describe the value, 164–165; give feedback in person, 163; lend a hand, 165; let the other person respond, 165; make an observation, 164; offer confidence, 166; receiving feedback, 166–172; use "I" statements, 163–164

Feedback Wanted activity, 177

Feelers personality type: comparing thinkers and, 149–150; description of, 148–149; review of how to work with, 211; soft skills for, 149–150

Feelings: angry, 182–195; how acceptance creates positive, 68–69; how words reflect, 74–75. *See also* Emotions

Ferrucci, P., 45

"Fireside chats," 80

Fleenor, J., 11

Folkman, J. R., 10, 79

Follower role, 125

Forced Choice Activity, 41–42

Ford Motor Company, 8
Frank the security guard, 209, 212
From Me to You Activity, 59
From Negative to Positive Activity, 58
Frustration, 183–184

G

Gestalt therapy, 13
Gifts from the Universe Activity, 58
Giving solution invalidation, 65
Goffman, Erving, 24
Golden Rule, 43
Gordon, T., 68
Gray, J., 48, 101

H

Hair! (musical), 14
Harmin, M., 39
Harmonizer role, 124
The Heart personality type, 27–28
Help Seeker role, 125
"Higher power," 56
Higher Self Activity, 56
Hostile aggressives (exploders), 189
Hostile aggressives (Sherman tanks), 186–188
Hostile aggressives (snipers), 188–189
Hotchkiss, S., 186
How I Learned activity, 200
"Human potentialities," 14
The Human Side of Enterprise (McGregor), 206
Humanistic education movement: focus on self-knowledge by, 13; positive outcomes of the, 14
Huxley, A., 14

I

"I Appreciate You!" activity, 179
"I" statements, 163–164
Indecisive stallers, 192
Information Seeker role, 124
Ingham, H., 161
Initial Team Assessment activity, 133
Initiator role, 124
Insights and Endings activity, 204
Intentions: paraphrasing to increase understanding of, 71–74; reasons for intention to communicate, 20–21. *See also* Motives
Interactions: C Shield theory of, 23–25, 208; examining what's behind our, 19–20; how acceptance improves, 68–69; how behavior changes depending on circumstances of, 24–25; how clear motives produce clear action and, 22; intention to communication, 20–21; perceived injustice impacting, 21–22; "sign vehicles" conveying information about, 24
Interpersonal Coach role, 125
Interpersonal skills: soft skills defined as type of, 12–13; typical list of, 10
Introvert personality type: energy of the, 141–142; review of how to work with, 211; soft skills for, 143–144; testing for the, 138–139
Intuition: decision making and problem solving role of, 99; intuitive personality preference for, 144–147, 211
Intuitives personality type: characteristics of, 146–147; how information is gathered by, 144–145;

review of how to work with, 211; soft skills for, 147
Invalidation: as emotional abuse, 63; how not listening results in, 63–64; ten ways to cause, 64–66; Validation or Invalidation? Activity on, 84

J
J.C. Penny commercials (2012), 76
Johari Window, 161*fig*
Journals, 194
Judgers personality type: characteristics of, 152; description of, 150–151; review of how to work with, 211
Jung, C., 139
Just What I Need to Know activity, 178

K
Kanungo, R. N., 196
Kaplan Thaler group, 209
Kennedy, John F., 98
Kiersey, D., 140
Kindness: gender differences in the expression of, 48–49; how being a good listener is, 67–68; parting thoughts on being right versus being, 212–213; self-esteem promoted through, 46–47; transformational power of, 45
King, Martin Luther, Jr., 148
Kipling, Rudyard, 91, 106, 181
Kouzes, J., 16
Koval, R., 207, 208–209

L
Lady Chatterley's Lover (Lawrence), 44–45
Laing, R. D., 14

Law of Attraction: description of the, 44; key principles of, 44–45; leader's connection by being catalyst in, 54–55; "no" as not recognized by the, 44, 51; philosophical review of the, 208–209; questions and tips on the, 54, 55; self-appreciations based on the, 46–47; Token of Appreciation (TOA) campaign story example of, 45. *See also* Positive thoughts
Law of Attraction activities: An Attitude of Gratitude, 57–58; From Me to You, 59; From Negative to Positive, 58; Gifts from the Universe, 58; Higher Self, 56; Random Acts of Kindness, 59–60; Thoughts That Serve, 59; What Do You Want?, 57
Lawrence, D. H., 44
Leader personality type, 28–29
Leaders: soft skills development supported by, 11, 16; "super contagious" nature of emotions shown by, 196
Leader's connection: to clear communication, 37; to conflict resolution, 196–197; to constructive use of feedback, 173–175; to effective teams, 129–130; to facilitating potential of personality styles, 153–154; as Law of Attraction catalyst, 54–55; to problem solving and decision making, 102–103; to soft skills development, 16; to workplace practice of listening, 79–80
The Leadership Challenge (Kouzes and Posner), 16

Leading questions, 76
Lecturing as invalidation, 65
Light Bulbs personality type, 26
Listeners: decoding of message by, 32; practicing diplomacy by being good, 66–68
Listening: assertive behavior as beginning with, 192–194; five steps to effective, 69–75; invalidation by not, 63–64; as a kindness, 66–68; leader's connection to workplace, 79–80; learning and developing skills of, 33; the power of questioning as part of, 75–79; questions and tips on, 79, 80; understanding the importance of, 62–64; when receiving feedback, 170
Listening steps: step 1: focusing, 69–70; step 2: encouraging, 70–71; step 3: paraphrasing, 71–74; step 4: reflecting feelings, 74–75; step 5: summarizing and supporting, 75
Luft, J., 161

M

Making observations, 164
Mandela, Nelson, 148
Marx, G., 71
Maslow, A., 14
May, R., 14
McGregor, D., 206
Mehrabian, A., 23
Men Are from Mars, Women Are from Venus (Gray), 48
Men Are from Mars, Women Are from Venus workshops, 48–49
Merit belief, 53–54

Messages: hearing, listening, and responding to, 33–34; how channels give context to, 31–32; listener's decoding of, 32; receivers' interpretation of, 32–33; speaker encoding of, 31; when it becomes a barrier to communication, 34–36. *See also* Communication
Messina, J., 14
Microsoft, 8
Minimizing as invalidation, 65
Miracle questions, 77
Mitchell, J., 14
Motivation: Law of Attraction impact on, 43–47; the reciprocity effect on, 47–51; recognition as most powerful form of, 45; Theory X and Theory Y on, 206–207
Motive activities: Forced Choice, 41–42; Values Ranking, 39–41
Motives: aligning and clarifying your, 25–26; of bullies, sociopaths, and narcissists, 29–30; clear versus ulterior, 22; of the Cynic, 26–27; as expression of values, 39; factors that influence, 20; of the Heart, 27–28; how behavior is driven by, 208; how perceived injustice impacts, 21–22; of the Leader, 28–29; of the Light Blub, 26; philosophical review of, 208; of the Spirit, 28; of thinkers personality type, 148. *See also* Communication; Intentions
"My Fair Lady" (song), 66
Myers-Briggs Type Indicator, 130, 139–140, 142, 150, 203

Index

N

Namie, G., 30
Namie, R., 30
Narcissists: description and motives of, 30; how to deal with, 30
NASA, 142
Nasty People: How to Stop Being Hurt by Them Without Becoming One of Them (Carter), 63, 185
Negative behavior: responding with strength without attack back, 126–127; suggestions for dealing with specific types of, 126
Negative thoughts: From Negative to Positive Activity on, 58; how "no" creates, 51–52; ways to transform, 52
Negativists, 190
Nelson, B., 45
Newton's first law of motion, 90, 92
"Nice" behaviors, 207–208
Nixon, R., 15
"No": body language that conveys, 53; negative reactions to being told, 51–52; as not recognized by Law of Attraction, 44, 51; ways to say "yes" instead of, 52
The No Asshole Rule (Sutton), 186
"Noise" listening distraction, 67
Nominal group technique, 107–108
Nonverbal communication. *See* Body language

O

One-way communication, 33
1001 Ways to Reward Employees (Nelson), 45

Open-ended questions, 75
Opinion Giver role, 124
Opinion Seeker role, 124
Ordering as invalidation, 64
Orienter role, 124
Ornish, D., 14
Osborn, A. F., 107

P

Paralinguistic communication, 23
Paraphrasing, 71–74; description and use of, 71–72; examples of effective and ineffective, 73–74; for reinforcing positive team progress, 128
Parent Effectiveness Training (P.E.T.) [Gordon], 68
Partnership for 21st Century Skills, 8
Past success questions, 77
Pavlina, S., 206
Pearson Education, 8
Perceived injustice, 21–22
Perceivers personality type: characteristics of, 152; description of, 151–152; review of how to work with, 211
Perls, F., 13
Personal Development for Smart People (Pavlina), 206
Personality conflicts, 101
Personality style activities: Demonstrate Differences, 157–158; Relationships, 156–157; Types and Teamwork, 156; Your Ideal Work Environment, 157; Your Personality Type, 155–156
Personality style assessments: Myers-Briggers Type Indicator (MBTI),

130, 139–140, 142, 150, 203; taking A1 and B1 test, 138–139, 141–142; Temperament Sorter, 140

Personality styles: demonstrating principle of preferences for, 142–143; extraverts, 138–139, 141, 143–144, 211; feelers, 148–150, 211; increasing your soft skills by understanding, 140–141; introverts, 138–139, 141–142, 143–144, 211; intuitives, 144–145, 146–147, 211; judgers, 150–151, 152, 211; leaders' connection on facilitating potential of, 153–154; perceivers, 151–153, 211; philosophical review on working with different, 211; questions and tips on, 152–153, 154; sensors, 144–146, 147, 211; Theory X and Theory Y on, 206–207; thinkers, 148, 149–150, 211; understanding significance of different, 137–141

Phillip Morris, 8

Philosophy: debate over being right or kind, 212–213; how it grounds practice, 205; reviewing soft skills in context of, 207–212; your purpose in life and personal, 205–207

Platinum Rule, 43

Please Understand Me series (Kiersey), 140

Positive thoughts: body language that conveys, 53; the merit of, 53–54; self-appreciations through, 46–47. *See also* Law of Attraction

Posner, B., 16

The Power of Kindness (Ferrucci), 45

The Power of Nice (Thaler and Koval), 208–209

Powerlessness, 183

Practice Sorting activity, 202

Practice the Model activity, 105

Preaching as invalidation, 65

Problem solving: defining the problem as critical to, 92–93*fig*; generating and evaluating options for, 94–95; importance of having effective, 87–88; leader's connection to process of, 102–103; other issues to consider during, 100–102; philosophical review of, 210; questions and tips for, 102, 103; role of intuition in, 99; scenario notes on turnover problem, 109–110. *See also* Decision making; Solutions

Problem solving activities: Practice the Model, 105; Tech Confusion, 106; What Is the Problem?, 105–106

Problem solving issues: beliefs and values, 101; cultural differences, 100–101; finding the right person, 101–102; legal, 100; personality conflicts, 101

Problem-solving model: Brad's department turnover problem solving using the, 109–110; illustration of the, 89*fig*; introduction to Trulson's, 88; nine steps of the, 88–99; overview of the, 104–105

Problem-solving model steps: step 1: problem awareness, 89–90, 104; step 2: gather data, 91–92, 104, 109; step 3: define problem and root cause, 92–93*fig*, 104, 109; step 4: generate options, 94, 104–105, 109; step 5: evaluate options, 94–95, 105, 109; step

6: make decision, 95–97, 105, 110; step 7: develop plan, 97, 105, 110; step 8: implement, 97–98, 105, 110; step 9: evaluate, 98–99, 105, 110
Problem-solving teams, 113*t*
Problems: becoming aware of the, 89–90, 104; Brad's department turnover, 90; defining the root cause of the, 92–93*fig*, 104; gathering data on the, 91–92, 104
Procedural Technician role, 124
Process improvement teams, 113*t*
Psychology Today, 39, 54

Q

Quality teams, 113*t*
Question types: closed-ended, 75–76; leading, 76; listening and the power using, 75–76; open-ended, 75; Socratic, 76–77; solution-focused, 77–78
Quick Decision Tool, 96

R

Rand Corporation, 108
Random Acts of Kindness Activity, 59–60
Random Acts of Kindness Foundation, 45
Random Acts of Kindness movement, 45
Rapport, 79
Raths, L., 39
Receivers: "catching" the message, 32; how their interpretation can impact communication, 32–33
Receiving feedback tips: acknowledge the feedback when, 170–171; be open to improvements when, 168–169; being willing to hear others' perceptions when, 166–168; clarify in order to understand when, 171; listen when, 170; make a plan for correction after, 172; recognize your strengths when, 168; say thank you after, 172
Reciprocity: benefits in the work environment, 48; description of, 47–48; gender differences in the expression of, 48–49; how we keep score of, 49–50; philosophical review of, 208–209; positive and negative, 50*t*–51*t*; principles of, 48
Recognition Seeker role: dealing with negative behavior by, 126; description of, 125
Reflecting feelings words, 74–75
Reiss, S., 39
Relationships activity, 156–157
Rogerian listening techniques, 13
Rogers, Carl, 13, 148
Role Plays activity, 203
Rolf, I., 14

S

Scaling questions, 78
Sebastian, J., 14
The Secret (Byrne), 44
Secretary's Commission on Achieving Necessary Skills, 10
Security guard story, 209, 212
Self-assessment of soft skills, 12–13
Self-awareness: Johari Window to develop, 161; of your life purpose, 205–207; of your triggers for anger, 185
Self-Confessor role: dealing with negative behavior by, 126; description of, 125

Self-esteem: bullies' lack of, 30; how kindness and positivity can improve, 46–47; humanistic education movement outcomes for, 14

Self-knowledge: humanistic education movement focus on, 13; positive outcomes of educational focus on, 14

Sensitivity training, 14

Sensors personality type: characteristics of, 145–146; how information is gathered by, 144–145; review of how to work with, 211; soft skills for, 147

Shankar, R., 14

Sheats, P., 124

Sherman tanks (hostile aggressivers), 186–188

Siegel, D., 182

"Sign vehicles," 24

Simon, S., 13, 39

Since Strangling Isn't an Option (Crowe), 186

Six Sigma team, 113t

Skills: list of applied, 9t; list of basic knowledge, 9t; list of interpersonal, 10. *See also* Soft skills

Skills Test activity, 201–202

Skype, 163

Snipers (hostile aggressives), 188–189

Snoop Dogg (Snoop Lion), 160

Snow White (fairy tale), 160

Social Interest Pleader role: dealing with negative behavior by, 126; description of, 125

Society for Human Resource Management, 8

Sociopaths: description and motives of, 30; how to deal with, 30

Socratic questions, 76–77

Soft skills: as being able to positively present ideas and thoughts, 52; building team relationships by using, 111–136; change in perception of, 11; evolution and applications of, 13–14; expansive list of descriptors of, 7–8; how understanding personality types can increase your, 140–141; importance in business, 8–9; for introverts and extroverts, 143–144; leadership support of, 16; new opportunities for, 10–11; philosophical review of, 207–212; progressively defined as interpersonal skills, 12–13; questions for self-assessment of, 12–13; reason for new emphasis on, 9–10; for sensors and intuitives, 147; a simple definition of, 8; teaching, 14–15; for the 21st century, 15. *See also* Skills

Soft skills practice: four wishes for your journey toward, 213; leader's support required for effective, 16; philosophical review of, 207–212; questions and tips on, 16–17

Solution-focused questions: exception-finding questions, 78; miracle questions, 77; past success questions, 77; scaling questions, 78

Solutions: "cone of probabilities" for implementing a, 95; develop a plan and implementing the, 97–98; "devil's advocate" role played during assessing, 94; evaluating decision

Index

on the, 98–99, 105; generating and evaluating options for, 94–95, 105; making a decision on a, 95–97. *See also* Problem solving

Sorensen, T., 98

Sorting technique: dealing with difficult behaviors with, 192–194; Practice Sorting activity on, 202

"Source energy," 56

Southwest Airlines, 142

Speakers: clear communication by, 31; encoding messages by, 31

The Spirit personality type, 28

Springer, Jerry, 71

Stages of rage: feeling enraged, 184; feeling frustrated, 183–184; feeling powerless, 183; understanding the physiological factors of, 182

Stages of Rage activity, 202

Standard Setter role, 125

Standing committee, 113t

State Farm, 8

Streep, Meryl, 148

Strengths: acknowledging and allowing others,' 46–47; self-esteem by identifying your, 46

Summarizing/supporting skill, 75

Super-agreeables, 191

Sutton, R., 186

T

"T" groups, 14

Tact: description of, 61; examining consequences of insensitivity and lack, 61–62; five steps to effective listening as paramount to, 69–75; philosophical review of, 209–210; the positive impact of, 61–64; the power of questioning as part of, 75–79; rapport established through, 79; taking care of yourself by being firm while using, 195. *See also* Diplomacy

Tact activities: Dialog, 84–85; Tact and Diplomacy Baseline, 81–84; Validation or Invalidation?, 84

Tact and Diplomacy Baseline Activity, 81–84

Take a break, 195

Take Care of You techniques: assessing if it is personal, 195; be firm and tactful, 195; journals, 194; questions and tips for, 195–196; take a break, 195

Task committee, 113t

Task force team, 113t

"Teaching Ways to Gain Group Agreement": brainstorming, 107; Delphi technique, 108; nominal group technique, 107–108; for team decision making, 94

Team adjourning stage, 123

Team Assessment activity, 135–136

Team building activities: Brainstorming, 136; Determine Ground Rules, 131–132; Initial Team Assessment, 133; Team Assessment, 135–136; Team Functioning Questionnaire, 134–135; Transportation, 136; What Is Not for Teams to Decide?, 132; Why Teams?, 131; Your Trust Factor, 133–134

Team Feedback activity, 177

Team Forming stage: description and behaviors during, 116–117;

interventions that encourage results during, 122
Team Functioning Questionnaire activity, 134–135
Team ground rules: determining team, 114–115; including respect for all members in the, 126; sample list of, 115*fig*
Team growth: stage 1: Forming, 116–117, 122; stage 2: Storming, 117–118, 122; stage 3: Norming, 118–119, 123; stage 4: Performing, 119–121, 123
Team interventions: during forming stage, 122; during norming stage, 123; during performing stage, 123; during storming stage, 122
Team member roles: common roles shared by all members, 127; the facilitator, 128–129; negative, 125–127; questions and tips on, 129; related to maintenance functions, 124–125; related to task functions, 124; significance and implications of, 123–124; ways to practice positive, 127–128
Team members: philosophical review of soft skills used by, 210–211; roles played by, 123–129; suggestions for dealing with negative behavior by, 126–128
Team Norming stage: description and behaviors during, 118–119; interventions that encourage results during, 123
Team Performing stage: description and behaviors during, 123; interventions that encourage results during, 123

Team Storming stage: description and behaviors during, 117–118; interventions that encourage results during, 122
Teams: determining ground rules and process for, 114–115*fig*; differences between a group and, 112; function and people sides of, 112, 114*fig*; leader's connection to function of, 129–130; philosophical review of soft skills used within, 210–211; questions and tips on leading, 130; stages of growth, 115–121; teaching 21st century soft skills to, 15; types and uses of, 112, 113*t*
Tech Confusion activity, 106
Temperament Sorter, 140
Teresa, Mother, 53, 148
Thaler, L. K., 207, 208–209
Theory X, 206, 207
Theory Y, 206–207
Thinker personality type: comparing feelers and, 149–150; description of, 148; review of how to work with, 211; soft skills for, 149–150
Thoughts: negative, 51–52, 58; positive, 46–47, 53–54
Thoughts That Serve Activity, 59
Threatening as invalidation, 64
360-degree feedback, 162
Tillich, P., 14
Token of Appreciation (TOA) campaign story, 45
Toynbee, A., 14
Traditional work unit team, 113*t*
Transportation activity, 136
Triggers, 185

Index

Trulson, G., 87, 88, 105–106, 210
Trump, Donald, 148
Trust Builder role, 125
Types and Teamwork activity, 156

U

Ulterior motives, 22
University of Massachusetts School of Education, 13, 15
University of Wisconsin, 107
Unresponsive clams, 191
"Until the cows come home," 71
U.S. Census Bureau, 101

V

Validation or Invalidation? Activity, 84
Value activities: Forced Choice, 41–42; Values Ranking, 39–41
Values: activities on processes of valuing or identifying, 39–42; choosing, prizing, and acting processes of, 39; criteria for defining a, 39; motives as expression of, 39; as problem solving issue, 101
Values Ranking Activity, 39–41
Van de Ven, A., 107
Voice tone, 23–24

W

Weinstein, G., 13, 15
Weiss, H. M., 196
What Do You Want? Activity, 57
What I Will Do activity, 201
What Is Not for Teams to Decide? activity, 132
What Is the Problem? activity, 105–106
What is your purpose in life?, 205–207
"What Work Requires of Schools: A SCANS Report for America 2000" report (1991), 10
Why Is It Always About YOU? (Hotchkiss), 186
Why Teams? activity, 131
Wildermuth, C., 101
Win-lose mindset, 22
Winfrey, Oprah, 71
Work environment: common behavioral expectations in the, 49; feedback in the, 162; Law of Attraction impact on the, 44–47; reciprocity effect on the, 47–51; soft skills supported in, 16
World Kindness Movement, 45

Y

Your Ideal Work Environment activity, 157
Your life purpose, 205–207
Your Personality Type activity, 155–156
Your Trust Factor activity, 133–134

Z

Zenger, J. H., 10, 79